Reading the Bible in Australia

"What does it mean to read the Bible on the Country of Aboriginal and Torres Strait Islander nations, occupied by the settler colony of Australia? This question remains largely unanswered nearly 250 years after colonization. In this significant new work, a diverse group of authors, beginning with leading First Nations scholars, respond to this question in insightful, challenging, and innovative ways. This is a critically important contribution to Australian biblical scholarship."

—**JOANNA CRUICKSHANK**, associate professor in history, Deakin University

"I am excited about this book. Why? As an Australian Christian who has read the Bible all his life, it never occurred to me to ask what it means to read it in Australia. I had read it devotionally. I have tried to read it internationally. I have read it as a church member. This book helps me to read it as an Australian in the light of our tragic history with Indigenous people and our response to this continent's natural environment. I commend it."

—**TIM COSTELLO**, executive director, Micah Australia

"This astonishingly rich collection of essays is both a compelling introduction for Australians as to how they engage with the Bible, and for the world of biblical scholarship to the exceptional context of Australia. The first three chapters by First Nations Australians are essential reading for anyone seeking to understand the Bible in Australia."

—**PETER SHERLOCK**, vice-chancellor, University of Divinity

"What an exciting collection of ideas are gathered in this book! Here are readers of the Bible from Australia who pay close attention to their important (and fascinating) social, cultural, and geographic 'contexts'—both past and present. Included here are insights on Scripture from Indigenous scholars, critiques of politicized uses and abuses of the Bible, and frank confrontations with the challenges of history and contemporary issues. If you are curious about why many of us maintain a keen interest in biblical scholarship in Australia, start here."

—**DANIEL L. SMITH-CHRISTOPHER**, professor of theological studies, Loyola Marymount University

"This rich mix of scholars and practitioners brings unique stories and experience of the biblical text. The result is a book that dives deeply into the defining issues of our time and reveals themes that colonization, settler theology, and capitalist economic interests have suppressed. I highly recommend this book to all who long for new and hopeful insights into the biblical text as they grapple with the consequences and implications of our colonial, capitalist world."

—**Sylvia C. Keesmat**, adjunct professor of biblical studies and hermeneutics, Institute for Christian Studies

"This fascinating collection of essays explores the biblical text in the context of a colonizing history of appropriation. It offers new ways of reading and responding to the Bible from within the Australian context, with its complex cultures and its ancient landscape. The book is invaluable both for its innovative interpretations and for raising acutely the question of what it means to interpret the Bible for today within particular cultural contexts."

—**Dorothy A. Lee**, research professor of New Testament, University of Divinity

Reading the Bible in Australia

Edited by
Deborah R. Storie
Barbara Deutschmann
and Michelle Eastwood

WIPF & STOCK · Eugene, Oregon

READING THE BIBLE IN AUSTRALIA

Copyright © 2024 Wipf and Stock Publishers. All rights reserved. Except for brief quotations in critical publications or reviews, no part of this book may be reproduced in any manner without prior written permission from the publisher. Write: Permissions, Wipf and Stock Publishers, 199 W. 8th Ave., Suite 3, Eugene, OR 97401.

Wipf & Stock
An Imprint of Wipf and Stock Publishers
199 W. 8th Ave., Suite 3
Eugene, OR 97401

www.wipfandstock.com

PAPERBACK ISBN: 978-1-6667-7941-7
HARDCOVER ISBN: 978-1-6667-7942-4
EBOOK ISBN: 978-1-6667-7943-1

VERSION NUMBER 12/29/23

The chapter by Anne Elvey draws on material published in chapters 1 and 4 of Elvey *Reading the Magnificat in Australia*, 2020. Used with permission of Sheffield Phoenix Press.

The chapter by Ray Minniecon was first published in *Zadok Perspectives* S2, Spring 2019, entitled "Job: An Aboriginal Story." Used with permission.

The cover art, *Healing Prayer*, by Safina Stewart is used with her permission.

The chapter by Megan Turton cites lines from Judith Wright's poem, "Black Cockatoos." Used with permission of HarperCollins.

Scripture quotations, unless otherwise indicated, are taken from the New Revised Standard Version Bible, copyright 1989 National Council of the Churches of Christ in the United States of America. Used by permission. All rights reserved worldwide.

Scripture quotations marked (NIV) are taken from the Holy Bible, New International Version, NIV. Copyright 1973, 1978, 1984, 2011 by Biblica Inc. Used by permission of Zondervan. All rights reserved worldwide. www.zondervan.com. The "NIV" and "New International Version" are trademarks registered in the United States Patent and Trademark Office by Biblica Inc.

Contents

Acknowledgements | vii
Healing Prayer: A Story Prayed through Art | ix
Contributors | xiii
Abbreviations | xix

Introduction | 1

Part I: First Nations' Readings

Reading the Bible in Australia: A Place for Aboriginal and Torres Strait Islander Peoples? | 15
   Naomi Wolfe

Job: An Aboriginal Story | 32
   Ray Minniecon

Colonial Bondage: Liberating Biblical Narratives and Theological Education | 50
   Anne Pattel-Gray

Part II: Questions of Culture and Translation

In the Beginning, Pundgyl Marman: Translating Creation at the Edges of Empire | 69
   Mark G. Brett *and* Deborah Shuh Yi Tan

Judges and Kings: A Distinction Without a Difference? Translating the Pitjantjatjara Bible in Central Australia | 85
   Samuel Freney

"Arriving Like a Fish of the Night" ("*Tōʻai faa-Iʻa a le Po*"): An Australian-Samoan Diasporic Reading of *Pasah* in Exodus 12:12–13 through a Samoan Fishing Proverb | 102
    Brian Fiu Kolia

Part III: Revisiting Colonial Mythologies

Whores and Saints: Glimpses of Eve in Early Australian History | 123
    Barbara Deutschmann

"Money Made Us": Reading Australia Through Jesus' Teachings on Money | 139
    Jonathan Cornford

"The Rust in the Wheat and the Dearth of the Dry Season": Ned Kelly's Victorian Apocalypse | 159
    Glen O'Brien

Part IV: Political and Personal Readings

The "Free Enterprise Parable"? Contesting John Howard's Appropriation of a Story Told by Jesus | 177
    Deborah R. Storie

Truth Within the Public Square: Morality, Rhetoric, and the Australian Christian Lobby | 199
    Michelle Eastwood

Solid Rock, Sacred Ground: Reading the Hebrew Bible within a Five Kilometer Radius | 219
    Megan Turton

Magnificat, Invasion, Reception, and the Call to Listen | 236
    Anne Elvey

Part V: Response

Reading the Bible in Australia, Maundy Thursday 2023 | 259
    Meredith Lake

Acknowledgements

WITH MORE ENTHUSIASM THAN experience, three researchers got together at a University of Divinity Research conference and proposed a book which responded to the invitation from Meredith Lake to continue conversations about the Bible's place in Australia. Meredith was contacted, expressed immediate interest in the idea, and agreed to write the reflective chapter that now concludes the book. Without her enthusiastic endorsement the book would not have got off the ground. The steady and experienced hand of Glen O'Brien guided us in the early stages and provided valuable encouragement as the book was being finalized.

We are grateful to ANZATS (Australian and New Zealand Association of Theological Studies) and FBS (Fellowship of Biblical Studies) who encouraged our endeavors and provided conference platforms to showcase our work. Authors interested in contributing pieces to this book presented ideas to other scholars and received fruitful feedback from the wider academic community.

Some twenty reviewers read early drafts of chapters and gave peer advice to authors. A bracing review is a gift to writers and we appreciated the generosity of our reviewers who gave their time, wisdom, and encouragement to the project.

The contributing authors have been on the journey with us, navigating through COVID-19 delays, lockdowns, cancelled conferences, and other disruptions, yet have each produced a unique and valuable chapter. The book reflects the mosaic of perspectives from different parts of the theological and ecclesiastical spectrum. We believe our authors have done wonderful work. Our heartfelt thanks to them.

The cover art, *Healing Prayer* by Safina Stewart is a reading of the Bible in itself. Thank you, Safina, for sharing your art and accompanying words so generously. We acknowledge Dalton McCaughey Library staff who helped us with resources and a collaborative working space when we put the book together. We acknowledge with gratitude a grant from the Australian Research Theology Foundation Inc. (ARTFInc.) to assist with publication costs.

Thanks are also due to George Callihan, our editor and other staff at Wipf & Stock for shepherding the publication process. Finally, to those personal supporters, the intimates, confidantes, and pilgrims who listened patiently, heard well, advised wisely, made tea, and baked bread: to these unnamed heroes, our heartfelt thanks.

We hope you enjoy the result of the labors of the many people named above whose collaborative endeavors have produced *Reading the Bible in Australia*.

Deborah R. Storie
Barbara Deutschmann
Michelle Eastwood

Healing Prayer
A Story Prayed through Art

Safina Stewart

The painting on the cover, Healing Prayer, was given to me in a dream at a time when my life was very painful. Despite all the disturbance I was going through, the Holy Spirit inspired a painting that speaks of God's peace and calm. It is simple, crisp, clear, confident, and well-balanced.

The vivid orangey red is our land and the blood spilled on the land. The blue-grey-green is the sea, the ocean. The cream line represents the shorelines of Australia, the beaches and cliffs of the mainland and of all the islands. The U prints are the marks we leave when we sit cross-legged in the sand. There are seven U prints in a circle facing inwards orientating on a central focus. The central large U print, outlined with dots, is Jesus. Wherever Jesus sits, wherever Jesus chooses to sit, that is holy ground.

The circle of U prints around Jesus represents both the Indigenous peoples of Australia and the colonizers, all painted a beautiful cream color because we are all made in the image of Creator. Their relationship is a difficult and complex one. The straight journey lines are pathways that show people coming into the center. The wavy journey lines show how people travelled going out from the center.

My prayer is that people would come together at the feet of Jesus, to sit together with Jesus and learn how to do right relationship and healing in this land, in this Country. We are all family now. Whether by good adoption or by bad relationship, we are now joined to each other. My prayer is about understanding and healing for the relationship between First and Second peoples. There has been extreme violence and injury, devastation and irreplaceable loss of so much that is precious: species, ecosystems, communities, families, children, culture, lore, song, traditions, and language. What is each of our responsibility for the restoration process? How do we fulfill our destiny and calling as children of God, enabling healing change, right relationship, reckoning with the past and building a better future?

This painting is not about healing through religion. I intentionally ignored things that can dismantle people's hopes and faith: buildings, roles, institutions . . . Healing is about relationship, not religion. This is an inclusive circle. Everyone, no matter their heritage, background, experiences, faith constructs, and affiliations, everyone knows what it is like to sit with, to be with, and to connect well with others.

The first part of my prayer is that we would come and sit together. Each straight line is a track of footprints coming in. These people need to get to the central destination as fast as they can. Weighed down by their burdens, they look down at the ground. All they can do is put one foot in front of the other. The straight lines come from every direction. Everyone from every place, all of us wounded, all of us with bad history, all seeking peace, we are all invited. Sitting in a circle, we are all on the same level. We come in humility, cherishing creation, honoring each other, our time together, and our conversation.

The second part of my prayer is that Jesus would meet with us. Everything in the Bible tells me that Jesus *will* meet with us! Jesus invites all who are tired and weary and burdened—that's us! The way of Jesus, the yoke of Jesus, is easy and light. My prayer is that Jesus would sit with us in our blood, mud, pain, disillusionment, and mixed-up confused identity; that he would sing the magnificent songs of truth, love, and healing to us; and that we would be healed. The invitation is beautiful, but listening takes time and trust.

The third part of my prayer is that we would carry healing back out to all our places, families, communities, and workplaces needing care and love, strength and inspiration, vision and purpose. Each wavy line shows people going out from the circle with joyful movement. Having laid our burdens down at the campfire, we travel out lighter, with a spring in our step, dancing to the song that Jesus has sung over us. Heads high, we carry healing back to wherever the truth and life-giving healing power of Jesus is needed. This healing and vision are practical, grounded in truth and justice, leading to action.

Healing Prayer reminds me that we can do healing in Australia. It reminds me that our healing depends on each other's willingness. Our willingness to come together is more powerful than we could ever imagine. Just a little yes, even a whispered yes, is still a yes.

Safina Stewart is an Aboriginal and Torres Strait Islander artist based in Wonthaggi in Victoria. Her Aboriginal heritage comes from Wuthathi Country in Far North Queensland. Her Torres Strait Islander heritage comes from Mabuiag Island. Her non-Indigenous heritage comes mainly from Scotland.

Contributors

Mark G. Brett

Professor Mark Brett teaches Hebrew Bible in Wurundjeri Country. He was raised in Papua New Guinea, which has yielded a lifelong interest in the cultural contexts of education. His most recent book is *Locations of God: Political Theology in the Hebrew Bible* (OUP, 2019), and he is currently writing on the history of Indigenous rights in international law.

Jonathan Cornford

Doctor Jonathan Cornford is the co-founder of Manna Gum, a not-for-profit organization that seeks to help Christians reclaim a biblical vision of economic life. He has doctorates in political economy and theology, and a background in international development. His research interests centre around the intersections of politics, economy, ecology and theology. Jonathan lives in Bendigo, Victoria, with his wife and two daughters, where they are members of Seeds, a small intentional Christian community seeking to live simply, justly and generously.

Barbara Deutschmann

Doctor Barbara Deutschmann worked in international development with Interserve and with Tearfund Australia for many years and is now a post-doctoral research associate at Whitley College, and occasional tutor at Trinity College, Melbourne. Her interests include gender in the Hebrew

Bible and early Australian feminism. She has published a book entitled *Creating Gender in the Garden* (T&T Clark, 2022). She lives on Wurundjeri Country and shares life with husband, Peter, three adult children and a clutch of grandchildren and is part of St Mark's Anglican church, Spotswood, Victoria.

Michelle Eastwood

Doctor Michelle Eastwood is Director of Research at Australian Lutheran College. Her research interests include gender and sexuality, Hebrew Bible, and worship and liturgy. She has degrees in psychology, history, education and theology and enjoys working at the intersections of these areas of interest. Michelle lives and works on the lands of the Wathaurong People of the Kulin Nation.

Anne Elvey

Doctor Anne Elvey lives on Boon Wurrung Country in Seaford, Victoria. Her publications include *Reading with Earth: Contributions of the New Materialism to an Ecological Feminist Hermeneutics* (Bloomsbury T&T Clark, 2022) and *Reading the Magnificat in Australia: Unsettling Engagements* (Sheffield Phoenix, 2020). Anne is an honorary research fellow, Pilgrim Theological College, University of Divinity, and an adjunct research fellow, Monash University.

Samuel Freney

Doctor Samuel Freney is a translation consultant with the Bible Society of Australia, an honorary post-doctoral research associate with Morling College, and an ordained deacon in the Anglican diocese of Sydney. Interested in many languages, Sam works with teams around Australia and the South Pacific as they communicate Scripture in their contexts. He, his wife Kristy, and his daughter Elissa are part of All Saints' Anglican Church in North Epping.

Brian Kolia

Doctor Brian Fiu Kolia is a second-generation Australian-born Samoan. He is a lecturer in Old Testament studies at Malua Theological College, Samoa.

He holds a PhD from the University of Divinity, Naarm (Melbourne), Australia. His research interests include diasporic, decolonizing readings/interpretation, and cultural and indigenous/native knowledge. More importantly, he is a husband to Tanaria and a father to Elichai.

Meredith Lake

Doctor Meredith Lake is an historian and broadcaster interested in how Australians understand the big questions of faith and meaning. She currently hosts *Soul Search*, a weekly ABC podcast about the lived experience of religion and spirituality. Her most recent book is the multi-award-winning *The Bible in Australia: a Cultural History* (NewSouth, 2020). Her PhD examined religious ideas about the environment in Australian colonial history.

Ray Minniecon

Doctor Ray Minniecon is a descendant of the Kabi Kabi and Gurang Gurang nations of South-East Queensland, and Ambrym Island in Vanuatu. He is honorary pastor of Scarred Tree Ministry at St John's Anglican Church, Glebe, Sydney, serves on the boards of other Indigenous ministries, and advises welfare and development organizations. Ray has a BA in theology (Murdoch University) and an honorary doctorate from NAIITS where he helped establish the first fully accredited International Indigenous University.

Glen O'Brien

Reverend Professor Glen O'Brien is Research Coordinator at Eva Burrows College within the University of Divinity. He is also Professor of Christian Thought and History and Chair of Examiners in the University. A Uniting Church minister, he has been employed by The Salvation Army as a theological educator since 2009 and is a member of the Methodist-Roman Catholic International Commission. His main research area is Wesley and Methodist studies, and his books include *Methodism in Australia: A History*, edited with Hilary Carey (Ashgate, 2015), *Wesleyan-Holiness Churches in Australia* (Routledge, 2018) and *John Wesley's Political World* (Routledge, 2023).

Anne Pattel-Gray

Professor Anne Pattel-Gray is head of the School of Indigenous Studies at the University of Divinity, Melbourne, Australia. Anne has a PhD from the University of Sydney with the major focus on Aboriginal religion and spirituality and a Doctor of Divinity from India. She is a recognized scholar, theologian, activist and prolific writer. Anne is a descendant of the Bidjara/Kari Kari Nations in Queensland and a renowned Aboriginal leader within Australia. She has dedicated her life to the struggle of Australian First Nations as a campaigner and lobbyist seeking justice, equity, and equal representation for First Nations people.

Deborah R. Storie

Reverend Doctor Deborah Storie lived and worked in a conflict-affected region periodically over several decades while also supporting Tearfund Australia in governance, project review, theological reflection, and other roles. Now Senior Pastor at East Doncaster Baptist Church and lecturer in New Testament with the University of Divinity, she seeks to read and respond to the Bible in ways that build peace and promote ecological, social and economic justice. Deborah now lives on Wurundjeri Land. She enjoys walking.

Deborah Shuh Yi Tan

Deborah Shuh Yi Tan has a longstanding interest in languages and intercultural studies, which she pursued in Malaysia, and in a minor thesis for the completion of her masters degree in theological studies in Australia. She is currently a PhD candidate in applied linguistics at Monash University.

Megan Turton

Doctor Megan Turton is lecturer in Hebrew Bible and Language at Whitley College, the University of Divinity. She has a PhD in biblical studies from the University of Sydney. Her doctoral dissertation on the textual fluidity of law and narrative in Exodus 19–24 will be published through Mohr Siebeck. Her research interests include the Pentateuch, the character and functions of biblical law, and ecological hermeneutics.

Naomi Wolfe

Naomi Wolfe is a trawlwoolway Aboriginal woman with Jewish German and Irish heritage who lives on Wurundjeri Country. Naomi is an academic at Australian Catholic University where she teaches indigenous and ancient histories. She has the privilege of being the director of academic programs for NAIITS College, Sydney College of Divinity. Naomi has a love of history of all types and enjoys discussions of history and theology. Naomi shares a home with her nephew Ollie and is a member of the Roman Catholic and Anglican traditions of Christianity.

Abbreviations

Biblical Texts and Versions

CEB	Common English Bible
CEV	Contemporary English Version
CSB	Christian Standard Bible
ESV	English Standard Version
GNT	Good News Translation
KJV	King James Version
LXX	The Septuagint
NCB	New Catholic Bible
NIRV	New International Reader's Version
NIV	New International Version
NJB	New Jerusalem Bible
NKJV	New King James Version
NLV	New Life Version
NRSV	New Revised Standard Version
NRSVUE	New Revised Standard Version Updated Edition
RSV	Revised Standard Version

Journals, Periodicals, and Major Reference Works

BAR	*Biblical Archaeology Review*
BibInt	*Biblical Interpretation*
CBQ	*Catholic Biblical Quarterly*
HALOT	Ludwig Koehler, Walter Baumgartner and Johann J. Stamm, eds. *The Hebrew and Aramaic Lexicon of the Old Testament*. Translated by Mervyn E. J. Richardson. Leiden: Brill, 1994–1999.

JAJ	*Journal of Ancient Judaism*
JBL	*Journal of Biblical Literature*
JETS	*Journal of the Evangelical Theological Society*
JSNT	*Journal for the Study of the New Testament*
JSOT	*Journal for the Study of the Old Testament*
JSRNC	*Journal for the Study of Religion, Nature and Culture*
TDOT	G. Johannes Botterweck and Helmer Ringgren, eds. *Theological Dictionary of the Old Testament*. Translated by John T. Willis et al. Grand Rapids: Eerdmans, 1974–2006.

General

ABC	Australian Broadcasting Corporation
ACL	Australian Christian Lobby
AIATSIS	Australian Institute of Aboriginal and Torres Strait Islander Studies
ANE	Ancient Near East
ANU	Australian National University
ANZAC	Australian and New Zealand Army Corps
APY	Anangu Pitjantjatjara Yankunytjatjara (lands)
ATF	Australian Theological Forum
ATS	Association of Theological Schools
BCE	Before the Common Era
CE	Common Era
CSIRO	Commonwealth Scientific and Industrial Research Organisation
FOBAI	Forum of Bible Agencies International
HB	Hebrew Bible
ISPCK	Indian Society for the Propagation of Christian Knowledge
IVP	InterVarsity Press
JPS	The Jewish Publication Society
LGBTQIA+	A term used to describe lesbian, gay, bisexual, trans and intersex people collectively
MT	Masoretic Text
NAIDOC	National Aborigines and Islanders Day Observance Committee
NAIITS	North American Institute for Indigenous Theological Studies. NAIITS is used as a name rather than an acronym by NAIITS College, Sydney, and NAIITS: An Indigenous Learning Community.

NCLS	National Church Life Survey
NT	New Testament
ODA	Official Development Assistance
OT	Old Testament
SBL	Society of Biblical Literature
SBS	Special Broadcasting Service
SCM	Student Christian Movement
SOGIESC	A term to describe sexual orientation, gender identity and expression, and sex characteristics collectively for the purposes of law and policy
SPCK	Society for the Propagation of Christian Knowledge
UNDP	United Nations Development Programme
WWF	World Wildlife Fund for Nature

Introduction

THE BIBLE DOES NOT interpret itself. When isolated from the broader traditions to which they belong, biblical texts can have almost limitless functions. For many Australians, for instance, the words of John 15:13 are familiar, but they may be unaware that the words have a history prior to the public readings on Anzac Day.[1] In common use, the saying honors combatants killed in foreign wars as those who "laid down their lives" for the sake of kin and country, enacting and embodying "the greatest love." Some Australians worry, however, that this use of words attributed to Jesus romanticizes war as a noble, even heroic, endeavor, and discourages any interrogation of the mixed motives and fraught consequences of Australia's more recent military involvements (Afghanistan, Iraq, Vietnam), and the militarization of our international relations, economy, and society.[2]

This book responds to Meredith Lake's *The Bible in Australia: A Cultural History*, and aims to shine a light on the various ways that the Bible is read in Australia today.[3] Lake described the Bible in Australia as "a many-splendoured thing: an object, a text, a source of stories and ideas; a word read, gossiped, preached, tattooed; and seen as everything from a resented imposition to the very Word of God." Her book disrupts any notion that Australia is "a doggedly secular society."[4] In the 2021 census, 49 percent of the population identified as having no religion with just under 44 percent claiming affiliation with Bible-reading religions, Judaism and Christianity.[5]

---

1. The NKJV of John 15:13 reads, "Greater love has no one than this, than to lay down one's life for their friends." On Anzac Day, see Australian War Memorial, "ANZAC DAY."
2. See, for example, Leunig, "Anzac Epitaph"; Campbell, "Anzac Day Lament."
3. Lake, *Bible in Australia*, 5.
4. Lake, *Bible in Australia*, 4.
5. Australian Bureau of Statistics, "Religious Affiliation in Australia"; Peter Kohn,

Religious identification is, however, a highly unreliable guide to religious practice. Other research estimated that only 7 percent of Australians consider themselves "active practisers" of the Christian faith.[6] This does not, however, reduce the need for critical study of the Bible and its history of influences.[7]

The Bible has not always been read well. The unfortunate alliance between interpretations of Bible texts and the colonial project has had disastrous consequences for Indigenous and Pasifika peoples and for their traditional lands. Gendered readings of texts have weaponized the Bible against women and non-binary people. Those who revere the Bible as a holy book have adroitly sidestepped biblical traditions which condemn the amassing of wealth, affirm the equal dignity of all people, and enjoin love of neighbor and enemy.

※

Lake envisages the Bible in Australia operating in "three main guises."[8] The "globalising Bible" matters as "part of the colonial inheritance from Britain" and because it "connects Australians to other places and peoples." As understood by the colonists, the Bible provided a warrant to seize the land, dispossess and oppress its peoples, on the one hand, and as a word of God that denounced colonization and its atrocities on the other. As Indigenous Australians made the Bible their own, they used its cultural authority and religious language to affirm their dignity, demand agency, and recover hope.

The "cultural" or "Enlightenment Bible" matters to Australia because of its deep and pervasive influence on its national life. Valued as the source of "shared cultural assumptions, rather than faith," the Bible "informed new visions of citizenship" and "influenced the ways people imagined themselves and their community, the kind of society they were building."[9] Biblical imagery, ideas, characters, and language exert a pervasive and powerful influence on Australian culture and its national life, often dancing unrecognized through conversations and dreams.

The "theological Bible" ("the Bible as the word of God") matters to Australians "because of its role in the life of faith."[10] The theological Bible is not apolitical. As individuals and communities are inspired by its vision of

---

"Record Number of Jews." 43.9 percent of the Australian population identified as Christian and 0.4 percent as Jewish.

6. McCrindle, *Faith and Belief in Australia*, 7.
7. Lake, *Bible in Australia*, 12, 428.
8. Lake, *Bible in Australia*, 5–18.
9. Lake, *Bible in Australia*, 12.
10. Lake, *Bible in Australia*, 13.

the good, they have taken on "an informed posture of altruistic engagement towards wider society."[11]

Reading the Bible in Australia invites deeper reflection on the difference that the Bible, variously understood, has made, still makes, and could make, to Australia. Its contributors probe the intersections between vital debates about Australian identity (who Australians have been, are, and aspire to become) and the Bible, bringing a range of perspectives to critical themes—indigeneity, colonization, and migration; landscape, biodiversity, and climate; gender and marginality; economics, ideology, and rhetoric. Most chapters explore the past and present influence of a particular biblical text or theme, offer a fresh contextually and ethically informed reading, and interrogate the wider consequences of reading the Bible that way. Most authors are careful to locate themselves socially and in relation to local and global networks of power and privilege. Unapologetically Australian in inflection and focus, each chapter testifies that the Bible and how it is read mattered to Australia—and still does.

All contributors to *Reading the Bible in Australia* approach the Bible as residents or recent residents of the lands now called Australia. Their reading locations vary in other respects, as do the predispositions, commitments, and interests with which they read. All study the Bible academically as biblical scholars, theologians, or historians, and are cognizant of the globalizing purposes for which the Bible has too often been used. We editors are convinced that the purpose of biblical research should be the pursuit of communal shalom (peace, wholeness, well-being) as well as encouraging and equipping Bible-reading communities to interpret the Bible in life-giving ways that promote justice and peace and restore the earth.[12] *Reading the Bible in Australia* does not pretend to represent the rich diversity of Australian society nor the multiple ways in which the Bible is read on these lands. It does, however, afford a glimpse of how, when interpreted carefully and communicated respectfully, the Bible can enrich and deepen national conversations.

The editors of this volume are white women of Anglo-Saxon heritage who speak English as a first language, and live, without significant physical disability, on the lands of the Wurundjeri and the Wathawurrung peoples of the Kulin Nations. Although we have each experienced periods of subsistence anxiety, we are acutely aware of our relative economic and social privilege. All Australian citizens, two of us are Australian-born.

Contrasting life experiences shape our approaches to the Bible and to this book. After graduating as a veterinarian, Deborah lived and worked in

---

11. Lake, *Bible in Australia*, 17–18.
12. Wolterstorff, *Educating for Shalom*, 10–26.

rural Australia before moving to a conflict-affected region of Central Asia. Taught from childhood to read the Bible devotionally and doctrinally, she began to read differently while living in a context where the foundational middle-class assumptions and dualisms of her native culture did not apply. While Deborah still reads the Bible theologically (as the word of God), the questions that now frame her reading are located, communal, practical, and political as well as personal.

Raised in the western suburbs of Melbourne, Barbara trained and worked as a teacher before moving to India with her husband where she parented three children while working in health programs facilitated by an Indian-led medical mission organization. After returning from India, she worked for many years with Tearfund Australia in both international and local Indigenous programs. The Bible has always been part of her journey. She reads it confessionally, that is, listening for the divine voice, and as a scholar, and sees no conflict between these two perspectives.

Born during a flood in Warwick, South East Queensland, Michelle has lived most of her life in Geelong. The daughter and granddaughter of Lutheran ministers, she grew up in culturally-Germanic and fairly conservative traditions, always aware that her ancestors emigrated to Australia in the mid-1800s in order to practice their faith without state interference. Theological studies widened, deepened, challenged, and nurtured her passion for the Hebrew Bible. She now reads the Bible from a literary perspective as a compilation of texts rather than a single cohesive "book," and retains a sympathy for those who read from a wide variety of perspectives.

Overview

First Nations Perspectives

Three First Nations authors emphasize the need for Aboriginal and Torres Strait Islander Christians to decolonize the Bible, theological education, and the church, in order to overcome the ongoing trauma visited upon them by racist interpretations of biblical texts. Raymond Minniecon, Anne Pattel-Gray, and Naomi Wolfe remind us that God has always been with and been known by First Nations peoples: God and knowledge of God were not imported by the British colonizers. Minniecon and Pattel-Gray both question theologies that start with Genesis 3 and focus on sin and judgment.

Naomi Wolfe, a trawloolway woman, offers "firesticks to light a wider fire of recognition, reception, and inclusion." Explaining that the colonizing practices of the church continue to exclude and constrain Indigenous

Christians, Wolfe urges readers to join the quest to "separate the Christianity that brings salvation, redemption, and transformation to all, from colonial Christianity that has been the vehicle of so much suffering and trauma." Wolfe's personal journey toward "decolonization" testifies to the importance of Aboriginal and Torres Strait Islander Christians being able to participate in theological education in authentically Indigenous contexts. A tantalizing glimpse of her reading of the Parable of the Good Samaritan (Luke 10:30–37) demonstrates how the readings of those who read "from the place of being Aboriginal and/or Torres Strait Islander" are likely to differ from the readings of other Australians.

Raymond Minniecon reads Job as an Aboriginal story. His story-telling approach invites readers to read Job *as if* looking over Minniecon's shoulder and, so, experience the story in his company and *as if* from his perspective. Minniecon explores four of Job's dialogues (three with his friends, one with God) in the context of the suffering of Aboriginal and Torres Strait Islander peoples. The themes of "blotting out" the day of their birth, being told that their suffering is because of their own sin, and Job's call for an advocate, all resonate with the experience of Aboriginal and Torres Strait Islander peoples. In the final dialogue, God calls Job "back inside the beginning of creation . . . inside the beginning of all things." "This," Minniecon explains, "is what God is saying to my people also. God is inviting us as Indigenous peoples to come back to the beginning . . . to see our suffering from a different starting point."

Anne-Pattel-Gray describes the intimate relationship Aboriginal peoples enjoyed with the Creator Spirit, the Land, and its creatures for thousands of years before turning her attention to the colonizers who invaded Aboriginal land and Aboriginal faith. Unable to see the Creator Spirit's presence with Aboriginal peoples, and blind to their rich spirituality, the colonizers' imperial interpretations of biblical texts "white-washed" the Bible, and denigrated Aboriginal people as "cursed, pagan, and racially inferior." Pattel-Gray personalizes her broad-brush account by describing the impact of "racist heretical interpretations" on herself when the only Aboriginal child in her Sunday School class. Now head of the University of Divinity's School of Indigenous Studies, Pattel-Gray calls "Black and White Australians" to liberate the Bible and theological education "from the bondage of colonialism."

Questions of Culture and Translation

Two chapters in this book reflect on the issues of translation into Indigenous languages. Mark Brett and Deborah Shuh Yi Tan focus on translations of Genesis 1 from the 1840s by William Thomas, Assistant Protector of Port Phillip and Westernport Districts. Thomas was one of the few early settlers who saw the significance of learning Indigenous languages. Brett and Tan analyze Thomas's translations of Genesis 1 from the King James Bible as examples of colonial contact and discuss the Indigenous terms that Thomas used to translate "God." The authors of this chapter reflect on a term finally employed by Thomas for God: *Pundgyl Marman* ("big/high/great father"), a combination of the Eastern Kulin word for the Creator eagle (now commonly spelt *Bunjil*) and *marman* (father). This cultural naming of God follows the inclusive impetus of the Hebrew text of Genesis 1, that "leaves open the naming of God" through its adaption of an Indigenous Canaanite name "El" as the grammatically ambiguous "Elohim." Brett and Tan further note that the term *Pundgyl Marman* was not widely adopted by Aboriginal people, pondering whether this was due to its "associations with imperial invasion."

Both Brett and Tan's work and the following chapter raise awareness about the wider consequences of Hebrew-English translation choices. Samuel Freney takes a different perspective, that of a modern Bible translation consultant. Bible translation has been an important way of preserving Indigenous languages, but Freney's contribution shows how difficult this process can be. His chapter documents the inner working of a Pitjantjatjara translation team as it considers how to translate the word "king" in the book of Samuel. Freney's discussion highlights something that we can often forget: an English-language Bible is itself a translation conveying imperfectly the thought-world of ancient times.

Brian Kolia is a second-generation Australian-born Samoan who introduces us to a Samoan reading of a familiar text. In his chapter, Kolia uses a Pasifika lens to read Exod 12:12–13, the account of the LORD "passing over" the land of Egypt. He employs a *talanoa*, a story-telling, conversational method of biblical investigation unfamiliar to many readers, to read the divine "passing over" alongside a fishing proverb. A diasporic Samoan, Kolia recounts the history of migration of Samoans to Australia, refreshing our reluctant memories about a dark period of mistreatment of Pacific islanders almost two centuries ago. His view of the Exodus text compares God's actions with the movement of a "fish in the night," a phenomenon known to Pasifika fishing communities. Kolia ends with an image of a respectful cultural practice that moves carefully into another's cultural space:

"The challenge is for us to read our Bibles bearing in mind that we are in a new context. We must learn to read in light of the new realities, with respect to the traditional custodians of these lands, and in pursuit of social justice."

Revisiting Colonial Mythologies

Myths are made from stories that we repeatedly tell ourselves, as we participate in a process whereby early impression solidifies into present verity. In this section of the book, authors take an interrogatory scalpel to three areas where myth has abounded.

Glen O'Brien investigates for its "religious instincts" and biblical themes, the *Jerilderie Letter*, a letter dictated by Ned Kelly to gang member Joe Byrne in 1879. O'Brien describes the fabric of Kelly's impoverished Irish-Catholic life where life, faith, and education were interwoven and interactions with churchmen not uncommon. What little education Kelly received, he received from the church and its book which together ". . . formed part of the social imaginary he inhabited . . ." O'Brien argues that Kelly adopted the posture of a divine Avenger, who threatened to reign down vengeance on anyone "who resisted his right to roam the country and redistribute its wealth at his own whim." He concludes that Kelly's religious instincts were genuine and informed by his reading of Scripture and membership in the Catholic Church.

Kelly's law-breaking life was shaped by exclusion and poverty. Jonathan Cornford's chapter queries the existence of any remnant of "commonwealth" within modern Australia. Although settlers brought well-thumbed Bibles with them, their pattern of settlement belied the economic vision contained within its pages. He describes Australia as a nation shaped by the quest for wealth. The series of "rushes" for seal skins, minerals, and agricultural land, were characterized by violence (to land and Indigenous peoples), and by exclusion (of non-whites). The capitalist accommodation within European Christianity was well-established before settlement and the link between faith and ethics long sundered before it took violent form in the wide spaces of Australia. Cornford discusses the economic and ecological vision of the Torah (first five books of the Old Testament) and sees its amplification in the words of Jesus. Starkly placed against this vision are the author's description of the effects of climate change and the contemporary rush for personal wealth. Cornford describes Australia as "a post-Christian nation haunted by a Christian conscience" and suggests that biblical visions of commonwealth can still be heard if we listen deeply.

While Cornford focusses on land as the place of access and control, Barbara Deutschmann turns the reader's attention to women's bodies as similar locations of access and control in early Australian colonies. She notes the abusive views of convict women obvious in the writings of ruling men as well as the highly racialized assessment of Indigenous women. Deutschmann focuses on the stereotypical views of these women as "whores" in early Australian colonies and links the development of these ideas to the interpretation of the Eve story in the book of Genesis. She demonstrates that these notions of women were part of a bigger literary debate on the nature and place of women known as the "*querelle des femmes*" or "woman question" in which discussions of biblical Eve had a prominent place. Deutschmann shows that this defective Eve story had been challenged by many women in their writing and in their activism through the centuries. Early Australian feminists wrote their own versions of the story of the first woman, finding liberative interpretations that gave rise to the successful campaigns for control of alcohol and for woman suffrage.

Political and Personal Readings

The personal and the political are not readily distinguished. The chapters by Deborah Storie and Michelle Eastwood are overtly political (in that they engage and challenge public discourse that attributes certain meanings to particular biblical texts) and also deeply personal. The chapters by Megan Turton and Anne Elvey relate their personal, even intimate, engagement with biblical texts. Both intentionally locate their readings in time and place, and draw on those texts to raise broader political-and-personal questions.

Deborah Storie focuses on former Prime Minister John Howard's "free enterprise" appropriation of "the Parable of the Talents" (Matt 25:14–20). Howard presented the parable as a divine exhortation: ". . . those of us in possession of assets have a responsibility to add to those assets." Storie argues that Howard's use of the parable, although a seemingly logical extension of one tradition of its interpretation, overlooks interpretive signals provided by its narrative, canonical, and historical contexts, and reinscribes misconceptions about Jesus' teaching concerning economic relations. Storie reads the parable as a fictional abstract yet realistic story that critiques the accumulation of wealth and the structures that promote it. She introduces readings of Nicaraguan *campesinos*, an American maximum-security prisoner, and two biblical scholars (German and Nigerian) to offer further insights into the parable and its contemporary implications. Pointing out that Howard's reading of the parable aligns with his ideological repositioning of Australian society as "aspirational" rather than "egalitarian," Storie asks how publicly promulgated interpretations of biblical texts to serve political agendas might be more effectively contested.

Anne Elvey shines a light on another subversive biblical text as she creatively engages the song of Mary (Luke 1:46–55), known from its Latin translation as the *Magnificat*. Elvey embraces it as a song of protest against white settler aggression which challenges readers to listen deeply to the songs of protest from First Nations' writers and artists: "As a woman's song, steeped in ancestral knowledge and resistance, the song can be understood not only as a song of praise but also as protest." She asks how, in a context of ongoing colonial invasion of First Nations Country, non-Indigenous Australians can respectfully read biblical texts that arrived as the material artifacts of colonization. Elvey draws on instances of the use of the *Magnificat* in settler Australian art and writing, notably, the short story of writer Henrietta Drake-Brockman published in *The West Australian* newspaper in January 1939. Her chapter describes a stance toward reading the *Magnificat* in a contemporary Australian context that reads the song with restraint, intertextual engagement, and creative witness. Toward the end of her chapter, Elvey offers an example of her own creative writing practice, a poem entitled: "On Visiting Elizabeth in the Western Australian Wheatbelt Mary Sings a Song." She ends with a call to settler readers to listen carefully and deeply, to hear what responses are appropriate from the perspectives of First Nations peoples.

While the *Magnificat* speaks of overturning places of power, Michelle Eastwood highlights the use of selective biblical quotation to buttress positions of power and privilege. Eastwood takes Australian Christian Lobby (ACL) leaders to task for their use of the definite article, ("the truth"), to suggest that simple, agreed moral positions, especially on sexuality and gender, are accessible from the Bible. Eastwood argues for the plurality of Christian voices and speaks for the many who feel that the ACL does not speak for them. Exploring former leader Martin Iles' use of Isaiah 59:14 ("Justice is turned back, and righteousness stands at a distance: for truth stumbles in the public square"), she counters that this passage, when read in the context of the wider book of Isaiah, serves to critique the ACL's interpretation. Eastwood notes that the ACL positions itself as the righteous and moral individual who is bravely speaking into the hostile public square on behalf of Australian Christians, but ironically, "is less concerned about the rights of LGBTIQA+ people to live in safety, the rights of Indigenous people, . . . who would benefit from voices speaking about the injustice they face within Australian society."

Megan Turton's chapter is a personal reflection occasioned by the COVID-19 lockdowns she experienced in Melbourne. Lockdown restrictions required the closure of sacred spaces. Turton found, however, with human movement limited to 5 km, urban wildernesses assumed a new aura of holiness. She proposes that we read local landscapes with passages in the Hebrew Bible that reveal that "tree and soil, stone and water, wind and bird, are capable of the state of holiness and of holding the divine presence." Turton demonstrates this sensibility through her reflection, using biblical texts, on her local area, the Yarra Flats. She writes of majestic river red gum trees, the kingfisher bird, and the flows of the Merri Merri Creek. Turton concludes that, read with and through our local landscapes, the biblical texts offer profound possibilities for "re-sanctifying" the land. In recognizing the awe and privilege of standing on solid rock and sacred ground, "we may also encounter new possibilities for our own redemption and sanctification."

We, the editors, are very grateful for the enthusiastic involvement of Meredith Lake in this project. Her response chapter closes the book. She begins by noting the "Judas" allusion used by prominent Aboriginal leader, Noel Pearson. The reader will notice that Lake, as well as many of the authors, write cognizant of the history of colonization and its effects on First Nations people. The final stages of this book project are being conducted in the context of a public debate of great national import: whether to enshrine in the Australian constitution an Indigenous Voice to Parliament. The right of Indigenous peoples to recognition and voice in locations of power has finally percolated to the surface of public consciousness. It is no accident that the campaign has brought biblical language to the surface. Such references speak not only to a common literary heritage but to the disruptive potential of biblical texts. The Bible is a text taken up sometimes as cudgel, sometimes as comfort, but it remains, as Lake has noted, "a public text."

Deborah Storie, Barbara Deutschmann, Michelle Eastwood
June 2023

Bibliography

Australian Bureau of Statistics, "Religious Affiliation of Australians: Exploration of the changes in reported religion in the 2021 Census." 4 July 2022. https://www.abs.gov.au/articles/religious-affiliation-australia.

Australian War Memorial. "ANZAC DAY." 25 April 2013. https://web.archive.org/web/20130501085852/http://www.awm.gov.au/commemoration/anzac/.

Campbell, Wes. "Anzac Day Lament." *Crosslight*. 21 April 2017. https://crosslight.org.au/2017/04/21/anzac-day-lament-reflection/.

Deutschmann, Barbara. *Creating Gender in the Garden: The Inconstant Partnership of Eve and Adam*. London: T&T Clark, 2022.

Kohn, Peter. "Record number of Jews." *The Australian Jewish News*. 30 June 2022.

Lake, Meredith. *The Bible in Australia: A Cultural History*. Sydney: NewSouth, 2020.

Leunig, Michael. "Anzac Epitah." 22 April 2015. https://www.leunig.com.au/works/recent-cartoons/313-epitaph.

McCrindle. *Faith and Belief in Australia: A national study on religion, spirituality and worldview trends*. Sydney: McCrindle, 2017.

Wolterstorff, Nicholas. *Educating for Shalom: Essays on Christian Higher Education*. Grand Rapids: Eerdmans, 2004.

Part I

First Nations' Readings

Reading the Bible in Australia
A Place for Aboriginal and Torres Strait Islander Peoples?

Naomi Wolfe

The Lord our God be with us, as he was with our ancestors;
may he not leave us or abandon us.

1 Kings 8:57 NRSV[1]

It is an age-old cultural and social protocol to acknowledge and pay respects to the Ancestors, traditional owners, and custodians of the land on which we are gathered.[2] I live on Wurundjeri lands and have done so for over half my life now. I pay my respects to the thousands of generations of Wurundjeri peoples who care for the land upon which I live and work. I am a trawloolway[3] woman with Jewish German and Irish heritage, and it is my great privilege to give back to community by working as an academic, historian and theologian within Australian Catholic University and NAIITS: An

---

1. Throughout this chapter I use several different biblical translations, a practice I owe to Dr. Sr. Barbara Stead, RSM, who encouraged her students to read multiple translations, comparing the translations themselves and the implications of those translations. Any errors remain mine, not Barbara's!

2. I capitalize "Ancestors" and certain other terms to denote respect and relationship rather than a casual unconnected mention-in-passing.

3. Our language does not use capitalization. trawloolway country is in North East lutriwita/Tasmania.

Indigenous Learning Community.[4] I acknowledge and thank my Ancestors for the love, care, and guidance that they teach me—I am because we are.

I invite you, the reader, to think about the lands on which you live, work, and play. Do you know the names of the local traditional owners and custodians? Do you know the history of the lands, waters, and skies of where you live? Do you know the shared histories of the local Indigenous peoples and your history—your personal story, your work story, your church story? These may well be questions that you may or may not have considered previously. But they are important—for the words of 1 Kgs 8:57 remind us that God was with the Ancestors of this land, and of every land.

I often see folks struggling to understand how God could have been here before colonial Christianity. After all, the Bible, Jesus, and ways of doing church came on the First Fleet, right? Well, if we remind ourselves that God is the Alpha and the Omega (Rev 1:8), then it becomes infinitely possible to see how God was already here in these lands before European ships and peoples arrived.[5] Otherwise, we get ourselves into theological somersaults that could be unhelpful to all concerned. We need to spend more time finding ways to separate the Christianity that brings salvation, redemption, and transformation to all, from colonial Christianity that has been the vehicle of so much suffering and trauma, both here in Australia, and around the world.

Meredith Lake writes:

> From the outset, the Bible was associated with the colonising projects of transporting convicts, appropriating Aboriginal land, and forming settler societies. To understand its long-term significance in Australian life, we need to consider not only the transmission of its European cultural products, but the messy realities of culture contact and the dynamics of colonial power.[6]

With these words in mind, what space does the wider church and its supporting institutions—universities and theological colleges, mission and community service organizations—make for the reception, inclusion, and leadership of Aboriginal and Torres Strait Islander theologians and their

---

4. NAIITS: An Indigenous Learning Community evolved from the formalization of the North American Institute for Indigenous Theological Studies and the involvement of Indigenous communities in Australia, the Philippines, South America, and Central America. Now truly international, NAIITS: An Indigenous Learning Community no longer uses NAIITS as an acronym.

5. It should be remembered that while the ships were "European" the peoples on board were not all European. Pybus, "Black Caesar," reminds us that people of African and African American descent were aboard the First Fleet.

6. Lake, *Bible in Australia*, 8–9.

communities? How might reading the Bible from the place of being Aboriginal and/or Torres Strait Islander be different from those who originate from settler societies or recent patterns of immigration? How might we come together to address issues at the heart of continuing colonization, and explore matters such as Indigenous readings of text and tradition? It begins with listening and reflecting. This chapter aims to bring these matters to a discussion as an offering from community to community, as firesticks to light a wider fire of recognition, reception, and inclusion of Aboriginal and Torres Strait Islander communities and their theologians.

> *The Lord is the One who goes before you. He will be with you.*
> *He will be faithful to you and will not leave you alone.*
> *Do not be afraid or troubled.*
>
> DEUTERONOMY 31:8 NLV

Deuteronomy 31:8 was one of my grandmother's favorite verses. I can remember her telling it to us grandkids over and over when we were small, and again when we grew up. It was one of the Bible verses she would quietly utter in her final weeks. I know of other Elders who also clung to this verse in times of trouble. A beloved Mutta Mutti Elder and Catholic Christian, Aunty Joyce Smith, who has since returned to the Dreaming after a battle with cancer, told me that she liked this verse because, even though it did not change the bad things, or the uncertainty, it reminded her that she was never alone, that our God knew what was happening, and so the verse gave her comfort. She believed very firmly that God and the Ancestors were with her in every step of the journey regardless of whether she wanted to be on that journey or not. It was one of the reasons why she and others felt led in faith and in determination to begin the Aboriginal Catholic Ministry in Melbourne.[7] For many non-Indigenous Christians, and many Indigenous peoples who have been wounded by colonial Christianity, it might be strange to seek comfort in a text that arrived on these shores in 1788. But as many Indigenous Christians know the world over, the text might have arrived on Country in 1492, or 1788, but God the Creator was already here, and we can connect and recognize that in both text and Country.

As Indigenous Christians, we know that Creation is found here as much as anywhere and that the Creator has always been here with us. Colonial Christianity arrived with the First Fleet in 1788, but God was already

---

7. Aboriginal Catholic Ministry would grow and expand throughout Victoria. On which see, http://www.cam1.org.au/acmv and https://melbournecatholic.org/live/aboriginal-catholic-ministry.

here with Aboriginal and Torres Strait Islander communities. So for Indigenous Christian communities, it is both possible and urgent that we find ways of decolonizing the texts, the traditions, and the viewpoints of colonial Christianity for the health of all of us—not just for Indigenous peoples. The texts of 1 Kgs 8:57 and Deut 31:8 are reminders for us that the work of answering all the questions posed above is not some new or "woke" thing that seeks to destabilize or corrupt the church, but a mission that seeks to bring healing and wholeness to the story of Creation in Australia.

> *Turn your ear toward wisdom*
> *and stretch your mind toward understanding.*
>
> PROVERBS 2:2 CEB

This might seem like a rather daunting task to achieve but the words of the writer of Proverbs give us a moment to breathe and to reflect before turning our ears and stretching our minds towards understandings, Indigenous understandings. These that were ignored at best, and at worst labeled as evil, as disposable, not only by early colonial Christianity, but by continuing forms of it today. These understandings of the relationship between Creator and Creation in these lands are not new to Indigenous communities. We Indigenous communities have tried for generations and generations to get the church and its agencies to listen, accept, and make space for the gifts given to them by the Creator. Aboriginal and Torres Strait Islander men and women have answered the call to ministry and service over generations, seeking to create reconciliation, and to build bridges between Indigenous Christianity and colonial Christianity.

Bidjara Professor Anne Pattel-Gray writes:

> Aboriginal pastors were tired of white (British-descended) churchmen and missionaries telling the Indigenous people they were subhuman. Aboriginal people were fed up with white people (mis)speaking with authority on the Indigenous people while labelling their culture as primitive and uncivilized[8]

Aboriginal and Torres Strait Islander communities still struggle with this viewpoint in churches and institutions today. These are the lived experiences of the "messy realities of culture contact and the dynamics of colonial power."[9]

Wiradjuri scholar Professor Mark McMillan writes:

---

8. Pattel-Gray, "Methodology in an Aboriginal Theology," 278.
9. Lake, "Bible in Australian History and Culture," 15.

> Australians seem to be always in need of re-education. Our embrace of the past is conveniently selective. We go to extraordinary lengths to keep the flame of ANZAC alive at the same time as we reduce the history of our frontier to a mere 'blemish' in the story of the nation's success. Over the last half-century, our political leaders have lurched from humble recognition of dispossession to shameless evasion.[10]

It would seem that whenever Indigenous peoples seek to commemorate Indigenous memories of the past, the wider Australian society shudders and demands we move on.[11] Some voice their concerns in a less than pleasant fashion across social media, the digital media, and in gatherings across homes and schools, and also in churches.[12]

Racism towards Indigenous peoples is not just acknowledged by Indigenous communities themselves; it is also acknowledged by the wider Christian community. The National Church Life Survey found that, when asked "whether racism towards Aboriginal people is still a concern," seventy-five percent of survey respondents agreed.[13] Perhaps the Australian Christian population might understand this racism better if the various traditions, theological and bible colleges, and mission agencies dedicated the space and time to acknowledging and to understanding. It will only be then that the hope of dismantling systemic and individual racism and prejudices might come to fruition.

Ah, I can hear an echo of, "But it's not my fault, I'm not guilty." I hear you, and I acknowledge that you as the individual reader may not have contributed to the marginalization of communities or to racist acts. But I want to take a moment to refocus this emotion and this response. I want us to take it out of the realm of "guilt" for a moment. I believe that guilt is deeply problematic for two reasons (and others but let us stick to these two!). Firstly, assuming or wearing the emotion of guilt leads to anger and a shutting down of relationships, of conversations, and of sharing our understandings together. The guilt-laden person is so angry at being mislabeled that they shut down any hope of communicating in an honest fashion that could lead to new beginnings or healed relationships. A second response is to become so overwhelmed by a sense of guilt that the projection of emotions takes up all emotional, spiritual, and intellectual energy, so that, again, there is a shutting down of relationships. This burden, furthermore, is often

---

10. Cited by McKenna, *Moment of Truth*, 26.
11. See McGrady, "The past isn't in the past."
12. Carlson et al. "Trauma, Shared Recognition," 2–6.
13. Bevis, Pepper and Powell, "Indigenous and Non-Indigenous Relations," 11.

transferred to the affected or marginalized community to somehow make the guilty one feel better or be reassured that they are one of the good ones. Both responses are unnecessary and unhelpful. They are also unrealistic in the aim of decolonizing the church experience, the theological education experience, the mission experience, and so on.

If we want a way forward that does not see sections of the Christian community continue to be marginalized, then we must realize that it is a much bigger task than relying only on an individualistic response. It is time for us within communities to recognize our locality. Most non-Indigenous Christians participate in systems, structures, and organizations that are unequal, often unintentionally. Guilt is useless, unwanted, and unhelpful in communities recognizing the systemic dismantling, healing, and creation that is necessary. It is time to set aside guilt, and work towards healing our broken churches and agencies so that future generations might engage differently. If this sounds hard, then yes, yes, it is. There is no apology for how hard the journey can be. It has been no picnic for Aboriginal and Torres Strait Islander communities either. There are numerous Elders all across the country who faithfully continue to enter into relationships with churches and agencies in the possibility that their understandings and gifts that the Creator gave to them might be received and celebrated. These are faithful Aboriginal and Torres Strait Islander Christians who have continued to believe and to hope when all evidence suggested that it might be in vain.

> *He has shown you, O mortal, what is good.*
> *And what does the Lord require of you?*
> *To act justly and to love mercy and to walk humbly with your God.*
>
> MICAH 6:8 NIV

What then is required? What is required is more than willingness, more than good intentions, more than plaques upon walls, reconciliation gardens, and so on. All these are important but do very little to dismantle and to decolonize. What is required now is action, action that is long-term, sustainable, and appropriate. This means churches and agencies doing the work to discover their place in the colonial Christian story. This means doing this work before expecting Indigenous peoples to take on yet another reconciliation project or to speak at your church's NAIDOC Week event.[14] Again, these are important and wonderful, but rarely lead to the long-term

---

14. NAIDOC (National Aborigines and Islanders Day Observance Committee) Week celebrates the history, culture, and achievements of Aboriginal and Torres Strait Islander peoples.

sustainable dismantling and recreating or healing required. Chris Budden writes that "churches in Australia have internalized the values of an invading society" yet most churches would be unaware of how, or perhaps even what, that meant.[15] It is past time for the churches to do the difficult work to uncover what this means for them. This work needs to form the foundation for future relationships, for it is only then that we can truly work together to address issues at the heart of continuing colonization. Without this foundation, attempts are transient and unsustainable, leading us all on a merry-go-round of frustration and brokenness.

Thankfully, there are already pockets within the wider church that have been faithfully hard at work. Take heart! There are examples of those hard-working communities and also the incredibly important work of both Christian and non-Christian historians and theologians—Meredith Lake, Mark Brett, Chris Budden, to name a few—whose work and commitment can assist communities to do the foundational work so that they are ready to engage with Aboriginal and Torres Strait Islander Christian historians and theologians such as Uncle and Aunty Graham Paulson, Garry Deverell, Aunty Patricia Courtenay, and Aunty Betty Pike, to name a few.[16] Such foundational work will develop a readiness for creating space and hearing the experiences of Aboriginal and Torres Strait Islander Christians.

> *A time to tear, and a time to sew;*
> *a time to keep silence, and a time to speak.*
> ECCLESIASTES 3:7 ESV.

The burden is not just on churches and agencies but should be shared by theological and Bible colleges too. If the next generations of ministers, priests, pastors, and lay workers are to assist their communities, they need to be equipped for the journey. It is past time for lip service and the casual inclusion of Aboriginal "perspectives" in curricula. Our theological colleges need to answer the call to equip our communities for the work that needs to be done, albeit in different ways depending on whether Indigenous or not, so that we all might heal and share in the continuing gifts of Creation. It is within our colleges that valuable and appropriate research in partnership with Indigenous communities might happen that can transform the knowledge (or ignorance) of our shared stories.

In 1914, the Society for Promoting of Christian Knowledge (SPCK) published missionary Herbert Pitts' treatise entitled *The Australian*

---

15. Budden, *Following Jesus in Invaded Space*, 7.
16. Noongar Elder Aunty Betty Pike entered the Dreaming in February 2023.

Aboriginal and the Christian Church. The church, Pitts maintained, had a duty to its conscience:

> We owe the aboriginals [sic] a tremendous act of reparation. Grievous have been the misdoings of our own guilty past. We have stolen from them their ancestral hunting grounds and given them nothing in return. We have outlawed and disinherited them and made their existence well-nigh impossible except by crime. We have exploited their labor for our own ends.[17]

This is but one example of the problematic reality of colonization upon Aboriginal and Torres Strait Islander peoples being known by missionaries and church people for a long time. Indeed, the Honorable Paul J. Keating, then Prime Minister of Australia, could have echoed the words of Herbert Pitts when he gave what became known as the Redfern Address in 1991:

> The starting point might be to recognize that the problem starts with us non-Aboriginal Australians. It begins, I think, with that act of recognition. Recognition that it was we who did the dispossessing ... It was our ignorance and our prejudice. And our failure to imagine these things being done to us.[18]

*To everything there is a season,
and a time to every purpose under the heavens.*

ECCLESIASTES 3:1 KJV

It is now time for these realities to be rediscovered by the churches as part of their work to own their part of the colonial project. Theological education has a vital role in educating not only future theological academics, but those directly in the field working in ministry, support, and evangelization. In 2009, Rev Dr Charles Sherlock delivered the final report of the project, *Uncovering Theology: the depth, reach and utility of Australian theological education*. This report recommended that higher theological education providers:

> consider more fully how learning is affected by the varied Australian contexts in which teaching, and ministry take place, in particular the opportunities afforded by engagement with indigenous [sic] theologians and colleges.[19]

---

17. Pitts, *Australian Aboriginal and the Christian Church*, 132.
18. https://pmtranscripts.pmc.gov.au/sites/default/files/original/00008765.pdf.
19. Sherlock, *Uncovering Theology*, 115.

For many years the Vocational Education and Training sector work of Wontulp-Bi-Buya College in Cairns and Nungalinya College in Darwin have been preparing Aboriginal and Torres Strait Islander peoples on their journeys of theological education.[20] Both colleges do amazing work with little support, encouraging and teaching Indigenous peoples, and responding to the growing needs of non-Indigenous peoples who want cultural awareness and cultural competency. The burden should be upon non-Indigenous providers not upon Indigenous organizations. Thankfully the tides of imbalance are beginning to turn with the launch of the University of Divinity's School of Indigenous Studies,[21] the appointment of Rev Dr Rex Rigby to Eva Burrows Salvation Army College,[22] and, more recently, the establishment of NAIITS College as a full member institution of the Sydney College of Divinity (SCD) and the first Indigenous designed, developed, delivered, and governed stand-alone theological college.[23] NAIITS previously had a Memorandum of Understanding with Whitley College and the University of Divinity to deliver postgraduate coursework programs and an Indigenous PhD cohort. During this time over a dozen Indigenous postgraduate students achieved graduation. Several PhD students are nearing completion as the Indigenous PhD cohort concludes from that Memorandum of Understanding.

As we head into late 2023, it is both monumental and astounding that there have been more Indigenous theology graduations at postgraduate level in the last five years than at any other time. As the wider Australian community grapples with the Uluru Statement of the Heart,[24] the proposed Voice to Parliament, and matters of treaty and reparation, now is the time for mainstream colleges to work with Indigenous providers to increase their cultural capacity and their willingness to put their ears and hearts as well as their bricks, mortar, and money into decolonizing theological education. The time is now!

Let wise people listen and add to what they have learned.
Let those who understand what is right get guidance.

PROVERBS 1:5 NIRV

---

20. https://www.wontulp.qld.edu.au/; https://www.nungalinya.edu.au/.

21. https://divinity.edu.au/university/school-of-indigenous-studies/.

22. Rev. Dr. Uncle Rex Rigby is the first Indigenous leader of a mainstream Christian denomination, the Wesleyan Methodist Church. On his life and ministry, see https://historymakersradio.com/podcast/rex-rigby.

23. https://www.naiits.com/.

24. https://ulurustatement.org/.

NAIITS College allows Indigenous and non-Indigenous Elders, faculty, and students to experience the best of all worlds through its active approach to decolonizing ourselves, our college, our scholarship, and our praxis. NAIITS College is a fully compliant higher education provider that seeks to actively center Indigenous ways of knowing, being, and doing.

NAIITS: An Indigenous Learning Community is a truly global organization. In the 1970s and 1980s, a curious thing began to happen in organic and isolated ways. Indigenous peoples across the world began to question how they might bring together their identity within their Indigeneity and their identity as followers of Jesus. Aboriginal and Torres Strait Islander communities were included in these communities that sought to find new ways of being Indigenous and Christian. The NAIITS Community is an Indigenous theological community that exists across many countries including Australia, the United States of America, Canada, the Philippines, and South America. It has memoranda of understanding with theological institutions such as Tyndale Seminary (Toronto), Acadia Divinity School (Nova Scotia), and the Sydney College of Divinity (Australia). With no bricks and mortar campuses other than those of its partners, NAIITS seeks to utilize its limited funds for student- and community-responsive theological education.

> *Let your hope keep you joyful,*
> *be patient in your troubles, and pray at all times.*
>
> ROMANS 12:12 GNT

Elders and their communities started to ask why it was not possible for God to be among us before the arrival of Western or colonial forms of Christianity given that God was omnipresent. From time-to-time, Indigenous communities around the world traveled and met with other Indigenous peoples, discovering that they too had similar questions. These connections led to a 1992 pilgrimage to the Middle East which resolved to meet together and discuss the possibility that God might be calling together a global alliance of Indigenous peoples. It was decided to hold the first World Christian Gathering on Indigenous Peoples in Rotorua City, Aotearoa (New Zealand) in the following years. In 1996, several thousands of people from across the globe attended, including a delegation of fifty-one Indigenous North Americans. During the week of gatherings, their study and analysis led participants to return home and build upon this Indigenous intercultural expression of Christian faith that was simultaneously Indigenous and Christian.

It was out of this movement that NAIITS: An Indigenous Learning Community, originally incorporated as the North American Institute for

Indigenous Theological Studies in December 2000, was birthed with the objective of addressing the dearth of theological research, scholarship, and writing by and for Indigenous people. It became immediately obvious that, not only did the content of the instruction need to be more inclusive, but the epistemological, ontological, and sociocultural frameworks of teaching needed to be more clearly amenable to Indigenous ways of knowing and being. Furthermore, instructional attitudes and methodologies needed to shift from the more didactic and reductionist approaches to knowledge acquisition that appeared to them to characterize Western thought, to an understanding that knowledge, and ultimately wisdom, was something that one entered into but could not acquire. It was also obvious that our student demographics in any program created would be older and more experienced in ministry and in life, but in high probability would have incomplete or interrupted academic progression upon their entry into graduate studies.

We identified the need to create a theological educational framework and delivery mechanisms that would include the unique histories and experiences of Indigenous peoples, initially in North America, then in other parts of the globe. Given that the Western systems with which they would need to interact were disposed to a relatively constrained way of delivering and tracking tertiary theological education, it also became evident that such an enterprise would, of necessity, be far messier in their teaching than their Western counterparts. Hence, in the NAIITS Community we often speak of being a well-trained, highly dedicated janitorial team, cleaning up the messes created when Indigenous people encounter the Christian institutions of tertiary theological education.

Those who place their hope in the Lord will regain their strength.
They will soar as with eagles' wings,
they will run and not grow weary,
they will walk and not become faint.

ISAIAH 40:31 NCB

NAIITS: an Indigenous Learning Community initially operated to create space for Indigenous peoples to be admitted to tertiary theological and biblical education leading to advanced degrees in a wide range of disciplines within the broad compass of divinity. Having developed capacity to do so, NAIITS began to offer non-accredited bridging programs designed to allow greater numbers of Indigenous people to enroll in theological education. NAIITS subsequently created a curriculum for a masters level degree designed, developed, and delivered by qualified Indigenous faculty. It then sought a partner school through whom to deliver the program as an accredited degree. Following its initial achievement in North America, our Australian, New Zealand, Philippine, and other Indigenous global family asked to be included in the work.

In Australia, Elders and academics were meeting regularly with church leaders, theological colleges, Bible colleges, and universities, asking for the opportunity to develop Indigenous undergraduate and postgraduate programs in theology. Unlike our North American cousins, these hopes and dreams were raised and dashed many times over, leaving Indigenous Christians bruised but never defeated. Prayer and planning continued with conferences at Whitley College spurring us on and encouraging us that it would one day happen! It was a fortunate meeting of Uncle Ray Minniecon and me with Professor Gary Heard and Professor Mark Brett from Whitley College that decided to invite Uncle Terry LeBlanc and his team to Australia to deliver trial postgraduate units, and to meet together to talk about partnership possibilities.

As part of the response to invitations around the world, the name of NAIITS was changed to reflect our commitment to the global context of Indigenous people. Retaining the acronym, NAIITS, we simply added, "An Indigenous Learning Community" to reflect the growing number of Indigenous communities across the world joining together to decolonize biblical studies and theological education. NAIITS: An Indigenous Learning Community has been our legal name ever since. In 2020 we became the first Indigenous institution to gain full accreditation with The Association of Theological Schools (ATS) meaning that we could deliver and accredit our own graduate programs within the North American context. This status gives NAIITS the same accreditation to offer stand-alone coursework and doctoral programs as Harvard University Divinity School, Yale University Divinity School, and Fuller Theological Seminary, among others. As an accredited member of ATS, and in compliance with accreditation standards, NAIITS participates in ongoing, systematic evaluation of the educational efficiency of each of its degree programs: Master of Divinity (MDiv), Master of Theological Studies (MTS), Master of Arts Intercultural Studies (MAIS), Master of Arts Indigenous Community Development Studies (MA-INCD), and Doctor of Philosophy (PhD). In 2022 we took a new bold and historic step: the creation of NAIITS College in Australia.

Why is it important for us to have stand-alone Indigenous institutions? We are often asked, Why not simply create support mechanisms for students in the existing institutions of theological education? NAIITS leadership believes that that would simply gloss the continued lack of deeply rooted theological reflection undertaken within a fully Indigenous paradigm and context. In other words, there would be little added to the wider body of theological investigation and understanding that would specifically and clearly emerge from Indigenous contexts. There would be a greater probability of a simple regurgitation process of Western-constructed and mediated theological understanding with some Indigenous window-dressing. That is not the way forward for Indigenous theological education. Nor is it the way forward for non-Indigenous theological education that seeks to decolonize and engage with Indigenous peoples, their traditions, and their experiences.

> *Let us examine and probe our ways and turn back to the Lord.*
> LAMENTATIONS 3:40 CSB

For me, the NAIITS Community has been a theological lifeline. I was at the point of being burnt out by educational institutions and by churches. This worried me greatly as I wanted, and still want, to be fully the person that I was created to become. I could not do that in mainstream theological reflection. It always felt like "black cladding," an afterthought, or a special occasion. I wanted something more tangible. I needed something that would challenge and affirm me. Before my work with NAIITS, I was looking to walk away from an active faith which saddened me deeply. As I got to know the diverse community of Aboriginal and Torres Strait Islander, North American, South American, and Philippine Indigenous Christian communities, I felt that finally I had a spiritual and an intellectual home. It was a home with fellow seekers, a home where gifts and challenges were received. NAIITS is a community where I can learn and listen and yarn about theological and historical interests, puzzles, and problems. I finally felt like I was making traction on decolonizing myself, and on decolonizing my research and pedagogy/andragogy. For the first time, I did not feel like I was a square peg in a round hole. It was both invigorating and disconcerting! It was within the NAIITS Community that I could begin again my love of the Hebrew Scriptures and the New Testament, and begin to unpick the familiar stories of Sunday school to interpret them through the lens of my own family instead of through a faux Greco-Roman or colonial approach.

Decolonizing the Parable of the Good Samaritan[25]

The Parable of the Good Samaritan (Luke 10:25–37) was one of the first texts I revisited.

25. My PhD thesis will include a more detailed reading of the Parable of the Good

An expert in the law stood up to test Jesus. 'Teacher,' he said, 'What must I do to inherit eternal life?' He said to him, 'What is written in the law? What do you read there?' He answered, 'You shall love the Lord your God with all your heart and with all your soul and with all your strength and with all your mind and your neighbour as yourself.' And he said to him, 'You have given the right answer; do this, and you will live.' But wanting to vindicate himself, he asked Jesus, 'And who is my neighbour?' Jesus replied, 'A man was going down from Jerusalem to Jericho and fell into the hands of robbers, who stripped him, beat him, and took off, leaving him half dead. Now by chance a priest was going down that road, and when he saw him, he passed by on the other side. So likewise a Levite, when he came to the place and saw him, passed by on the other side. But a Samaritan while traveling came upon him, and when he saw him, he was moved with compassion. He went to him and bandaged his wounds, treating them with oil and wine. Then he put him on his own animal, brought him to an inn, and took care of him. The next day he took out two denarii, gave them to the innkeeper, and said, 'Take care of him, and when I come back, I will repay you whatever more you spend.' Which of these three, do you think, was a neighbour to the man who fell into the hands of the robbers?' He said, 'The one who showed him mercy.' Jesus said to him, 'Go and do likewise.' (NRSV)

I have heard this parable include Indigenous or "other" in a couple of different ways, but none really resonated with me. I can remember a Sunday school teacher describing the robbers as "black, dirty, and evil" leaving no doubt as to what she thought about Indigenous peoples and people of color in general. Leaving aside the racism, I was intrigued by the story with its motifs of empire, injustice, and otherness. I was already very interested in history, particularly my own cultural history and that of other ancient worlds such as the Roman Empire, so I read up more about the Roman Empire and those intriguing Samaritans. I asked questions in Sunday school and then at university, but little encouragement or space was forthcoming to continue to unpack the Good Samaritan story. Years later, I heard another Aboriginal woman speak about the Good Samaritan in a different way. Brooke Prentis, a Wakka Wakka woman, speaks about Aboriginal people being:

> robbed, stripped, and beaten each and every day since colonization. Stolen land. Stolen wages. Stolen Generations. Stolen

---

Samaritan.

lives . . . Battered and bruised by an Australia that does not know and does not learn its true history.[26]

This is all true, these things have happened, and continue to happen.

I want to delve a little deeper and a little differently into the story in a way that perhaps turns it on its head, but in a way that seeks to decolonize the story and to open up further discussions. Let's think about what it might mean if Aboriginal people were neither the robber nor the victim in this parable. What might we learn if we begin to think about Aboriginal people as the Good Samaritan, the outsider of mainstream society, who stops to assist the broken and beaten victim? What might we learn if we see colonial Christianity as the robber, the violent thief that inflicts harm and disruption?

It seems to me that we must begin to see the experiences of Aboriginal people as compassionate helpers as much as the broken or the violent. Why cannot we as Aboriginal peoples, as Torres Strait Islanders, as global Indigenous peoples, connect with the merciful Samaritan? These are questions that a decolonizing space such as NAIITS allows for the unpacking, for discussion, and prayer. Imagine what might happen if our own non-Indigenous brothers and sisters did not immediately associate Indigenous peoples as violent criminals or as helpless victims! How can we make this happen if the status quo is maintained? No growth, no healing, can come from that stance. No doubt this will make some people very uncomfortable, but decolonizing the Bible, theological studies, church communities, and, importantly, ourselves, is—and will be—uncomfortable.

The Time for Renewal Is Now

It is time for renewal within Australian Christianity. Aboriginal and Torres Strait Islander peoples have a vital role to play in wider mainstream Christianity if it will allow us a seat at the table. Many Indigenous Christians are faithful but cynical that renewal and our involvement will come to fruition. Uncle Ray Minniecon writes about the lived experiences of Aboriginal and Torres Strait Islander Christians:

> The stealing, killing, and destroying of all that is sacred and meaningful to our identity is still an everyday experience for us. We have no idea what abundant life looks like anymore. We thought Christianity and the Church would deliver the promise of Jesus in abundance. Our expectations of the second part of this verse are an unachievable reality, even though we long for

26. Prentis, "Parable of the Good Samaritan."

its promise every day. Sadly, history has shown us time and time again that abundant life from the Church is not achievable.[27]

Yet despite all this, Uncle Ray and others remain faithful and open to conversations and working to achieve abundance for all!

> *A gift opens the way and ushers the giver*
> *into the presence of the great.*
>
> PROVERBS 18:16 NIV

Meredith Lake reminds us that Aboriginal and Torres Strait Islander theologies and our communities have significant gifts to offer:

> One of the insights of Indigenous theology . . . may be a recovered understanding of the land and, even more deeply, of the stewardship of creation. Indigenous readings of the Bible not only challenge imperial assumptions about the inferiority of non-European societies, but they may also help overturn poor Western theologies of environmental domination.[28]

Will you and your church family join with Aboriginal, Torres Strait Islander, and our global Indigenous cousins throughout Aotearoa, South America, the Philippines and beyond? Will you commit yourself to working towards knowing the uncomfortable aspects of our shared stories, including our shared colonial Christianity? If you do, you will find communities of others, Indigenous and non-Indigenous, trying to do the same. Whether you do, or whether you do not, I will be praying for you.

---

27. Minniecon, "To Dream the Impossible Dream," 24.
28. Lake, *Bible in Australia*, 142.

Bibliography

Bevis, Steve, Miriam Pepper, and Ruth Powell. "Indigenous and non-Indigenous Relations in Churches." *NCLS Research Occasional Paper* 33. Sydney: National Church Life Survey, 2018.

Budden, Chris. *Following Jesus in Invaded Space: Doing Theology on Aboriginal Land.* Eugene, OR: Pickwick, 2009.

Carlson, Bronwyn Lee, Lani V. Jones, Michelle Harris, Nelia Quezada, and Ryan Frazer. "Trauma, Shared Recognition and Indigenous Resistance on Social Media." *Australasian Journal of Information Systems* 21 (2017) 1–18.

Lake, Meredith. *The Bible in Australia: A Cultural History.* Updated Edition. Sydney: NewSouth, 2020.

———. "The Bible in Australian History and Culture." *St Mark's Review* 240 (2017) 12–33.

McKenna, Mark. *Moment of Truth: History and Australia's Future.* Collingwood, Victoria: Schwartz, 2018.

McGrady, Karla. "The past isn't in the past and I can't just get over it." *Indigenous X*, January 2016. https://indigenousx.com.au/the-past-isnt-in-the-past-and-i-cant-just-get-over-it/.

Minniecon, Ray. "To dream the impossible dream." *Zadok Perspectives* 153 (2021) 24.

Pattel-Gray, Anne. "Methodology in an Aboriginal Theology." In *The Cambridge Companion to Black Theology,* edited by Dwight Hopkins and Edward Antonio, 278–97. Cambridge: Cambridge University Press, 2012.

Pitts, Herbert. *The Australian Aboriginal and the Christian Church.* London: SPCK, 1914.

Prentis, Brooke. "The Parable of the Good Samaritan: A Lenten Study." Common Grace, 2019. https://www.commongrace.org.au/parables_the_good_samaritan.

Pybus, Cassandra. "Black Caesar: Our First Bushranger Was a Six-Foot African Man Who Arrived on the First Fleet." *Arena Magazine,* February (2002) 30–34.

Sherlock, Charles H. *Uncovering Theology: The Depth, Reach and Utility of Australian Theological Education.* Adelaide: ATF, 2009.

Job

An Aboriginal Story

Ray Minniecon

This chapter began as an oral presentation for the 2019 NAIITS Symposium at Whitley College, Melbourne.[1]

I REMEMBER A STORY about a missionary who went among our people in the desert a long time ago. He started introducing the God of the Bible and talked about Jesus being the Son of God. After a while, an old man stopped him from speaking, saying something along these lines, "Brother, thank you for your interesting story, but we've already got God here. He's always been here with us before you people came. He's always looked after us and he's still looking after us. He's caring for us all the time. We don't need another God. Why do we want another God?" As I reflected on this conversation between the missionary and the old man, I realized that the old man's response to the missionary says a lot about how Christianity was introduced to my people in the past, and about what Christianity might still mean to many Aboriginal and Torres Strait Islander people today.

In this chapter, I would like us to consider our history in the light of Job's story and look at the ways in which the book of Job is similar to our Aboriginal story here in Australia. I start by exploring very briefly the impact that two hundred and thirty-five years of colonization has had on Aboriginal

---

[1]. An earlier version of "Job: An Aboriginal Story" was published in *Zadok Papers* in 2019.

and Torres Strait Islander peoples. I will focus on the criminal neglect and the exclusion policies and practices of the church that have had a demoralizing impact on my people. I will explore this historical impact through three of the dialogues between Job and his friends (Job 2:11—3:26; 4:1–21; 8:1—10:22). The themes of "blotting out" the day of your birth (Job 3:3, CEV), being told that your suffering is because of your own sin (Job 4:7–9), and Job's call for an advocate (Job 9:32–35), all resonate with the experience of Aboriginal and Torres Strait Islander peoples. And finally, I will consider Job's dialogue with God (Job 38–42). We will find that God's dialogue and response to Job is much broader and more instructive than those of Job's friends. I would like to suggest that an Aboriginal and Torres Strait Islander theology of suffering gives us a better understanding of justice and love and reconciliation because it starts with Genesis 1, which is where God begins his dialogue with Job, in contrast to Western theology, which too often begins with Genesis 3.

Some Analogies

As we begin our reflection on the story of Job, let us consider our country's history over the past two hundred-plus years. Like Job, Aboriginal and Torres Strait Islander nations and peoples were living in their own land for many millennia, enjoying the fruits of their own labor, on their own lands and in relative freedom, innocent to the histories and stories of other nations. Job's story is disrupted when robbers and murderers came into Job's estate, plundered his lands, stole his treasures and assets, murdered his children, and left him bereft of any legal recourse to justice and recompense. In a similar fashion, our lands were invaded and our sacred treasures were forcibly taken and removed from us. Our land. Our children. Our language. Our heritage and assets. Our culture and religion. Within a matter of a few years, these sacred treasures were all forcibly removed and smashed beyond recognition!

When the Australian Constitution was enacted in 1901, we were seen through the eyes of social Darwinism and the evil doctrine of *terra nullius*.[2] This doctrine was instituted under the notion that we did not resemble human beings at all. Australia's first constitution included the enactment of racist laws that "justified" the invaders' behaviors and attitudes toward us. Let us remember also that not until 1967 was a national referendum conducted with the intention of overcoming some of the prejudices, behaviors, and injustices committed against Aboriginal people that were embedded in the 1900 Constitution. The focus of the 1967 Referendum to amend the

---

2. *Commonwealth of Australia Constitution Act 1900.*

Constitution was on the civil and political rights of my people.[3] No attempt was made to recognize First Nations' sovereignty at that time.

It was only in 1992 that the Mabo decision finally put the evil doctrine of *terra nullius* to rest.[4] This decision gave a measure of recognition to Aboriginal and Torres Strait Islander peoples' laws and customs—if they could be proven in a common court of an imposed and foreign law. Subsequent legislative changes provided for compensation to be paid for the loss of native title in certain circumstances, such as where native title rights had been extinguished through government action and affected Indigenous groups had suffered loss as a result. The Mabo judgment refused to question the validity of the British assertion of sovereignty.

My people have suffered the worst human rights atrocities and abuses, rightly described as genocide.[5] We need to remember the numerous massacres that occurred throughout the country and the forced removal from our ancestral lands. We were seen to be non-human and were denied the dignity of being treated as human, made in the image of God. Our children and our parents were forcibly removed from their ancestral lands, family and community. Many were treated as slaves. Our ancestral lands were stolen and desecrated. Many perpetrators of these heinous crimes called themselves Christian. They went to church in the morning and hunted, shot, and massacred us in the afternoon. Today, we are working feverishly to repair the damage of this devasting history, heal our people, and restore what has been lost, beginning from the starting point of healing our deep hurts, loss, and trauma. Our history of trauma and suffering places us in a similar situation to that of Job.

The Failure of the Church and an Aboriginal Theology

We now need to discuss the history of the Christian church and theology in Australia. The understanding of Christian theological concepts among our people is very thin. We don't have the numbers of Aboriginal and Torres Strait Islander theologians that other nations have with the capacity to explore, interrogate, and develop our understandings of theology in

---

3. The 1967 Referendum proposed alterations to the Constitution to enable Aboriginal and Torres Strait Islander people to be counted as part of the population, like all other Australians, and to enable the Commonwealth to make laws for them. On its result and significance, see National Library of Australia, "The 1967 Referendum."

4. For a brief overview of the Mabo Case and its implications, see Australian Institute for Aboriginal and Torres Strait Islander Studies, "The Mabo Case."

5. See, e.g., Tatz, *With Intent to Destroy*.

relationship to Christian theological concepts and our cultural principles and traditions. While we honor the inspiring protests of past leaders such as William Cooper,[6] our theological struggle is just beginning.

As an Aboriginal Christian, I have been critical of the church because of this criminal neglect and because of the exclusionary policies and practices of the church toward my people for such a long period of time. If you consider all the institutions of the Australian church (yes, we group all the denominations together from our perspective), and their lack of connection with and understanding of the Australian context and our people, you begin to realize that there is an even more deeply painful aspect of that historical trauma, suffering, and neglect. Many of our Aboriginal and Torres Strait Islander Christian leaders have knocked on the doors of many churches to ask these basic questions: "You've been in my country for over two hundred years . . . Where are my pastors? Where are my bishops? Where's my church? Has this message of the good news that you preach and teach failed my people? Or have you, the messengers of the good news, failed my people? Where are our pastors?" When we look behind us, trying to find those young people coming through and looking for the opportunity to become followers of the teachings of Jesus and his message, they are even harder to find. It is within this historical context that we have to live and work out the meaning of the good news amongst our Aboriginal and Torres Strait Islander peoples, amid the everyday traumas and crises that plague our communities, and without the support and encouragement of the church in Australia.

I now work within the Anglican system. I have worked in the Uniting Church system. I trained and have worked in the Baptist system. I came out of a Pentecostal tradition, the Assemblies of God. And now our people ask me, "Ray, why do you follow that foreign religion? It's just another imported religion into our country." And they are right, it is foreign! Yet, the Australian Bureau of Statistics tells us that the proportion of First Nations people who identify with the Christian religion is roughly the same as the proportion of other Australians.[7]

What then makes the Christian message so attractive to so many Aboriginal and Torres Strait Islander people? I have pondered that question many times, and I continue to ponder it. I was brought up under the old Queensland *Aboriginals Preservation and Protection Act of 1939–65*. I remember that, back in the old Mission days, the things that fascinated our old people most about the Bible were its prophetic insights and teachings.

---

6. See, for example, Barwick, "Cooper, William."
7. Australian Bureau of Statistics, "2071.0—Census of Population and Housing."

Perhaps the prophetic became so real to our old people because the Bible gave them some kind of reference point for what justice can be from God's perspective. The Bible's prophetic insights and teachings spoke about what was going to happen to all humanity at the judgment of God that was to come. Our old people were always asking deeper questions like: "Who gave these people permission to invade my country? Did God give them that permission? Who gave them permission to do all these killings and massacres, this genocide of our people? Who gave them permission to forcibly remove our children with such impunity, destroying our languages and our God-given culture? Who gave them that right?"[8]

When the old people read the Bible, they saw all these commandments in the Scriptures. The old people said: "Aren't they being disobedient to their own laws, and not only to the words that are in the Bible, but also to the laws of God? The Bible declares, 'Do not steal! Do not kill!' Don't they believe in the God of this Book that they teach and preach about?" So, I recognized that the prophetic passages of the Bible became very, very real to them. They knew that our old laws, given to our people by our Creator, were the very same laws that our people lived by for millennia. Even British law has those same time-honored laws. Why did they break their law and God's law? They knew that if you break God's law there is going to be judgment. You cannot get away with breaking God's divine law. There must be punishment. There must be judgment. And so, the old people instructed us on the old Mission that if God is going to judge these people, we had better be prepared to listen and obey God's laws so that we could escape God's wrath on that terrible judgment day.

The good news becomes real to us from the perspective of this history of injustice. We found a way to read the Bible that taught us, not only that the God of the Bible brings justice, but also that God's Son is reconciling and healing the whole world. This is good news to me and my people. This theology of justice and a judgment day became our main reference point in relation to accepting and responding to the Christian message and the Bible. We did not have any theologians in the Western sense. We did not have any trained ministers amongst us in those days, but I guarantee you that, if you heard some of those Aboriginal and Torres Strait Islander preachers that I had the privilege to sit under, you would have heard them proclaim the Good News of Jesus daily. They provided this incredible exegesis of the Scriptures without formal training! As a young Christian, I didn't need a Bible college professor to teach me the Good News because I had these ministers and pastors living amongst us—God's chosen!

---

8. Cf. Jennings, *The Christian Imagination*.

Job: An Aboriginal Story

It is within this brutal and traumatic historical context and the theology of justice and judgment day that I see my Aboriginal and Torres Strait Islander people in the biblical narrative of Job. I want to explore how the Job story can help bring a deeper understanding to our contemporary challenges and an insight into how our Creator works out a plan and a future restoration for my people. Let us read the Job story in juxtaposition with our own people's story. Let us read it as an Aboriginal story.

To start with, let us see how the Bible introduces us to the fascinating story of Job and his family:

> In the land of Uz there lived a man whose name was Job. This man was blameless and upright; he feared God and shunned evil. He had seven sons and three daughters, and he owned seven thousand sheep, three thousand camels, five hundred yoke of oxen and five hundred donkeys, and had a large number of servants. He was the greatest man among all the people of the East. His sons used to hold feasts in their homes on their birthdays, and they would invite their three sisters to eat and drink with them. When a period of feasting had run its course, Job would make arrangements for them to be purified. Early in the morning he would sacrifice a burnt offering for each of them, thinking, 'Perhaps my children have sinned and cursed God in their hearts.' This was Job's regular custom. (Job 1:1–5)[9]

Like my ancestors, Job is a very spiritual man. He believes in a righteous God. He eagerly seeks to please God and follow God's ways for himself and his family. His spiritual practices and rituals please God so much that, from God's point of view, God could say, "There is no one on earth like him; he is blameless and upright, a man who fears God and shuns evil" (1:8). This dedication to God's laws is similar to the practices of my ancestors! They loved God's law and were committed to following it carefully.

Then, at the end of the first chapter, we see this blameless man stripped of everything that was treasured by and valuable to him. He lost his sheep, his camels, his yoke and oxen, his donkeys, his servants, his reputation, even his children were murdered and destroyed (1:13–20). And it was God who seems to have allowed it to happen! In the last picture of Job in the second chapter, you see him sitting down in the burnt-out ashes of his beautiful ranch house scratching his sores with a bit of cow manure and his distraught wife challenges him.

---

9. Biblical citations are from the NIV except where otherwise noted.

> His wife said to him, 'Are you still maintaining your integrity? Curse God and die!' He [Job] replied, 'You are talking like a foolish woman. Shall we accept good from God, and not trouble?' In all of this Job did not sin in what he said. (2:9–10).

Job's response is maturity at his highest level! Job did not sin or charge God with any wrongdoing! Now that is maturity. When you have lost everything you treasure and value, then to react with that kind of response is breath-taking and awe-inspiring. That is why I say that this book is an Aboriginal story. When you consider what we have lost, and how our people have responded with grace and dignity through and in our pain and suffering, it is always astonishing and inspiring.

I want to offer four further observations as to why I see this story as an Aboriginal story. First, Job's sufferings and his losses and his trauma are very similar to our sufferings and our losses and our traumas. I outlined above a few of the atrocities that my ancestors faced. Let me reinforce the fact that, since the invasion of our country in 1788, the so-called *Aboriginal Protection Acts* and the doctrine of *terra nullius* continue to cause much suffering and trauma because of the loss of all the things that we treasured and valued. These are current realities and not only legal suppositions from the past.

Second, it is important to notice that Job is not an Israelite. He does not have any relationship with the biblical ancestors like Abraham and is not connected to the Abrahamic or Mosaic covenants. He does not fit into the nation of Israel's story. He seems to live outside their national story.

Third, Job is an innocent man. Even God boasts about him: "There is no one on earth like him; he is blameless and upright, a man who fears God and shuns evil" (1:8). Job is not seen as a sinner in God's eyes.

Fourth, Job is a prayer warrior and a spiritual practitioner. He prays to God for the protection of his children and the prosperity of his estate. Job respects God's sovereignty even when he does not experience God's justice.

I also want to highlight a saying from Jesus that adds weight to Job's story and to our story. It highlights the challenges that we face as Indigenous people here in Australia. When exploring the theme of the Good Shepherd, Jesus said: "The thief comes only to steal, kill and destroy. I came that they may have life, and have it abundantly" (John 10:10, NRSV). I can say quite categorically that our people know the first part of this text, but I can guarantee you that we do not know what it is like to experience the last part of this text. We are very familiar with the actions and behaviors of the thief, but what is "abundant life"? What does abundant life mean to my people who have been robbed of everything? That is the reason why this story is so powerful for me. We know what it is like to have everything stolen. We know what it is like to suffer from genocidal policies, to be utterly destroyed. Yet, we would like to know what Jesus meant by the last part of this saying, "to have life, and have it abundantly."

We know also that the thief in our experience has been very arrogant, very cunning. In Job's story, the thief moved very swiftly, callously, and brutally. He took his treasures, his assets, his animals, and his children. Our people are so familiar with the dealings of the thief. Job's story is so similar and so familiar to our context here in Australia. I can take you to so many massacre sites and show you where that suffering is still felt in our country. That is part of our story. The Australian churches are just now coming to grips with their complicity, participation, and responsibility in this country's brutal history.

The Job Dialogues

I turn now to three of Job's dialogues on his sufferings. I have chosen these dialogues because they help us to understand the story from an Aboriginal and Torres Strait Islander perspective.

The First Dialogue: blot out the day of my birth

The first of the three texts (3:1–26) does not come in response to the speech of Job's three friends; it comes in response to their seven days of silence. Silence can be part of Job's dialogue as well. Eliphaz, Bildad, and Zophar have recognized Job's suffering, they have wept together with Job, and finally Job speaks (3:3–6):

> May the day of my birth perish,
>   and the night that said, 'A boy is conceived!'
> That day—may it turn to darkness.
>   may God above not care about it;
>   may no light shine on it.
> May gloom and utter darkness claim it once more;
>   may a cloud settle over it;
>   may blackness overwhelm it.
> That night—may thick darkness seize it;
>   may it not be included among the days of the year
>   nor be entered in any of the months.

I hear this cry from many of our old people. "We are innocent people! Who gave them permission to invade, steal, and murder us? What have we done to deserve this suffering and misery? What sin or crime did we do? Where did we go wrong with these invaders? Why are my children in jail? Why do we have to sit under this oppression every day? Where's the freedom we once enjoyed? Where is the liberty we once possessed? Where can we find justice?" That is also the cry here from Job. He too is in the depths of despair. He is at the nadir point of his sufferings and one of the first things he says in this, his first dialogue in response to his sufferings, is very powerful and relevant: "May the day of my birth perish'" (NIV). Or as another translation puts it: "Blot out the day of my birth" (CEV).

Aboriginal and Torres Strait Islander peoples make a similar point about celebrating Australia Day on the twenty-sixth of January. Like Job, our people are saying, "Just blot out that day. Do not celebrate it! It is Invasion Day! It is Survival Day! It is the day our good world ended! That day was the dawning of our sufferings, traumas, and nightmares." The thief has come to destroy us! But, like Job, we cannot eradicate that day from our national or personal life. We cannot eradicate our story from the earth. Like my people, Job is in deep trauma and deep grief. Today, all Aboriginal and Torres Strait Islander peoples know that every day is invasion day. Every day we wake up to a sun that shines upon us as an oppressed people. Every night we go to sleep under a colonized moon. And we hear the voice of our Ancestors saying continuously that we are an innocent people. We did not do anything wrong to deserve this constant slaughter and punishment. Our cry is similar to the cry of Job (3:24–26):

> For sighing has become my daily food;
>   my groans pour out like water.
> What I feared has come upon me;
>   what I dreaded has happened to me.
> I have no peace, no quietness;
>   I have no rest, but only turmoil.

The Second Dialogue: weighing our sufferings

In the second dialogue (6:1—7:21), Job responds to his friend Eliphaz the Temanite. Eliphaz is trying to convince Job that his suffering is due to the (alleged) fact that he has sinned against God and, therefore, that God, in his righteousness and judgment, is punishing Job for his wrongdoing. Eliphaz's accusation of Job is based on that type of theological understanding.

> Consider now: Who, being innocent, has ever perished?
>   Where were the upright ever destroyed?
> As I have observed, those who plow evil
>   and those who sow trouble reap it.
> At the breath of God they perish;
>   at the blast of his anger they are no more. (4:7–9).

I am of the opinion that Western evangelical theological tradition has its roots in this kind of theological thinking. As I mentioned before, much of Western theology finds its starting point in Genesis 3 rather than Genesis 1. Western theology has proposed, time and again, that our Aboriginal and Torres Strait Islander peoples' culture, spirituality, and traditional practices are pagan, un-Christian, and evil, an embarrassment and shame to God. Therefore, the reason for our sufferings and trauma is that we have committed some imperceptible, invisible, and undetectable sins against the Creator of the universe; that Western theology has found us out; and, therefore, that only Western theology can save us. The implication is that only through a politically implemented Western cultural replacement process can we be saved from God's wrath and anger. Our people need to be "transformed" by replacing our culture, our theology, and our spirituality with the Western understanding of being human culturally, theologically, and spiritually according to their interpretation of the Bible.

Job's reply to this accusation from Eliphaz, of Job's alleged "plowing of evil" and "sowing of trouble," does not arise from a sense of having committed any sin. Rather, his response is grounded in a theology of suffering and trauma. Job cries out from the depths of his suffering (6:2–3):

> If only my anguish could be weighed
>   and all my misery be placed on the scales!
> It would surely outweigh the sand of the seas—
>   no wonder my words have been impetuous.

Job is asking the deeper theological question. How do you measure suffering? Where are the weights and measures that can say, "OK, here's my suffering, now let's weigh it in the scales of justice'?" Like Job, we too are asking similar questions: "How do you measure and weigh our suffering? How many more consultants, researchers, politicians, and commentators can really plumb the depths of our sufferings and offer us a solution that brings us reconciliation, restoration, and healing? Can Western theology weigh us in their scales of justice and describe to us the depth of our sufferings? What policy or program can any government implement to Close the Gap?"¹⁰ What about the church's scales of justice? Can it measure our suffering and trauma? What can the church do that will give us this "life in abundance?" It seems that thirty billion dollars is spent on us Aboriginal people each year.¹¹ Apparently, I'm worth about forty-eight thousand. Is that how you measure the depths of our suffering, by the number of dollars you spend on us? This is the question that Job is raising for us here today: How do you weigh and measure suffering and trauma that comes from historical injustices? What computation or calculation can you use to account for this tremendous loss and trauma from which all of our people are suffering?

Much of my ministry work is with and among our Stolen Generations.¹² I know what their loss and trauma cost them. I hear their stories. I do not know how to weigh that loss in the scales of justice, because I do not know what the scales look like. I certainly don't know who owns the scales of justice. Recently, I had a phone call from my wife when she was over in Perth in Western Australia at a conference. She had had a call at 6am over there from a young Aboriginal fella in Sydney. She was possibly the only one that he trusted to talk to about this. And he said to her, "Look, the friend I have in my house, who's just moved in, he's just hung himself on the clothesline in my backyard." And so, I get the phone call and go and have a talk to him. He is from the Stolen Generation. He is completely devastated. And I am trying to figure out . . . what do I do?

Maybe the real question was not, "What do I do?" or "How do I help him?" but "How do you measure this injustice?" How do you weigh this pain that he is experiencing right now? How do you sit with that? How do you walk with him in his suffering for his friend who just suicided? How do you measure that kind of trauma and suffering? We know as Christians that we can try and filter this pain and this struggle through the sufferings of Jesus on the cross. We can try to measure all sufferings through and with the cross of Jesus. But that is for us who believe . . . What about those who do not believe? Also, how do you plumb the depths of suffering and trauma that Jesus experienced for all humankind?

---

10. "Close the Gap" refers to the entrenched inequality faced by Aboriginal and Torres Strait Islander people and the need to reduce "the gap" between their life outcomes and those of other Australians. For an advocacy perspective, see https://closethegap.org.au. For a government perspective, see *The National Agreement on Closing the Gap*, https://www.closingthegap.gov.au.

11. Biddle, "Fact Check Q&A."

12. "Stolen Generations" refers to the Aboriginal children who were forcibly removed from their families by government agencies and church missions in an attempt to assimilate them into the culture of white Australia, a practice that continued until the 1970s.

The Third Dialogue: who will be my advocate?

The third dialogue I want to discuss is Job's call for an advocate, a mediator between him and God (9:1—10:22). Job introduces this dialogue when he says (9:32–35):

> He is not a mere mortal like me that I might answer him,
>   that we might confront each other in court.
> If only there were someone to mediate between us,
>   someone to bring us together,
> someone to remove God's rod from me,
>   so that his terror would frighten me no more.
> Then I would speak up without fear of him,
>   but as it now stands with me, I cannot.

"Where is my advocate? Who is my advocate? Who's going to speak up for us? Is there anyone in heaven or earth who will defend me and speak up on my behalf? Is there an angel responsible for this role? What is his name? Can a negotiator mediate between me and God, be an advocate and fight to uphold my position and cry of innocence?" This is what Job was asking. It is also what our people are asking. Do we have to go outside this country to the United Nations and present our case every year, describing all the things that have happened to us? Is there another person or country to whom we can appeal who will mediate on our behalf? We have got to continue to press our case of injustice. But to whom? We need an advocate because the government will not listen to us.

And so, we are left to our own devices as we try and navigate this traumatic dilemma and come to some means of managing our suffering and pain in our struggle—politically, socially, spiritually, and culturally. This is our constant cry for justice every day: Who will mediate and negotiate and act as an advocate for justice and accountability on our behalf?

In the story of Job's friends, they accuse him of wrongdoing. They say, "You have sinned. You're guilty before God." These are the words of Job's "comforters." I find these attitudes also in many encounters with the Church. I have come across five attitudes in the Church that I cannot seem to penetrate or break through. The first is arrogance. The second is hypocrisy. The third is ignorance. The fourth is apathy. The fifth is cynicism. In regard to arrogance, the first colonial wave of Christianity was very arrogant and this arrogance is still with us. I cannot deal with that, I do not have an answer for it, but I know that it is there, along with hypocrisy, ignorance, apathy, and cynicism.

We could do with a mediator, but who? Like Job, we are confronted with a blame-the-victim philosophy. Some developmental theories suggest that we have developed a "culture of poverty" and that we are responsible for our own suffering, trauma, and pain.[13] We come up against these attitudes and challenges all the time within the church, within society, and in government policies. That is how we deal with this type of suffering in this country—we blame the victims. Who will listen to us in our suffering, trauma, and loss? Who will be our mediator and our advocate?

God's Dialogue and Intervention

In Job's story, after all the dialogues with his friends are completed, we see God intervene in Job's suffering and trauma (40:1—41:34). After all the human arguments are finished, God enters into the dialogue through a whirlwind. This grand entry by God fits with Indigenous spirituality and expectations. Our people believe that whirlwinds are spirit beings. We know that our Creator uses creation to speak to our people. Our people are so connected to creation that we can hear a certain bird and know that someone has died or that someone is coming. All living things in creation are related to us like family through totems and stories.

So, when Job hears a whirlwind, we Aboriginal and Torres Strait Islander peoples know that this is God talking. The first thing that God says are these words (38:2–7):

> Who is this that obscures my plans
>   with words without knowledge?
> Brace yourself like a man;
>   I will question you,
>   and you shall answer me.
> Where were you when I laid the earth's foundation?
>   Tell me, if you understand.
> Who marked off its dimensions? Surely you know!
>   Who stretched a measuring line across it?
> On what were its footings set,
>   or who laid its cornerstone—
> while the morning stars sang together
>   and all the angels shouted for joy?

Now this part of Job's story is frustrating and fascinating from an Indigenous perspective.

---

13. On "the culture of poverty" and the misuse of related theories, see Harvey and Reed, "Culture of Poverty."

You will recall that it was God who allowed this tragedy to happen to Job in the first place (1:9–12). Even though he is seen by God as a righteous man, an innocent man, Job loses everything, including his children. The first thing you would expect from God is an apology to Job! You would think that he would say to Job, "Well brother, I'm sorry for what I allowed to happen to you." But there is no apology! There is no explanation! Job is not even given the right to know that there was a big executive meeting with Satan, and that Satan and God decided to test Job's character, integrity, faith, and sincerity. In this whole story, Job has got no frame of reference whatsoever as to why this happened to him. Instead, God challenges Job to think about creation, the beginning of all things.

The first challenge with this dialogue between Job and God is language. My people encounter problems of language and translation whether we are reading from an English translation of the Old Testament or a Kriol Bible. English is a foreign language to my people and to this country. The English translations of the Bible are problematic. The original language of the Old Testament Bible is Hebrew, but I have taught myself to approach the Bible from the perspective of translators who were foreigners to the Hebrew language, culture, context, and meanings. We filter the language of the Bible from Hebrew to English, then to our own language, then back to English.[14]

English is a foreign language when it comes to interpreting the original Hebrew of the Old Testament. How, for example, do you interpret the first words in Genesis, "*Bereshit bara elohim*"—"In the beginning, God"?[15] Nevertheless, this is where God begins when He approaches Job: "Where were you when I laid the earth's foundation? Tell me if you understand. Who marked off its dimensions? Surely you know! Who stretched a measuring line across it?" (38:4–5). In other words, Job, were you there in the beginning of creation?

What I see God doing to Job in his pain—remember, Job is still in his suffering and trauma here, still suffering the loss of his children and the loss of his goods and everything else. God has not healed him! Nor compensated him! What I see God doing is inviting Job back to the beginning of all things: "Come back here, inside the beginning." This is what God is saying

---

14. Aboriginal and Torres Strait Islander peoples engage the Bible by storytelling and living-in-story. Within our oral cultures, we tell and live the stories as we remember them. We are not constrained by particular English versions of the Bible.

15. The Hebrew of Genesis 1:1 begins, *Bereshit* (in the beginning) *bara* (created) *elohim* (God) . . ." The verb generally precedes its subject in biblical Hebrew. In English and in Kriol, the verb generally follows its subject, rendering Genesis 1:1, "In the beginning, God (created) . . ."

to my people also. God is inviting us as Indigenous peoples to come back to the beginning.

That is why this story is so powerful and so important to us. God offers us a way to see our suffering from a different starting point. Job started with his birth by stating "blot out the day of my birth," but God took him further back beyond time and history: "*Bereshit bara elohim*". . . "In the beginning, God." When it was proclaimed to our people, Western theology only took us back to Genesis 3, to a judging God who cursed the ground because of Adam and Eve's disobedience. According to this reading of Genesis, we are all sinners "in Adam" and we deserve God's righteous punishment. The outcome of that theological starting point is that it pointed us to an angry God. We already understood that message clearly! Our old laws taught us that God will punish us if we do not obey his laws. But Indigenous theology does not start in Genesis 3. It begins in Genesis 1: "*Bereshit bara elohim*". . . "In the beginning, God". . . "In the Dreaming, God!" It is interesting that the name of God throughout this first chapter of Genesis is *Elohim*, the name of God for all peoples, not just the name of God that Israel knew. In fact, the old Indigenous (Canaanite) name for God, *El*, is used fifty-six times in the book of Job![16]

As Indigenous peoples, when we start in Genesis 1, we know that we have been created in God's image, the image of *Elohim*. We understand the habitation of all human beings as an integral part of God's creation. We understand the significance of redemption, reconciliation, and salvation through the cross and the resurrection of Jesus.

How many times do we have to be saved from our sins (evangelists make the same point over and over), when we also need to be saved from those who have sinned against us? Why do people continue to preach this message of guilt to my people? Who has offended our Creator more grievously? Can the invaders of my country respond to their guilt and shame? Western theology starts from Genesis 3 but that is not our Good News. We have a better understanding of justice and love and reconciliation if we begin from Genesis 1 and from our understanding of the Dreaming. From this vantage point, we have a better understanding of what redemption, justice, and reconciliation look like and the means by which they are accomplished. We can look down through the lens of the whole biblical story, from inside the beginning to inside the end of all things, and see God's full plan of redemption, justice, reconciliation, and restoration for all humanity and for all of God's creation.

---

16. See further, Brett, *Political Trauma and Healing*.

One of my favorite texts in the New Testament is Col 1:15–16. It reads like an early church creed: "The Son is the image of the invisible God, the firstborn over all creation. For in him all things were created: things in heaven and on earth, visible and invisible." From this cosmic perspective, we understand what it means to have "the mind of Christ" (1 Cor 2:16) and to think theologically about all creation.

One of the cultural practices that we have as Indigenous peoples is "to walk backwards into the future." In order to know where we are going, we must know where we come from, and that means going all the way back inside the beginning of creation. We have got to know who we are, what our old people taught us and trained us to think and do, how we need to think, act, and be. Western culture tries to turn our young people away from our historical ancestors' teaching and cultural and spiritual anchors. The moment our young people turn their backs on our history and creation story, they become lost. And yet, if God spoke to Job out of creation material, a whirlwind, revealing again the greatness of his power, the wonders of his workings, the splendor of his skill and his wisdom, then we can also be confident that God continues to speak to Indigenous peoples through our culture, traditions, and ancestors' teachings, in Spirit and in Country. God has always spoken and revealed himself to us and God *Elohim*, to use that old Indigenous name, continues to take us back inside the beginning where we find his healing, justice, and consolation.

When we come *back inside this beginning* as Aboriginal people, then the notion of *terra nullius* is itself rendered null and void. In 1819, Bishop Samuel Marsden wrote: "The Aborigines are the most degraded of the human race . . . The time is not yet arrived for them to receive the great blessings of civilization and the knowledge of Christianity."[17] *Inside the beginning of all creation*, that statement becomes null and void. In 1902, a member of the newly federated parliament said: "An Aboriginal is not as intelligent as a Māori. There is no scientific evidence that he is a human being at all."[18] *Back inside the beginning*, this statement is also null and void.

My prayer is that, as we encourage our people to go *back inside the beginning of all creation*, we can say with Job (42:2–3, 5):

> I know that you can do all things;
>   no purpose of yours can be thwarted . . .
> Surely I spoke of things I did not understand,
>   things too wonderful for me to know . . .

---

17. Elder, ed., *Letters and Journals of Samuel Marsden*, 232.

18. Commonwealth of Australia, *Parliamentary Debates, House of Representatives*, 1902, 119–41.

> My ears had heard of you
> but now my eyes have seen you.

It was God who approached Job in his traumas and sufferings. God initiates the connection and the conversation. God speaks, Job listens. God does speak to us in our trauma and sufferings. God speaks, we listen. Perhaps, one day, even the church will say to my people, "Now I see you." Perhaps, one day, with this wonderful opportunity here in Australia, we may be able to take the hand of the church and lead the church *back inside the beginning*, back behind Genesis 3 to start with *"Bereshit bara elohim"*... Inside the beginning of all things.

This is a personal reflection on the story of Job. To me, Job is an Aboriginal story. I remember an old Aboriginal Elder saying, "Religion is for those who believe in hell, spirituality is for those who've been there." It seems like it is when we have lost everything of value, everything we treasure, all our possessions, all that we see as important, that we finally have the eyes to see God. This story teaches us that we do not measure our Creator's blessings by how much we accumulate, or even by how much we have suffered. It teaches us that we can take God to task. We can put *Elohim* on trial and say, "Hey, we want an audience with you. We've got some things we want to talk to you about." I know that *Elohim* will hear us and respond, just like God responded to Job. Jesus always opens the door and his ears to hear us.

Bibliography

The Aboriginal Preservation and Protection Act of 1939 (Queensland). https://media.sclqld.org.au/documents/digitisation/v01_pp7-30_Aboriginals_Aboriginals%20Preservation%20and%20Protection%20Acts,%201939%20to%201946.pdf.

The Aborigines' and Torres Strait Islanders' Affairs Act of 1965 (Queensland). www.legislation.qld.gov.au/view/html/asmade/act-1965-027#act-1965-027.

Australian Bureau of Statistics. "2071.0 Census of Population and Housing: Reflecting Australia—Stories from the Census, 2016." 28 June 2017. https://www.abs.gov.au/ausstats/abs@.nsf/Lookup/by%20Subject/2071.0~2016~Main%20Features~Religion%20Data%20Summary~70.

Australian Institute of Aboriginal and Torres Strait Islander Studies. "The Mabo Case." 6 Dec 2022. https://aiatsis.gov.au/explore/mabo-case.

Barwick, Diane. "Cooper, William (1861–1941)" *Australian Dictionary of Biography. Volume 8*. National Centre of Biography, Australian National University, 1981. https://adb.anu.edu.au/biography/cooper-william-5773/text9787.

Brett, Mark G. *Political Trauma and Healing: Biblical Ethics for a Postcolonial World*. Grand Rapids, MI: Eerdmans, 2016.

Biddle, Nicholas. "Fact Check Q&A: Is $30 billion spent every year on 500,000 Indigenous people in Australia?" *The Conversation*. 5 September 2016. https://theconversation.com/factcheck-qanda-is-30-billion-spent-every-year-on-500-000-indigenous-people-in-australia-64658#.

Commonwealth of Australia Constitution Act 1900. https://www.foundingdocs.gov.au/resources/transcripts/cth1_doc_1900.pdf.

Commonwealth of Australia, Department of the Prime Minister and Cabinet. *The National Agreement on Closing the Gap*. 2002. https://www.closingthegap.gov.au/national-agreement/national-agreement-closing-the-gap.

Commonwealth of Australia, House of Representatives. *Parliamentary Debates*, 23 April 1902 (King O'Malley, Member for Tasmania). https://www.aph.gov.au/Parliamentary_Business/Hansard.

Elder, John Rawson, ed. *The Letters and Journals of Samuel Marsden, 1765–1838*. Dunedin: Otago University, 1932.

Harvey, David, and Michael Reed. "The Culture of Poverty: An Ideological Analysis." *Sociological Perspectives* 39 (1996) 465–95.

Jennings, Willie James. *The Christian Imagination: Theology and the Origins of Race*. New Haven, CT: Yale University Press, 2010.

The National Library of Australia. "The 1967 Referendum." https://www.nla.gov.au/research-guides/the-1967-referendum.

Tatz, Colin. *With Intent to Destroy: Reflecting on Genocide*. London: Verso, 2003.

Colonial Bondage

Liberating Biblical Narratives and Theological Education

Anne Pattel-Gray

As a First Nations scholar, theologian, author, and activist I have written this paper solely from an Aboriginal perspective. For several decades I have been on my own journey of discovery to explore the rich religious, cultural, and spiritual heritage of my people and to affirm and embrace my people's teachings and epistemology within the development of my own academic research.

An Aboriginal Worldview

Aboriginal cosmology, worldview, and epistemology are central to a First Nations ontological quest and fundamental to what we know and embrace. The basis of this research is that we are the oldest living culture in the world, and it has always amazed me how little this means to White Australia and how they give little recognition, respect, or value to this immense treasure of knowledge and wisdom that Australia has at its fingertips. It is important to note that the Creator Spirit was with us long before the British invaded our lands and our faith has been nurtured over thousands of years. As a result, we have a very intimate relationship with the Creator Spirit. When we speak of this relationship, we invoke the Creator Spirit in our midst.

Our Ancestral Narratives reflect this relationship, and our ceremonies give praise to our Creator Spirit and remind us of our obligations to one another, to land, to the environment and the whole of creation, to our law, and to the responsibilities given to us by the Creator Spirit via our Spirit Ancestors. Among First Nations people there are power-filled stories about the Creator Spirit's acts in the time of creation. Aboriginal Christian leaders tell of their Ancestral Narratives that speak about our knowledge and beliefs of the Creator Spirit who through our Spirit Ancestors formed our world and forged our identity, culture, and law. This process highlights the relationship of Aboriginal peoples to the land, to the whole of creation, and to the spiritual world of our Spirit Ancestors and the Creator Spirit. They were and still are all linked to each other and dependent upon this interconnection. Our faith and the spiritual world are the life force and foundation of our life existence and survival. The land is the source of life for us, and we cannot survive without our connection to the life source as stated by our spiritual leaders.

First Nations people have a deep understanding of the mysticism associated with the Creator Spirit which has been nurtured over some one hundred and ten thousand years.[1] The Creator Spirit is the creator of our world, and the creator of our humanity. We are created in the image of the Creator Spirit, and we are who we are because of the Creator Spirit. We have an intuitive sense of God as the Creator Spirit, as a wisdom teacher on Country, and as Spirit. The Creator Spirit bestowed upon us our land and entrusted this world to us, and we are to protect, care for, and to rejuvenate our Earth Mother. The Creator Spirit handed down our Law, which dictated every aspect of our life and permeates our spiritual life, and taught us how to care for our country and our obligations and responsibilities to our kinship system, religious and spiritual life. The Creator Spirit gave us our ceremonies, songs, and rituals to both honor the Creator and remind us of the Creator's presence. The Creator Spirit is always with us.

What the Colonizers failed to see was the rich spiritual life in which Aboriginal people lived and the presence of Creator Spirit in us. Their understanding of God was different from ours and because of this they could not see that we were a deeply spiritual people. The Colonizer could not see past our blackness, nor could they comprehend how our relationship with the land was and is spiritual in nature, and that our connectedness was defined by the bestowal of land to us by the Creator Spirit.

In this study, I will explore the impact of colonial imperialism on the lives of Australia's First Nations peoples and the racism that permeated all aspects of western Christianity and influenced their interpretation of biblical narratives. Racist interpretations doomed First Nations people to a life of servitude and inferiority. There is a need for First Nations theologians to

---

1. Sherwood, *Prologue*.

decolonize the western biblical narratives and to reinterpret biblical narratives through an Indigenous lens. By undertaking this process, First Nations people find affirmation of their humanity and drive a deeper theological understanding that draws on their ancient wisdom and spirituality.

Western Colonial God and Domination

When the British empire invaded our lands in 1788, so began the forced indoctrination of western Christendom which would be the beginning of our nightmare. "Empire was baptized by Christianity, and Christianity on many occasions served as the 'running dog of imperialism.'"[2] The collusion between Church and State was such that every aspect of our lives would be literally dominated and the "Good News" would be anything but good. The British invaders were consumed with an imperial delusion of superiority, that they were commissioned by God, king, and country to take land that they deemed to be unutilized. British imperialists saw themselves as God's chosen people to be agents to take possession of land that they deemed not exploited to its maximum potential. To deliver the advancement of western civilization to First Nations people was the foundation to their mission.

Nasili Vaka'uta details how empires are founded on delusions, that is, idiosyncratic beliefs, doctrines, or ideologies invented, maintained, and/or propagated despite being contradicted by reality or reason:

> Imperial delusions inspired the most violent forms of injustice pertaining to people and land in colonised contexts, such as being subjected to dehumanizing measures—like racism, religious violence, ethnic cleansing, and cultural deracination—because imperial expansion operated upon the delusion that people with certain skin colour, belief, ethnicity and culture are inferior and less human.[3]

Aboriginal nations would experience a version of God that was not only foreign but also racist, dehumanizing, and dominating and as one who demanded total submission to the British empire and colonists.

The Bible was used as a tool to justify all manner of dehumanizing actions of the Colonizers and Aboriginal people would quickly learn how the Colonizers dominated every aspect of the Bible from biblical interpretation and translation. The text was used to justify racist views, colonial theft and dispossession, subjugation and oppression, massacres and cultural

---

2. Vaka'uta, "Delusion of Empire," 121.
3. Vaka'uta, "Delusion of Empire," 111.

genocide, and the rape of women and children. This racist biblical view also formed the basis on which we were deemed cursed, pagan, and a racially inferior race of people. Many First Nations people ask, "What can turn the same people who call themselves by Christ's name into a people who will kill, steal, and destroy land and nature with genocidal passion?"[4]

The colonial invaders, based on their racist views, believed their "whiteness" made them superior and they considered First Nations people as inferior and morally bankrupt.[5] It was imperative for the Colonizer to dominate and take total control over the lives of First Nations people and to force them into submission. The Colonizers imposed their control through military might, political dictatorship, and through the racist attack on First Nations people's self-image. This happened through the destruction of First Nations people's culture, art, dance, religions, history, geography, education, and the outlawing of the use of traditional language and being forced to take on western culture, behaviors, and language. The Bible that came to Australia was also white-washed and every person depicted in the Bible was white and even Jesus was white—blond hair, blue eyes and white skinned. How could First Nations people ever hope to identify with the Bible when all black people were slaves in bondage to the white rulers and blackness was viewed as sinfulness, wickedness and evil? This had an enormous impact on the psychological make up of First Nations people around the globe. This led to the mental abuse of First Nations people suffering at the hands of the colonial structure and systems. Robert C. Young writes about psychological colonization as ". . . 'a metaphorical displacement' of realities; the engineering of a 'creative lie' whereby Colonizers (irreversibly) transformed the geographical, cultural, political, educational, linguistic, religious, ecological, economic landscapes of many countries and peoples."[6]

These days, First Nations people continue to experience racial discrimination. A good example is when the Federal government suspended the *Racial Discrimination Act 1975* which protects the human rights of Australia's First Nations people leading to the continuing removal of our children from their families and community. This includes governments taking control of our people's incomes, high incarceration rates of Aboriginal people, children and young people, high suicide rates of our children, the denial of cultural rights and heritage, and successive governments' failure to formalize a treaty with the First Nations people. The horrific acts that have been inflicted upon Australia's First Nations peoples have had a deep

4. Woodley, *Indigenous Theology*, 98.
5. Pattel-Gray, *Great White Flood*, 312.
6. Vaka'uta, "Delusion of Empire," 115.

psychological impact on the lives of Aboriginal people which has left them traumatized.

The most frightening aspect of the church's complicity in the subjugation of First Nations peoples is the heartfelt sentiment that it was done "with the best of intentions." This, however, does not alleviate the enormous trauma inflicted upon Aboriginal people by the forced imposition of the Christian missionaries and the fact that those churches worked among Aboriginal communities, partnering with the Government in the genocide. Unwittingly no doubt, and done always "with the best of intentions," nevertheless the missionaries and churches were guilty of complicity in the destruction of First Nations cultures and tribal social structures—complicit in the devastating intergenerational impoverishment and death of the people to whom they preached.

Other genocidal acts led to the crushing of Aboriginal people's cultural identity, religious and spiritual beliefs. The history of colonization is seen as the domination of the western world. Whether this is good or bad, it has impacted upon the physical, emotional, and psychological lives of Aboriginal Nations people resulting in intergenerational trauma through the means of colonization and missionization. The legacy of "colonial Christianity" and its effects on both First Nations people and colonial participants in the colonization and missionization processes meant that there was, and still is, a critical need for Aboriginal people to identify and reaffirm our spirituality and cultural heritage as the first step in our struggle for religious self-determination. This was the first step in the process for Australia's First Nations people to re-interpret the biblical narratives and to decolonize our theology and to remove all western bias.

As an Aboriginal scholar I have always struggled with the colonial narrative that was presented to us that portrays a Colonial God who favors one race over another. Although this is an Israelite narrative, it has been taken over and co-opted by the western world and used to justify western Colonizers who identify themselves as the "Chosen Ones." I cannot believe that this Colonial God is the one and the same as the Creator Spirit that we know and understand, and in whose spirit we breathe. This Colonial Imperial God that the Colonizer brought to our land was, and still is, hell bent on destroying First Nations people. We could not tolerate bearing the image of this God; nor could we find comfort in, or communion with, a God who acted like a colonial landlord.

Randy Woodley, a Native American Indian theologian, describes the western worldview as being "physically dualistic, morally dualistic, essentially spiritual, religiously intolerant, individualistic, extrinsically categorical, hierarchical, competitive, greed based, utopian, White supremacist, anthropocentric, triumphalist, and patriarchal."[7] This description is one that Aboriginal people would agree with as this has been their experience. The Australian church, however, taught—either directly or by implication—that the people in the Bible were white, and that to be white was a good thing because it was to be "like God." If this was so, Aboriginal people realized that they could never be white, so they were doomed to eternal damnation.

Unfortunately, the Colonial Christianity transported to our lands in a flower plot remains in its original flowerpot and was never transplanted into the land of my people and therefore never took root in this country. This is visible in the fact that theological education still looks to the north and is only engaged in its research and discourse with Europe and North America. We therefore see in Australia that the majority of theologians have very little engagement with the landscape where they actually live or with the political and theological context or with First Nations people whose lands they live upon and call their own. It is important to understand that the "illegitimate use of power via White supremacy and religious cultural hegemony, especially as used against others structurally, is among the primary failures of western Colonizer Christianity."[8]

This western imperial God embodies all that is evil—colonialism, patriarchalism, misogyny, racism, and homophobic disdain which unfortunately permeates ecclesiology and theological education today. Therefore, it is important for Aboriginal people to return to the image of the Creator Spirit prevalent in our culture and spirituality, as the source through which to understand our relationship with the Creator Spirit. In order to do so, Aboriginal people must deconstruct and decolonize the western Colonial God brought to us by the colonial church.

De-Colonizing Biblical Narratives

Since the late 1980s significant cutting-edge theological research has begun to emerge from the African American theological tradition from researchers such as James Cone, Cornel West, Katie Cannon, Mary Shawn Copeland, Jacquelyn Grant, and Willie James Jennings and biblical scholars identifying the black people and races in the Bible. Other examples are scholars such as Charles B. Copher, Cain Hope Felder, Randell C. Bailey and Jacquelyn Grant, Hugh R. Page Jr., and Itumeleng J. Mosala. These scholars had a significant impact on biblical and theological perspectives of First Nations peoples around the globe. Black people had for the first

---

7. Woodley, *Indigenous Theology*, 98.
8. Woodley, *Indigenous Theology*, 98.

time a different interpretation of the biblical narratives, and this brought a whole new dimension and discourse to the table. This would bring a whole new revelation for Aboriginal theologians because now the biblical narratives took on a totally new dimension with the identification of black people and people of color in the biblical narratives. This brought new insight as to how we read and understood the Old and New Testaments which was revolutionary for Aboriginal people. This affirmed Aboriginal Christians as it became clear that the Bible was not just about white folk and if this were the case then perhaps there were other areas that we needed to investigate. For example, if the Colonizer distorted the identities of people in the Bible, did they also distort the texts? Were they changed to provide justification for colonialism, greed, and the abhorrent treatment of First Nations people?

Over the next several decades First Nations scholars would spend considerable time investigating this area. In 2019 Professor Norm Habel and I began discussions and together we commenced working to decolonize biblical narratives, beginning with Genesis, with the development and exploration of the hermeneutical process that we would use. Together we held a number of week-long workshops with Aboriginal Christian leaders from across the country to share our work and findings.[9] Arising out of these workshops came three publications.[10] Another Australian biblical scholar, Mark G. Brett, has made a significant contribution in his publication titled, *Decolonising God: The Bible in the Tides of Empire.*[11]

It is imperative for Christians to understand that the Bible has been read, translated, and interpreted from a colonial perspective whether with a conscious or non-conscious awareness. The Bible has been used by the Colonizers and missionaries as a tool to justify invasion, conquest, theft of land, massacres, cultural genocide, racism, hatred, prejudice, exclusion, forced assimilation, and the ongoing social and political injustices that Aboriginal people face every day. The history of our country can be summarized as "colonial terrorism." Steve Heinrichs writes:

---

9. I wish to take this opportunity to express my deepest gratitude to Norm as we acknowledge his courage to give us insights into the Hebrew narratives of Genesis and to open this world to us as a non-biblical scholar. Norm's incredible willingness to deconstruct and to decolonize the biblical narratives with us has exposed the colonial bondage that has encapsulated the Colonizers' interpretation of biblical narratives to legitimate the colonization that is expressed through their theology.

10. Pattel-Gray and Habel, *De-Colonising the Biblical Narrative: The First Nations De-Colonising of Genesis 1–11*; *De-Colonising the Biblical Narrative: The First Nations De-Colonising of Genesis 12–25*; *De-Colonising the Biblical Narrative: The Colonial God YHWH, Progressive Revelation of the Character of YHWH in the Book of Exodus.*

11. Brett, *Decolonising God.*

> The Bible has been used as a tool of colonialism, xenophobia, exclusion, and cultural genocide. It still is. But this does not have to be. For centuries, communities of radical compassion and courage have read and re-read the sacred page in creative and critical fashion, so that these old memories shake the powers from their thrones and bring actual change to those who have been kept down.[12]

The Australian church practiced racist heretical biblical exegesis and hermeneutics. Aboriginal peoples' experiences of the transcendent were expected to be limited to white western understandings and viewed only through their cultural lens. Indeed, their expressions of God, church, faith, and life were forcibly limited to white Australian ones.[13] Most European "Christians" came to prosper from the "new" land, but the presence of Indigenous peoples restricted this process. Thus, Aboriginal people were taught falsehoods and heresies to rationalize the takeover of their land.

The Australian church played right into this plan, with its racist heretical biblical exegesis and hermeneutics. From the very first missions to the later more organized denominations, the Australian church read out the meaning of the actual text of the Bible in a way that distorted much more than just words.[14] The biblical injunction found in Gen 1:28 provides an excellent example:

> God blessed them, and God said to them, 'Be fruitful and *multiply*, and fill the earth and *subdue* it; and have *dominion* over the fish of the sea and over the birds of the air and over every living thing that moves upon the earth' (Emphasis added).

Heretical colonial exegesis and hermeneutics turned this passage into a mandate for the "conquest" (colonization) of the land and the "dominion" (subjugation) of the "native."[15] Reinforced by western racism and pretentions to "superiority," they supported the denigration of Aboriginal peoples. A passage that originally was intended to have humanity propagate the earth was twisted into one justifying theft, enslavement, imprisonment, terrorism, brutality, and colonial domination.

The Australian church had the benefit of literally thousands of years of analytical study of the biblical text, complemented more recently by the development of critical tools (tools which would subsequently be refined

---

12. Heinrichs, *Unsettling the Word*, xvii.
13. Attwood, *Making of Aborigines*, 1.
14. Reynolds, *Dispossession*, 5.
15. Harris, *Thinking for Ourselves*, 18, 20.

into textual, historical, grammatical, literary, form, tradition, and redaction criticisms).[16] What did the Australian church do with all this teaching? It warped it to serve its own self-interest.

Another example is found in the Australian churches' teaching of the heretical (so-called) "Curse of Ham."[17] People were taught by the church one of the most notorious examples of western theological deceit across Australia. This "church teaching" of the Hamitic curse supposedly condemned all "black-skinned peoples" to eternal inferiority based on a very specific kind of interpretation of the story in Gen 9:18–27.[18] Sadly, some missionaries were quite efficient, and a few older Aboriginals still believe they are condemned by God to be "less than whites."[19] I was taught this heresy at the Mundingburra Uniting Church in a Sunday School lesson, and I can remember it as if it was yesterday, the shame and humiliation I felt being the only Aboriginal child in this class. I wanted to disappear as the other white children looked at me with racist contempt. I recall being extremely traumatized by this experience and it has stayed with me all these years. I cried to my mother asking her why God would make us black, didn't God like us, what had we done to be hated by everyone? I cried to God asking why he did this to us. Very little thought was given by the white Sunday school teacher as to what effect that this biblical interpretation would have on my person as no compassion was ever given nor demonstrated by her. This experience would define me in so many ways and it would shape my theological research for the future.

Randy Woodley reflects on his people's questions as they wrestle as to what truth is and what is lies:

> ... White men who translated the Bible probably kept stuff out that they didn't want us to know, and they put things in that they did want us to know that weren't there originally. So, in some circles there is little trust that the scriptures are in the best interest of Indigenous people ... The scriptures were oral before they were written. And we don't have the original oral content of the Aramaic-speaking Jesus.[20]

There is an important and critical need for academic scholars to examine how colonization holds both white and black Australians in bondage as we are all indoctrinated to hold a certain colonial worldview. We must be aware

16. Hayes and Holladay, *Biblical Exegesis*, 14–23.
17. Paulson, *Issues We Confront*, c.f. Evans, Saunders, and Cronin, *Exclusion*, 11–12.
18. Pattel-Gray, *Great White Flood*, 124.
19. Harris, *One Blood*, 169.
20. Woodley, *Indigenous Theology*, 125–26.

that the very structures that we participate in and function in each and every day are founded on colonial racist values to maintain colonial power, wealth, and privilege. An individual who participates in these structures may not be racist but the structure itself can be and we work in these structures that maintain racist and exclusionary systems to benefit the dominant culture. We need to be able to name this if we are ever to be free and liberated from this colonial mindset that holds us in bondage. While this worldview, structure, and value remain in place we—both black and white Australians—will never be liberated or freed from a life of division. Aboriginal people will be forever confined to a life of inequality, subjugation, racism, and perpetual poverty. If ever there was a time to transform our theological education the time is now.

The white churches have consistently omitted from their exegesis the numerous positive instances of black people and people of color in the biblical text. In my theological studies in the 1980s and 90s at the University of Sydney I was exposed to the black identity of many biblical figures through the academic literature written by black biblical scholars from America and Africa. This became a turning point for me as it confirmed what I had believed, namely, that Jesus was black and so were many other biblical figures such as Hagar (Gen 16, 21),[21] Moses' wife (Num 12),[22] Tirhaka, king of the Ethiopians (2 Kgs 19:9; Isa 37:9), Pharaoh of Egypt,[23] the Queen of Sheba (1 Kgs 10),[24] Simeon who was called Niger (Acts 13:1),[25] and various others. To the contrary, black people in the Bible were portrayed by the Australian church to be either white or "colorless," or simply were avoided. This kind of selective exegesis of the biblical narrative kept Aboriginal people from having possible racial identification and positive role models.[26] It also deprived Aboriginal people of the full and complete biblical text which showed blacks not only as full members of the community of believers, but also as wealthy people, leaders and rulers. What became clear is that the Australian church exegesis was not only racist but heretical.[27]

Therefore, we Aboriginal theologians encourage the academic theological institutions to question how the church has literally whitewashed biblical narratives and to examine the racist overtones found in the western

---

21. Waters, "Who Was Hagar?" 187–205.
22. Felder, *Troubling*, 42.
23. Felder, *Troubling*, 32–36; c.f. Snowden, *Blacks in Antiquity*.
24. Felder, *Troubling*, 32–36.
25. Felder, *Troubling*, 47.
26. Trompf, *Gospel is Not Western*, 7–9.
27. Pattel-Gray, *Great White Flood*, 312.

cultural biases and racist exegetical and hermeneutical practices. Where do we begin to develop a theological truth that names western racist treatment inflicted upon Aboriginal people in order to deconstruct our racist western hegemony of white Australia and to recognize the integrity, strength, and resilience to survive? There is a critical need to eradicate those aspects that hold us in bondage and begin a process to deconstruct and decolonize our Christian beliefs and theological education to be able to speak with integrity into the world in which we live.

The Bible, as taught by the colonizing church, teaches First Nations people that God is a distant ruler who has handed over to the white Colonizer the whole created order as a resource under their oversight and for their own use and benefit. God is a faraway king who has ceded control of all the animals and plants to the white landlord. This God instructs the white landlord to rule over what has been entrusted to them. If God, the heavenly monarch, has handed the whole created order over to the white colonists as the landlords, the outcome is that they, in turn, are free to do what they want with it.[28]

It is important that the churches and Christians realize how essential it is to de-colonize both the biblical and theological narratives. We need to restore our relationship first and foremost with the Creator Spirit and next to make a radical transformation that sees us reconnecting physically and spiritually with the land and our common kinship with each other and all creation. We need to understand our human necessity to see ourselves as part of creation but not as nature itself, or as a power over nature. We must regard ourselves as living in creation and with creation being important to our very existence. We long for our primordial sense of belonging to mother earth: our existence is dependent on her.

Aboriginal people have stated over the past several decades that Adam and Eve could not have been Aboriginal because, if they were, they would have eaten the snake and not the apple. Based on this understanding, Adam and Eve would not have been the basis for sin entering the world. However, Aboriginal people see the basis for sin entering this world through colonization and this as the foundation for evil to thrive. Nevertheless, through western colonization and Christianity, this became the means in which they brought their cultural views and baggage to make others inferior to them and the source of their superiority.

The development of First Nations theology could not be done without setting the experiential context of the suffering, subjugation, and oppression of our people under the weight of colonization. Their lived experience, both

---

28. Woodley, *Indigenous Theology*, 101.

historical and current, defines the First Nations peoples' anguish because of the cruelty of western colonization and missionization in Australia, through the theft of land, massacres, genocidal acts, slavery, segregation, the forced removal of thousands of Aboriginal children from their mothers (referred to as the Stolen Generations), not to mention the environmental destruction of Aboriginal land, seas, waterways and lifeways.[29]

The role of First Nations women is considered critical to the maintenance, continuity, and survival of the entire societal structure. First Nations society depends on the equal participation of women. Today, the status and position of First Nations women within Australia differs, depending upon the impact and absorption of the colonization, missionization, western patriarchal beliefs, and misogynist acts in our society. This biblical interpretation and these western values have done much to undermine the status and role of First Nations women throughout our land. That is why it is critical for biblical narratives to be decolonized so that they dismantle and hopefully eradicate colonial power and domination and will give way to the empowerment of all First Nations people around the world.

From our perspective, this blatant colonial tradition which confirms the original harsh mandate to dominate the land and all living creatures of the land (Gen 1:26–28), also reflects the colonial worldview and colonial actions of the European peoples who invaded and colonized the land of Australia. Our response is to discern the falsity of this biblical tradition, recall the truths of our First Nations' relationship with the land and the land beings of our country, and to endorse the alternate interpretation. As First Nations theologians, we are not only free to take this stand because of our rich spiritual relationship with the land and the Creator Spirit in the land, but because we believe that Christ has liberated us from the sin of colonial control and freed us to correct ancient biblical narratives and retrieve the underlying spirit of the gospel that is colonial-free.

The Australian church's racism is evident in its abysmal failure to stand united against racism in this country. Recognizing the existence of racism *in general* is the easy part, and so, many churches decry this evil. Some churches even go the next step and recognize the existence of racism *in the* church itself. The church's silence is deafening; its lack of action is shocking. By keeping quiet, the Australian churches are accepting the situation of racism against Aboriginal people, and implicitly espousing the cause of the privileged white majority. The churches are reinforcing their own racism, as well as that of society in general. They are endorsing inequality and injustice.[30]

29. Pattel-Gray, *Great White Flood*.
30. Pattel-Gray, *Great White Flood*, 159.

Liberating Theological Education

As the head of the newly established School of Indigenous Studies at the University of Divinity, I have a very important role to play at this critical time in Australia. The School of Indigenous Studies has the opportunity to influence theological education, to bring an Aboriginal theological insight, hermeneutics and exegetical process, to share an Aboriginal biblical interpretation, and to share ancient knowledge and wisdom. We have the chance to provide Aboriginal Christians with access to academic theological education to raise up the next generation of Australia's First Nations leaders.

Richard Twiss, a Sicangu Lakota theologian, sums up the aspirations of Aboriginal people:

> What we are seeking is a place where the gospel brings freedom and spiritual power to follow Jesus with all our hearts, souls, minds and strength, while still fully embracing our tribal identity, traditional customs, cultural forms, worldview and rituals. We seek a place where we are no longer seen as the perpetual mission field of the dominant culture church, but rather a place where we are honestly embraced as coequal participants in the life, work and community of Christ's followers—as Indigenous people.[31]

The School of Indigenous Studies allows us to be coequal participants to influence theological education and to share our theological insights, our cutting-edge scholarship, and groundbreaking research.

The School of Indigenous Studies will be a national platform to raise up the First Nations voice and speak into all social and political areas that are of concern and relate to securing justice and equity for our people. It is important to note that the School would not have been established if not for the University of Divinity's capacity to hear the aspirations of Australia's First Nations people who wanted a recognized place within theological education and institutions. The Council of the University of Divinity moved to make our aspirations a reality with the establishment of the School in 2022, the first academic theological institution of its kind in Australia. It is vital to acknowledge those council members and Christian individuals who saw our value, our worth, and made this happen through their own generosity and personal investment which saw First Nations theological scholars moved from the periphery to the center of theological education. So doing has raised the status of Aboriginal academic scholarship into the heart of theological scholarship, with the potential to be a critical paradigm shift in theological education.

31. Twiss, *Rescuing*, 93.

The School of Indigenous Studies provides Aboriginal theologians the opportunity to now speak into this world and to challenge racist biblical interpretation and culturally biased theological concepts. It is important that Aboriginal people move beyond western imperialism, colonization, and missionization, and advocate by seeking guidance from our Creator Spirit "made known among us in Jesus, who is Christ."[32] Aboriginal spiritual leaders ask if 2023 is "the year of the Lord's Favor" to bring "good news" to the poor and downtrodden Aboriginal people of this land. As Lal Fernando says, "liberation is seen here through the lens of God's covenant with the poor through Jesus Christ, which is seen as unique to Biblical tradition."[33] If we are to have any hope of reconciliation and restoring wholeness in creation, then we First Nations people must first begin by challenging the way colonial inheritors do theology on stolen land, and questioning what it means for them to be seen as colonial inheritors. It is time for "truth telling," exposing the lies, the brutality and the power, privilege and wealth colonial inheritors have gained at the expense of First Nations people—"and the truth will set you free" (John 8:32 NIV).

To begin the "truth telling" process we must start with the objects and subjects, this being the Aboriginal people themselves, examining the import of Christianity and the measures taken by the colonist to civilize the Aboriginal people through western Christianization and missionization.

Meredith Lake provides details of Aboriginal peoples' encounter with the Christian missionaries.[34] The missionaries held a racist belief that Aboriginal people were inferior to them, and a Eurocentric attitude that Aboriginal people were savages and needed to be saved and civilized. This racist lens epitomized the missionaries' colonial trappings and saw biblical narratives held in bondage by their cultural bias. Lake states, "Though colonists and especially missionaries often imposed the European Bible on Aboriginal communities, from very early on, Indigenous people found ways to reappropriate and reinterpret it for themselves."[35] This is evident in how Boorong rejected western culture and all its trappings. Lake refers to Boorong's son Dickey as being the "first Indigenous Australian evangelist"[36] who died shortly after his baptism. The same was said of Jemmy, another young Aboriginal convert[37] who also died shortly after his conversion. It

---

32. Twiss, *Rescuing*, 46.
33. Lal Fernando, "People, Land and Empire," 131.
34. Lake, *Bible in Australia*, 518.
35. Lake, *Bible in Australia*, 9.
36. Lake, *Bible in Australia*, 56.
37. Lake, *Bible in Australia*, 60.

was not surprising to see that most Aboriginal people rejected the Bible as it was packaged in western culture. Some Aboriginal people who encountered the Bible would in fact take it to far greater dimensions by interpreting the Bible into their language.

A renowned Aboriginal scholar and linguist Biraban (meaning "Eaglehawk") claimed his Awabakal cultural heritage, fulfilled the requirements of cultural Law of initiation and become fully immersed in cultural practices. Biraban taught his language, culture, and spiritual beliefs to a missionary named Lancelot Threlkeld, who had been commissioned by the London Missionary Society in 1825. They would work together the next seventeen years translating the English Bible into Awabakal language. Anne Keary states:

> . . . he [Biraban] did not see Christianity as an exclusive religious truth nor view the missionary as his superior in spiritual knowledge. At the same time as he learned about Christianity, it is evident that he tried to teach Threlkeld about the significance of Awabakal Beings and sites.[38]

I had the good fortune of living on the Awabakal land for a period and my home was only several hundred meters from the site where Biraban and Threlkeld met and translated the Bible into Awabakal language. During this time, I met with several elders who had known Biraban. Joe Hampton, Chair of the Aboriginal Elders Council, told me a lot about Biraban and the establishment of the Biraban Local Aboriginal Land Council in 2012, of which Hampton was a member. He spoke about how Biraban tried to tell white fellas about Awabakal spiritual beliefs and their cultural practices, but this fell on deaf ears. He went on to speak about how Biraban became a broken man as he watched the white colonialist consume his land, dispossess his people, leaving them in poverty, destroying his peoples' cultural and spiritual beliefs, and committing cultural genocide and sexual abuse of women and children.[39] This drove him to drink. The hurt and destruction of his people was too much to bear, and it destroyed his soul. He tried so hard to educate the white man about his people, that the Creator was already here in our midst, but the white fellas did not understand.[40]

Nevertheless, it is necessary for Aboriginal people to decolonize themselves and to realize that the Bible is still being used by some to colonize us and we must break free of the colonial shackles in order to be free from the colonial might. It is encouraging to know that Aboriginal people since the

---

38. Keary, *Christianity, Colonialism*, 129.
39. Pattel-Gray, *Great White Flood*, 312.
40. Joseph Hampton, oral testimony, 2016.

1960s have begun to define their own theology through their cultural lens drawing on our cosmology, epistemology, and ontology to interpret biblical narratives. We want to shape our theological thoughts and expressions by embracing our own language that gives meaning to who we are as a people. Our theology is born from this land, founded on our relationship with the Creator since time began, and it is this deep ancient wisdom that sustains us and provides our resilience to survive. It is only together that black and white Australians can make a difference as we wrestle with these challenging questions, recognize how colonized we are, and begin the process of decolonizing ourselves in the endeavor to liberate our theological education from the bondage of colonialism.

Bibliography

Attwood, Bain. *The Making of the Aborigines*. Sydney: Allen & Unwin, 1989.

Bailey, Randall C. and Jacquelyn Grant. *The Recovery of Black Presence: An Interdisciplinary Exploration: Essays in Honor of Dr. Charles B. Copher*. Nashville, TN: Abingdon, 1995.

Barrett, John. *The Better Country: The Religious Aspect of Life in Eastern Australia, 1835–1850*. Melbourne: Melbourne University Press, 1966.

Brett, Mark G. *Decolonising God: The Bible in the Tides of Empire*. Sheffield: Sheffield Phoenix, 2008.

Evans, Raymond, Kay Saunders, and Kathryn Cronin. *Exclusion, Exploitation and Extermination: Race Relations in Colonial Queensland*. Sydney: Australia and New Zealand Book Company, 1975.

Felder, Cain Hope, ed. *Stony the Road We Trod: African American Biblical Interpretation*. Minneapolis, MN: Fortress, 1991.

———. *Troubling Biblical Waters: Race, Class, and Family*. Maryknoll, NY: Orbis, 1989.

Harris, Charles. "Thinking for Ourselves." *Koori Mail*, 15 January 1992.

Harris, John. *One Blood: 200 Years of Aboriginal Encounter with Christianity: A Story of Hope*. Sutherland: Albatross, 1994.

Hayes, John H., and Carl R. Holladay. *Biblical Exegesis: A Beginner's Handbook*. London: SCM, 1983.

Havea, Jione, ed. *People and Land: Decolonizing Theologies*. Washington, DC: Lexington, 2019.

Heinrichs, Steve. *Unsettling the Word: Biblical Experiments in Decolonization*. Maryknoll, NY: Orbis, 2019.

Keary, Anne. "Christianity, Colonialism and Cross-Cultural Translation: Lancelot Threlkeld, Biraban and the Awabakal." *Aboriginal History* 33 (2009) 117–55.

Lake, Meredith. *The Bible in Australia: A Cultural History*. Sydney: NewSouth, 2018.

Lal Fernando, Jude. "People, Land and Empire in Asia: Geopolitics, Theological Imaginations and Islands of Peace." In *People and Land: Decolonizing Theologies*, edited by Jione Havea, 123–38. Washington, DC: Lexington, 2019.

Mosala, Itumeleng J. "Reconstructing the Azanian Mispähot (Clans): Land, Class and Bible in South Africa Today." In *Text and Experience: Towards a Cultural Exegesis of the Bible*, edited by Daniel Smith-Christopher, 238–46. Sheffield: Sheffield Academic, 1995.

Page, Hugh R., ed. *The Africana Bible: Reading Israel's Scriptures from Africa and the African Diaspora*. Minneapolis, MN: Fortress, 2021.

Pattel-Gray, Anne, *The Great White Flood: Racism in Australia*. Atlanta, GA: Scholars, 1998.

Pattel-Gray, Anne, and Habel, Norman, eds. *De-Colonising the Biblical Narrative: The First Nations De-Colonising of Genesis 1–11*. Brompton: ATF, 2020.

———. *De-Colonising the Biblical Narrative: The First Nations De-Colonising of Genesis 12–25*. Brompton: ATF, 2023.

———. *De-Colonising the Biblical Narrative: The Colonial God YHWH, Progressive Revelation of the Character of YHWH in the Book of Exodus*. Brompton: ATF, 2023.

Paulson, Graham A. *The Issues We Confront*. From Mission to Church Conference, Australian Council of Churches' Commission on Mission. Sydney, NSW, 27 August 1993.

Reynolds, Henry. *Dispossession: Black Australia and White Invaders*. Sydney: Allen & Unwin, 1989.

Sherwood, John E. "Prologue—of People, Birds, Shell and Fire." In *The Moyjil Site, South-West Victoria, Australia: Fire and Environment in a 120,000-Year Coastal Midden—Nature or People?*, edited by Jim M. Bowler, David M. Price, et al., 7–13. Melbourne: The Royal Society of Victoria, 2018.

Snowden, Frank M. Jr. *Blacks in Antiquity: Ethiopians in the Greco-Roman Experience*. Cambridge, MA: Harvard University Press, 1970.

Trompf, Garry W., ed. *The Gospel is Not Western: Black Theologies from the Southwest Pacific*. Maryknoll, NY: Orbis, 1987.

Twiss, Richard. *Rescuing the Gospel from the Cowboys: A Native American Expression of the Jesus Way*. Westmont, IL: IVP, 2015.

Vaka'uta, Nasili. "Delusion of Empire: On People and Land in Oceania." In *People and Land: Decolonizing Theologies*, edited by Jione Havea, 111–22. Washington, DC: Lexington, 2019.

Waters, John W. "Who Was Hagar?" In *Stony the Road We Trod: African American Biblical Interpretation*, edited by Cain Hope Felder, 187–205. Minneapolis, MN: Fortress, 1991.

Woodley, Randy S. *Indigenous Theology and the Western Worldview: A Decolonized Approach to Christian Doctrine*. Grand Rapids, MI: Baker Academic, 2022.

Part II

Questions of Culture and Translation

In the Beginning, Pundgyl Marman
Translating Creation at the Edges of Empire

Mark G. Brett *and* Deborah Shuh Yi Tan

For historic Protestantism, translation of the Bible into vernacular languages was a constitutive element of religious identity, and this emphasis on translation carried over into the majority of Protestant colonial missions in the nineteenth century.[1] But in contrast with other British colonial territories, there were remarkably few attempts to engage with the Aboriginal languages spoken in New South Wales, Tasmania, South Australia, and Victoria.[2] Our focus in this paper will be on translations of Genesis 1 from the 1840s by William Thomas (1793–1867), who was an Assistant Aboriginal Protector from 1839 in the Port Phillip District—at the time, an area within the colony of New South Wales. His world was entirely Eurocentric, but his translations clearly diverge from a common picture painted of the earliest Australian colonists as actively hostile towards the learning of Aboriginal languages.[3] The question arising is why his efforts at translation ceased after little more than a decade.

1. Among many other studies, see especially Sanneh, *Translating the Message*.

2. The creation narratives of Genesis, for example, were translated into the Wiradjuri language in 1834 (NSW) by William Watson, a CMS missionary. A similar effort to translate the creation narratives by Thomas Wilkinson in Wybalenna (Tasmania) was condemned by Governor Arthur as imprudent, and Wilkinson was dismissed by 1834. A Ngarrindjeri rendering of Genesis 1–4 (South Australia) was published in *Tungarar Jehovald* in 1864, and the translation is available in the Trove database at nla.gov.au. See Harris, *One Blood*, 66, 99, 363–64, 810.

3. His published translation of the creation narrative appeared as part of a submission to the Select Committee of the Legislative Council on the Aborigines of 1858–59, reprinted in Thomas, "Succinct Sketch," 118–33, with Genesis 1 on 130–32.

The Port Phillip Protectorate was born out of the Buxton Committee Report of 1837, which reflected the humanitarian movement within the British Parliament at the time. It sought to temper the ill-effects of colonial settlement while delivering the assumed benefits of civilisation and Christianity.[4] This would necessarily include a defence of "the rights and interests of the Natives," and from "any encroachment on their property, and from acts of Cruelty, of oppression or injustice."[5] These were rights and interests as understood in English law, but the new Protectors were also to represent Aboriginal "wants, wishes or grievances" to the colonial government. This would hardly be possible without some knowledge of the Indigenous language, and accordingly, when describing the appointment of the Protectors, Lord Glenelg instructed Governer Gipps:

> In reference to every object contemplated by the proposed Appointment, it is exceedingly desirable that the Protector should, as soon as possible, learn the language of the Natives so as to be able freely and familiarly to converse with them.[6]

Thomas was not a linguist, and we can only wonder how his biblical translations would have been received by the Taungurung, Wurundjeri and Boonwurrung clans.[7] However, our paper does not seek to explore the history of the Kulin languages as such, a research topic which properly belongs in the hands of current Aboriginal leaders and linguists.[8] (For similar reasons, this paper cannot be seen as a contribution to Aboriginal Christian theology.) Instead, we will analyze William Thomas' translation as an example of colonial contact,[9] and then venture some comparisons with the ancient text of Genesis 1 in its own intercultural context. This ancient biblical text was first composed in Hebrew, most likely after the fall of the Judean state in 587 BCE, at a time when the Israelite and Judean peoples were subjected to the rule of the Babylonian and Persian Empires. We will highlight some features of the biblical text that remained unknown to Thomas but which

---

4. Carey, "Christian Colonisation," 322–30.

5. Letter from Lord Glenelg to Governor Gipps, 31 January 1838, *Historical Records of Australia*, 1, xix, 254.

6. Letter from Lord Glenelg to Governor Gipps, 255. Similarly with reference to linguistic competence, *Report of the Parliamentary Select Committee on Aboriginal Tribes (British Settlements)*, 126.

7. Stephen Morey, "Previously Unexamined Texts," 45–60.

8. We are grateful to three linguists at Monash and La Trobe Universities who have offered comments on the colonial records: Stephen Morey, Andrew Tanner, and from the Dja Dja Wurrung people, Harley Donolly-Lee.

9. On translation projects in the colonial contact zone, see, e.g., Errington, "Colonial Linguistics," 19–39; Carey, "Lancelot Threlkeld," 447–78.

are, in some ironic ways, analogous with his own situation as a translator at the edge of empire.

Naming "God" in Port Phillip

The first chapter of Genesis appears to be one of the earlier texts that Thomas sought to translate. Having arrived at Port Phillip in January 1839,[10] he recorded in his journal some fifteen months later that "In the evening had service & for the 1st time spoke in the native tongue, on the Creation of all things."[11] His major informant during these early years was Budgery Tom, but when he referred to his translation efforts in July of 1841, he did not directly name the "one who was assisting me in the Translation of Genasis [sic]."[12] During the previous month, he had also been reflecting on creation with Old Tottoy.[13]

Translations of Genesis 1 appear in four volumes of his language records. Three are clearly identified as translations of Genesis,[14] but one example from April 1840 is more generally headed "On the Creation."[15] In this latter context, Thomas referred to God using the term *Woodi Bullito Marminarta* ("big/high/great father").[16] Similarly, Thomas relays several conversations with Aboriginal people in his journals in February and March 1840 in which he referred to God as *Big Marminarta, Bulito/Bullito Marminarta*.[17] In another of his translation records, Thomas begins Gen 1:1 with *Koonge Marnameek Marman* ("excellent father"), followed thereafter by *woody/ woodi bullito marman* ("big/high/great father"), sometimes written with a shorthand formulation, *w. b. marman*.[18]

10. Stephens, *Journal of William Thomas*, 1:iv.

11. Sunday 19 April 1840, Stephens, *Journal of William Thomas*, 1:156.

12. Stephens, *Journal of William Thomas*, 1:340, 342. Marie Fels suggests Budgery Tom. Fels, "*I Succeeded Once*," 6.

13. On 27 June, 1841, Thomas notes the conversation with Old Tottoy. Stephens, *Journal of William Thomas*, 1:320–21.

14. See Volume 22 (Item 02), Volume 23 (Item 04), and Volume 24 (Item 10) in State Library of New South Wales, "William Thomas Papers, 1834–1868, 1902," Manuscripts, Oral History and Pictures Catalogue, n.d.

15. Volume 26 (Item 44) in State Library of New South Wales, "William Thomas Papers."

16. Unless stated otherwise, word meanings are taken from: Marguerita Stephens, *Journal of William Thomas*, Volume Four: Kulin Language. Meaning of *Marminarta* from: Fels, "*I Succeeded Once*", 90, n177.

17. Stephens, *Journal of William Thomas*, 1:132, 142.

18. Volume 22 (Item 02) in State Library of New South Wales, "William Thomas

In his final published version, however, Thomas rendered the name of God as *Pundgyl Marman*, adopting a traditional name also spelt *Pungil*, *Ponjel* or *Bingyal* in the nineteenth century, although today's spelling is more often *Bunjil*. The combination of an Eastern Kulin word for the Creator eagle with *Marman* ("Father") deserves some reflection.[19] Referring to God as Father is a common Christian practice, but the word "father" does not appear in the ancient text of the creation narrative (in Hebrew we would expect to see *'av*), and neither does it appear in the King James Version of Genesis 1, which was the text that Thomas used as the basis of his translation. Instead, the Hebrew version adopts a peculiar plural noun for God, *Elohim*, for reasons that we will discuss later in this paper.

Interestingly, the Hebrew text does suggest that the spirit of God "flutters" or "hovers" like a bird in Gen 1:2, and an association with the flight of an eagle would have been possible for a nineteenth-century translator versed in the original language. Thomas set out his translation of Gen 1:1–2 in parallel with the King James Version, which overlooks the birdlike imagery and adopts instead a generic rendering of the verb as "moved":

KJV	Thomas' Translation
1. In the beginning God created the heaven and the earth	1. *Ganbronin Pundgyl Marman monguit woorworer bar beek.*
2. And the earth was without form, and void, and darkness was upon the face of the deep. And the Spirit of God moved upon the face of the waters.[20]	2. *Nier beek nowdin netbo, beek tandowring tarkate ; nier boit, nier mill, nier taul, nier turrong, nier uungo ; bar boorundara kormuk bumile. Bar Moorup Pundgyl warrebonuk narlumbanan parn.*

It is evident here that Thomas rendered the phrase "Spirit of God" as *Moorup Pundgyl*, but he decided that the leading metaphor for configuring *Pundgyl* would be father. Instead of rejecting the idea that God in Genesis 1 could be rendered in Aboriginal languages (or rejecting the very idea of religion in Aboriginal societies), Thomas renders the God of Genesis 1 with a combination of "eagle (ancestor)" and "father."[21]

Papers".

19. Newton, "Two Victorian Corroborees," 121–49, at 131 notes the possibility of Christian influence, following Swain, *Place for Strangers*, 114–58.

20. Thomas, "Succinct Sketch of the Aboriginal Language," 130.

21. John Green was later to produce a word list in which God was rendered simply as *Bonjel*, published in Brough Smith, *Aborigines of Victoria*, 102. Working in the 1840s in Dja Dja Wurrung (Western Kulin) Country, Assistant Protector Parker adopted *Marmingorak*, "father of all," according to Parker, *Aborigines of Victoria*, 20–21. Our thanks to Harley Donolly-Lee for pointing this out.

An association of *Pundgyl* and "father" appears in the 1880s in the writings of A. W. Howitt, reflecting on a few Aboriginal sources. There is one tantalizing record of a traditional Woiwurrung song composed by Wenberi (also spelled Winberri or Winberry) using the term *Bŭnjil mainmenngala* (*Bunjil*, our father).[22] In Gippsland, Howitt also heard reference to a great being above the sky who was named *Mungan-ngaura* ("Father ours"), which he reported in a letter to the anthropologist E. B. Tylor in Oxford.[23] However, the earlier records from John Bulmer suggest that he had heard *bingyal* called "father" or "brother" in one part of Victoria, but not in Gippsland:

> Colin Hood of the Western District tells me the name of their God is *bingyal* and that they call him father & brother (*maamee* father, *wahwee* brother). They also look upon *bingyal* as possessing all things. Thus the sun is *whyepook bingyallu* i.e. God's. I have tried to get this from the Lake Tyers men but they have no idea of fatherhood of the *ngulambiu* (the first).[24]

It is unclear when Thomas decided to start using *Pundgyl Marman* for God, but this probably happened by the end of 1843.[25] Among the creation stories that Thomas heard, he records one in his diary as explained to him by Poleorong, as they watched a man working with clay:

> Pundgyl make em Koolins—Pundgyl worked up the clay with his big one knife and when all soft commenced to make Man, beginning at the feet and the legs and so on upwards, he made a man on each piece of bark when he had made them he looked at them a long while was pleased danced round them he then got some stringy bark made hair of it and put on their heads once straight and the other he curled, Pundgyl was big one pleased and danced round them he gave each a name.[26]

---

22. Howitt, "Notes on Songs and Songmakers," 327–35, at 331. We are grateful to Stephen Morey for pointing out these examples from A. W. Howitt.

23. The letter dated February 2, 1884, is available in the Oxford anthropology records: https://web.prm.ox.ac.uk/sma/index.php/primary-documents/primary-documents-index/414-howitt-tylor-papers-prm.html.

24. Campbell and Vanderwal, eds, *John Bulmer's Recollections*, 39. Regarding Colin Hood (Merang, from the Djab Wurrung), see Critchett, *Untold Stories*, 79–106.

25. By the time Thomas translated a hymn sung for the first time in language on Sunday 5 November 1843, *Pungil Marman* was the term he used. The day after the hymn was sung, Thomas records "the Goldbourn Blacks came over . . . to hear Blacks sing to Pungil Marman." Stephens, *Journal of William Thomas*, 1:557.

26. Undated, quoted in Fels, "*I Succeeded Once*", 39.

The suggestion that *Pundgyl* used clay in making humans resonates more with Genesis 2 and Psalm 104. In Gen 2:4, the *'adam* ("man") is taken from the *'adamah* ("land")—evidently a wordplay—and instead of seeing God speaking from a lofty distance in the heavens, Psalm 104 describes a divine spirit immanent in the earth and in all creatures (Ps 104:27–30).[27] This cosmic concept of the Spirit of God resonates with the *Moorup Pundgyl* who moves over the face of the deep in Gen 1:2, but Thomas generally does not envisage God as immanent in earth and waters.

He frankly reports that his translations received mixed reviews, and his work did not become influential in later years. In one confrontation with an Aboriginal man, Nerrimbinek, he was evidently admonished for promoting his Christian ideas, with the notable conclusion that "my Pundgyl was not his Pundgyl." Thomas found this exchange difficult, but acknowledged it nonetheless.[28] On the other hand, he also recorded the generosity of his friend, Derrimut,[29] who reportedly spoke of *marman Bundgyl* in the hours before his death: "there good *marman Bundgyl, Murrumbuk bar Murrum binna marman, bondup nge*" ("The good father Bunjil is there, Father of you and me, it is good, he is close by").[30] There are many ambiguities in this poignant exchange, which we will leave to Aboriginal historians to interpret.

Instead, as indicated at the outset of our paper, we turn to the intercultural exchanges reflected in the Hebrew text of Genesis 1 itself, which will then allow us to frame a number of questions about the ancient and modern politics of translation. We are not suggesting that William Thomas would have been aware of this ancient compositional history that sits behind the modern English translations of Genesis, but a brief excursus at this point will provide another lens through which the significance of his translation efforts might be considered.

The Ancient World of Genesis 1

The ancient Hebrew compositions of Genesis 1 come from a cultural world unknown to the translators of the King James Version, which was

---

27. Krüger, "'Kosmo-theologies' zwischen Mythos und Erfahrung," 49–74. See further, Schmid, "Himmelsgott, Weltgott und Schöpfer," 111–48.

28. Stephens, *Journal of William Thomas*, 2:305; cf. 2:53, where an Aboriginal woman seems to associate *Pungil Marman* simply with the God of the white settlers.

29. On Derrimut, a Yalukit-willam clan leader among the Boonwurrung, see especially Clark, "You have all this place," 107–32.

30. 26 April 1864, in Stephens, *Journal of William Thomas*, 3:444. We have followed the translation in n.268 of Stephens (3:444), which differs slightly from the earlier transcription and translation in Clark, "You have all this place," 123 and n.104.

first published in 1611. As already indicated, this is the English version that guided Thomas in his translation efforts, rather than the Hebrew text. There is a very broad consensus in historical biblical research since the late nineteenth century that Genesis 1 belongs to a so-called Priestly school of thought, which is different from the second creation narrative in Gen 2:4—3:24.[31] There are ongoing debates about the dating of the composition, and perhaps successive editorial additions, but most of the controversial details can be left to one side for the purposes of our discussion. We begin by reflecting on the consistent and peculiar choice for the divine name in the ancient Hebrew versions of Genesis 1.

Within the Priestly compositions in the book of Genesis and Exodus, the earliest ancestors never learnt Israel's own name for God: YHWH (which is rendered LORD in capital letters in most English translations). According to the Priestly account, Israel's ancestors in Genesis knew only the divine name "El," because the name "YHWH" (LORD) was revealed for the first time during the exodus from Egypt (Exod 6:2–3).

Genesis 1 does not, however, use the name "El," and instead, it consistently adopts a grammatically curious plural noun, *Elohim*, even though the associated verbs are singular. God therefore becomes singular but nameless, plural but also in some sense singular, and the paradoxical grammar is part of a novel attempt to construct a version of monotheism that is actually "inclusive" in an important sense: the Creator can be named in a huge variety of ways, even by using the Indigenous Canaanite name "El."[32] In short, *Elohim* (without a definite article) is not so much a name as a tantalizing abstraction, like "divinity" in English, which leaves open the naming of God. In contrast with any "national" theology that calls for a uniformity of religion (such as in the case of the Yahwism in the book of Deuteronomy), Genesis provides a more ecumenical social vision.

The Priestly creation theology was evidently forged in debate with the Mesopotamian mythologies of creation and flood. The biblical account accepts much of the cosmic geography while also contesting some key points.[33] Apparently, there was general agreement across ancient Western

31. In the mid-nineteenth century, the Priestly literary source was recognized under other names. For example, Bishop Colenso, who will be discussed below, called this material "Elohist." The distinctive use of the divine name Elohim in Genesis 1 was one factor in this earlier scholarly designation. See Rogerson, *Old Testament Criticism*, 232.

32. See especially de Pury, "Gottesname, Gottesbezeichnung und Gottesbegriff," 25–47. Regarding the alternative "Yahwistic" traditions in Genesis, see Brett, "YHWH among the Nations," 113–30.

33. See especially Hendel, "Genesis 1–11 and Its Mesopotamian Problem"; Frahm, "Counter-texts, Commentaries, and Adaptations"; Carr, "Precursors to the Priestly Creation Account."

Asia, for example, that the waters above the heavens were held back by a hard dome, as is also depicted in Gen 1:6–8. In the Babylonian myth, Enuma Elish, this cosmic order was established only after a violent conflict with Tiamat, a sea goddess whose name is reflected in the Hebrew word that is commonly translated as "deep" in Gen 1:2 (*tehom*). In the Priestly version of the flood narrative, the waters burst up from the "great deep" (Gen 7:11) as well as falling as rain through the windows of heaven, and this cosmic geography was shared across many cultures.

Instead of preserving a divine conflict at the foundation of the world, however, the Priestly narrative in Genesis 1 asserts that all this happened through the actions of *Elohim*, the grammatically enigmatic Creator. And most importantly, all human beings were made in the image of *Elohim*, according to Gen 1:27, and thus not made in the image of Israel's YHWH, who was yet to be revealed in the exodus story. According to the Priestly tradition, the ancestors of Israel could freely use the Canaanite name for Creator, "El," and they had no knowledge of the name "YHWH." Retrospectively, it was revealed to Moses' generation that El and YHWH were in fact the same God under different names (Exod 6:2–3).

A similar conceptual point is made in Genesis 14, even though this chapter contradicts the chronology suggested in Exod 6:2–3. The wording in Gen 14:13 implies that Abram lived in a treaty relationship with the local Indigenous people, who are called the "treaty partners" of Abraham.[34] A respect for the old Canaanite traditions of El is explicitly articulated when Abram acknowledges "El Elyon, Creator of heaven and earth" in Gen 14:22. The Hebrew text also suggests that Abraham identified YHWH with El Elyon. There are some variations among the ancient manuscripts at this point, but the inclusive implications are essentially the same, regardless of the textual variations: Abraham acknowledges El Elyon as the Creator, and thus adopts an Indigenous name for God.[35] This is not likely to be a composition that stems from the Priestly writers (since it contradicts their idea that none of the ancestors in Genesis knew the name YHWH), but the theological point being made in Genesis 14 implicitly agrees with Exod 6:2–3 on the need for an inclusive theism. The different traditions in Genesis converge on the point that "YHWH" refers to the God who is also named "El."

---

34. Lewis, "The Identity and Function of El/Baal Berith," 413–14.

35. Smith, *God in Translation*, argues that "YHWH" was later added to emphasize Abraham's orthodoxy.

Reflections from the Edges of Empire

Modern translators of Genesis 1 have often debated the appropriateness of adopting divine names in the intercultural manner that was commonplace in the ancient world.[36] The South African biblical scholar Nathan Esala, for example, argues that most of the missionary Bible translations in Ghana were so imperialistic in character that they can be characterized as cultural invasion.[37] One of the many ironies that we find in the Hebrew composition of Genesis 1, however, is that this creation narrative was itself born out of ancient Jewish struggles to survive in the face of empire. In this respect, invasive missionary translations in colonial contexts have reversed the underlying impetus in the biblical material.[38] Cultural impositions are sociologically the inverse of ancient struggles to survive in the face of empire.

Many comparisons could be made across Africa, Asia, and the Pacific, and some of the key issues arising have come into focus in an engagement between two Black theologians, Lamin Sanneh and Willie James Jennings. The contours of their disagreement offer a helpful framework for considering the questions of Bible translation in Australia.

Sanneh draws attention, for example, to the translations into the Zulu language in the nineteenth century in which Methodist missionaries resisted an Indigenous name for God, *uNkulunkulu*, and adopted instead a kind of transliteration from Hebrew, *uJehova*.[39] This is essentially what happened also in Awabakal Country in 1820–30s New South Wales, where the missionary translator Lancelot Threlkeld adopted transliterations from Hebrew: *Eloi* derived from *Elohim*, and *Yehoa* (or Jehovah).[40] Threlkeld took this approach against the advice of Biraban, his language teacher and co-translator, who argued for a local ancestral name. The missionary's reasoning was that "there is no word in the [Awabakal] language but of an equivocal character."[41] Acknowledging evidence of "some instinctive feeling of dependence on the great 'Unknown Being,'" Threlkeld nevertheless concluded that the Awabakal were "without God in the world."[42]

As in the example of Biriban's point of view, Sanneh emphasizes that it was Zulu Christians in the African context who advocated for *uNkulunkulu*, the local name that eventually prevailed in Bible translations. The choice of

36. See the expansive list of ancient examples in Smith, *God in Translation*.
37. Esala, "Translation."
38. See, for example, Brett, "Imperial Context."
39. Sanneh, *Translating the Message*, 171–72.
40. Keary, "Christianity, Colonialism," 129–32.
41. Threlkeld, *Key to the Structure*, 51.
42. Threlkeld, *Australian Reminiscences*, 62–63.

uNkulunkulu was also accepted in the long run by the first Anglican Bishop of Natal, John Colenso, who had originally suggested an alternative divine name derived from Latin. His change of heart was in large measure the result of his friendship with William Ngidi, a Zulu Bible translator.[43] The German linguist Jacob Döhne argued that *uNkulunkulu* was simply a "proto-ancestor," but he also relented in the end.[44] In Sanneh's account, the European missionaries initially tended to favor loan words when it came to naming God, and African Christians generally affirmed local names for divinity.

The emphasis on vernacular translation ironically sowed the seeds of later cultural resistance in many contexts, however, and Colenso himself supported a Zulu emancipatory movement in the nineteenth century. Translation yielded effects that the missionary translators could not control, a dynamic that is affirmed by Sanneh.[45] Especially in the hands of African Independent Churches, the Bible was wrested from the hands of imperial interests.[46]

The controversial Bishop Colenso is the focus of a long chapter in the landmark work, *The Christian Imagination: Theology and the Origins of Race*, by Willie James Jennings. The critique of Colenso in this chapter does not question the idea that the bishop was genuinely concerned for the well-being of the Zulu people and that he therefore supported their resistance to English rule. The core problem for Jennings is that Colenso could not escape a nationalist imaginary; certainly the Anglican bishop switched sides, but the question for Christian theology is why he could not deconstruct the binary option of supporting either the English or the Zulu. As Jennings puts it:

> For Colenso, God was already present among the Zulus. They had a name for God and knowledge of God rooted in their religious consciousness. . . . Yet at another level, what is apparent in Colenso's conclusions is the formation of a cultural nationalism that fully captures Christian theology. It is theology of and for the nation, for a people, any people, and every people. And

---

43. See, for example, Colenso, *Bringing Forth Light*; Draper, *Eye of the Storm*. The isiZulu translations of Genesis published by the Bible Society of South Africa in 1959 and 1997 reflect this outcome when they use *uNkulunkulu* in Genesis 1 and *uJehova uNkulunkulu* (for the Hebrew combination YHWH Elohim) in the second creation story from Gen 2:4 and following. Available at www.bible.com/bible/286/GEN.1.ZUL59.

44. Sanneh, *Translating the Message*, 171–72.

45. Sanneh, *Translating the Message*, 106. So also Errington, "Colonial Linguistics," 20: "Actions of colonial agents outran their own intent."

46. Esala, "Translation," 190–239, emphasizes the anti-colonial uses of the Bible among African Independent Churches. Cf. Dube, *Postcolonial*; West, *Stolen Bible*.

> in this conceptualization, Israel is historicized as an exhausted theological moment because God is now with everyone else.[47]

This influential theological argument deserves to be considered from many different perspectives, but we will consider its relevance mainly in the Australian context, and especially in relation to the translations of William Thomas.[48]

In Thomas' case, he appears to have rejected his own earlier use of more abstract terms for divinity ("big/high/great father") and adopted the proper name *Pundgyl Marman*, but his diaries do not provide the reasons for this shift. We can be sure, however, that he was not building links to Aboriginal nationalism in the 1840s or 50s. It must be confessed that his writing does not betray anything like the sophisticated scholarship of Bishop Colenso. And unlike the South African context where the local name *uNkulunkulu* became popular among Zulu Christians, very few Aboriginal people seem to have taken up the name *Pundgyl Marman*. Could it be that the associations with imperial invasion were too great to bear?

After the Protectorate ended in 1849, Thomas no longer refers to translation work in his journals. There may have been several reasons for this, but among the most important factors was the size of the Aboriginal population in the 1850s. Thomas reported that the Aboriginal people in his charge together numbered only thirty-one people in 1858, a decline from three hundred people in the course of two decades.[49] Having met with an Aboriginal person incarcerated in Melbourne, he wrote in 1855 that "It is lamentable that this Blk knows nothing of his native Tongue,"[50] so he clearly regretted the loss of traditional languages.

Yet only three years later, he could recommend English-only schools and the removal of children from their parents for educational purposes. He acknowledges the brutality of the suggestion—that it "may appear relentless and emanating from a breast devoid of feeling"—yet he saw it as a measure that could avert, in his view, "the extinction of the Aboriginal race." When in school, these children "will still be among their race."[51] The teaching of English was in this sense a counsel of despair, yet astonishingly, it did not

---

47. Jennings, "Colenso's Heart," 166.

48. Accordingly, we do not explore the range of alternative approaches to vernacular translation taken up in the South African context by Ngoetjana, "A Critical Comparison."

49. *Report of the Select Committee of the Legislative Council*, 1. So also Carey, "Threlkeld, Biraban," 459.

50. 1 August 1855, in Stephens, *Journal of William Thomas*, 3:49.

51. *Report of the Select Committee*, 40. See further, Tan, "Language Ideologies."

provoke questions for William Thomas as to the overall validity of English colonial rule. Instead, he tried to intervene with measures that could achieve some level of justice in his own eyes.

In a letter to the Commissioner of Lands and Survey on 20 July 1859, he detailed a plan for providing provisions at regional depots, and allocating "extensive tracts of land" to Aboriginal communities across the colony, with "a comprehensive scheme of Guardianship." The plan included the removal of squatters from allocated land, and compensating them if necessary. As for the cost of these measures, he argued that "the Aborigines of Victoria have equal if not superior claim on us than the Africans had upon the British purse," referring here to the compensation costs arising from the *Slavery Abolition Act* of 1833.[52]

The proposal fell on deaf ears, and here we will mention just one among many examples that could be given. In early March of 1859, Thomas took a delegation of seven Aboriginal people to meet with the Commissioner of Lands in Melbourne, where they requested and were ostensibly granted land in the Northern Goulburn area. Some forty-five hundred acres were surveyed within a matter of weeks, and Thomas referred to this as their "Promised Land," and subsequently as their "Goshen."[53] Taungurung people began working with enthusiasm on Acheron Station, as it was subsequently known, but by the end of the year the grant of land was revoked under pressure from squatters. Thomas wrote an angry letter to his superiors: "This, the fate of Aboriginal industry, is enough to deter Aborigines from ever after having confidence in promises held out to them."[54] One might infer that Thomas had here failed in his official obligation to defend the Aboriginal people from "encroachment on their property."[55] No doubt such failed

---

52. Letter "Proposing a plan to provide support of the Aborigines throughout the Colony of Victoria," 20 July 1859, *Journal of William Thomas*, 3:221–25 (corresponding to NAA: B312, Item 3, Folios 4–5). As Thomas Piketty has outlined in his comparative economic study of abolition, the former slaveholders were richly compensated by the British government in the 1830s, but not the enslaved persons themselves. *Capital and Ideology*, 203–303.

53. Stephens, *Journal of William Thomas*, 3:196–97. The diary entry for 18 March, 1859, refers to this "Promised Land" for the Goulburn people as Nyageron, the earlier name for Acheron. In his comprehensive plan of 20 July 1859, he refers to "their ('Goshen') promised land" when advising that "It would be well for the Aborigines to themselves select the localities." This alludes to the Goshen story in Genesis, rather than to a Promised Land within the exodus-conquest imaginary. See Brett, *Locations of God*, 135–37 on "Goshen" land, with a response to Lydon, "Experimental 1860s," 89–91.

54. Thomas to Central Board, 22nd November, 1860. NAA: B312, Item 3, Folio 44.

55. As already noted, this was among the stated objectives of the Protectors, as set out by Lord Glenelg in his letter to Governor Gipps, 31 January 1838, *Historical Records of Australia*, 1, xix, 254.

promises and injustices also undermined the credibility of the colonizers' religion, which makes the advent of Aboriginal Christianity in this context even more remarkable—a form of Christianity, however, that was not so much shaped by nationalism as by protest against injustice.[56]

Conclusion

The original composition of Genesis 1 was framed by Priestly authors as a matter of survival for Israelite and Judean communities living under the shadow of empire.[57] The biblical scribes evidently knew the Enuma Elish from Babylonian imperial culture and even made some concessions to it. But the biblical authors rejected the violence of the Babylonian myth and the implication that only kings were made "in the image of God."[58] Instead, Gen 1:27–28 says that all human beings, male and female, were made in the image of Elohim, and the Priestly narrators went on to assert that Israel's ancestors acknowledged the Canaanite deity El, rather than the national deity, YHWH. With the demise of the Babylonian empire, many of the Judean exiles returned to their traditional country at the Western edge of the Persian imperial jurisdiction, having reshaped the ancestral theology of creation.

Perhaps these Priestly authors can be said to have foreshadowed, in some respects, the choices of *uNkulunkulu* and *Pundgyl* in biblical translations of the nineteenth century, and provided a precedent for the cultural resistance expressed in Indigenous Christianities in many parts of the British Empire. Reading from the side of imperial administration, William Thomas seems to have discerned some of the potential of the Priestly theology in Genesis. Yet he did not absorb the kind of biblical criticism advanced by Bishop Colenso in South Africa, or the more radical challenge to British rule. Given the rank injustice of colonial administration that purported to be Christian, it is no wonder that Aboriginal people generally made little sense of Thomas' efforts to present another story about *Pundgyl Marman*.

---

56. Regarding nineteenth century resistance in Victoria, see, for example, Barwick, *Rebellion at Coranderrk*; Attwood, *William Cooper*.

57. See especially Markl, "Babylonian Exile"; Brett, *Locations of God*, 54–74.

58. Middleton, *Liberating Image*, 160–81, 185–231.

Bibliography

Attwood, Bain. *William Cooper: An Aboriginal Life Story.* Melbourne: Miegunyah Press, 2021.

Barwick, Diane E. *Rebellion at Coranderrk*, edited by Laura E. Barwick and Richard E. Barwick. Canberra: Aboriginal History Inc, 1998.

Brett, Mark G. "The Imperial Context of the Pentateuch." In *The Oxford Handbook of the Pentateuch*, edited by Joel S. Baden and Jeffrey Stackert, 443–62. New York: Oxford University Press, 2021.

———. *Locations of God: Political Theology in the Hebrew Bible.* New York: Oxford University Press, 2019.

———. "Yhwh among the Nations: The Politics of Divine Names in Genesis." In *The Politics of the Ancestors: Exegetical and Historical Perspectives on Genesis 12–36*, edited by Mark G. Brett and Jakob Wöhrle, 113–30. Tübingen: Mohr Siebeck, 2018.

Campbell, Alistair and Ron Vanderwal, eds. *John Bulmer's Recollections of Victorian Aboriginal Life, 1855–1908,* Occasional Papers 3. Melbourne: Museum Victoria, 1999.

Carey, Hilary M. "Christian Colonisation and Its Critics." In *God's Empire: Religion and Colonialism in the British World, c.1801–1908,* 311–40. Cambridge: Cambridge University Press, 2011.

———. "Lancelot Threlkeld, Biraban, and the Colonial Bible in Australia." *Comparative Studies in Society and History* 52/2 (2010) 447–78.

Carr, David M. "Precursors to the Priestly Creation Account (Gen 1:1—2:3)." In *The Formation of Genesis 1–11: Biblical and Other Precursors,* 7–29. New York: Oxford University Press, 2020.

Clark, Ian D. "'You have all this place, no good have children . . .' Derrimut: Traitor, Saviour, or a Man of his People?" *Journal of the Royal Australian Historical Society* 91/2 (2005) 107–32.

Colenso, John William. *Bringing Forth Light: Five Tracts on Bishop Colenso's Zulu Mission,* edited by Ruth Edgecombe. Pietermaritzburg: University of Natal Press, 1982.

Critchett, Jan. *Untold Stories: Memories and Lives of Victorian Kooris.* Melbourne: Melbourne University Press, 1998.

Draper, Jonathan A. *The Eye of the Storm: Bishop John William Colenso and the Crisis of Biblical Inspiration.* London: Bloomsbury, 2003.

Dube, Musa W. *Postcolonial Feminist Interpretation of the Bible.* St. Louis, MO: Chalice, 2000.

Errington, Joseph. "Colonial Linguistics," *Annual Review of Anthropology* 30 (2001) 19–39.

Esala, Nathan Adam. "Translation as Invasion in Post-Colonial Northern Ghana." PhD diss., Pietermaritzburg, University of Natal, 2020.

Fels, Marie Hansen. *"I Succeeded Once": The Aboriginal Protectorate on the Mornington Peninsula, 1839–1840.* Canberra: Australian National University Press, 2011.

Frahm, Eckart. "Counter-texts, Commentaries, and Adaptations: Politically Motivated Responses to the Babylonian Epic of Creation in Mesopotamia, the Biblical World, and Elsewhere." *Orient* 45 (2010) 3–34.

Harris, John. *One Blood: 200 Years of Aboriginal Encounter with Christianity*, 2nd ed. Sutherland, NSW: Albatross Books, 1994.

Hendel, Ronald. "Genesis 1–11 and Its Mesopotamian Problem." In *Cultural Borrowings and Ethnic Appropriations in Antiquity*, edited by Erich S. Gruen, 23–36. Stuttgart: Franz Steiner Verlag, 2005.

Howitt, A. W. "Notes on Songs and Songmakers of Some Australian Tribes." *Journal of the Anthropological Institute of Great Britain and Ireland* 16 (1887) 327–35.

Jennings, Willie James. *The Christian Imagination: Theology and the Origins of Race*. New Haven, CT: Yale University Press, 2010.

Keary, Anne. "Christianity, Colonialism, and Cross-Cultural Translation: Lancelot Threlkeld, Biraban, and the Awabakal." *Aboriginal History Journal* 33 (2009) 117–55.

Krüger, Thomas. "'Kosmo-theologies' zwischen Mythos und Erfahrung: Psalm 104 im Horizont altororietalischer 'Schöpfungs' Konzepte." *Biblische Notizen* 68 (1993) 49–74.

Lewis, Theodore J. "The Identity and Function of El/Baal Berith." *JBL* 115 (1996) 401–23.

Lydon, Jane. "The Experimental 1860s: Charles Walter's Images of Coranderrk Aboriginal Station, Victoria." *Aboriginal History* 26 (2002) 78–130.

Markl, Dominik. "The Babylonian Exile as the Birth Trauma of Monotheism." *Biblica* 101/1 (2020) 1–25.

Middleton, Richard J. *The Liberating Image: The Imago Dei in Genesis 1*. Grand Rapids, MI: Brazos, 2005.

Morey, Stephen. "Previously Unexamined Texts in Victorian Languages—The Manuscripts of Rev. William Thomas (1793–1867)." *Monash University Linguistic Publications* 2/1 (1999).

Newton, Janice. "Two Victorian Corroborees: Meaning Making in Response to European Intrusion." *Aboriginal History* 41 (2017) 121–49.

Ngoetjana, Lucas Mogashudi. "A Critical Comparison of the Concepts of MODIMO [God] in Sotho Traditional Religion and the Concepts of the Christian God as a Missiological Problem." PhD diss., Pietermaritzburg, University of Natal, 2002.

Parker, Edward Stone. *The Aborigines of Victoria*. Melbourne: Hugh McColl, 1854.

Picketty, Thomas. *Capital and Ideology*. Translated by Arthur Goldhammer. Cambridge, MA: Harvard University Press 2020.

de Pury, Albert. "Gottesname, Gottesbezeichnung und Gottesbegriff: 'Elohim' als Indiz zur Entstehungsgeschichte des Pentateuch." In *Abschied vom Jahwisten: Die Komposition des Hexateuch in der jüngsten Diskussion*, edited by Jan C. Gertz, Konrad Schmid, and Markus Witte, 25–47. Berlin: de Gruyter, 2002.

Report of the Parliamentary Select Committee on Aboriginal Tribes (British Settlements): reprinted, with Comments, by the "Aborigines Protection Society." London: William Ball, Aldine Chambers, Paternoster Row, and Hatchard & Son, 1837.

Report of the Select Committee of the Legislative Council on the Aborigines; Together with the Proceedings of Committee, Minutes of Evidence and Appendices 1858–59. Melbourne: John Ferres, Government Printer, 1859.

Rogerson, John W. *Old Testament Criticism in the Nineteenth Century: England and Germany*. London: SPCK, 1984.

Sanneh, Lamin. *Translating the Message: The Missionary Impact on Culture*. Maryknoll: Orbis, 1989.

Schmid, Konrad. "Himmelsgott, Weltgott und Schöpfer; 'Gott' und der 'Himmel' in der Literatur der Zeit des Zweiten Tempels." In *Der Himmel*, edited by Dorothea Sattler und Samuel Vollenweider, 111–48. Neukirchen-Vluyn: Neukirchener, 2006.

Smith, Mark S. *God in Translation: Deities in Cross-Cultural Discourse in the Biblical World*. Grand Rapids, MI: Eerdmans, 2010.

Stephens, Marguerita. *The Journal of William Thomas: Assistant Protector of the Aborigines of Port Phillip & Guardian of the Aborigines of Victoria 1839 to 1867*. Volume One: 1839 to 1843. Melbourne: Victorian Aboriginal Corporation for Languages, 2014.

———. *The Journal of William Thomas: Assistant Protector of the Aborigines of Port Phillip & Guardian of the Aborigines of Victoria 1839 to 1867*. Volume Two: 1844 to 1853. Melbourne: Victorian Aboriginal Corporation for Languages, 2014.

———. *The Journal of William Thomas: Assistant Protector of the Aborigines of Port Phillip & Guardian of the Aborigines of Victoria 1839 to 1867*. Volume Three: 1854 to 1867. Melbourne: Victorian Aboriginal Corporation for Languages, 2014.

———. *The Journal of William Thomas: Assistant Protector of the Aborigines of Port Phillip & Guardian of the Aborigines of Victoria 1839 to 1867*. Volume Four: Kulin Language. Melbourne: Victorian Aboriginal Corporation for Languages, 2014.

Swain, Tony. *A Place for Strangers: Towards a History of Australian Aboriginal Being*. Cambridge: Cambridge University Press, 1993.

Tan, Deborah Shuh Yi. "Language Ideologies and Language Loss in 19th-Century Victoria: The Translations of William Thomas." *Journal of Australian Studies* 47 (2023) 298–413.

Thomas, William. "Succinct Sketch of the Aboriginal Language." In *The Aborigines of Victoria*, edited by Smyth, Robert Brough. Vol. 2. Melbourne: John Ferres, Government Printer, 1878.

Threlkeld, L. E. *Australian Reminiscences & Papers of L.E. Threlkeld, Missionary to the Aborigines, 1824–1859*. Edited by Niel Gunson. Vol. 1. Canberra: Australian Institute of Aboriginal Studies, 1974.

———. *A Key to the Structure of the Aboriginal Language*. Sydney: Kemp and Fairfax, 1850.

West, Gerald O. *The Stolen Bible: From Tool of Imperialism to African Icon*. Leiden: Brill, 2016.

Judges and Kings: A Distinction Without a Difference?

Translating the Pitjantjatjara Bible in Central Australia

Samuel Freney

TRANSLATIONS INTO TRADITIONAL LANGUAGES that are spoken across this country are critical in enabling many First Nations people to read the Bible at all. At a fundamental level all our modern Bibles are translated Bibles—we normally read in English (or whatever our native tongue happens to be) and not Greek, Hebrew, and Aramaic. Translation into languages of this country seeks to provide the same possibility of reading Scripture to others as we have in English. As Pitjantjatjara translator Makinti Minutjukur[1] has put it, "We need to have all of God's Word in our language, so that we can all understand it well."[2] Her parents worked on the New Testament translation and she recognized the importance of local language translation: "We saw the strength it gave them and the people that read it."[3] In this case "reading" is understood very broadly as accessing a written text, or listening to it, or otherwise engaging with it. Translation choices impact the possibilities for accurate and sophisticated Bible reading within these communities and can even bring about change to the languages themselves.

    1. In the Pitjantjatjara kinship system into which the translators have included me, Makinti is my *ngunytju* (mother).
    2. Eckert, "We're Just Trying to Keep Up."
    3. Delbridge and McLellan, "Bible Translation Runs in the Family for These Indigenous Women."

This chapter will give a brief introduction to the modern shape of translation projects in Australia in light of the early translation efforts outlined by Meredith Lake in *The Bible in Australia*. I will then move to consider one particular Pitjantjatjara translation issue in 1 Samuel concerning judges and kings. This question of accurate terminology will enable us to consider what set of assumptions are operative in our reading of the monarchical history of ancient Israel in English Bibles, what issues may be present for First Nations Australians in light of colonial history, and the opportunities this can give for sophisticated reading of this text and others in the future.

The question of accurate terminology I want to consider is this: the important offices of "judge" and "king" in ancient Israel's monarchical period are important to differentiate in translation. The translators of the Bible into the Pitjantjatjara language of central Australia have come up with interesting ways of reflecting different types of hierarchical leadership in the text according to their translation idiom. One Pitjantjatjara word, *mayatja*, is used to refer to many different leadership positions throughout the Bible, from ancient Israelite judges to masters of slaves to Jesus himself. To avoid confusion in the initial draft translation of the Old Testament book of 1 Samuel, therefore, descriptive and contextual qualifiers are often added to this one term to determine the type of leader in view. In this chapter I will recount the translation team's deliberations over this translation choice in 1 Samuel and demonstrate that an accurate description of a "king" must take into account, not only the target language and the immediate context of translation, but also a broad canonical view, and an understanding of how these texts might be read in the present context of Indigenous Australia and colonial history.

I write as one both connected and at a remove to this project. Pitjantjatjara is a Western Desert language in central Australia and I live on the east coast. I am neither a Pitjantjatjara person nor a fluent speaker of the language, but I am involved with the ongoing translation of the Pitjantjatjara Bible as a consultant. I have been included as an outsider into the Pitjantjatjara kinship network, and my *ngunytju* (mother) Caroline Windy especially assisted me in understanding the relational networks and translation history at work here.[4] The issues I discuss in this chapter arose as I worked with translators on the text of 1 Samuel over 2019–2021.

Translation into Aboriginal and Torres Strait Islander languages has been a small but persistent stream in the story of the Bible in Australia over the past couple of hundred years. Meredith Lake's account of translation efforts in the early colonial period, principally Biraban and Threlkeld's

---

4. Caroline is Makinti's kinship sister, hence she is also my mother.

work on Awabakal, highlights well the challenges inherent in translating the Scriptures into the languages of Australia. Lake writes, "Looking over some of the [Awabakal] manuscripts, it is obvious that translation is hard."[5] There is significant continuity here with the modern scene of Bible translation in Australia: translation is still hard! Many of the difficulties of translating abstract concepts or foreign objects remain in modern translation projects.[6]

While the total amount of Scripture translated into First Nations' languages is no longer approximately "nothing,"[7] even today it is not as great as we might wish it to be. The number of translations is certainly not the same as the estimated one hundred and twenty-three currently-spoken Aboriginal and Torres Strait Island languages.[8] The sad reality is that many First Nations people cannot read the Scripture in their own languages—the long history in Australia of colonization has resulted in many people without connection to their language at all, and many others who still have a connection being less literate in their languages than they may want to be. In addition, there is a lack of available Scripture. Many languages across Australia have portions of the New Testament translated.[9] Fifteen languages have a full New Testament. A few have portions of the Old Testament translated in addition to a New Testament. Of these different translation projects, Pitjantjatjara is the most advanced with approximately a third of the Old Testament fully translated, driven by multiple generations of motivated Indigenous translators. Only Kriol has a complete Bible translation.

The level of agency Indigenous people have in Bible translation is a significant change from the early colonial scene as described by Lake. She writes of that era, "The scope of [Indigenous people's] opportunities for interpretation were usually constrained: it was typically the missionaries who decided which passages to emphasize, the kind of access people would have to them, the interpretative gloss or framework that would accompany them,

---

5. Lake, *Bible in Australia*, 80.

6. It is interesting to note the different solutions found in various translation projects to similar issues of vocabulary or abstract concepts. Biraban and Threlkeld left untranslated Mark's "camel through the eye of a needle" in Mark 10 (Lake, *Bible in Australia*, 84). The Warlpiri translation modified this particular metaphor to communicate the meaning, rendering this verse as: "Does a camel go into the hole of an ant's nest? No. Likewise a rich person won't go into God's kingdom."

7. Lake, *Bible in Australia*, 79.

8. Australian Institute of Aboriginal and Torres Strait Islander Studies (AIATSIS), *National Indigenous Languages Report*, 42.

9. A number of Bible translations in Aboriginal and Torres Strait Island languages can be accessed online at https://aboriginalbibles.org.au, including Biraban and Threlkeld's Mark's Gospel in Awabakal.

and the range of acceptable readings."[10] In contrast on this point at least, current translation projects are initiated and carried out by Indigenous people for their own communities, with external assistance given when requested. This is true across Australia and is generally the case around the world. The stereotypical image of a missionary sitting under a tree translating the Bible for the community he or she has travelled to is, if it ever was an accurate picture, certainly not the case now. The text is translated by fluent speakers of a given language, who are Christian people who desire to have Scripture available in their own language. Importantly, translation is not done by a missionary or another external person for whom the target language is a second or additional language but by mother-tongue translators; nor is the completed translated work imposed on a community from outside. Agencies such as the Bible Society of Australia (my employer) provide services to enable translation projects to proceed, but the impetus and local language expertise comes from Indigenous communities themselves.

My own involvement with the Pitjantjatjara Bible translation came about through this modern shape of translation projects. What follows is a short description of a long process that is followed whether a translation is of only a few verses, or a whole book of the Bible.[11] Generally speaking, Indigenous translators work from an English source text. It is my hope that this will change in the future, but presently they do not usually have any facility in the original biblical languages (Greek, Hebrew, and Aramaic). Occasionally the source text will be another Indigenous language translation that is closely related or well understood. I know of current translation projects currently using New Testament translations in Kriol, Djambarrpuyŋu, and Kunwinjku as their source texts. When an English source text is used, it is frequently modified slightly to form a "front-translation," which puts the text in a form more easily translated into the target language with respect to spelling, syntax, and sometimes larger-scale organization. For example, many Australian languages do not have the passive voice, so John 1:17a ("For the law was given through Moses") might be rendered as "For God gave the law through Moses" in a front-translation. This front-translation is then translated by a fluent speaker of the target language, forming a first draft. This draft gets checked by a separate translator for accuracy and fluency, and this re-drafting process is often repeated. It is worth noting that as most translations done in Australia are from already-translated texts, these

10. Lake, *Bible in Australia*, 62.

11. The process described here is somewhat specific to Australian requirements but reflects the "Basic Principles and Procedures for Bible Translation" agreed to by the Forum of Bible Agencies International (FOBAI), of which the Bible Society of Australia is a member.

texts inevitably somewhat reflect their own cultural milieu and potential colonial frameworks, which need to be recognized in the stages of translation.

The translated text then undergoes a community check with other speakers of the language to assess how natural the translation is (Does it sound like a translation, or normal speech?), if it is acceptable (Does it use terminology that is, for example, taboo in a certain context?), as well as its comprehensibility (Do community members understand what is being said?). When the team is happy with the state of the translation, a back-translation into English (or the relevant local trade language) is usually made so that a translation consultant can help check the translation for accuracy. The back-translation is a straightforward, relatively wooden, "literal" translation of the final draft in the target language back into the trade language, so that the translation can be assessed by someone who is not fluent in that target language.[12] This accuracy check serves to compare the communicated meaning of the original biblical texts with the communicated meaning of the translated text, and the consultant may offer suggestions to the team where issues arise. Finally, after all these checks for naturalness, acceptability, clarity, and accuracy, a text is considered ready to be published.

I am one such Bible Translation Consultant with the Bible Society of Australia, and this is how I have come to be associated with this project, and why I am interested in this particular translation question surrounding kings and judges. My training is in biblical studies, the biblical languages, and linguistics. I hold a PhD in theology and biblical studies; my dissertation examined quotation techniques of New Testament authors in *Koine* Greek as they used the Septuagint, but I am not a Pitjantjatjara person, nor do I have any Australian Indigenous ancestry. I am in no way a sophisticated speaker of Pitjantjatjara. I am writing this chapter on Wallumedegal land of the Darug people, a part of the country far from the central desert, so I am therefore very thankful for the input of *Aṉangu*[13] and my Bible Society Australia colleagues in understanding the historical background and linguistic issues involved in this chapter. My academic and social background has necessarily shaped me in ways different to the rest of the translation team. My role in the project is to ask the translation team questions based on the back-translation and my understanding of the texts in the original

---

12. The example of the Lord's Prayer beginning with "Our Father on top sky" given in Lake, *Bible in Australia*, 79, is an example of a back-translation. The *Nyul Nyul* translation has been back-translated into English so we, as English speakers, can see what is being said in the target language.

13. *Aṉangu* is the Western Desert language term for "people," "person," "human being," and so on, and is used by these Aboriginal people to describe themselves.

language(s), and then provide some suggestions where it appears the translation could be more accurate to the source texts as I and others understand them.

Sometimes these are simple errors in transmission, such as the time in 1 Samuel 16 where Jesse presented only six sons to Samuel. One of David's brothers had gone missing in translation. Other errors, such as this chapter's central issue of judges and kings, are more subtle and require more thought from the team as to how to best translate. The final determination of how a text ought to be rendered in Pitjantjatjara is not my call. This Bible is translated by Pitjantjatjara speakers for the Pitjantjatjara people. It is their text, not mine.

Pitjantjatjara itself is a dialect of the Western Desert language of central Australia.[14] It is mutually intelligible with other Western Desert dialects, and most closely related to Yankunytjatjara. The 2021 census records 3,199 people who speak Pitjantjatjara at home (8,416 for Western Desert language as a whole).[15] Pitjantjatjara people are located predominantly in the Aṉangu Pitjantjatjara Yankunytjatjara (APY) lands of north-west South Australia. Historically Pitjantjatjara lands were around and south of Uluṟu into South Australia, but Pitjantjatjara speakers have moved eastwards more recently into lands that were traditionally of the Yankunytjatjara people. The town of Pukatja (also known as Ernabella) in South Australia, historically the epicenter of the Pitjantjatjara Bible translation project, has a great many Pitjantjatjara speakers while being traditionally Yankunytjatjara land.

The Pitjantjatjara Bible project is long-standing. Having started in the 1930s, a *Shorter New Testament* was published in 1949, and a full New Testament in 2002.[16] The New Testament has been recorded in a dramatic

---

14. The distinction between "dialect" and "language" for Australian Indigenous languages is at times contentious. Here I follow several sources identifying Pitjantjatjara as a dialect of Western Desert language, although the intention is simply to note that speakers are mutually intelligible with several neighbouring people groups. See Walsh, "Languages and Their Status," 1; Dixon, "Australian Languages," xxxvii; Goddard, *Dictionary*, 4.

15. The *National Indigenous Languages Report* from AIATSIS (2020) notes the significant limitation of census data for Indigenous languages, summarized on p. 46: "There are no questions in the Census about how people are using language and the contexts and depths to which language is being spoken. Nor does it easily recognize language varieties. The Census also only allows for one language other than English to be listed. This does not reflect the occurrence of multilingualism, which is common in some communities. The Census also does not capture information about people learning an Indigenous language, who may for example use that language for cultural, spiritual or ceremonial purposes."

16. Aboriginal Bibles, "Pitjantjatjara (Palya)."

audio version, completed in 2018.[17] Portions of the Old Testament were included with the New Testament publication. The *Shorter Pitjantjatjara Bible* includes these portions of the Old Testament along with other sections that are brief re-tellings of Bible stories and has been updated several times (most recently in 2019).

Leadership in 1 Samuel

Traditional Pitjantjatjara culture, like that of many other Aboriginal peoples, has a strong and complex kinship network. An individual is related to the rest of their community through a network of relationships that define respect, responsibilities, community roles, potential partnerships, justice, and more.[18] When the early translators of the Bible came to articulating authority relationships of ancient societies found in the Scriptures, however, they chose to use a term that sat outside these kinship relationships. The word used for "leader" or "boss" in the present day is *mayatja*, which is itself actually a loan-word from English.[19] It was sourced from either "mayor" or "major" back in the Presbyterian mission days of the early twentieth century, and has come to be a generic term for someone who is some form of leader. It is, however, essentially the only term for leadership external to family. Elders have a certain standing within the community by virtue of their age, and there are terms such as *tjiḻpi* ("old man") that have a measure of respect, but from the early days of Bible translation the translators decided there was no term such as "elders" that refers to any form of office or category of leadership independent of kinship networks.[20] In the Pitjantjatjara New Testament, therefore, Jesus is *mayatja* because he is Lord, and often is called *mayatja puḻka* (the "big *mayatja*") to distinguish him from other (plural) *mayatja* such as the teachers of the law. The Sanhedrin, for example, are *Jewku mayatja* (e.g., Mark 15:1; "*-ku*" here is a genitive suffix, so *Jewku* translates "of the Jews"). The Lord God is translated as *Mayatja God*. Prayer is often addressed to *Mayatja God* or *Mayatja Jesus*.

In the book of 1 Samuel, leadership of God's people is the major narrative arc. Coming out of the exodus period with Moses leading the people

---

17. McLellan and Payne, "Pitjantjatjara New Testament Audio."

18. Dousset, *Australian Aboriginal Kinship*, 75–94.

19. Many other loan-words exist in Pitjantjatjara, such as *mutuka* (car), *taraka* (truck), and *tjuwa* (store).

20. As Whellum says, "There are no tribal or language group heads or chiefs acting as community-appointed leaders." "Administration of Justice," 102. Cf. Edwards, *Aboriginal Societies*, 53; Aboriginal Customary Law Committee, Preliminary Report, 28.

through the desert and Joshua leading them in the conquest of the land, the book of Judges outlines the leadership of "judges" raised up by God. These judges are presented in contrast to the nations around who have kings, for "there was no king in Israel" (*'en melek be yisra'el*, Judg 21:25). Through the book of Judges, these judges (*soptim*) are relatively localized warlords who through the narrative of the book function to save the people from oppression, although they also proclaim Torah to the people (Judg 2:16), and settled matters not able to be dealt with by local tribal leaders (Judg 4:4–5).[21] In 1 Samuel, Samuel is gradually presented as the chosen leader of the people. Coming so soon after the book of Judges, we would expect him to be a judge raised up for the people in a time of need just as were Gideon, Samson, and other judges. Sure enough, in 1 Sam 7:6 we read that Samuel was performing a similar judicial function in the community that Deborah performed under the tree in Ephraim, "Samuel was judging the Israelites at Mizpah" (*wayyispot semu'el 'et-bene yisra'el bammispah*).

In the preliminary Pitjantjatjara translation and revisions of 1 Samuel, this role of Samuel the judge is rendered using this word for "leader/boss," *mayatja*, so in 1 Sam 7:15 the draft Pitjantjatjara back-translation read "And for many years Samuel continually lived as the Israelites' boss/leader [*mayatja*]." The leadership narrative arc of 1 Samuel represents a transition from the leadership of these judges to the institution of the monarchy. The "judges" as leaders of the people of Israel give way, from Saul on, to "kings."[22] 1 Samuel 8 is a particular focal point of this transition and presents the opportunity for confusion. In Samuel's old age, his sons are appointed as leaders/bosses (*mayatja*, pl.) of the people.

Therefore, in 1 Sam 8:4, the elders of the people (*mayatja*, pl.) come to Samuel to demand a king (a *mayatja*, sg.) like all the other nations. In 8:20 it is clear what the people's demand is: they want a king who will judge them, go out before them, and fight their battles. (The draft Pitjantjatjara back-translation read as a "different *mayatja*" who will "protect" us and "lead us with authority when we go out for battle"). Having only one word to describe a leader can create some confusion when the text is concerned with delineating different types of leadership, although readers of the text

---

21. Webb, *Judges*, 14, 144–45.

22. Saul, David, Solomon, and later kings are identified as *melek* ("king") over Israel, as opposed to Gideon, Deborah, etc, who are identified as *soptim* ("judges"). Occasionally other terms such as *nagid* ("prince, ruler, head of a family") are used, but they are paralleled to nominal or verbal forms of "king," e.g., 1 Kgs 1:35; 2 Sam 5:2. Priests and prophets were other leadership offices within Israel, but these do not present the same translation issue in Pitjantjatjara as I am considering for judges/kings.

during a checking workshop I attended were comfortable enough with the different categories of leadership in 1 Samuel 8.

Elsewhere in the draft translation, however, to alleviate that potential confusion when it is not clear from the narrative, these terms "judge" and "king" were translated as qualified instances of *mayatja*. "Judge" is rendered as "a boss (*mayatja*) who decides between us" or "a boss who helps us [with problems]" (e.g., 7:14–16). The term "king" is either "big boss (*mayatja pulka*)" (e.g., 10:1; 11:15) or "the boss who protects us" (e.g., 12:1).[23] That is, the descriptions of the offices are *functional* descriptions, outlining what the person in that office does when fulfilling their duty. The questions before us are therefore: Are these functional descriptions adequate given the context of 1 Samuel? What effect might alternative vocabulary choices make?

Translation Technique

The Pitjantjatjara Bible over the decades has adopted a *dynamic equivalence* approach to translation, following Nida's work in the 1960s.[24] At the heart of this approach, a dynamic equivalence translation *decodes* the meaning of the original text from the original language, and then *encodes* that meaning using target language text. The formal features of the original text (such as word order, particular vocabulary, or grammatical features) are not prioritized for preservation in this approach.[25]

The terms "judge" and "king" were translated in the early Pitjantjatjara drafts of 1 Samuel with a qualifier that describes their function—either a judge in the discernment or judicial sphere, or a king in the national protection sphere. Given that the target language does not have specific terms for these categories, a functional description of the office suffices for a meaning-to-meaning transfer. It mirrors the way each of these two offices are talked about in the text of 1 Samuel itself and differentiates them sufficiently that one can be distinguished from the other. Within the scope of the book of 1 Samuel, these functional descriptions appear to be quite accurate: a judge has their role centered around administering justice to the people, and the king is the protector of the realm. The overall narrative of Samuel is certainly not entirely positive about kings: Saul is very far from the perfect candidate;

---

23. The qualifier "big" (*pulka*) often connotes importance or prominence, e.g., Eli is called "the big priest" of Israel in 1 Sam 4:18.

24. Nida, *Toward a Science of Translating*; Nida and Taber, *Theory and Practice of Translation*.

25. A translation approach that prioritised such features would be termed a *formal equivalence*.

David's treatment of Bathsheba or her husband is far from protective; the "judgements" or "habits" of the king in 1 Samuel 8 are given by Samuel as a litany of terrible consequences for the people in enabling the king to be a king. In the eyes of the people asking for a king, however, protecting the realm and leading its people in battle is what a king does at his best. This is what distinguishes him from a judge.

This description of function, however, masks a bigger issue that requires a discourse-level or even a canonical-level approach.[26] First Samuel sits in a broader biblical context of Deuteronomistic history, the literary group of books in the Hebrew Bible that outline Israel's history in light of the covenant stipulations, promises, and curses in Deuteronomy. Given the immediate narrative context of Judges, read together with the Torah's description of how judges and kings ought to live in Deuteronomy 17, it appears that the proper *functional* difference between a judge and a king is slight. An institutional difference based on heredity is clear, but the distinction on how they exercise leadership is less so. Kings should be individuals who judge the people, just like those Moses appointed as judges under his leadership, or, indeed, Moses himself. Kings ought to be subject to Torah, with the chief task of being "the instrument of Yahweh's justice and covenant blessing" (cf. Ps 72:1–2).[27] The famous episode of Solomon handing down a judgment between two women fighting over a child is an example of this proper exercise of kingly judicial power (1 Kgs 3:16–28). David also administered justice and righteousness as king to the people of Israel under his rule (2 Sam 8:15). In Deuteronomy's vision for kings, what kings are *not* to do is to amass military strength so they can fight for the people. Solomon is once more an example for us here, albeit a negative one this time. This is borne out through Judges and the ark narrative of 1 Samuel 4–6, where it is evident that *God* is the one who fights for Israel, not their leader. Kings, therefore, should judge the people and be clear—like David in his interaction with Goliath—that God fights for them.[28] There is not a great distinction in the Deuteronomic vision of judges and kings in terms of the exercise of their role. The significant difference between these offices is one of the institution of monarchy itself: national stability based on hereditary transfer of power.

---

26. A weakness of Nida's approach is identified by Mojola and Wendland as being focused too narrowly on "sentence-level-and-below linguistics." See "Scripture Translation," 6.

27. Mowinkel, *He That Cometh*, 94. Cf. also Birch, *Let Justice Roll Down*, 220–21.

28. I am thankful to Dr Michelle Knight for this particular insight into David's kingship from a conversation we had on Twitter (@mlizknight, July 15, 2020) https://twitter.com/mlizknight/status/1283064381446725632.

As mentioned above, within 1 Samuel glossing "king" as "a leader who protects us" is an apparently good summary of the function of the king. It is literally what the people ask for, and what the king goes on to do throughout the rest of the narrative. What then is the communicative effect of (even occasionally) translating "king" like this? It runs the risk of embedding within the reader's conception of the office itself that part of the people's request that was considered sinful. In 1 Sam 8:20 the people requested a king so they would be "like the other nations" (*kekal-haggoyim*)—a king to "judge us" (*usepatanu malkenu*), but also to "*go out before us and fight our battles*" (*weyasaʾ lepanenu wenilham ʾet-milhamotenu*). This language of "protection" echoes the function of other nations' kings—leading the people out in battle and championing them in war. A king like this in 1 Samuel 8 displaces God as the protector of Israel, and so the request of the people here is a rejection of God as their king. To therefore gloss "king" as a "protector leader" embeds that rejection within the term itself.

Many of the prophets view the monarchy as instrumental in furthering this rejection of God throughout Israel's history (e.g., Amos 5:26; Hos 7:3). The monarchy, however, is not always an institution that is opposed to God. David was promised by God himself that his descendants would continue on the throne forever (2 Samuel 7), and the prophets are saturated with Messianic expectation of the coming Davidic king. Messianic psalms are positive in their depiction of the monarchy (e.g., Pss 2; 45; 89). Josiah's reforms are not principally about protection of the people (2 Kgs 22), rather he is concerned with the central place of Torah in the life of the king and the people. Jesus tells Pilate that his "kingdom is not of this world" (John 18:36 in Pitjantjatjara translates as, "I am a *mayatja* not like those of this earth"). If memory of Israel's rejection of God is part of the language used to describe the king, even if only a marginal memory from occasional use, then later revelation about the centrality of God's king in the life of his people has the potential to be compromised.

A more accurate *definitional* description of the category of king is a long-term institutional view related to hereditary leadership and nation-state stability. But a description like this in the narrative of 1 Samuel results in contextual information that hinders understanding. Imagine reading the book of 1 Samuel, and when you came across the term "king" there was instead a phrase something like, "a boss/leader of Israel, who united all the people and became the boss/leader because his father was also the leader of the people." It is worth noting that the Pitjantjatjara translation does often operate like this elsewhere: significant explanation is very frequently given within the text itself. The Pitjantjatjara Bible is lengthy! The term altar, for example, is usually accompanied by a phrase along the lines of "you know, to worship God with sacrifices." Natural acceptable Pitjantjatjara can require a phrase describing what an object is used for in addition to its name. Contextual information is given along with the term so that the reader/hearer can grasp the significance quickly, at the expense of processing a (considerably!) longer sentence. But in the terms of Gutt's relevance theory, this additional information carries with it a processing cost, and that cost of additional attention and understanding should not overload the recipient with information that is not relevant to the context of the utterance.[29] The processing cost for incorporating a *definitional* distinction between judge and king in terms of heredity into the term for "king" would be simply too high, and would overload the hearer/reader by not sufficiently linking up to the context. The "protector leader" version of "king" could be considered optimally relevant. It is linked in the clearest contextual way to the function of that leader within the narrative of the book of 1 Samuel. It is relevant in this contextual scope, however, at the expense of creating unintended implications.

As a result, it is best not to adopt a definition for "king" as "protector" from the immediate context on the basis of a broader literary analysis.[30] For the original readers and hearers of the Hebrew Bible, the term "king" (*melek*) is not only a well-defined cultural category, but is also a significant office that is filled with meaning through thick intertextual connections all across Scripture. Defining it narrowly has the potential to shut down literary connections to elsewhere, thinning out the possibilities of what one might reasonably expect the king to be and do. None of us are blank slates when we read these texts, and we bring interpretations of terms and offices from elsewhere. Even so, the addition of "protection" language to the term for leader in this case does seem to tip the balance too far.

Cultural Assumptions

Acknowledging the cultural category and intertextual connections for the original recipients of this part of Scripture presupposes that we can acknowledge our own cultural baggage. For someone like myself, I implicitly acknowledge when I read of Israelite kings that they are in some ways like the current English monarch, Australia's head of state, but in many ways are different. My first thought is to my cultural interpretive map, which helps me to connect certain ideas and reject others as I read. An ability to recognize this type of interpretive background is a necessary component of

29. Gutt, *Relevance Theory*.
30. Wendland, "Literary (Artistic-Rhetorical) Approach," 277.

sophisticated reading. This raises excellent questions for translation teams as they consider how their own cultural features might be used in translating the source. For example, must traditional Pitjantjatjara culture and language be used to describe ancient Israelite leadership, or can modern Australian terms be used as well? There is an obvious disjunction between traditional Pitjantjatjara culture and ancient Israelite practices and hierarchies.[31] To what extent should outside influences be imported and explained as opposed to using traditional terms?

These questions provide useful opportunities for non-Pitjantjatjara people to re-assess our own assumptions of the text. Communicating hierarchy is difficult in Pitjantjatjara. Is hierarchy necessary to communicate here, either in Pitjantjatjara or in English? On one hand the king is clearly one of the people: he should not be a foreigner (Deut 17:15); he is to be humble among the people (Deut 17:20); King Saul even does very mundane work out ploughing in the field (1 Sam 11:5). Mary J. Evans rightly demonstrates from 1 Samuel that there should not be any aristocracy in God's kingdom as it is incompatible with the theology of the covenant.[32] Once a king is chosen from among the people, however, there is an inescapable sense of hierarchical appointment in the language of the text itself. The king is said to reign "over" the nation (he is king over Israel, *'l-yisra'el*, e.g., in 1 Sam 13:1 and numerous other instances).[33] Samuel's description of the rights of the king describe an extreme power imbalance (1 Sam 8:11–18, cf. Deut 17:14–17).[34] Even David, who has a far more generous assessment of the kingship than Samuel does in 1 Samuel 8, describes Saul in his confrontation with him as "the Lord's anointed" and his "master" (*'don*, 1 Sam 24:6). The office of king has a power differential over the rest of the citizens of Israel. There is a hierarchy here.

What of judges? The Hebrew term connotes administering God's justice to the people; the English term conjures up (in my mind, at least) a

---

31. Lawrence Venuti's dynamic of foreignization and domestication is useful to consider. Venuti's concern is translation, broadly conceived, and his target is "ethnocentric violence" caused by domestication of a text causing it to be swallowed up by the target culture. "Modernism seeks to establish the cultural autonomy of the translated text by effacing its manifold conditions and exclusions, especially the process of domestication by which the foreign text is rewritten to serve modernist cultural agendas." *The Translator's Invisibility*, 188. Cultural imperialism of Pitjantjatjara over against ancient Israel is not really the question here, but the categories are still enlightening for translators as to the dynamics of what may be fronted or suppressed.

32. Evans, *Samuel*, 62–63.

33. This description of the Israelite king being "over Israel" uses the same vocabulary as the rule of foreign kings "over Israel," e.g., Judg 3:12; 6:2.

34. McCarter, Jr., *I Samuel*, 161–62.

black-robed courtroom figure perhaps conditioned more by *Law and Order* or countless other courtroom dramas than the ancient Israelite office.[35] To what extent do such modern conceptions of a judge interfere with our reading of the Deuteronomistic history? The United Bible Societies' *A Handbook on Judges*, a commentary intended as an aid for translators, argues for using a term for "judge" in a target language that reflects the salvation or deliverance brought about by these people such as "hero" or "savior," rather than a judicial term that carries a "false impression."[36] There is of course a judicial function to the work of the judges (e.g., Samuel travelling around holding court to sort out issues in 1 Samuel 7; or Deborah doing the same in Judges 4). But the false impression conveyed by prior conceptions of courtrooms is surely greater for translations into Indigenous languages in Australia than it is for English readers, given that those who read these Indigenous languages are far more likely to be on the receiving end of the judicial system. The image of a judge sitting in judgement has high levels of recognition. There is no-one more familiar with the workings of the courts in Australia than Aboriginal people. That familiarity, of course, is set within a history of colonialism and extreme disadvantage, and a complicated present-day relationship of Indigenous people with Western settlement in Australia. The history of a people, even very recent history, necessarily shapes translation choices. In light of all these considerations, the translation of the book of Judges uses an unqualified *mayatja* throughout for Israel's judges.

Maintaining vocabulary about biblical categories that are alien to a target culture—such as the monarchy—helps to challenge a reader's world-view. This happens by maintaining a level of difference to one's own traditional culture, thus outlining new ideas and possibilities, while still necessarily being accessible to a general reader. As an example, I suggest that "sacrifice" (of the visceral kind we find in Leviticus) is a foreign cultural concept for us today. As English speakers we have the vocabulary to express it (partly because of long association with the Bible), but the practice is foreign and therefore challenging to tease out the implications. In the same way, kingship is an important but often foreign category throughout the Scriptures. Jesus connects himself to that history of Israel from his very first announcement that "the kingdom of God is near" (Mark 1:15), and thereby challenges readers to acknowledge the external authority and claim of God's kingdom. "King" is still an alien term for Pitjantjatjara culture, but less alien than a couple of generations ago. This cultural category is not

---

35. *Law and Order* is an American police procedural and legal drama produced by Wolf Entertainment and Universal Television that began screening on television in 1990. https://wolfentertainment.com/television/current/law-order/.

36. Ogden and Zogbo, *Judges*, 9–10, 107.

present in their communities, but it is more intelligible than it was a century ago. For example, the Ernabella choir has sung for Queen Elizabeth II. There is first-hand knowledge of a European version of royalty even within the community itself, to say nothing of knowledge of kingship through exposure to outside influences in wider Australia. I am not suggesting that the British royal family are identical to the ancient Israelite monarchy, and most certainly not that being ruled by a European monarch is necessary for biblical interpretation. But general cultural knowledge of an institution called "monarchy" has a terminological connection to "king" in the Scriptures in terms of vocabulary and associated ideas. Vocabulary of "king" and "kingdom" are now available to use in translation in a way that wasn't true in the past, and this allows for new challenges for readers.

Conclusion

After discussing the issues of differentiating the office of king from other leaders, the translation team have adopted *kinga* as a Pitjantjatjara word for "king." In light of the discussion above, what effect will this have? First, discussion of how this will impact reading the Scriptures in community is at this point tentative and prospective. These Pitjantjatjara chapters of 1 Samuel only went through the full translation process in early 2021, so there is no history of reading this part of the Bible in Pitjantjatjara within communities to assess. Furthermore, travel to remote communities, especially by external visitors, has been virtually eliminated due to pandemic restrictions, so in writing this chapter I've been severely restricted in what further interaction I could have with translators about how this translation might impact the church community. The impact of interpretation of this translation choice must be left to a later investigation.

An introduced term such as *kinga* retains and reinforces the distance of the ancient narrative from the contemporary target language and culture. This is obviously not a traditional Pitjantjatjara word; it is something foreign. For a term that is used in narratives of ancient Israel and not central Australia there is a certain logic and fitness in doing this. At the same time, the term is not totally alien. Pitjantjatjara culture is not the same today as it was a century or more ago. Hierarchical terminology and monarchical office are not traditionally part of the culture, but they are sufficiently well-known as external realities that they can be adopted without constant explanation or description of another external structure. This term, at least, does not result in biblical text that suffers from death by footnotes.

That level of cultural knowledge is a necessary assumption for this term to be an adequate translation. Discussions of where a translation lies on a formal equivalence—dynamic equivalence spectrum are more commonly centered on grammatical questions than solely lexical issues, but it is still worth considering for this particular lexical issue. To fulfil the aim of a meaning-based translation—communicating the same effect the original would have had rather than the formal features of the original text—this translation choice requires readers to fill that term with meaning from elsewhere. Literary sophistication in pulling external cultural knowledge together with intertextual biblical references is necessary to construct a cognitive map of what *kinga* means, so that when a Pitjantjatjara person reads *kinga David* they have the background to understand what this foreign word means in context. If that additional work isn't done, then the effort to transfer the meaning of "king" to the term *kinga* will end up, effectively, being simply a formal equivalent, roughly akin to a title. In short, this choice requires people to be sophisticated readers as they are not given all the information in the moment, requiring more processing to properly situate the office within the narrative. In my opinion this extra effort from readers of the Pitjantjatjara Bible will result in greater rewards. This judgement, however, is not mine to make. It is ultimately one for the Pitjantjatjara community.

Bibliography

Aboriginal Bibles. "Pitjantjatjara (Palya)." 2019. https://aboriginalbibles.org.au/pitjantjatjara/.

Aboriginal Customary Law Committee. *Preliminary Report of the Aboriginal Customary Law Committee*. Adelaide, 1979.

Australian Institute of Aboriginal and Torres Strait Islander Studies. *National Indigenous Languages Report*. Commonwealth of Australia, 2020.

Birch, Bruce C. *Let Justice Roll Down: The Old Testament, Ethics, and Christian Life*. Louisville, KY: Westminster, 1991.

Delbridge, Tess and Bryce McLellan. "Bible Translation Runs in the Family for These Indigenous Women." *Eternity*, 10 July 2017. https://www.eternitynews.com.au/good-news/bible-translation-runs-in-the-family-for-these-indigenous-women/.

Dixon, Robert. M. W. *Australian Languages*. Cambridge: Cambridge University Press, 2009.

Dousset, Laurent. *Australian Aboriginal Kinship: An Introductory Handbook with Particular Emphasis on the Western Desert*. Marseille: pacific-credo, 2011.

Eckert, Paul. "We're Just Trying to Keep Up." *Coordinate*, 2013. https://www.coordinate.org.au/regions/central-australia/"we're-just-trying-keep-up".

Edwards, William. H. *An Introduction to Aboriginal Societies*. Tuggerah, NSW: Social Science, 2004.

Evans, Mary J. *The Message of Samuel: Personalities, Potential, Politics and Power.* Nottingham: IVP Academic, 2004.
Forum of Bible Agencies International. "Basic Principles and Procedures for Bible Translation." April 2017. https://forum-intl.org/wp-content/uploads/2019/03/FOBAITranslationBasicPrinciplesandProceduresApril2017.pdf.
Goddard, Cliff and Rebecca Defina. *Pitjantjatjara/Yankunytjatjara to English Dictionary.* 2nd ed. Alice Springs: Institute for Aboriginal Development, 2020.
Gutt, Ernst-August. *Relevance Theory: A Guide to Successful Communication in Translation.* Dallas, TX: Summer Institute of Linguistics, 1992.
Lake, Meredith. *The Bible in Australia: A Cultural History.* Sydney: NewSouth, 2020.
McCarter, Jr., P. Kyle. *I Samuel: A New Translation with Introduction, Notes and Commentary.* New York: Doubleday, 1980.
McLellan, Bryce and Kaley Payne. "Pitjantjatjara New Testament Audio to 'Last Forever.'" *Eternity*, 7 March 2018. https://www.eternitynews.com.au/australia/pitjantjatjara-new-testament-audio-to-last-forever/.
Mojola, Aloo Osotsi and Ernst Wendland. "Scripture Translation in the Era of Translation Studies." In *Bible Translation: Frames of Reference*, edited by Timothy Wilt, 1–26. London: Routledge, 2003.
Mowinkel, Sigmund. *He That Cometh: The Messiah Concept in the Old Testament and Later Judaism.* Translated by G. W. Anderson. Grand Rapids: Eerdmans, 2005.
Nida, Eugene A. *Toward a Science of Translating.* Leiden: Brill, 1964.
Nida, Eugene A. and Charles R. Taber. *The Theory and Practice of Translation.* Leiden: Brill, 1982.
Ogden, Graham S. and Lynell Zogbo. *A Handbook on Judges.* Miami, FL: United Bible Societies, 2019.
Peng, Kuo-Wei. "Contemplating the Future of Chinese Bible Translation: A Functionalist Approach." *The Bible Translator* 63/1 (2012) 1–16.
Venuti, Lawrence. *The Translator's Invisibility.* London: Routledge, 1995.
Walsh, Michael. "Languages and their Status." In *Language and Culture in Aboriginal Australia*, edited by Michael Walsh and Colin Yallop, 1–14. Canberra: Aboriginal Studies Press, 2010.
Webb, Barry G. *The Book of Judges.* Grand Rapids MI: Eerdmans, 2012.
Wendland, Ernst, "A Literary (Artistic-Rhetorical) Approach to Biblical Text Analysis and Translation." *Journal of Biblical Text Research* 16 (2005) 266–363.
Whellum, Peter. "The Administration of Justice in the Aṉangu Pitjantjatjara Yankunytjatjara (APY) Lands: A Front Line in Tensions Between Traditional Aboriginal Culture and the Criminal Law." PhD diss., Adelaide, University of Adelaide, 2018.

"Arriving Like a Fish of the Night"
("*Tō'ai faa-I'a a le Po*")

An Australian-Samoan Diasporic Reading of *Pasah* in Exodus 12:12–13 through a Samoan Fishing Proverb

Brian Fiu Kolia

Diaspora is defined by movement. The movement of bodies and peoples from one place to another, from one region to a different district, from homeland to foreign lands. Put simply, without movement/migration, there is no diaspora. As a diasporic Samoan in Australia, understanding movement is an integral part to comprehending identity, and at the same time negotiating space/s for oneself. Because movement is an essential aspect of diaspora and so understanding diaspora involves deciphering the kind of movement it involves. Hence, movement in diasporic terms entails the need to negotiate space/s for oneself in the new environment that results from this movement, and the impact all this has on one's understanding of personal identity.

The Hebrew Bible, for many parts, is a book about migration and about moving bodies: bodies of water, earthly bodies, human bodies, non-human bodies, divine bodies. The creation moves, the wind blows, birds fly, the water rises/subsides. Humans migrate between lands—sometimes willingly, sometimes unwillingly, other times a complex combination of both. Patriarchs traverse, matriarchs navigate, children levitate (rise above elder siblings!). All these movements are found just in the first five books of the Hebrew Bible.

For this chapter, I want to focus on the movement of a particular body: the divine body of God in Exodus 12. First, this will entail a form of probing known throughout Pasifika as *talanoa*, an approach that will allow us to consider questions, perspectives, dimensions, and experiences that Western methodologies do not usually consider. A *talanoa* re-reading of God's movements from an Australian-Samoan diasporic perspective may provide alternative nuances for us to consider. This may then provide significant implications for not only interpreting Exod 12:12–13, but for rethinking our own movements in the current transnational world.

Talanoa as a Way of Interrogating Texts

Before I proceed further, I want to take some time in laying out my approach for (re)reading Exod 12:12–13. There will no doubt be some problems in this reading, particularly for traditional and western(ized) readers of the Bible. However, the ever-changing landscape of Australia should reflect the multiplicity of voices and perspectives, and as an Australian of Samoan heritage, I want to utilize the way my parents and ancestors interrogate the world around them (cultural and visual texts), which is through *talanoa*. Using *talanoa* as a way of investigating texts (literary, oral, cultural, visual, etc.), is not a new phenomenon, nor is it restricted to one definition.[1] In light of the many discussions of how *talanoa* takes place, I want to adopt a few standpoints for my *talanoa*. Firstly, I want to frame this *talanoa* around Jione Havea's understanding of *talanoa* as:

> [t]he confluence of three things: story, telling and conversation. Talanoa is not story without telling and conversation, telling without story and conversation, or conversation without telling and story. Talanoa is all three—story, telling, conversation—as one.[2]

This explicates the fluid nature of *talanoa* but, at the same time, emphasizes the necessity for conversation to materialize. What is the point of a story if it does not stimulate conversation and dialogue?

At the same time, I want to utilize my own Samoan understanding of *talanoa* which sees the word as a construct of the words *tala* and *noa*. The observatory nature of Samoan culture and wisdom contributes to the formation of many of its words. The word *tala* can mean a host of things. As a verb it can mean "to open," "to unpack," "to untie," or "to extend." As a noun,

---

1. For a thorough discussion on the various meanings and uses of *talanoa* in theorizing and analyzing texts, see Tomlinson, "Talanoa as Dialogue," 35–46.
2. Havea, "Bare Feet Welcome," 210.

it can mean "story" or refer to the front and back of a Samoan *fale* (house). The word *noa* also has a variety of meanings, such as "nothing," "emptiness," "void," or it can also mean "knot." Much of Samoa's wisdom stems from the oceanfront and here I argue that the word *talanoa* results from observations of its sea-life, in particular, fishing. *Talanoa* thus can be taken to mean an untying of knots, as envisioned in the untying of knots in an *upega* (fishing net).[3] Before a *tautai* (fisher) goes out to use the *upega*, they must first untie the knots so that it can be used for fishing. For this exercise, I seek to *tala* (untie) the *noa* (knots) of the text, where the *noa* refers to the ambiguous and problematic elements of the text in reading. As a second-generation Australian-born Samoan, there is an obvious tension in how I perceive the text as a child of migrants, as a settler with an awareness of the colonial tendencies of my residence and that of other settlers, and also as a biblical scholar who seeks to decolonize western readings and understandings of the biblical text/s.

I follow the conversational manner of Havea, and take *talanoa* to also mean an extension into the unknown. In other words, I seek to *tala* (extend) the conversation regarding the story of Exod 12:12–13 into the *noa* (void) of inquisitory reflection. Ironically, the mind is like the *moana*, where it drifts, ebbs and flows, to other places and spaces. But what if we pursue those voids and take the conversation further? What if we push the boundaries in biblical interpretation beyond the western paradigms, and ask questions that seek to probe the text but also challenge us as readers? What if we push the envelope in terms of how we see God's movements in the text? It may seem unconventional and even outlandish, but for too long, Samoans and other Pasifika peoples have been told/advized/colonized in how to read the Bible. *Talanoa* allows for a decolonized reading that frees itself from the colonial legacies of mission-taught biblical reading.[4]

This indeed is an alternative (alter-native?) way of interrogating biblical texts that endeavors to break the mould of western methods, seeking to *continue* the conversation and not just confine interpretation to a programmed robot-like framework. Like the waves of the *moana*, *talanoa* is fluid, so let us ride the waves of *talanoa* and feel its ripples.

---

3. A similar understanding of *talanoa* (*taranoa* in Solomon Islands) was shared by Robert Fakafu, a Solomon Islands native and PhD candidate at Otago University, during the Legacies of Slavery and Colonisation in Aotearoa and Pasifika Virtual Conference, hosted by the Council for World Mission in 2021.

4. See Vaka'uta, *Reading Ezra 9–10 Tu'a-Wise*, 2n5.

The Movements of God in Exodus 12

In this *talanoa*, I want to begin with a word study of the Hebrew terms used for God's movements. In Exod 12:12–13, the two verbs used are: *'abar* (v.12) and *pasah* (v.13). I invite us to consider not just the context of the story, but also to imagine the context of the original readers or listeners of this story. It is often lost on traditional Western interpreters of the biblical text that such stories originated from oral traditions. It is important to reclaim the orality of these texts as stories once heard and told through mouth. This is one reason why *talanoa* is key for our reading, because Samoan and Pasifika cultures are oral cultures, where we deal mainly with cultural, verbal, and visual texts, as opposed to written literary texts. Thus, in our word study, I want to consider how these verbs might have been heard, and the thoughts that such words may have stirred in hearing. While the terms used for God's movements can both be translated as "pass over," as they have been in English translations, in the Hebrew they possess other interesting nuances for us to consider and perhaps reflect on a bit more. Intriguingly, the use of two verbs could actually be an invitation to consider God's movements more closely and, hence, to hear the text more clearly.

As we *talanoa*, let us *tala* (untie) the *noa* (knots), while *tala* (extending) into the *noa* (void). Let us consider that while *'abar* presents a more commanding entrance by God, *pasah* portrays an ambivalent picture of God because *pasah* can be taken to mean "to be lame" or "to limp" or "to jump" or "pass over." The possibilities in translation will be important for this essay in stimulating a *talanoa* around God's movements, and how they may invite us to think of movement and migration in the biblical text.

'abar

The term *'abar* denotes "[a]n anthropomorphism, or ascription to God of human activity, in order to make His active Presence in history more vividly and dramatically perceived."[5] The word *'abar* can denote a variety of things, ranging from the common meanings "to traverse" and "to pass," to other rare denotations such as "to transgress" and "to offer as sacrifice." Ironically, the word *'abar* ("to traverse" and "to pass") sounds similar to the word *habiru* (Hebrew) which denotes the travelling/migrating people of God. In other words, while God passes over (*'abar*), the Hebrew people (*habiru*) pass over as well.[6] In these nuances of *'abar* there is a sense of an unwelcome entrance,

---

5. Sarna, *Exodus*, 56.
6. For an extensive discussion on the word *habiru*, see, Na'aman, "Habiru and

especially when read with the understanding of "transgressing." Even the meaning of being offered as sacrifice brings about a sense of transgression, whether it is the abomination of sin for which the offering is made, or an animal that is to be slaughtered against its will.

pasah

The word appears in noun form in Exod 12:11, denoting the Passover feast. In the verb form, it "occurs very infrequently outside of Exodus 12. It appears in Isa 31:5 with the connotation 'to protect.'"[7] Elsewhere, the verb means something else: "In 1 Kings 18:21 this verb means 'to limp,' and the cognate adjective means 'lame' frequently in the Old Testament."[8] In Exodus 12, the verb is to be understood in the context of the Passover feast mentioned in 12:11. This latter meaning is particularly intriguing given the difference to the word *'abar* as discussed above. When read intertextually with 1 Kings, it is difficult to ignore the resonance of *pasah* with the meaning of "to limp." Ancient hearers of this story may have wondered the same thing. Hence, I want to further explore this meaning of "limping" in this essay.

How might the varying connotations of *pasah* and *'abar* help us reimagine God's "passing" in Exod 12:13? This question will provide the impetus for this *talanoa*. Perhaps *pasah* resonates with the movement of diasporic bodies, particularly from third world countries to first world nations such as Australia, who limp into new lands after moving from adversity, poverty, and hostility in their homelands. The word *'abar*, on the other hand, might echo the experience of colonial settlers entering foreign lands in commanding fashions. Which diasporic movement does God resonate with? Is it one or the other or both? How might my experience as a diasporic Samoan in Australia help to understand God's movements? To answer these questions, I want to utilize a fishing proverb from my Samoan culture: "*To'ai faa-I'a a le Po*" (to arrive like a fish of the night), which I will discuss in the next section.

Proverb: "*To'ai faa-I'a a le Po*"

The proverb "*To'ai faa-I'a a le Po*" (to arrive like a fish of the night) has its origins in Samoan sea fishing. The proverb speaks of the sudden jumping of fish out of the seawater during night time fishing. Usually, the fish is a shark

---

Hebrews."

7. Childs, *Book of Exodus*, 183.
8. Cole, *Exodus*, 115.

or another large species of fish.[9] Metaphorically speaking, the meaning of the proverb is to denote the unexpected and uninvited arrival of guests.

For this essay, I read Exod 12:12–13 from a diasporic Samoan perspective in order to discern particular nuances of the verbs describing God's movements. To be clear, my reading position is a migrant one; one that moves between spaces and, as such, engages in negotiating different standpoints. I read as a Samoan who negotiates the Samoan culture and Samoan Indigenous knowledge of the land (*fanua*) of my ancestors in perceiving and interpreting. At the same time, I read as an Australian born on "these lands now called Australia."[10] I also read as a descendant of Samoan migrants, as I navigate the host land/foreign land in search of a position to "fit in." In this dynamic of reading, I consider myself a "hybrid" where my two cultures are in conversation as opposed to one culture dominating the other. This understanding of hybridity is defined by Homi Bhabha as:

> the sign of the productivity of colonial power, its shifting forces and fixities; it is the name for the strategic reversal of the process of domination through disavowal (that is, the production of discriminatory identities that secure the 'pure' and original identity of authority).[11]

Disavowal denotes that hybrids cease from a mimicry of the lifestyle instructed by the colonial powers, but instead create a "third space" where the cultural symbols of the homeland are "appropriated, translated, rehistoricized and read anew" in the diaspora.[12] Reading from this hybridized position, I want to wrestle with this Samoan proverb, knowing that this knowledge brings forth a unique perspective for someone born on Gadigal Country. This in some respects constitutes a "fusion of horizons"[13] with the purpose of finding new and alternative meanings. To gain further insight into the "third space" which Australian diasporic Samoans occupy, I will give a brief discussion of the mass migration of Samoans to Australia.

Samoan Migration to Australia

Mass migration of Samoans to Australia began in the late 1970s and continued to the early 1980s. Before that, Samoans would migrate to Australia on

   9. Cf. Schultz, "Proverbial Expressions," 150.
   10. Prentis, "What Can the Birds?," 31.
   11. Bhabha, "Signs Taken for Wonders," 154.
   12. Bhabha, *Location*, 6.
   13. See Gadamer, *Truth and Method*.

individual pursuits for a variety of reasons. Since the late 1970s, Samoans began to migrate in large numbers via New Zealand. When the friendship treaty began between New Zealand and Samoa, migration was a free enterprise for Samoans to New Zealand until the beginning of a quota system in the 1980s. New Zealand was not to be the last frontier however, as Samoans sought to explore job and education prospects over the opposite side of the Tasman. As migration was free between New Zealand and Australia, Samoans would use New Zealand as a springboard to move to Australia.[14]

However, in recent times, New Zealander-Samoans have experienced a stumbling block in their emigrational efforts to Australia, with the Australian government enforcing stricter residency conditions for migrating New Zealanders. The fact that many New Zealand migrants were Pacific Islanders may have been a factor, as Paul Hamer argues:

> the freedom of entry for Pacific Islanders won in 1973 has been regarded by some as one of the key reasons for Australia's imposition of renewed restrictions on the rights of New Zealanders in Australia ever since. This includes the severe limitation of New Zealanders' access to welfare payments imposed in 2001.[15]

As a result, restrictions had been put in place by Australian government authorities since 1973. As Paul Hamer explains:

> In 1981, for example, Australia introduced the requirement for travellers between the two countries to carry passports. From 25 January 1984, New Zealanders had to be an Australian citizen in order to be able to vote unless they had been registered to vote before that date. In 1986, Australia introduced a six-month waiting period for newly arrived New Zealand citizens before they could become eligible for welfare payments. In 1994, Australia created a 'Special Category Visa' (sub class 444) for New Zealanders living in Australia, and in 2000, it extended the stand down period for welfare payments to two years.[16]

Looking at the restrictions since 1973, there may be an implicit form of discrimination taking place, especially given the relationship between New Zealand and its Pacific neighbors. Countries like the Cook Islands and Tokelau are granted automatic New Zealand citizenship, while countries like Samoa can enter through a quota system of eleven hundred people

---

14. Howes and Surandiran, "The NZ Pathway."
15. Hamer, "Unsophisticated," 94.
16. Hamer, "Unsophisticated," 106.

annually.[17] Perhaps Hamer is right that in spite of the 1975 *Racial Discrimination Act*, section 9(1) that makes it "unlawful to discriminate on the basis of 'race, colour, descent or national or ethnic origin' . . . there has remained a suspicion that at least some of the renewed restrictions have represented a form of indirect discrimination against Pacific Islanders."[18]

There are now large communities of Samoans living in Australia, particularly across the eastern states of New South Wales, Queensland, and Victoria, with rising numbers of Samoans also living in Perth.[19] However, given the restrictions put in place, some of which target low-income earning migrants, Samoans, who are largely disadvantaged due to these unfair conditions, are found "limping" into these lands now called Australia.

Blackbirding: A "forgotten" form of migration

Further to the theme of migrants "limping" into Australia, I want to draw attention to another lesser-known form of migration. Prior to the mass numbers of Samoans migrating to Australia in the late 1970s–1980s, many Samoans and other Pacific Islanders were victims of a scheme known as "blackbirding." Blackbirding involved the:

> recruitment of labour in the Pacific Islands, but was used particularly to refer to the worst forms of kidnapping and FORCED MIGRATION, the virtual slave trading of islanders. This began with instances of illegal and forced recruitment and transportation of Melanesians to Australia after 1847 and of Polynesians to South America in 1862–64.[20]

The early term used for South Sea Islanders during the blackbirding era was the term "Kanaka" which was "originally a Polynesian word for rural or uneducated person."[21] The Samoan equivalent is the word *tagata* but in informal conversations it is pronounced with a "k" as *kagaka* (pronounced "ka-nga-ka"), thus it may be that this early word, which is common among Polynesian dialects, may refer to Samoans as well as other Polynesians.

In recent times, indentured labour schemes operating throughout Australia seem to evince a modern form of blackbirding. As Pacific Islanders

---

17. Hamer, "Unsophisticated," 115.
18. Hamer, "Unsophisticated," 107.
19. For 2016 Census figures, see Australian Government Department of Home Affairs, "Samoa-born Community Information Summary."
20. Fortune, "Blackbirders," 208.
21. Moore, "Australian South Sea Islanders," 156.

were tricked into joining ships in the 1800s, Australian farmers dangled a similar carrot in front of Pacific Islanders to travel to Australia on three-year visas for seasonal work picking fruit and working in abattoirs. Yet, like the Pacific Island slaves working under poor conditions and with little to no remuneration and often dying away from home, some Pacific Island seasonal workers experience similar slave-like conditions, usually earning less than half of what they signed up for due to various deductions from their bosses, and living and working under poor conditions.[22] This new wave of Samoan migrants to Australia may seem to be presented with new opportunities but, as it turns out for many, reminders of Australia's blackbirding history and the mistreatment of Pacific Islanders almost two centuries ago rear their ugly heads even if former Australian Prime Minister Scott Morrison has forgotten about it.[23]

"To'ai faa-I'a a le Po" (Like a fish of the night): Native Wisdom for the Diasporic Samoan

For this essay, I want to utilize the proverb "*To'ai faa-I'a a le Po*" as a lens for reading. I need to establish such a reading perspective before discussing how it can be used for discerning the meaning of the text. So, what sort of viewpoint does this proverb bring? As mentioned earlier, the meaning behind this saying speaks to the instance of unexpected (uninvited!) guests. The feelings of shock and surprise seem to be reflected in the proverb, and as a result, the subsequent feelings may either be of happiness or disappointment. When considering the deeds of the *tautai* (fisher) in the night, they could perceive the sudden appearance of the fish as a threat. On the other hand, the *tautai* could see the sudden fish as an opportunity should they accept the fish as catch.

Approaching the Text: *Talanoa*

In reading, I want to decolonize our approach to the text by utilizing the various parts of the proverb. While Western methodologies have been used extensively, as a diasporic Samoan I ask the question: Why must I privilege the Western forms when I could approach the text from my own Samoan perspective? The patterns in my own Samoan worldview may offer an alternative to Western ideas that may enrich the reading experience. At the same

---

22. Tamer, "Pacific Islander farm workers demand justice."
23. Hayne and Hitch, "Scott Morrison says slavery comments."

time, I also acknowledge that this exchange works both ways, and I must allow for my own Samoan perspective to be scrutinized. As such, I offer a *talanoa* from my Samoan perspective, using the elements of the proverb or the Samoan *muagagana* to discuss my approach.

To'ai (Arrived at)

The word *to'ai* comes from the word *to'a* which means "to settle," "to arrive at," or "to position."[24] In *talanoa* with Exod 12:12–13, the reader and text *to'ai with* each other. As the fish arrives (*to'ai*) the *tautai* assesses the situation to determine if the sudden appearance of the fish is cause for concern or an opportunity. Analogously, it is at this *to'ai* that a "fusion of horizons" occurs so that meaning is made. The reader assumes the position of *tautai* as the text becomes like the fish in the night; that is, the text becomes an unknown anomaly that requires further probing.

Faa I'a a Po (Like a fish of the night)

The word *fa'a* means "like" or "as," while the word *I'a* means "fish." The words *a Po* mean "of the night" where *Po* refers to the night. What is intriguing is the association of the fish with the night, a time of uncertainty and ambiguity. Undoubtedly, what happens during the night usually comes as a shock, particularly a fish shooting out of the water, even to an alert *tautai*. But as the *tautai* encounters the fish, they do not avoid the fish, but remain committed. In reading, the reader is like the *tautai* who may be watchful, but when terror occurs in the text, feels shocked or surprised. Like the *tautai*, the reader does not avoid the text, but is drawn to it and determined to make meaning of it. This is done not in order to avoid ambiguity in the text, nor to reject stories of a controversial nature, but to confront such tales head-on as the *tautai* tackles the fish of the night. Through such an encounter, the reader can expect to find an alternative meaning/reading as the *talanoa* with the text takes a turn.

The moana (the ocean)

The *moana* (ocean) is not mentioned explicitly in the proverb, however, it is the context of the proverb (*muāgagana*). I bring the *moana* into the conversation as an extension of the main text (the fish). The *moana* provides an apt

---

24. Cf. Pratt, *Samoan Dictionary*, 205.

analogy for the world of the text. When we see the *moana* at surface level (*fogasami*), we can only see the waters and the moving waves, yet below the surface level lies the diversity of sea life. In reading, the surface level equates to a superficial reading of the text that pays attention to the main voices, whereas diving below surface level is analogous to a deeper reading that draws awareness to and scrutinizes the details in the text that are less obvious. More importantly, reading below surface level allows for unravelling of marginalized voices that have been supressed through traditional, colonial, and androcentric readings.

As an alternative, the proverb can frame our *talanoa*, (re)imagining the text and its world through the *moana* and conceiving our engagement with the text through the rendezvous between the *tautai* and the fish. The waves of the *moana* and the fishing expedition thus reflect the "non-linear, inclusive and fluid" nature of *talanoa*.[25] In *talanoa*, we allow the waves to take us on a journey and to feel the ripples through our reading senses. In our re-reading of Exod 12:12–13, we probe like the *tautai* and anticipate the text encroaching upon us like a fish of the night yet, like the unpredictability of the *moana* waters, our *talanoa* can also become unpredictable as we are shocked and surprised by meaning.

A *To'ai faa-I'a a le Po* Reading of Exodus 12:12–13

How might my Samoan Indigenous wisdom be employed to gain further insights into *pasah*. In answering these questions, I will create a *talanoa* with the Exodus text and the Samoan proverb. For this intertextual *talanoa* of the biblical text with the cultural text, I break up the proverb into its parts as a way of re-envisaging God's movements. This will see the word *to'ai* used to reimagine *pasah* in terms of the Israelite experience (opportunity) and in light of the Egyptian standpoint (threat). This *talanoa* will also look at God/YHWH and whether God is like the fish of the night (*I'a a le Po*")

To'ai (Arrived at): Opportunity

Verse 13 reads:

> The blood shall be a sign for you on the houses where you live: when I see the blood, I will *pass over* (*pasah*) you, and no plague shall destroy you when I strike the land of Egypt (NRSV).

---

25. Cammock et al, "Strengthening Pacific Voices," 122.

In reclaiming the text's orality, how could we hear God's "passing over" through a *to'ai faa-I'a a le Po* perspective? Reading the text as *moana*, we find on the surface level those who are marked by the blood, namely, the Israelites. There is an opportunity here for the Israelites as they are given the chance for life as a result of the blood. There is humor here when reading *pasah* because, as we *talanoa* with verse 13, we are reminded of one meaning of *pasah* which is 'to leap'.[26] Perhaps the original hearers of the text may have been wondering about this word *pasah* in a similar manner. In *talanoa* style, what is unusual here and constitutes a *noa* in the text, is the question of why God needed a sign. Walter Brueggemann makes a similar observation by noting that, "[i]n all the previous places where Yahweh makes a distinction (8:23; 9:6, 26; 10:23), Yahweh has known where the special people are and has needed no marking signal."[27] Perhaps there is humor in this verse. I argue that there is humor in that God actually needs a sign to know where God's children are, and to add further bite to the comical event, it may be that God *pasah*—leaped—at the sight of the blood! In light of the events in Exodus and the context of the literary text, my reading here would seem bizarre. However, the question of why God needed a sign is a *noa* (void) that directs us to re-consider God's movements, particularly when considering that the multivalent nature of the word *pasah* may generate different responses.

Another question worth asking is: What about the blood itself? Douglas Stuart argues that "the sight of dried blood by itself had no power to deter death."[28] So what was the actual purpose of the blood? In the Hebrew Bible, blood symbolizes a number of things. Sacrifices for the atonement of sins require blood offerings so that the offending person can be cleared of sin.[29] Intriguingly, blood in the Hebrew Bible can also be seen as a protective barrier for a person against curses and evil spirits.[30] However, Israel may well have been expecting God to pass over the bloody doors in another way. Understanding the significance of blood in the context of offering and atonement as well as of protection against curses, means that there is still a level of uncertainty in what proceeds the sign of blood. In a positive sense, the blood marks a *to'ai*-opportunity for Israel.

---

26. Kaiser, "Exodus," 426.
27. Brueggemann, "Book of Exodus," 777.
28. Stuart, *Exodus*, 278.
29. Sklar, *Sin, Impurity*, 105–36.
30. See Durham, *Exodus*, 154. Also see: Lee, "Forgiveness and Reconciliation," 34.

To'ai (Arrived/Settled at): Threat and Neglected Voices

When reading Exod 12:12–13 below the surface, we find nameless characters, humans and non-humans, who have often been neglected. While the Israelites suffered under Pharaoh's regime, they are not the only ones who suffer in the story. Also in anguish are those who played no part in Pharaoh's tyranny, such as women, firstborn Egyptian children, and firstborns in prison, as well as firstborn animals (Exod 12:29). These are the unheard voices who suffered at the hands of YHWH, and they are also often neglected in our reading. There is a Samoan saying: "*Ua lavea fua Foaga e le'i fai misa,*" which translates as: "Foaga has suffered despite not being involved in the quarrel." This proverb speaks to the suffering of those who were not part of a conflict, and in Exodus 12, we see the suffering of innocent Egyptians as well as animals who did not take part in this quarrel between Moses/YHWH and Pharaoh. In this sense, YHWH's *pasah* can be translated as "transgressing"[31] or "invading." YHWH's *pasah* as a result is seen as a threat for the lives of the innocent and of other members of creation.

Faa-I'a a le Po (Like a Fish of the Night): The Invading God?

As the *talanoa* ebbs and flows, there are questions that require untangling, and we must *tala* (open) the *noa* (knots). One *noa*-knot that requires *tala* is the question of whether God's "passing through" may be seen as invading? Perhaps this is reflected best through God's other name in Exod 6:3, "*El Shaddai,*" which is often translated as "God Almighty," speaking to God's military prowess.[32] Yet God's power is not for show but used to honor the covenant with Israel's forefathers. Thus, when Israel cries, God responds. This leads to God passing through to rescue Israel, with dire consequences for others.

Here, our *talanoa* shifts to another spectrum, that of how God's movements affect the natives of the land: the Egyptians. To highlight the extremity of God's passing for the Egyptians, it is interesting to note the events preceding the ten plagues, particularly how God decides to bring Israel out of bondage. Hence, the question of agency warrants further probing for this *talanoa*. In *talanoa* with Exod 3:7–9, God makes it clear that God will bring Israel out of Egypt, yet in verse 10 it appears that it is not God that will save Israel, but Moses, as God instructs Moses: "So come, I will send *you*

---

31. Hoogendyk, *Lexham Analytical Lexicon of the Hebrew Bible*.
32. Durham, *Exodus*, 76–77.

to Pharaoh to bring my people, the Israelites, out of Egypt."³³ While God/ YHWH gives the instruction, "It is Moses who will do what Yahweh said, and Moses who will run the risks that Yahweh seemed ready to take."³⁴ The agency here seems to lie with Moses or perhaps shifts to Moses.

Yet, despite God's call for Moses to bring the people out of slavery, it seems that God has decided to reclaim agency and take matters in his own hands in Exod 12:12 and thus pass through instead. Again, I see humor here. Has God lost patience with Moses? Or with Pharaoh? Is God frustrated that it has taken ten plagues to finally get Pharaoh's approval? When re-read in light of these questions, it seems ominous that God waits until the last plague to make his entrance and pass through the land of Egypt. Here, there is more to God's movements than we have come to expect, as God oversteps Moses, passes over Israelite houses/doors, and invades the lands of Egypt in order to strike down their firstborns.

Conclusion: Implications for Diasporic Communities

God's passing through Egypt has significant implications for migrants. It seems that God's movements in Exod 12:12 resonate with the colonial settlers in 1788. In the context of Exodus, my reading may appear preposterous, but as this volume is about reading the Bible in Australia, we may need to re-envisage how we hear this text. After all, the Egyptians are the natives in the text, and it is their land that is being inhabited. Perhaps when read with a settler mentality, this fact is lost on the reader. Yet, when reading the Bible in Australia, we must be reminded of and acknowledge the legacies of the colonial project. The colonial settlers overstepped the Indigenous peoples who had already inhabited the lands for over sixty thousand years; they passed over sacred sites and claimed British sovereignty, and invaded the lands and homes of the many Indigenous nations. They also violated the world's oldest culture and its ancient stories and spirituality, so that they could replace it (or so they tried!) with:

> hundreds of Scriptures, in hard copy, unloaded at Sydney Cove and distributed at the discretion of the chaplain. Fragments of the Bible were also transmitted by European colonists through common and formal speech, in various kinds of writing, and even in the inscriptions on convicts' bodies.³⁵

---

33. Brueggemann, *Theology of the Old Testament*, 364. Italics are mine.
34. Brueggemann, "Book of Exodus," 713.
35. Lake, *Bible in Australia*, 2.

The colonial project's lasting legacy upon the various lands in the South Pacific did not only claim physical territory, it claimed the spiritual landscape of Australia.

To *tala* (extend) further into the *noa* (void), and push the boundaries of interpretation even further, we may imagine that in 12:13 God's initial vigorous movements had perhaps been restrained. God goes from passing *'abar* to passing *pasaḥ*, a passing which, according to its other nuances, exhibits a more careful and less forceful approach, especially if we are to understand the term *pasaḥ* as "limping" or "lame." In the spirit of *talanoa*, this sense of the word brings God's "passing through" in a different light, one where God might just be aware of the destructive nature of his visit. It is this verb that is used "to explain the noun that gives its name to the festival [Passover]."[36] Perhaps then we are not to think of limping as though one is injured or lame, but to reimagine a different type of festival dance, one of a more somber mood. Certainly, this is not the dance which the colonial settlers performed, for they staged a more victorious dance on Sydney Cove at the expense of Indigenous peoples who had been dancing on their own lands for more than sixty thousand years.

This is the challenge for more recent migrants. In my case, I speak especially for diasporic Samoans who are a privileged group compared to refugees and asylum seekers. The latter are often locked away in detention centres for many years,[37] in isolation on Manus Island, with great uncertainty about what the future holds for them. Despite the restrictions the Australian government imposed on migrant Pasifika people who enter via New Zealand, Samoans are still more fortunate than those in refugee camps and detention centers. At least migrant Samoans can always return to the peaceful lands of Aotearoa or even back to Pasifika. For refugees, there is nowhere to which to return. The challenge for migrant and diasporic Samoans is not to replicate the enterprise of the 1788 colonizers, but to pass—*pasaḥ*—and limp. Who are we to dance in joy when Indigenous Australians are crying in sorrow? We must perform a more respectful dance in solidarity with our Indigenous sisters and brothers.

There is a Samoan dance known as the *taualuga* which is the final dance before the end of cultural festivities. The honour of dancing in the middle (or centre stage) is given to the *taupou* (the daughter of the village high chief) or the guest of honor. The villagers usually dance from a distance away from the *taupou*, a dance known as *aiuli* (the dancers themselves become known as *aiuli*). The *aiuli* show respect by dancing from a distance.

---

36. Cole, *Exodus*, 115.
37. Grewcock, "Our lives is in danger," 77.

They also dance in tandem with the *taupou*, moving to the same tune and beat, but always giving the spotlight to the *taupou*. In these lands now called Australia, the *taupou* is and has always been Indigenous Australians; the rest of us must dance—*pasah*, in the background as *aiuli*. For too often, non-Indigenous have claimed the right to be *taupou* without admitting that they had stolen the right from Indigenous Australians two centuries ago.

Limping also reminds me of treading carefully. In Pasifika, this is reflected through the practice of *tulou*. In Pasifika, "*tulou* acts as a pardon, or excusing a person out of respect for infringing a *tapu* [that which is sacred] with regard to another person or group of people."[38] The practice of *tulou* somewhat resembles a limping person as they "pass over" a sacred space but do so out of respect. When one says *tulou*, they bow down as a show of humility, knowing that they are about to intrude a person or family or village's sacred space.

Many of us Pasifika migrants also bring our own versions of the Christian Bible into these lands, translated in our various languages, but have done so without saying *tulou* to these unceded lands belonging originally to Indigenous Australians. The challenge is for us to read our Bibles bearing in mind that we are in a new context. We must learn to read in light of the new realities, with respect to the traditional custodians of these lands, and in pursuit of social justice. Hence, limping must remind us of our duty as *aiuli*, and of our culture of *tulou*, where we are cautious of the spaces we enter, and more importantly, that we are respectful of the spaces we intrude and pass through.

38. Kolia, "Lifting the Tapu of Sex," 86.

Bibliography

Australian Government Department of Home Affairs. "Samoa-born Community Information Summary." 2018. https://www.homeaffairs.gov.au/mca/files/2016-cis-samoa.PDF.

Bhabha, Homi. "Signs Taken for Wonders: Questions of Ambivalence and Authority under a Tree Outside Delhi, May 1817." *Critical Inquiry* 12 (1985) 144–65.

———. *The Location of Culture*. London and New York: Routledge, 1994.

Cammock, Radilaite, Cath Conn, and Shoba Nayar. "Strengthening Pacific voices through Talanoa participatory action research." *AlterNative* 17 (2021) 120–29.

Childs, Brevard S. *The Book of Exodus: A Critical, Theological Commentary*. Louisville, KY: Westminster John Knox, 1997.

Cole, R. Alan. *Exodus: An Introduction and Commentary*. Vol. 2. Downers Grove, IL: IVP 1973.

Brueggemann, Walter. "The Book of Exodus." In *New Interpreter's Bible*, edited by Leander E. Keck, Vol. 1, 675–981. Nashville, TX: Abingdon, 1994.

———. *Theology of the Old Testament: Testimony, Dispute, Advocacy*. Minneapolis, MN: Fortress, 1997.

Douglas K. Stuart. *Exodus*. Nashville, TX: Broadman & Holman, 2006.

Durham, John I. *Exodus*. Dallas, TX: Word, 1998.

Fakafu, Robert. Oral contribution to the Talanoa Oceania 2021: Legacies of Slavery and Colonisation in Aotearoa and Oceania Conference. Council for World Mission, 2021. https://www.facebook.com/watch/live/?ref=watch_permalink&v=538100970613076.

Fortune, Kate. "Blackbirders." In *The Pacific Islands: An Encyclopedia*, edited by Brij V. Lal and Kate Fortune, 208. Honolulu, HI: University of Hawaii Press, 2000.

Gadamer, Hans-Georg. *Truth and Method*. Translated by Joel Weinsheimer and Donald G. Marshall. New York: Continuum, 2004.

Grewcock, Michael. "'Our lives is in danger': Manus Island and the end of asylum." *Race & Class* 59 (2017) 70–89.

Hamer, Paul. "Unsophisticated and unsuited." *Political Science* 66 (2014) 93–118.

Havea, Jione. "Bare Feet Welcome: Redeemer Xs Moses @ Enaim." In *Bible, Borders, Belonging(s): Engaging Readings from Oceania*, edited by Jione Havea, David J. Neville and Elaine M. Wainwright, 209–22. Atlanta, GA: SBL, 2014.

Hayne, Jordan and Georgia Hitch. "Scott Morrison says slavery comments were about New South Wales colony, apologises for causing offence." *ABC News*, 12 June 2020. https://www.abc.net.au/news/2020-26-12/pm-apologises-offence-caused-slavery-comments-clarifies-remarks/12348716.

Hoogendykm Isaiah, ed. *The Lexham Analytical Lexicon of the Hebrew Bible*. Bellingham, WA: Lexham, 2017.

Howes, Stephen and Sherman Surandiran. "The NZ Pathway: How and Why Samoans Migrate to Australia." *Devpolicy Blog*, 1 February 2021. https://devpolicy.org/the-nz-pathway-how-and-why-samoans-migrate-to-australia-part-one-20210201-1/.

Hytner, Mike. "Israel Folau to be sacked by Rugby Australia over social media posts." *The Guardian: Australian edition*, 11 April 2019. https://www.theguardian.com/sport/2019/apr/11/israel-folau-to-be-sacked-by-rugby-australia-over-social-media-posts.

Kaiser, Walter C. "Exodus." In *The Expositor's Bible Commentary Revised Edition: Genesis—Leviticus*, edited by Tremper Longman and David E. Garland, 331–561. Grand Rapids, MI: Zondervan, 2008.

Kolia, Brian Fiu, "Lifting the Tapu of Sex: A Tulou Reading of the Song of Songs." In *Sea of Readings: The Bible in the South Pacific*, edited by Jione Havea, 85–102. Atlanta, GA: SBL, 2018.

Lake, Meredith. *The Bible in Australia*. Sydney: NewSouth, 2018.

Lee, Ann Suk Yee, "Forgiveness and Reconciliation in Old Testament Sacrifice." *McMaster Journal of Theology and Ministry* 13 (2011–2012) 24–44.

Moore, Clive. "Australian South Sea Islanders' narratives of belonging." In *Narrative and Identity Construction in the Pacific Islands*, edited by Farzana Gounder, 155–76. Amsterdam: John Benjamins, 2015.

Na'aman, Nadav. "Habiru and Hebrews." In *Canaan in the Second Millennium B.C.E.*, edited by Nadav Na'aman, 252–74. Winona Lake, IN: Eisenbrauns, 2005.

Pratt, George. *Samoan Dictionary: English and Samoan, Samoan and English with a Short Grammar of the Samoan Dialect*. Apia: London Missionary Society, 1862.

Prentis, Brooke. "What Can the Birds of the Land Tell Us?" In *Grounded in the Body, in Time and Place, in Scripture: Papers by Australian Women Scholars in the Evangelical Tradition*, edited by Jill Firth and Denise Cooper-Clarke, 31–44. Eugene, OR: Wipf & Stock, 2021.

Sarna, Nahum M. *Exodus*. Philadelphia, PA: Jewish Publication Society, 1991.

Schultz, E. "Proverbial Expressions of the Samoans." *The Journal of the Polynesian Society* 58 (1948) 150.

Sklar, Jay. *Sin, Impurity, Sacrifice, Atonement: The Priestly Conceptions*. Sheffield: Sheffield Phoenix, 2005.

Tamer, Rayane. "Pacific Islander farm workers demand justice after claims of 'modern slavery.'" *SBS News*, 6 February 2022. https://www.sbs.com.au/news/article/pacific-islander-farm-workers-demand-justice-after-claims-of-modern-slavery/ylxfok3wj.

Thompson, Geoff. "Why Christians disagree over the Israel Folau saga." *The Conversation*, 25 June 2019. https://theconversation.com/why-christians-disagree-over-the-israel-folau-saga-118773.

Tomlinson, Matt. "Talanoa as Dialogue and PTC's Role in Creating Conversation." *Pacific Journal of Theology* 59 (2020) 35–46.

Vaka'uta, Nāsili. *Reading Ezra 9-10 Tu'a-Wise: Rethinking Biblical Interpretation in Oceania*. Atlanta: SBL, 2011.

Part III

Revisiting Colonial Mythologies

Whores and Saints

Glimpses of Eve in Early Australian History

Barbara Deutschmann

"Figtree serpent and eve."

"Figtree serpent and eve" was the description of convict Thomas Sanders' tattoo, recorded on his arrival in New South Wales in 1832. It was not unusual for convicts to have biblical motifs pictured on their bodies.[1] To tattoo Eve alone, however, without partner Adam, was striking, and hints at Sanders' view that the first woman may have been implicated in his punishment.

Meredith Lake shows how those who colonized the land now called Australia in the eighteenth century often drew on the image of Adam and Eve's expulsion from Eden to describe their predicament, speaking of themselves as "exiles" or "banished sinners" and of their new surrounds as a "solitary waste of the creation."[2] This reference to the biblical image of Eden testifies to the way that biblical themes influenced perceptions at the time. While convicts felt themselves banished, the First Peoples of Australia suffered their own banishment as settlers pushed them off lands they had stewarded for millennia.[3]

Colonial settlers were unlike the inhabitants of biblical Eden in every way. In 1792, men outnumbered women five to one in New South Wales,

1. Barnard, *Convict Tattoos*, 27.
2. Lake, *Bible in Australia*, 34.
3. Attwood, *Telling the Truth*.

and, of the few women, many were convicts.[4] Sexist assumptions were part of the unexamined social baggage of colonizers, and a peculiarly antipodean gendering of the female sex can be seen in the terms applied to women of the time: "damned whores" and "God's police."[5]

It was Lieutenant Ralph Clark who first applied the term "damned whores" to female convicts: "[T]he damned whores the moment that the[y] got below fel a fighting amonst one a nother and Capt Meridith order the Sergt. not to part them but to let them fight it out..."[6] The descriptor merged assumptions about rampant female sexuality with notions of pollution and disorder. That these women were damned was a theological assumption that showed the opprobrium in which they were held.[7] In contrast, social reform campaigner Caroline Chisholm popularized the term "God's police" to promote the improving influence of free women in the colonies.[8] Respectable women, she argued, would do more than the clergy to elevate men.

Both terms, "damned whores" and "God's police," carried messages about sexuality. Contemporary accounts show that convict women's sexual behavior earned more censure than their crimes.[9] Lieutenant Ralph Clark's epithet revealed anxiety about the expressive sexuality of many convict women who lived outside the boundaries set by marriage and public expectations of sexual behavior. The hypocrisy of many men is revealed by the fact that some leading men, including Ralph Clark himself, kept convict mistresses and fathered children outside of marriage. "God's police," on the other hand, carried the opposite notion that women were pure and kept sexuality safely contained within marriage or within celibacy.

For First Australian women this negative stereotype took toxic shape when merged with racial notions that left them with little agency. Anne Pattel-Gray has drawn attention to the way that Indigenous women were cruelly caught in this dichotomy. "Mary became 'the mother of all good' ...

4. Grimshaw, *Creating a Nation*, 42.

5. Anne Summers drew attention to this dichotomy in her book, *Damned Whores*, 67, 313–15.

6. As recorded in Finlon and Ryan, *Letters and Journals of Lt. Ralph Clark*, 50.

7. Damousi, "Depravity," 30–45.

8. "For all the clergy you can despatch, all the school masters you can appoint, all the churches you can build and all the books you can export, will never do much good, without what a gentleman in that colony very appropriately called 'God's police'—wives and little children—good and virtuous women." Letter to Earl Grey, Secretary of State for the Colonies, as cited by Caroline Chisholm, *Emigration and Transportation Relatively Considered*, 17. The notion of women as God's police was further popularised by Coventry Patmore's poem *The Angel in the House*, published in 1894, celebrating the selfless wife, https://www.gutenberg.org/files/4099/4099-h/4099-h.htm.

9. Sturma, "Eye of the Beholder," 3–10, at 4.

While Aboriginal women, like Eve, were labelled as having no virtue, the White woman, like Mary was portrayed as having no sin."[10] Visual representations of Aboriginal women by settler colonialists reveal "a king-tide of malice" directed at Aboriginal women.[11]

I am interested in the origin of these gender archetypes, and the response to these labels by the women affected by them. My earlier work in international development brought me face to face with some of the narratives that oppress and humiliate women. I observed women who were malnourished, girls who could not go to school, mothers bringing dead babies into clinics for treatment, women delivering babies on the sides of roads. I wondered what beliefs about women could possibly lead to such parlous outcomes for women. My working assumption is that unexamined metanarratives profoundly influence the interrelationship of the sexes and I approach these injustices from the stance of being a white feminist and a Christian, committed to exposing and overcoming patriarchal dominance.

On what cultural narratives did descriptions of women as damned whores or God's police draw? To people familiar with the Bible, these descriptors sound strangely familiar. Similar tropes of sexuality, disorder, and pollution have long been employed to characterize the primeval woman, Eve.[12] A strong stream of interpretation has portrayed Eve as a seductress, insubordinate, and guilty of introducing sin into the world. Completing the dichotomy, portrayals of Mary show her as submissive, virginal, and sinless.[13]

In this chapter, I will focus on Eve, arguing that the Eden narrative in the biblical book of Genesis provides little basis for Eve as the model of the "damned whore" stereotype, and that tropes focused on Eve's sexuality were the development of a later interpretive period. It was gendered interpretations of the Eden story that had produced the negative stereotype. British colonial settlers imported as unexamined cultural baggage hierarchical views of gender that reflected a suspicion of Eve's allegedly unruly sexuality and then applied these views to convict and Indigenous women.

I will develop this case in four parts. The first section exposes the insubstantial case for seeing convict and Aboriginal women as whores. The second examines the Genesis 2–3 text to refute the case that the Bible associates Eve with its conception of the prostitute or seductress. Sections three and four

10. Pattel-Gray, "Hard Truth," 261.

11. Conor, *Skin Deep*, 368.

12. Phillips, *Eve*, 55–77; Loader, *Philo, Josephus, and the Testaments on Sexuality*, 10–141.

13. Phillips, *Eve*, 132–37.

trace the emergence of negative views of Eve in the interpretation history, and the development of alternative readings of Eve by pro-feminist writers.

Women as Whores in Australia

The perception that all female convicts in early Australia were whores was persistent but had little basis in fact. Of the twenty-four thousand women transported, Lloyd Robson estimates that about one-fifth had engaged in prostitution before leaving for Australia. Prostitution was not a transportable offence and records show that most transported women had committed property crimes.[14] The perception that all female convicts and most non-convict single women were prostitutes could only be explained by the peculiar conditions of the colonies and the gendered views of their observers.[15]

There was a low rate of marriage in the colonies and there were peculiar reasons for this.[16] Marriage was not possible for those who had a spouse in England, or those who could not afford the license fee. There were few employment options in townships for women who had completed their sentence. Unable to make their way back to England by working a passage on a ship, women were often forced into protective relationships due to the risky environment of rural settlements. By the time that free immigrant women began to arrive in numbers, the epithet of whore was still employed.[17] Single women were assumed to be living from sex work. The Rev. Samuel Marsden's 1806 *Female Register* counted as prostitutes all single women and those married under rites other than Anglican, revealing his own assumptions about marriage and singleness.

Given the weak case for regarding women in early settlements as whores, what could explain that persistent label? "Whore," "concubine," or "prostitute" were labels located more in the category of insult than of occupation. These terms, associated with notions of depravity and disorder, testify more readily to the attitudes of their male proponents than to the characters of their subjects. The punishments of the day further revealed their marginal status. Their motherhood was implicitly discredited when convict mothers were separated from their children, who in many cases were sent to Orphan

---

14. Oxley, "Female Convicts," 85.
15. Robson, *Convict Settlers*, 78.
16. Michael Sturma makes the point that marriage hesitancy was a feature of working-class life in England at the time and became a class-marker for English middle- and upper-classes. "Eye of the Beholder," 3–10.
17. Summers, *Damned Whores*, 322–24.

Schools. A common, much-hated punishment was the shaving of the head, depriving women of their most obvious feminine marker.[18]

While female convict bodies bore the imprint of male, ruling class attitudes, Aboriginal women's bodies carried an extra signification—that of a racialized subject. The right of imperialist extraction applied to the bodies of Indigenous women. On the edges of settlement misogyny merged with racial stereotypes to create a perilous environment for women.[19] Women were summarily punished for minor incidents and violent assaults were perpetrated with impunity. Liz Conor concludes that, "The intricate trails of ink, when traced, scanned and sampled across the typeset, confirm that sexual difference is complicated by race and confers intelligibility to it. Aboriginal women were cast in a starring and often salacious role as brutalized and docile."[20]

There was certainly more than simple discounting of women going on in colonial Australia. Anthropologist Mary Douglas drew attention to the way that separating subjects as "other" imposes order on an unruly society.[21] An exaggeration of female characteristics in highly stereotypical formats, created an easily recognizable "other" against which male qualities could be measured:

> ... ideas about separating, purifying, demarcating and punishing transgressions have as their main function to impose system on an inherently untidy experience. It is only by exaggerating the difference between within and without, above and below, male and female, with and against, that a semblance of order is created.[22]

The "untidy experience" of early colonial Australia provided an example of Douglas' conclusions. The project of definition and control was enacted on the bodies of women, both those found in the places of female incarceration (the so-called "female factories") and in the camps of Aboriginal people. The imposition of social order mirrored the manipulation of the physical landscape that was happening simultaneously. Land and female bodies beckoned as places for access and control. "The colonial project was buttressed by conceptions of a feminised landscape, through a similitude of body and land holding out the promise of sexual access..."[23]

18. Connolly, *Disorderly Women*, 48.
19. Conor, *Skin Deep*, 144–51.
20. Conor, *Skin Deep*, 151.
21. Douglas, *Purity and Danger*, 4.
22. Douglas, *Purity and Danger*, 4.
23. Conor, *Skin Deep*, 367.

Although these analyses are helpful, they do not fully explain the social antagonism between women and men that was so evident in early Australian life and which persisted through the temperance and suffrage movements in the late nineteenth-century. I suggest that these gender formulations had their origins in the wider debate known as the "woman question" or *querelles des femmes* which engaged the literary classes of Europe from the fifteenth- to the nineteenth-century. The Bible, and in particular, views of Eve, had a central role in this debate, evidenced by the repeated defense of her by women in literature of the period.[24]

Meredith Lake has established the presence of "an influential but contested Bible" in early Australia.[25] Given the mixed class and religious origins of settler society, there is no simple connection to be seen between Bible reading and social practice. In the societal mix, Catholic met Protestant, evangelical met high churchman, and rebel met conservative. "Sullen indifference" to religion probably best explains the attitude of both ruler and ruled.[26] This indifference to established religion does not mean that the Bible had no influence. Lake draws attention in many instances to the way this "cultural Bible" helped form "deepest attitudes about life, God and the world."[27] The debates around "the woman question" engaged by nineteenth-century Christian women, often referencing Eve and the Eden narrative, thus made their way into gender formulations of Australian life.

Eve the Seductress

How accurate a representation of biblical Eve is the image of her as woman guilty of seducing man? Because the notion of prostitution means different things in different settings, care should be taken not to relate contemporary understandings of commercial sex work to constructions of prostitution in the Hebrew Bible.[28] Although rarely expressed in such crude terms as "damned whores," the Hebrew Bible certainly knew about prostitutes (Gen 38:15; Josh 2:1; Judg 16:1). Prostitutes feature in several biblical narratives and prostitution was licit and tolerated. For men, sex with prostitutes, war prisoners, widows, and unmarried women not under a father's authority,

---

24. Benckhuysen, *Gospel According to Eve*, 1–22; Taylor and Weir, eds., *Let Her Speak*, 1–105.

25. Lake, *Bible in Australia*, 32–33.

26. Gascoigne, *Enlightenment*, 23.

27. Lake, *Bible in Australia*, 78.

28. Athalya Brenner summarizes the different Hebrew terms and their usage. *Intercourse of Knowledge*, 147–51.

was not proscribed although there were limits imposed by propriety. Texts such as Job 31:1, Hos 4:14, and Prov 5:15–23 show that, irrespective of any legal obligations, the Hebrew Bible expected moral fidelity of men. Biblical laws governing sexual relations were, however, constructed differently for men and women.

The verbal root *zna* carries the notion of extra-marital sexual activity.[29] In the Hebrew Bible the term is used both metaphorically and literally. In prophetic metaphorical use, Israel "played the prostitute" when she strayed from devotion to God (*tiznena*, Ezek 23:3). In literal use, the subject is always a woman and refers to actual or alleged sexually promiscuous behavior.[30] Although prostitution was not proscribed, the women who engaged in it were socially marginalized characters who nevertheless played important roles in Israel's story.[31] All uses of the verbal root, as opposed to the noun (*zona*, "a woman who is a prostitute," Deut 22:21; 2 Kgs 9:22), refer to promiscuity.[32]

The clearest picture of the prostitute is the *strange woman* (*issa zara*) of Proverbs 1–9. She is a woman of smooth speech. She is wily and adept in the sensual arts of seduction. She deceives her husband (Prov 7:10–23) and ultimately destroys her victim. The picture conveyed is of a woman who takes sexual initiative to seduce men, using all her mastery of the sensory arts as well as a good dose of womanly knowledge. She exists outside the social boundaries fixed by marriage or social convention, is a threat to order and the boundaries of family and social group, and exists on the margins of society. To what extent does the Eve of Genesis relate to this stereotype?

In Gen 2:24, woman joins the creation scene to fulfil the need for a *helper alongside* (*ezer kenegdo*), a term unique in the Hebrew Bible and best explained by her performance of the role in the circumstances of the couple's life as shown in Genesis 2–3.[33] The masculine form of the noun *helper* (*ezer*), is used and not the feminine, *ezrah*, indicating that the outcome of the experiment to find the helper, a woman, was not essential to the narrative.[34] There is no obvious sexual role foregrounded in the text for this partner. The joyful recognition by the human (2:23) may imply sexual awareness, *bone of*

---

29. Bird, "Play the Harlot," 76–79.
30. Lipka, "The Offense," 162.
31. Brenner, *Intercourse of Knowledge,* 151.
32. Lipka notes that promiscuity of an unmarried woman is not regarded as a punishable crime in Lev 19:29, while in Deut 22:20–21 it is considered a capital crime. "The Offense," 170. The behavior, according to Leviticus (18:24–30; 19:29), is a serious threat to the whole community leading to the defilement of the land. "The Offense," 175.
33. The expression *ezer kenegdo* is unique in the Hebrew Bible.
34. Eskenazi, "Non-Gender Equality."

my bone and flesh of my flesh (*esem me asamay ubasar mibbesari*), although a stronger case can be made that kinship is the main idea here.[35] In 2:24, an editorial note stamps the male/female relationship with approval and safely embeds any potential sexual congress in a recognised social institution. So far, there is no evidence of a seductive Eve. Could this be inferred from their naked state, *naked and not disconcerted* (*arummim welo yitbosasu*) in 2:25?

Nakedness is not a neutral term. In Hebrew Bible usage, it conveys the idea of defencelessness or moral lapse, refers to the exposure of genitals, and is often linked with shame (Gen 9:22–23; Hos 2:3–5; Nah 3:5). In the prophetic tirade against Israel in Ezekiel 16, nakedness suggests two things: the pubescent state of Israel over which God spread the edge of the divine cloak of marriage (16:8), and the nakedness of prostitution (16:38–39). Within this text, nakedness stands for blatant sexual expression, itself a metaphor for covenantal unfaithfulness and linked, as in Gen 2:24, with *shame* (*bos*) in 16:52 and 63. Although nakedness is associated with prostitution in Ezekiel, the connection is less obvious in Gen 2:25. The characters of Genesis 2 were both naked (not just the woman) and their nakedness was without the usual negative associations.

Readings of Eve the seductress often center on the moment of eating of the tree of knowledge good and bad (Gen 3:1–6). We note first that there is no seductive language or behavior obvious in the text. Eve does not persuade or cajole the man. She simply eats and gives to the man who, we are told, is with her and has heard, along with her, the persuasive argument of the serpent. She does not lure the man to eat. Unlike the *strange woman* of Proverbs, she does not use words at all. The seduction is worked by the serpent, not Eve, a truth to which she points in 3:13.[36] Far from seeking to seduce the man, Eve simply shares food with her partner.

We need to consider the possibility that eating from the tree of knowledge good and bad (*es haddaat tob*) implies an erotic awakening. The Hebrew lexeme *da-at* ("knowledge") and its verbal form *yada* have a range of meaning that includes sexual intercourse (Gen 4:1; Num 31:17). It is not clear how a sexual meaning could be intended by *da-at* within the phrase "knowledge good and bad." The same verb is employed when, after eating, the pair "know" they are naked and seek to hide. The Hebrew Bible has no trouble describing intercourse (Gen 4:1; 25), employing a range of

---

35. Brueggemann, "Same Flesh and Bone," 532–42; Chapman, *House of the Mother*, 82, 194–96.

36. The *hiphil* verb form of *nša* indicates she was deceived, not sexually seduced, although the Greek Septuagint parallel *epatesen* carries sexual connotations. Loader, *Making Sense of Sex*, 19.

expressions to do so, therefore it is difficult to see why a coyness should occur here if sexual awakening was a significant result of the disobedience.

Although Genesis does not initially characterize Eve as a sexualized temptress, we need to consider the possibility that the text portrays her as becoming a sexualized temptress following the partaking of the fruit of the forbidden tree. The divine pronouncement declares, "To your man is your desire (*tesuqah*) and he will predominate (*mesol*) over you." Does the penalty she received in God's pronouncement of 3:16 assume that henceforth she is placed under male rule as a result of her now-compromised state? Does "desire" imply her sexuality, hereafter something to be controlled? Genesis 3:16 raises many interpretive possibilities. The key problems are the meaning of *desire* (*tesuqah*) and *rule* (*mesol*), and the relationship implied between the woman's *tesuqah* and the man's *mesol*. The subtleties of meaning in these two key words of v. 16 are not carried in the common English translations, "desire" and "rule."[37] The repetition of these two terms in Gen 4:7 in a different context with reference to the relationship between two brothers highlights the problematic nature of gendered interpretations in Genesis 3. The lack of scholarly consensus on Gen 3:16 regarding the intent of the penalty on the woman makes it difficult to assume that she needs male rule to control her sexuality.

A full discussion will not be attempted here but the installation of hierarchy as a response to disordered sexuality is an unlikely conclusion.[38] The remainder of the verse sets her penalty into the context of her toil in childbearing. It is probable that this is a text explaining the origins of both the toil of childbearing and the toil of early rural life in the Levant, and the nexus of gendered roles that will sustain it.[39]

The Genesis account which honors Eve's motherhood provides further evidence against ideas of Eve as a prostitute. The word used for her offspring in Gen 3:15–16, and when she gives birth to Seth in 4:25, is *seed* (*zarᶜa*), the term often used in promises to the patriarchs. There is a gravity about this role that places her into the company of the patriarchs, responsible not just for bearing individual children but rather for bearing a succession of sons that carry on through the ages. Eve's maternal role is positively recognized in her man's declaration that she is the *mother of all living* (*em kol-ḥay*) in 3:20. Eve seems to have a sense of this as she exclaims on the birth of Cain: *I have acquired a man with YHWH* (*qaniti is et-yhwh*). This unusual expression

---

37. As seen in translations NRSV, NIV, NASB, ESV.

38. Deutschmann, *Creating Gender*, 44–68. Two recent studies illustrate the range of interpretive possibilities: Chapman, "Breath of Life," 262; Morse, *Encountering Eve's Afterlives*, 22–26.

39. Meyers, *Discovering Eve*, 118.

promotes the idea of a participatory divine agent. There is a strong case that the woman here is making a counterclaim to the notion of creation out of the side of man (2:22).[40] This time, together with YHWH, she has been the vehicle of new life. Seth's birth seems to place Eve as the progenitor of the Sethite line that is the first to practice worship of YHWH.[41]

In her two short speeches of Genesis 4, Eve demonstrates a desire to assert her own meanings for her childbearing (Gen 4:1; 4:25). We can conclude that there are few grounds in the Genesis 2–4 text for regarding Eve as the precursor of the damned whore stereotype. Given that Genesis 2–3 allows positive readings of Eve, the emergence of the notion of Eve as seductress requires explanation. I turn now to sketch the major phases of this re-casting of Eve, noting that fuller accounts of that negative history are available elsewhere.[42]

Early Interpretations of Eve

Eve became a prominent subject in many later extra-biblical works, a surprizing fact given that she is not featured in the Hebrew Bible at all after Genesis. Many elaborated versions of the Adam and Eve story circulated in the ancient world at the turn of the Common Era.[43] The impact of the Hellenistic environment of the ancient Near East in the Second Temple period is evident in many of these elaborations. Although Hellenistic constructions of sex and gender are complex, they are androcentric and often misogynistic.[44] In Platonic terms, put simply, woman, with her visible reproductive functions, was associated with matter, and man with the allegedly superior spiritual dimension.

In readings of the Eden narrative, Eve became a universal character standing for everywoman. It was but a small step to then associate woman and sexuality with the origin of sin, as seen in the Wisdom of Sirach in the second century BCE: "From a woman is the start of iniquity—and because of her, we waste away, all alike."[45] Woman became temptress, a

---

40. Pardes, "Beyond Genesis 3," 171–72, 173–93,

41. Morse, *Encountering Eve*, 137.

42. See for example: Reuling, *After Eden*; Flood, *Representations of Eve*; Becking and Hennecke, eds., *Out of Paradise*; Kvam, Schearing, and Ziegler, *Eve and Adam*.

43. There exists a textual tradition known as the *Life of Adam and Eve*, which includes twenty-seven manuscripts of the *Greek Life of Adam and Eve*, thought to have developed between 100 BCE and 300 CE.

44. Frymer-Kensky, *In the Wake*, 202–12.

45. Ellis, *Gender*, 222. Ben Sira is thought to have been a scribe based in the temple in Jerusalem in the late second century BCE.

designation already part of the symbolic lexicon of the age seen in the Lilith and Pandora myths.[46] Pandora lent credence to the allegedly inherent "troublesome" characteristics of women, such as curiosity, deceitfulness, and impetuousness, and to the notion of woman's "alluring" body as the site of both attraction and danger. Such mythical elaborations played a role in the sexualization of the Genesis fall story.[47]

Philo's works continued this trajectory. A Jewish philosopher living in Alexandria between 20 BCE and 50 CE, Philo authored an early exegesis of the Greek Septuagint translation of the Pentateuch very influential among medieval scholars.[48] In his retelling of the creation story, a primary androgyne was created in God's image (Gen 1:27). In a second stage, a male is created first representing *nous* (mind), and a female is created second, representing *aesthesis* (sense-perception), as helper and ally of mind (Gen 2:22). According to Philo, the woman was the source of the fall of man, her senses falling prey to the wiles of the serpent.[49]

Several first and second century commentators continued the tradition of reading Eve's fall as a sexual fall that implicated all women. Such interpretations are clearly evident in early Christian literature such as the *Acts of Andrew*, the *Martyrdom of Perpetua and Felicitas*, and the *Protoevangelium of James*,[50] and in epistles of the New Testament (1 Cor 11:7–12; 2 Cor 11:3; 1 Tim 2:13–15).[51] John the Seer records a more redemptive view of Eve (Revelation 12) where the toiling woman and her newborn child are snatched away by God to her special place "prepared by God."

Intense controversies developed in the second century around questions of marriage and celibacy and the Eden story featured strongly. Early

46. In Hesiod's version of this myth, dating from about 700 BCE, Pandora opens the jar of evil, releasing all the evils and diseases that silently and invisibly wander over the earth. Phipps, *Genesis and Gender*, 40–49. A closer link can be found between conceptions of Eve and the Mesopotamian Lilith myth. The earliest evidence of Lilith is found in a Sumerian list from 2,400 BCE that describes "Lilu-demons" who would visit sleeping men to seduce them and produce grotesque children. In legend, she became known as Adam's insubordinate first wife, created from the same clay in Gen 1:27. Hurwitz, *Lilith the First Eve*.

47. Irenaeus, Tertullian, Gregory Nazianzus, and Origen integrated the Pandora story into their work on Eve. Phillips, *Eve*, 21–23; Panofsky and Panofsky, *Pandora's Box*, 11–13.

48. Runia, *Philo*, 3; Flood, *Representations of Eve*, 17.

49. Philo, *On the Creation of the World*, LIII, 151–52. For a helpful discussion of Philo's thought on the two sexes, see Lloyd, *Man of Reason*, 22–28.

50. Anna Rebecca Solevåg finds positive comparisons of Eve and Mary in the Greco-Roman childbearing discourse of the time. *Birthing Salvation*, 112–32, 180–81, 254–56.

51. Solevåg, *Birthing Salvation*, 133.

Church Fathers skewed the image of Eve in three ways.[52] Firstly, they continued the Pandora theme, seeing Eve as a dangerous seductress. Second, they developed the idea that Eve, and in fact, all women, were marked with negative qualities from the moment of their creation, not from the transgression in the garden. Their third theme, seen particularly in the work of Augustine, was to highlight the sexualization of the Fall. Against these powerful, damaging ideas about Eve, however, another story was emerging. Away from the academic halls of men, emerging in the novels, lessons and letters, and other writings of women, was another view of Eve.

Another View of Eve

Pro-feminist research has uncovered many women who had positive views of Eve.[53] As early as the twelfth-century, Hildegard of Bingen named Eve as a precursor to Mary in her maternal role.[54] In the late fourteenth-century, Christine de Pizan, an early participant in the *querelle des femmes*, the literary debate about the nature of women, noted Eve's significant maternal role. She pointed out that humanity gained more through Mary than it lost through Eve: ". . . humanity was conjoined to the godhead, which could never have taken place if Eve's misdeed had not occurred."[55] These fresh, womanly perspectives on Eve brought under-recognized facets of her character to the foreground. They highlighted the important role of women not only in birthing but in rearing new generations.

Other positive features of Eve came to be recognized by women in the sixteenth- and seventeenth-centuries.[56] Some English pamphleteers saw Eve as a seeker of knowledge and a positive influence on *adam*. Rachel Speght, for instance, proposed that Eve was needed to help imperfect man.[57] Pamphleteers in the sixteenth- and seventh-centuries offered "a strong affirmation of the creative strength of women as life-givers, as well as figures of repentance and redemption."[58] In the late seventeenth-century, the theme of

---

52. Deutschmann, *Creating Gender*, 170–84.
53. Morse, *Encountering Eve*, 187
54. Newman, *Sister of Wisdom*, 93–95.
55. de Pizan, *Book of the City of Ladies*, 23.
56. This section owes much to the research of Amanda Benckhuysen and Holly Morse. Benckhuysen, *Gospel According to Eve*, 45. Morse, *Encountering Eve*, 187–96.
57. McManus, "Eve's Dowry," 193–219.
58. Morse, *Encountering Eve*, 188.

the creation of Eve to complete or improve the *adam* was taken up by many other early commentators.[59]

In the eighteenth-century, Eve was enlisted in arguments to reform marriage. Lucy Hutton, familiar with Hebrew, wrote *Six Sermonicles* for women in which she suggested that sex did not enter the world with Eve's disobedience but was part of the original creation.[60] She dared to suggest that woman as well as man experiences desire and passion in marriage as God's gift. Other women, writing children's Bibles and improving literature, conveyed sympathetic views of Eve as a forgiven sinner.[61]

By the late nineteenth-century fresh readings of Genesis 1–3 argued for Eve's spiritual and ontological equality with *adam*.[62] Sarah Grimké, Catherine Booth, and Frances Willard challenged notions of women's separate sphere.[63] Campaigns for women's suffrage and for other rights brought women out into public spaces and gave them experience of solidarity with others of their sex. Activists brought to their work competent, pro-feminist biblical exegesis and a cogent vision of women as social reformers. As such, they were the archetypal "God's police," not as the domestic angel imagined by men, but woman configured to fit their own aspirations.

Eve in Australia

This notion of the improving role of spiritually mature wives gained currency in Australian colonies and developed impetus from the work of early feminists in the late nineteenth-century. Women's organized voices began to be heard as lower- and middle-class women joined the cause for the control of alcohol. The Woman's Christian Temperance Union expanded in size and influence in Australia by the turn of the twentieth-century.[64] Employment and divorce rights, property and inheritance laws were advocated along with the robust campaign for alcohol control and women's suffrage. Australian activists such as Bessie Harrison-Lee were supported by the arguments of American Katharine Bushnell, a classics scholar and activist for women's causes. Bushnell's original translations from Hebrew and Greek undergirded her fresh interpretations of Genesis which offered

---

59. Benckhuysen, *Gospel According to Eve*, 35–41, 119–20.
60. Benckhuysen, *Gospel According to Eve*, 98–101.
61. Benckhuysen, *Gospel According to Eve*, 154–65.
62. Benckhuysen, *Gospel According to Eve*, 177–99.
63. Benckhuysen, *Gospel According to Eve*, 137, 140, 182.
64. There were 80 WCTU "unions" in Victoria alone in 1892. Reported in *Australian Star*, June 1892.

a positive view of Eve's role. Bushnell visited Australian colonies in 1892 and spoke extensively in towns and cities throughout Victoria, New South Wales, Queensland, South Australia, and Tasmania.[65] Her interpretive work on Eve reinforced her feminine sympathies for vulnerable women, those often called "damned whores."

Conclusion

The story of Eve in Australia teaches us many things. Where people have a vested interest in the power arrangements of the status quo, Scripture is often enlisted in its defense. In the fraught colonial period, ruling classes aspired to control an unruly mix of convicted men and women as well as Indigenous peoples. Biblical stories that could be used to reinforce the subject, inferior status of these groups, such as the narratives of Genesis 2 and 3, were readily employed to the task. In doing so, they drew from a long history of misogynist and racialized biblical interpretation in circulation throughout Europe and its colonies.

We have found also that when those who are affected by such readings are empowered to take up the Good Book themselves and begin to read anew, then God's revelation is extended and new horizons discovered. The "woman question" debate of the early modern period shows this process in operation. Interesting and rounded understandings of womanhood developed as a result of pro-feminist thinking about Eve. She was a seeker of knowledge who brought a wholeness to Adam. She was a revered childbearer who, through her influence on future generations, became a shaper of society. She reformed marriage to bring mutuality and partnership to patriarchal hierarchy. Australian women, like their pro-feminist forebears, enrolled themselves as "God's police," re-shaping the concept to highlight woman's wisdom, agency, and redemptive motherhood. Through all these re-imaginings of Eve's character, women negated the centuries of misogynist readings and laid claim to a consecrated life.

---

65. A survey of local newspaper reports indicates that she spoke to at least thirty-one public meetings in that period.

Bibliography

Attwood, Bain Munro. *Telling the Truth About Aboriginal History.* Crows Nest: Allen & Unwin, 2005.

Becking, Bob, and Susanne Hennecke. *Out of Paradise: Eve and Adam and Their Interpreters.* Sheffield: Sheffield Phoenix, 2011.

Benckhuysen, Amanda W. *The Gospel According to Eve: A History of Women's Interpretation.* Downers Grove, IL: IVP Academic, 2019.

Bird, Phyllis A. "To Play the Harlot: An Inquiry into an Old Testament Metaphor." In *Gender and Difference in Ancient Israel*, edited by Peggy L. Day, 76–79. Minneapolis, MN: Fortress, 1989.

Brenner, Athalya. *The Intercourse of Knowledge: On Gendering Desire and 'Sexuality' in the Hebrew Bible.* Leiden: Brill, 1997.

Brueggemann, Walter. "Of the Same Flesh and Bone, Gen 2:23a." *CBQ* 32/4 (1970) 532–42.

Bushnell, Katherine. *God's Word to Women: One Hundred Bible Studies on Woman's Place in the Divine Economy.* 4th ed. Self published, Piedmont, CA: Bushnell, 1930.

Chapman, Cynthia R. *The House of the Mother: The Social Roles of Maternal Kin in Biblical Hebrew Narrative and Poetry.* New Haven, NY: Yale University Press, 2016.

———. "The Breath of Life: Speech, Gender, and Authority in the Garden of Eden." *JBL* 138/2 (2019) 241–62.

Conor, Liz. *Skin Deep: Settler Impressions of Aboriginal Women.* Perth: UWA Publishing, 2016.

Cruickshank, Joanna, and Patricia Grimshaw. *White Women, Aboriginal Missions and Australian Settler Governments.* Leiden: Brill, 2019.

Damousi, Joy. "'Depravity and Disorder': The Sexuality of Convict Women." *Labour History* 68 (1995) 30–45.

Deutschmann, Barbara. *Creating Gender in the Garden: The Inconstant Partnership of Eve and Adam.* London: Bloomsbury T&T Clark, 2022. .

———. "One Becomes Two: The Gender Anthropology of the Eden Narrative and Its Reception Journey." PhD diss., University of Divinity, 2019

Fidlon, Paul G., and R. J. Ryan, eds. *The Journal and Letters of Lt. Ralph Clark 1787-1792.* Sydney: Australian Document Library, 1981.

Flood, John. *Representations of Eve in Antiquity and the English Middle Ages.* London: Routledge, 2011.

Greenblatt, Stephen. *The Rise and Fall of Adam and Eve: The Story That Created Us.* London: Vintage, 2017.

Grimshaw, Patricia, Marilyn Lake, Ann McGrath, and Marian Quartly. *Creating a Nation.* Melbourne: Penguin, 1994.

Hurwitz, Siegmund. *Lilith the First Eve: Historical and Psychological Aspects of the Dark Feminine.* Zurich: Daimon Verlag, 2007.

Kvam, Kristen E., Linda S. Schearing, and Valarie H. Ziegler. *Eve and Adam: Jewish, Christian, and Muslim Readings on Genesis and Gender.* Bloomington, IN: Indiana University Press, 1999.

Lake, Meredith. *The Bible in Australia: A Cultural History.* Sydney: NewSouth, 2018.

Lipka, Hilary. "The Offense, Its Consequences, and the Meaning of הנז in Leviticus 19:29." In *Sexuality and Law in the Torah*, edited by Hilary Lipka and Bruce Wells, 159–79. London: Bloomsbury T&T Clark, 2020.

Loader, William. *Making Sense of Sex: Attitudes Towards Sexuality in Early Jewish and Christian Literature*. Grand Rapids, MI: Eerdmans, 2013.

———. *Philo, Josephus, and the Testaments on Sexuality: Attitudes toward Sexuality in the Writings of Philo and Josephus and in the Testaments of the Twelve Patriarchs*. Grand Rapids, MI: Eerdmans, 2011.

McManus, Barbara. "Eve's Dowry: Genesis and the Pamphlet Controversy About Women." In *Women, Writing and the Reproduction of Culture in Tudor and Stuart Britain*, edited by M. E. Burke, J. Donawerth, L. L. Dove, and K. Nelson, 193–206. Syracuse, NY: Syracuse University Press, 2000.

Meyers, Carol. *Discovering Eve: Ancient Israelite Women in Context*. Oxford: Oxford University Press, 1988.

Moreton-Robinson, Aileen. *Talkin' Up to the White Woman: Indigenous Women and Feminism*. St Lucia: University of Queensland Press, 2000.

Morse, Holly. *Encountering Eve's Afterlives: A New Reception Critical Approach to Genesis 2–4*. Oxford: Oxford University Press, 2020.

Newman, Barbara. *Sister of Wisdom: St Hildegard's Theology of the Feminine*. Berkeley, CA: University of California Press, 1987.

Oxley, Deborah. "Female Convicts." In *Convict Workers: Reinterpreting Australia's Past*, edited by Stephen Nicholas, 85-97. Cambridge: Cambridge University Press, 1989.

Panofsky, Dora and Erwin Panofsky. *Pandora's Box: The Changing Aspects of a Mythical Symbol*. London: Routledge & Kegan Paul, 1956.

Pardes, Ilana. "Beyond Genesis 3: The Politics of Maternal Naming." In *A Feminist Companion to Genesis*, edited by Athalya Brenner, 173–93. Sheffield: Sheffield Academic, 1993.

Pattel-Gray, Anne. "The Hard Truth: White Secrets, Black Realities." *Australian Feminist Studies* 14/30 (1999) 259–66.

Phillips, John A. *Eve: The History of an Idea*. San Francisco, CA: Harper & Row, 1984.

Phipps, William E. *Genesis and Gender: Biblical Myths of Sexuality and Their Cultural Impact*. New York: Praeger, 1989.

de Pizan, Christine. *The Book of the City of Ladies*. Translated by Rosalind Brown-Grant. London: Penguin, 1999.

Reuling, Hanneke. *After Eden: Church Fathers and Rabbis on Genesis 3:16–21*. Leiden: Brill, 2006.

Robson, Leslie Lloyd. *The Convict Settlers of Australia*. Melbourne: Melbourne University Press, 1970.

Runia, David T. *Philo in Early Christian Literature: A Survey*. Minneapolis, MN: Fortress, 1993.

Schüngel-Straumann, Helen. "From Androcentric to Christian Feminist Exegesis: Genesis 1–3." In *Feminist Biblical Studies in the Twentieth Century: Scholarship and Movement*, edited by Elisabeth Schüssler Fiorenza, 123–44. Atlanta, GA: SBL, 2014.

Solevåg, Anna Rebecca. *Birthing Salvation: Gender and Class in Early Christian Childbearing Discourse*. Leiden: Brill, 2013.

Sturma, Michael. "Eye of the Beholder: The Stereotype of Women Convicts, 1788–1852." *Labour History* 34 (1978) 3–10.

Summers, Anne. *Damned Whores and God's Police*. Ringwood: Penguin, 1975.

"Money Made Us"
Reading Australia Through Jesus' Teachings on Money

Jonathan Cornford

From very early on, Australian settler colonists joined the most affluent peoples on Earth, a position retained to the present day. Indeed, Australian prosperity has been central to Australian identity since white settlement. Donald Horne, who coined the (originally derisive) term "the lucky country," considered Australia one of the most "economic" nations in the world. His 1976 book, *Money Made Us*, is less an economic history than an inquiry into how Australians see themselves. Explaining that, "Nations exist in the mind," Horne argues that the "worship of economic development," along with Britishness, Christianity, and Whiteness, has been a central and continuous thread of the complex chimera we call "Australian national identity."[1] All but one of Horne's four threads of national identity have since begun to unravel; only the worship of economic development remains.[2] Horne, thoroughly post-Christian himself, had little interest in the relationship between Australia's economic drive and its proclaimed faith. It is, however, a striking paradox of history that Australian colonists, for the most part, claimed allegiance to a religious text that, in many ways, *opposed* their economic vision. Indeed, the depth of this paradox might be measured by

---

1. Horne, *Money Made Us*, 16.

2. Although some voices still protest that Britishness, Christianity, Whiteness, or all three, should continue to be central to Australian identity, their need to protest suggests that they no longer represent the main current of Australian cultural and intellectual life.

the extent to which this last sentence sounds blasphemous to contemporary Australian Christians.

This thesis is admittedly contentious. Reading history and reading the Bible are both interpretive exercises. It is my intention to propose in broad brushstrokes the outline of an alternative narrative of Australian history, hitherto under-recognized, without debating all the complexities and contestations that such claims bring to the fore.

In this chapter I attempt to do three things: (i) explore the radical disjuncture between the economic visions that have shaped Australia and the economic visions affirmed by the Bible, to which, until relatively recently, most Australians attributed a degree of moral authority; (ii) demonstrate and, to some extent, explain the general failure of Australian Christianity to recognize or to come to terms with this disjuncture; and (iii) consider how the social, political, and ecological outcomes of twenty-first century Australia bear out, in a negative sense, the economic wisdom of the Bible.

As a descendant of British colonists who first emigrated in the 1850s, I approach this task, like so many Australians, as someone trying to make moral sense of the home they love, but whose existence as a nation is morally fraught. My sense of the acuteness of this moral dilemma is rooted in my reading of the Bible. The Bible is a complex assemblage of literature, written, compiled, and edited over a period of centuries. Contrary to more skeptical scholars, I approach it with the unfashionable conviction that the complexity of the Bible does not prevent a coherent moral ethic from being discerned in its pages and across its narrative arc, and that there are more and less authentic hermeneutics that can be brought to the text.[3] Such a conviction may not interest some readers, except that it bears a kinship to the conviction of many of the colonists who came here in the century after 1788. I hope to show that continuing to read the Bible in this country can, and should, contribute to "the unsettling of Australia."[4]

Australian Settler Colonization in a World Economy, 1788–1901

The immediate impetus for British colonization of Australia was primarily geopolitical (to head off French acquisition of the continent) and social (to alleviate the extreme pressure on Britain's prisons) rather than "economic." Britain's geopolitical and social objectives were themselves, however, requirements of its remarkable and expanding imperial economy: British

---

3. I describe my approach to interpreting the economic ethics of the Bible more fully in Cornford, *Coming Home*.

4. I am borrowing and adapting the thought behind Berry's, *Unsettling of America*.

competition with France was economic to the core;[5] its harsh penal system was a product and reflection of the intensifying social dislocations that characterized Britain's rising commercial (soon to be industrial) economy.[6] In a broader historical perspective, the existence of Australia as a modern nation founded by Europeans is a product of the dramatic material expansion of the European world-economy under the tutelage of British hegemony. In this regard, the settler colonization of Australia must be read from the same page of world economic history as the subjection of the Indian sub-continent by the East India Company, the Industrial Revolution, and the Opium Wars.[7]

To put it another way, Australia is an outgrowth of world capitalism. "Capitalism" is a contentious term. I use it here to describe an economic system that arose in Europe towards the close of the Middle Ages and has since come to dominate the globe.[8] The capitalist world-economy is an internationalized economic system competitively structured towards endless accumulation and expansion that externalizes or socializes the costs of its expansion.[9] Colonized in response to the competitive signals and incentives of this system, Australia's social and economic history has been tightly linked to the fluctuations of the international economy ever since.

Despite a shaky start, Australian settler colonialism was remarkably prosperous.[10] Australian incomes (GDP per capita) were the highest in the world from the mid-nineteenth century until around 1900 and have remained amongst the highest in the world since then.[11]

Australian prosperity is built upon the almost complete dispossession of the continent's Indigenous peoples. The grabbing of a whole continent by Europeans within the space of a century is *the* central fact that establishes Australia as a modern nation. This dark and tragic fact is irrefutable yet continues to be veiled in accounts of Australian prosperity. Ian McLean, for example, in his otherwise insightful economic history, *Why Australia Prospered*, attributes Australian prosperity to natural resource wealth without using the terms "dispossession," "land grab," or "theft."[12]

5. See, for example, Wallerstein, *Modern World-System II*, chapter 6.
6. See, for example, Hammond and Hammond, *Village Labourer*.
7. Arrighi, *Long Twentieth Century*, chapter 3.
8. See Kocka, *Capitalism: A Short History*.
9. Wallerstein, *Historical Capitalism*; Arrighi, *Long Twentieth Century*.
10. This was a feature of Anglophone settler colonialism as a whole. See Belich, *Replenishing the Earth*, 85.
11. McLean, *Why Australia Prospered*, 1.
12. McLean, *Why Australia Prospered*, 1.

Following colonization, the first century of Australian settler history is characterized by a series of rushes that Horne, not unfairly, describes as little more than a process of "looting."[13] The first of these was a rush for seal skins on the southern Australian and Tasmanian coasts and the Bass Strait islands. Responding to export demand from China, men with clubs set about annihilating Australia's massive seal colonies, rendering them almost extinct within an alarmingly short time. Whaling, timber, pastoral, gold, selection, and, finally, cropping and irrigation rushes followed in rapid succession. As Belich observes, similar patterns of plundering occurred throughout the nineteenth-century Anglo settler world: "the conviction that nature's bounty was inexhaustible . . . transcended the evidence."[14]

These rushes left a dramatic legacy in the landscape and ecology of the nation and on Australian conceptions of land, nature, economy, and place. They were all rushes to seize natural resources perceived to be there for the taking.[15] This set up the violent and wholesale dispossession of the peoples who stewarded and depended upon these resources. A sense of a God-given entitlement to plunder is evident in the righteous indignation and violent fury with which colonists often responded to Aboriginal resistance. Australian colonists saw the landscape through financial eyes with a view to returns that could be extracted in the short to medium term.[16]

The first phases of the various rushes were characterized by the crudest technologies and methods available: clubs, axes, men with guns moving mobs of sheep onto land, shovels, picks, and pans. Australia's pastoral rush coincided with England's celebrated agrarian revolution, a revolution that deployed organic methods of boosting and protecting the ecological productivity of soils. Despite this, Australian squatters, mostly men of education and capital, disregarded everything that had been learnt about agricultural improvement and knowingly overgrazed native grasses and fragile soils, all but destroying them, before moving their flocks on to the next run.[17] Some pastoralists in the 1840s took 100 percent returns on their investments every two-and-a-half years.[18]

Australian rushes for natural resources all responded to demand signals from a world market and the promise of windfall gains. The nascent

13. Here and following, Horne, *Money Made Us*, 24–42.
14. Belich, *Replenishing the Earth*, 204.
15. Horne, *Money Made Us*; McLean, *Why Australia Prospered*, 5.
16. I do not describe the colonialists as seeing the landscape through "economic eyes" because "economy" properly understood implies long-term management and stewardship.
17. Horne, *Money Made Us*, 27; Dingle, *Settling*, 23–26.
18. Broome, "Changing Aboriginal landscapes," 91.

colonies' domestic demand would have been unlikely to generate the rushes' frenzied character. The prodigious prosperity that settler Australia was establishing by the mid-nineteenth century was built on selling prodigious quantities of seal skin, cedar, wool, and gold overseas. This established the character of the Australian economy as an extractive economy servicing a world market.[19]

As histories of the gold rush demonstrate, the nature of the "rush" resembled a remarkable outbreak of mass fever.[20] Many of those who joined the gold rush made irrational and destructive choices, often sacrificing wives and children to the quest for gold. "Gold fever" was a kind of madness brought on by the promise of windfall riches—the dream of gold. Although most acute in the gold rush, this "fever" can be detected in other rushes as well.

The gold rush was remarkable in that it manifested a more democratic form of greed that gripped people across social and economic classes (in contrast to the greed of mill owners in "the old country" and the greed of the squattocracy in the new). Indeed, the combination of capitalist ambition alongside a strong vein of social democracy is a curious feature of Australian social and economic history. Influenced by Chartism[21] and trade unionism, many of those who came to Australia in the gold rush called for democratic government *and* economic justice.[22]

Labor movements flourished in the Australian colonies. Newly federated Australia became the world's first nation to elect a Labor Prime Minister.[23] The labor movements articulated the high ideals of a commonwealth shaped by justice and equal human dignity.[24] These ideals were, however, freighted with avarice. The Australian labor movement envisaged the commonwealth of equal human dignity as a commonwealth of whites. It grew

---

19. McLean, *Why Australia Prospered*, 18–19; Dingle, *Settling*, 23; Horne, *Money Made Us*, 24–26.

20. Broome *Arriving*, 67, subtitles a chapter on the gold rushes, "A Madness Descends." Belich, *Replenishing the Earth*, 200–206, documents how contemporaries used terms such as "fever," "madness," and "frenzy" to describe settler booms and rushes.

21. A British working-class movement in the 1830s and 40s seeking political enfranchisement.

22. Dingle, *Settling*, 58–60; McMichael, *Settlers and the Agrarian Question*, 208–10. Beyond movements for social democracy, there are many ways we could explore deviations from, or counter-currents to, the dominant capitalist mentality in Australia by, for example, paying special attention to gender and to ethnic and religious minority communities.

23. Andrew Fisher, Prime Minister of Australia (1908–1915).

24. Here and following, Buckley and Wheelwright, *No Paradise for Workers*, 147–53; Gollan, *Radical and Working Class Politics*, chapters 1 and 7.

in response to perceived wage competition from non-whites as much as it did in response to the depredations of employers. Prosperity was to be built upon tightly defined exclusions. Moreover, the labor movement shared the early colonists' vision of extracting wealth from the land.

The nation of modern Australia was foundationally shaped by the quest for wealth. At its best, this was a quest for an affluent social commonwealth. Nevertheless, it was a quest purchased by violence (to the land and Indigenous peoples) and by exclusion (of non-whites).

And yet, many of the first pastoralists who sat on their horses, toting a bevy of guns, pushing vast flocks of sheep out into the continent's expansive grasslands, and many of the diggers who tramped up the Mount Alexander Road to join the throng lugging pick and pan, each dreaming of new worlds of opportunity to be opened up by windfall riches, carried a book in their packs. This was a book whose moral authority was almost universally accepted by the colonists.[25] It was also a book that warned against economic visions of the sort stirring Australian colonists.

Biblical Visions of Economic Commonwealth

The Bible, in both its Hebrew and Christian Scriptures, recounts stories of the engagement of Israel's God, "the God of Abraham, Isaac and Jacob," and the people called and gathered in worship of Israel's God, "the people of God." From the creation stories of Genesis through to the final apocalyptic visions of Revelation, a recurrent and central thread of these stories is the concern to articulate a mode of economic life appropriate to the proper worship of Israel's God. Here I focus attention on the economic worldview inherent in the *Torah* (the Books of the Law in the Old Testament) and in Jesus' teachings about money in the New Testament. Not only do these texts provide striking examples of the gulf between biblical and colonial worldviews, they also, arguably, play a critical role in delimiting an economic hermeneutic of the Christian Bible.

Before unpacking this theme we must address the elephant in the room. The Bible contains narratives that portray Ancient Israel as divinely mandated to conquer and dispossess other peoples.[26] The question of how we should understand the dispossession mandates of the Hebrew Bible has

---

25. Meredith Lake demonstrates that whether one professed Christian faith or not, the moral authority of the Bible within colonial society, whether as a theological or cultural text, could not be evaded. Meredith Lake, *Bible in Australia*, 1–15.

26. For example, Deuteronomy 7:1–6; 9:1–3.

been addressed by others and will not be examined here.[27] For our purposes, it is sufficient to acknowledge that biblical exodus and conquest narratives were used to construct an all-too-easy biblical justification for the conquest of Aboriginal lands by Australian colonists. As I shall demonstrate, such a use of biblical texts resulted from a profound disjuncture in the ways Western Christians read their Scriptures.

In order to appreciate the enormity of this disjuncture, we need to investigate the ways in which the writings later collated into "the Bible" were understood in the ancient Mediterranean worlds from which they emerged. These writings, produced by peoples who were marginal to, and oppressed by, the ancient empires of Egypt, Assyria, Babylonia, Macedonia, and Rome, stand as a remarkable manifesto of an alternative vision of human civilization. Although the meaning and interpretation of these writings is contested, the following outline is consistent with understandings of the Bible that were widely attested by Jews and early Christians (the earliest Christians were nearly all Jews), and that continued to be attested by parts of the Christian church for much of its two-thousand-year history.

The biblical canon opens with two narrative poems that establish the place of humankind within creation (Gen 1:1–2:4; 2:4–25). Influenced by the Enlightenment and capitalism, modern western readers have generally overlooked the ecological dimensions and implications of Genesis 1 and 2. Contrary to Lynn White's oft-repeated claim that these creation stories "established a dualism of man and nature [and] insisted that it is God's will that man exploit nature for his proper ends,"[28] these texts place humanity, a creature amongst creatures, within a wondrous creation.

Genesis 1:1–2:4 was likely written during, or soon after, the period of exile of Jerusalem's leaders to Babylon following the traumatic destruction of Jerusalem and its temple (587 BCE). Read in this context, Genesis 1 presents as a striking counter-myth to the Babylonian creation narrative, the *Enuma Elish*. Whereas the *Enuma Elish* sees the world created out of the blood and gore of matricidal conflict between the gods, Genesis 1 praises the creation of the world by a good God's intention, telling us seven times that what God created was "good" in God's eyes (1:4, 10, 12, 18, 21, 25), seven being the number of completion. Whereas the *Enuma Elish* explains that humans are slaves to the gods destined to serve the gods' divine representative on earth, the Babylonian king, Genesis maintains that every human being—male *and* female—bears the image of God (1:26–27). The Bible

---

27. Brett, *Decolonizing God*, for example, reviews and contests the use of the Bible to support the colonization of Australia.

28. White, "The Historical Roots of the Ecological Crisis," 1205.

thus opens with a powerful statement of the intrinsic worth of the natural world and the radical equality of all people.[29]

There is a recognition in Genesis 1 that the human creature holds a special power not shared by other creatures, hinting at the vast destructive potential so evident today. The creation narratives seek to constrain human power with *responsibility*: the "dominion" God delegates to humankind (Gen 1:26) is not a licence to dominate, as Lynn White assumes, but a vocation to serve. The second creation narrative subordinates human power to service within the whole. The human is called to "work and keep" the garden (2:15). The Hebrew verbs translated "work" and "keep" mean "work for" and "protect," "nurture," or "observe" limits.[30] The human is called to serve and observe the earth.

The call to observe limits is central to the economic vision for "the Promised Land," the divinely inspired conception of an economic commonwealth. To understand what the Promised Land represents in social and economic terms, we need to return to its foundational myth, the story of liberation from slavery in Egypt (Exod 1–16). Just as Gen 1–2:4 can be read as a counter-myth to the Babylonian *Enuma Elish*, the Promised Land can be read as a counter-vision to the economy of Egypt, an economy that produced fantastic wealth *and* fantastic inequality. Exodus portrays Egypt as the embodiment of power, technological advancement, and wealth *and* as the place that enslaves. The story of Moses' struggles with God, with Pharaoh, and with the Israelite supervisors and elders (Exod 3–11), the Passover (Exod 12), and the crossing of the Red Sea (Exod 14–15:21), is a story of salvation from an oppressive economic system that forced enslaved peoples to do bad work, under bad conditions, and afforded them no rest. Conscripted to build Pharaoh's store cities (Exod 1:11), the Israelites were enslaved to systemic accumulation.[31]

The newly liberated Israelites were given a new economy in the wilderness. The provision of manna from heaven (Exod 16) established and demonstrated "an economy of enough" founded on three core practices: (i) collect only what you need for the day (16:4); (ii) don't accumulate excess—stored manna spoils (16:20); and (iii) rest from work on the seventh (Sabbath) day (16:23). The result of the manna economy was that "the one who gathered much did not have too much, and the one who gathered little did not have too little" (16:18). Within this economic system of shared

---

29. Howard-Brook, *"Come Out My People!"* 16–21.

30. Davis, *Scripture, Culture and Agriculture*, 28–33, 53–59.

31. Myers, *Sabbath Economics*, 10–15; Davis, *Scripture, Culture and Agriculture*, 66–79.

sufficiency, accumulated wealth was useless, concentrated wealth ("too much") was impossible, work was intentionally limited, and regular shared rest was enjoyed by all.

The law (*torah*) or commandment (*mitzvah*) of the covenant (*berit*) given through Moses provided the moral vision for how the Israelites were to inhabit the Promised Land. A series of economic instructions indicate that Israel was to be a *commonwealth*—a place where wealth benefits the whole community, human *and* non-human.[32] These instructions included: (i) prohibitions on charging interest, (ii) cyclic remission of debts and liberation of slaves; (iii) periodic restoration of land to its ancestral custodians (Jubilee); and (iv) legislation concerning credit provision, work relations, animal husbandry, agricultural practices, and redistributive mechanisms. Laws limiting the extractive efficiency of agriculture, mandating fallow periods and constraining harvest practices, were intended to conserve an ecological surplus to sustain the poor, wild animals, and the soil itself. These economic provisions give substance to the Genesis commission to serve and observe the earth, respecting its limits and those of human dominion. According to both Leviticus and Deuteronomy, the ecological abundance of the Promised Land—"a land flowing with milk and honey" (Deut 6:3)—is not the Israelites' ethno-religious birthright, but it is *conditional* upon their observance of these limits. Failure to keep covenant laws and commandments will result in ecological desolation (eg. Lev 26:14–25).

Whether or not Israel ever implemented Jubilee and Sabbatical laws, our interest here is in how the *economic vision* of the Torah projects an ideal to which Israel's prophets later appeal. It is this same economic vision that is taken up by the New Testament.

The New Testament fundamentally delinks the identity of "the people of God" from ethnicity, certain aspects of Torah observance (circumcision and food taboos), and territorial nationhood, and links it instead to a common *spirit*, the Holy Spirit. Amongst other things, this fellowship of the Spirit was expressed in a scandalously multi-ethnic and economically communitarian social ethic. The new "Christian" communities continued to deeply imbibe the vision of the Jewish Scriptures *without* perceiving any mandate for conquest or dispossession *while also* exploding the Torah's particularism (a commonwealth for the children of Israel) into a universal vision (a commonwealth for all people and all creation).[33] This radical re-reading of Scripture came straight from the movement's founder, Jesus.

32. Horsley, *Covenantal Economics*, 17–49; Davis, *Scripture, Culture and Agriculture*, 101–19; Myers, *Sabbath Economics*, 10–15.

33. Here and following, Hays, *Moral Vision of the New Testament*, 306–9; Wright, *Mission of God*, 502–30.

The Gospel of Matthew portrays Jesus as the one who brings the Jewish Scriptures to their fulfillment, with the Sermon on the Mount (Matt 5–7) evoking Moses bringing the law down from Mount Sinai (Exod 19–20). At the center of this sermon, Jesus provides a model prayer, the petitions of which draw on and affirm the moral vision of the Torah. The plea that God's will "be done on earth as in heaven" (6:10) is followed by a petition alluding to the manna economy ("Give us this day our daily bread," 6:11), followed by a petition that recalls the reciprocal obligation to cancel debts ("Forgive us our debts as we forgive those indebted to us," 6:12). Jesus complements this prayer for the institution of "the kingdom of heaven" (a commonwealth) with a stern warning about the perils of accumulation ("Do not store up for yourselves treasure on earth," 6:19), an encouragement to observe the economy of nature ("consider the lilies of the field," 6:28), and a reminder that one's own welfare is dependent on the flourishing of the common welfare ("strive first for the kingdom of God and his righteousness/justice," 6:33).[34]

The Gospel of Luke portrays Jesus as the climax in the salvation history of Israel in which God's self-revealing work is extended to all humanity. The Lukan Jesus announces his purpose by reading the prophet Isaiah: "The Spirit of the Lord is upon me, because he has anointed me to bring good news to the poor . . . to let the oppressed go free . . . to proclaim the year of the Lord's favour" (4:18–19 citing Isa 61:1–2; 58:6). In this last statement, Jesus, following Isaiah, invokes the Jubilee tradition of land restoration in Leviticus 25. In what follows, Luke presents a cascade of teachings about money and possessions in which the consistent theme is the lifting up of the poor and the bringing down of the rich.[35] Such texts presented a profound challenge to a world in which wealth was honored and injustice normalized.[36]

Two sayings of Jesus highlight the immensity of the gap between the economic vision of the New Testament and the Christianity of Australian colonists. (1). "You cannot serve both God and Mammon" (Matt 6:24; Luke 16:3). Jesus personifies money (Mammon) to place it in direct and absolute opposition to God. Mammon is not merely an idol (an object of false worship) but a *spiritual force*. The apostle Paul means something similar by "the ruler of the power of the air" (Eph 2:2), pointing to a powerful and pervasive spiritual/intellectual/cultural climate that directs and constrains

---

34. Horsley, *Covenantal Economics*, 99–114; Myers, *Sabbath Economics*, 20–24.

35. A table listing the Lukan teachings on money and wealth can be found in Cornford, *Coming Home*, 164–65.

36. Yoder, *Politics of Jesus*, 60–75; Myers, *Sabbath Economics*, 20–24, 36–39.

the possibilities of human thought, imagination, and action in ultimately self-destructive patterns.[37]

(2). "How hard it will be for those who have wealth to enter the kingdom of God" (Matt 19:23; Mark 10:23; Luke 18:24). Mark recounts the social shock this statement provokes, the disciples are "perplexed" and "astounded" (10:24, 26), but Jesus goes on to amplify the impact of his words: "It is easier for a camel to go through the eye of a needle than for the rich to enter the kingdom of God"(Mark 10:24; Luke 18:25; Matt 19:24). These sayings are not atypical. Virtually all of Jesus' sayings and actions in relation to money and wealth warn of their destructive potential and/or advise their relinquishment.[38]

The tenor of teaching about money and wealth continues throughout the New Testament.[39] Since space precludes even the briefest review, I draw attention only to how 1 Tim 6:9–10 reads like a commentary on the sayings of Jesus discussed above:

> Those who want to be rich fall into temptation and are trapped by many senseless and harmful desires that plunge people into ruin and destruction. For the love of money is a root of all kinds of evil, and in their eagerness to be rich some have wandered away from the faith and pierced themselves with many pains.

The Capitalist Accommodation of Australian Christianity

How might we reconcile the faith whose founder taught "Do not store up treasures for yourself on earth" and "You cannot serve God and Mammon" with an economic system characterized by the pursuit of, and endless accumulation of, wealth? How might we explain such a radical disjuncture between the Gospels' teaching on money and possessions and the outlook of many "Bible-believing" Australian colonists?

In foregrounding "the capitalist accommodation of Australian Christianity," I am drawing attention to an under-recognized strand within the complex constellation of factors shaping Christian belief and action in Australia. However, as we shall see, this accommodation was neither unique to Australian Christianity nor universal within it.

---

37. Wink, *Naming the Powers*, 83; Ellul, *Money and Power*, 75–77.
38. Ellul, *Money and Power*, 73–99; Collins, *Wealth, Wages and the Wealthy*, xv–xix.
39. Collins, *Wealth, Wages and the Wealthy*, 287–306.

The accommodation of capitalism within European Christianity began before the First Fleet set sail.[40] The adoption of Christianity as the official religion of the Roman Empire in the fourth century CE began the process by which Christianity became the scaffolding for the creation of European civilization: "Christendom." It also marked the effective abandonment of both the non-violence and the economic vision and practice of Jesus and the early church. The disjuncture between Australian religionists and their Scriptures began deep in history: whatever the personal convictions or denominational allegiances of Australian colonists, virtually all came as bearers of something that can be called "Christian civilization" which was never straightforwardly Christian.[41]

Nevertheless, despite the opulence of bishops and popes and their defence of feudal subjugation, the mediaeval church did not deny that the Christian Scriptures condemned "avarice" (the pursuit of wealth). Commenting on this contradiction, the economic historian R. H. Tawney wrote:

> If it is proper to insist on the prevalence of avarice and greed in high places [within Mediaeval society], it is not less proper to observe that men called these vices by their right names, and had not learned to persuade themselves that greed was enterprise and avarice economy.[42]

Not until after the Reformation did Christians adopt that hermeneutic trick.

The thesis that Protestantism gave birth to capitalism has been attributed to Max Weber. Although Weber's thesis was considerably more sophisticated, he did argue for a certain affinity between the psychological dispositions of Calvinism and the irrational rationalism demanded by capitalist enterprise.[43] Tawney made a stronger historical case in *Religion and the Rise of Capitalism*.[44] His intent therein was not to explain the rise of capitalism, but to describe the ways in which capitalism *changed Christianity*. As Tawney demonstrated, the religious individualism unleashed by the Reformation was transmuted, against the intentions of the Reformers, and

---

40. Indeed, attempts to reconcile the gospel of Christ with the religion of wealth took a more virulent form amongst North American Puritan colonists whose the quest for "a beloved community" assumed the form of a capitalist enterprise. See McCarraher, *Enchantments of Mammon*, 247–52.

41. Piggin and Linder, *Fountain of Public Prosperity*, 34, 258.

42. Tawney, *Religion and the Rise of Capitalism*, 72.

43. Weber, *Protestant Ethic and the Spirit of Capitalism*, 49: "[W]e have no intention whatever of maintaining such a foolish and doctrinaire thesis as that the spirit of capitalism could only have arisen as the result of certain effects of the Reformation, or even that capitalism as an economic system is a creation of the Reformation."

44. Tawney, *Religion and the Rise of Capitalism*.

through the pressure of events and economic change over a couple of centuries, into a possessive individualism shorn of social solidarity. Identifying an irreconcilable conflict between the economic ethics of Christianity and those of capitalism, Tawney set out to demonstrate how Christianity's accommodation to capitalism had evacuated its economic ethics. As he wrote elsewhere, "What was Christian in Christianity had largely disappeared."[45]

The sundering of Christian faith and economic ethics was long-established by the time Britain colonized Australia. It is not that the colonists were not religious—recent historians have demonstrated that they were—but rather that British Christianity had become secularized.[46] Disenchanted of spiritual potency, the "secular" cosmos was filled with a "capitalist enchantment," a glittering quest for prosperity animated by a divine call to conquer nature and transform raw materials into property and commodities to develop a glorious technological civilization.[47] Where societies failed in this quest, the divine willed that they be replaced—such was the moral ordering of "Progress." The "cultural Bible" (as Meredith Lake has called it) was used to clothe the modern quest for prosperity and progress in "Christianity."

This does not mean that the formation of colonial Australia was not influenced by biblical economic ethics. As in Britain, the labor movement nurtured visions of an economic commonwealth that were nurtured by the left-wing of Evangelicalism, Christian socialists, and Catholic social teaching. They also drew upon a deep well of moral economy amongst the lower classes that can be traced back through the Captain Swing rebellion of the 1830s, the Luddite revolts, the food riots of the eighteenth century, and the Diggers and Levellers of the seventeenth century, to pre-modern peasant revolts. John Ball's articulation of the lower classes' moral economic visions resonates through the centuries: "When Adam delved and Eve span, who was then the gentleman?"[48] As Tawney observed, "It was not the Church,

---

45. Tawney, *Acquisitive Society*, 18. Both Waterman and Oslington argue that the political economy of Adam Smith, William Paley, and Thomas Malthus was rooted in a natural theology that was a "deeply Christian enterprise" (Oslington, "Christianity's Post-Enlightenment Contribution, 62). These men were "Christian" in terms of cultural-intellectual heritage, and some of them in terms of self-identification and institutional affiliation. However, as John Milbank has pointed out, their "Christianity" was devoid of Christ. See Waterman, *Political Economy and Christian Theology*; Oslington, "Christianity's Post-Enlightenment Contribution"; Milbank, "Christianity and Late Capitalism," 38.

46. Charles Taylor understands modern secularity, not so much as a question of faith or non-faith, but as a foundational outlook that envelops all religious and moral questions. Taylor, *Secular Age*, chapter 1.

47. McCarraher, *Enchantments of Mammon*, 167–72.

48. John Ball was a leader in the Great Peasants Revolt (d.1381).

but revolting peasants in Germany and England, who appealed to the fact that 'Christ has made all men free.'[49] Nevertheless, the dreams of economic commonwealth harbored by Chartists and trade unionists in Australia departed from this older moral economy of "enough" to become one of *progressive* wealth held in exclusion of a racial "other."[50]

Piggin and Linder contend that the forward-looking reformist drive of Evangelicalism was a major factor in the "energising and civilizing of capitalism in colonial economies."[51] In Australia, Evangelicalism *energized* the pursuit of riches, coloring it with a religious hue, while also *moderating* and directing the use of wealth towards more public outcomes than in many other places. If the idea of "Australia" has a religious note, it is heard in how the interweaving of religious faith and the quest for prosperity, private or public, has produced a sense that Australian prosperity is pre-ordained. This, I suggest, is Australia's real religion. Having shed the vestments of institutional Christianity, it now manifests as a naked "growth fetish" to which all major political parties pay homage.

How Does the Bible Read Australia?

How does the Bible *read* Australia? Capitalism, as Tawney observed, "leaves a taste of ashes on the lips of civilization" even in the hour of its triumph.[52] Although Australian colonists were remarkably successful in building the prosperous democratic society they sought, that success came at a price. That price is anticipated by the wisdom of the holy book that accompanied the colonists, a wisdom that understands the natural and moral ecology upon which human societies are founded. Four outcomes of "the Australian project" validate the wisdom found in biblical moral economy. Two of these outcomes are legacies of invasion and conquest, two are legacies of the quest for prosperity. In the Hebrew Bible, "the word of the Lord" frequently comes as a word of "judgment" that unveils the moral failures which underlie social crises. To read the Bible in twenty-first-century Australia is, in many ways, to encounter such an unveiling.

---

49. Tawney, *Religion and the Rise of Capitalism*, 70.
50. Gollan, *Radical and Working Class Politics*, 86–87, 116–17.
51. Piggin and Linder, *Fountain of Public Prosperity*, 38.
52. Tawney, *Religion and the Rise of Capitalism*, 280.

First Nations Legacy

Persistent Indigenous disadvantage is an open wound in Australian national life.[53] The entrenched disadvantage of contemporary Indigenous Australians, reflected in health, education, housing, unemployment, and incarceration statistics, results in part from structural racism against people of color, from historic and ongoing policy failure at all levels of government, and also from something much deeper. The wound of Indigenous Australia in the twenty-first century is still fundamentally the wound of the original act of dispossession that was perhaps the most complete of any colonized people on earth.[54] The survival of Indigenous cultures in the face of sustained attempts to erase their ways of life—their *economies*—along with their structures of meaning, memory, relationship, law, and language, testifies to their strength.

Australia is a post-Christian nation haunted by a Christian conscience.[55] If ancient Romans, for whom conquest and brutality were central to moral order, had come to these shores, no moral ghost would have hovered behind the question of nationhood. But those who usurped the continent and committed genocide identified as Christian people. Appeals to Old Testament conquest narratives do not silence *New* Testament accounts that speak of God-in-human-form choosing to suffer rather than cause suffering, rejecting violence, and commanding the way of love. Defenses of dispossession, whether derived from Scripture or evolution, ring hollow against such a moral vision. Two centuries on, the New Testament's refusal to endorse or excuse invasion and dispossession haunts attempts to celebrate Australian nationhood. If, as Donald Horne suggests, "nations exist in the mind," then the words and life of Jesus leave the Australian mind with an existential doubt almost too terrible to utter.[56]

Ecological Legacy

Australian colonization rapidly transformed landscapes and ecologies.[57] The combined impact of grazing, clearing, farming, and mining resulted in a massive loss of topsoil, permanently changing terrestrial ecology and

---

53. See Australian Government, *Closing the Gap Report 2020*.

54. Boyce, *1835*, 204–5.

55. For an account of the enduring power of Christian ideas in post-Christian societies, see Holland, *Dominion*.

56. Horne, *Money Made Us*, 16.

57. Here and following, Charles Massy, *Call of the Reed Warbler*.

habitat, reducing fertility, and radically altering the hydrology of the continent. Whereas soft, ancient soils had stored water captured through rainfall, landscapes stripped of topsoil rapidly shed water and are prone to erosion and flash-flooding. Two centuries of European settlement significantly dried out the continent prior to any impact from global climate change. The El Niño Southern Oscillation weather system produced unreliable rainfall prior to colonization, but the radical *dryness* experienced by colonists as prolonged and severe drought was largely of their own making.

The degradation of landscapes, introduction of invasive plant and animal species, and enthusiastic hunting of native animals, combined to produce the highest mammal species extinction rate on earth. Now, as global climate change takes hold, Australia's drier and hydrophobic landscape makes it one of the most climate-vulnerable nations on earth.

The ecological vision of the Bible is resoundingly consistent. The British colonists who deployed a narrative of occupying "the Promised Land" evinced little interest in the *conditions* that the Hebrew Bible placed upon such occupation. Whereas the Hebrew Scriptures anticipate ecological desolation as an inevitable consequence of human failure to observe limits (economic *Sabbath*), the modernist capitalist European mindset mocked such outdated superstitions, abandoning the limitations and cautions of biblical wisdom. The question before us now, is whether we will observe our suffocating rivers, bleaching reefs, floods, fires, and droughts sufficiently deeply to heed the wisdom of the limits inscribed in nature, what the Bible describes as a *given order* which humans do not control and to which they must conform.

Affluenza

The achievement of national prosperity is central to Australian identity. From Federation until recently, Australian social democracy—influenced by biblical visions of economic commonwealth—was, by world standards, comparatively successful in distributing that prosperity. However, the ongoing national quest for prosperity has also paid a dark dividend, a striking social malaise that seems closely connected with the experience of affluence—"affluenza." Social analysts of various hues agree that the demands of consumer capitalist individualism have progressively unravelled the relational, social, cultural, and psychic foundations of wellbeing, all the while clothing us in an excess of food, goods, and leisure activities.[58]

---

58. See, for example, Hamilton and Dennis, *Affluenza*; Mackay, *Australia Reimagined*.

Affluenza describes a multidimensional assortment of malaises. It first became evident in the post-war years when happiness levels did not rise despite dramatic growth in real incomes, and a widely held belief that more money would make people happier. Indeed, rising incomes were correlated with a *decreased* sense of financial sufficiency.[59] More recently, rising affluence has been correlated with declining participation in community, religious, and sporting groups, high rates of primary relational breakdown and social isolation, and alarming rates of mental ill health across classes. This speaks of an unravelling of the social and relational connections foundational to wellbeing and, most alarmingly, of an unravelling taking place *within* people experiencing deep psychic and existential uncertainty.[60] As epidemiologist Fiona Stanley reminds us, individual deficiencies and pathologies do not cause epidemics of this sort:[61] affluenza is a disease rooted in the structure of Australian social life.

What is the link between affluence and this widespread social malaise? This is a difficult question for social science, and beyond the scope of this chapter. However, perhaps the ancient wisdom contained within the Bible cuts through the complexity with a truth we would sooner avoid:

> Those who want to be rich fall into temptation and are trapped by many senseless and harmful desires that plunge people into ruin and destruction. For the love of money is a root of all kinds of evil, and in their eagerness to be rich some have wandered away from the faith and pierced themselves with many pains. (1 Tim 6:9–10)

Similar folk wisdom has been shared by many cultures through the ages. Why are we Australians so reluctant to accept it?

Christianity in Crisis

Tawney lamented, "What was Christian in Christianity had largely disappeared."[62] He considered that the church's accommodation to capitalism had so hollowed out Christian faith that it was but a shell of belief. When cultural Christianity collapsed in 1960s Australia, the robustness of faith was revealed to be remarkably thin. Seven percent of Australians now consider

---

59. Layard, "Income and Happiness"; Hamilton, *Overconsumption in Australia*.
60. Mackay, *Australia Reimagined*.
61. Stanley, "Address to the National Press Club."
62. Tawney, *Acquisitive Society*, 18.

themselves "active practisers" of Christian faith.[63] Although unquantifiable, the most concerning indicator of a crisis within Australian Christianity may be the deep *uncertainty* within many congregants about the meaning of their faith in the face of twenty-first-century challenges and pressures.

Has the extent to which Australian Christianity has been bound up with the project of settler colonial capitalism, its ethics and visions of the good life, rendered it unable to speak wisely or hopefully into the existential crises of our time? If the Bible speaks a word of judgment, it is a word of judgment leveled first and foremost at those who identify as "the people of God": "For the time has come for the judgment to begin with the household of God" (1 Pet 4:17).

Coda

Donald Horne claimed that "money made us." Was he right? Jesus insisted, "You cannot serve both God and Mammon." Many of those colonists who arrived in the lands now called Australia with a Bible in their packs attempted to do just that. Seemingly deaf to Jesus' teaching on the economic dimensions of life, their pursuit of prosperity drove all before it, doing untold damage along the way. The consequences of our national obsession with money must be faced: "You reap whatever you sow" (Gal 6:7). Nevertheless, echoes of biblical visions of commonwealth are audible in those moments of Australian history when broadly communitarian consensuses were at their strongest and, despite sounding ever fainter, can still be heard if we listen deeply.

---

63. McCrindle, *Faith and Belief in Australia*, 7. The census data for affiliation with Christianity (43.9 percent in 2021) is dramatically inflated.

Bibliography

Arrighi, Giovanni. *The Long Twentieth Century: Money, Power, and the Origins of Our Times.* London: Verso, 2010.

Australian Government, Department of the Prime Minister and Cabinet, *Closing the Gap Report 2020.* Canberra: Commonwealth of Australia, 2020.

Belich, James. *Replenishing the Earth: The Settler Revolution and the Rise of the Anglo-World, 1783–1939.* Oxford: Oxford University Press, 2009.

Boyce, James. *1835: The Founding of Melbourne and the Conquest of Australia.* Melbourne: Black Inc., 2011.

Brett, Mark. *Decolonizing God: the Bible in the Tides of Empire.* Sheffield: Sheffield Phoenix, 2009.

Broome, Richard. *Arriving. The Victorians.* Sydney: Fairfax, Syme and Wheldon Associates, 1984.

———. "Changing Aboriginal landscapes of pastoral Victoria, 1830–1850." *Studies in the History of Gardens & Designed Landscapes* 31 (2011) 88–96.

Buckley, Ken, and Ted Wheelwright. *No Paradise for Workers: Capitalism and the Common People in Australia 1788–1914.* Oxford: Oxford University Press, 1988.

Cornford, Jonathan. *Coming Home: Discipleship, Ecology and Everyday Economics.* Melbourne: Morning Star, 2015.

Davis, Ellen. *Scripture, Culture, and Agriculture: An Agrarian Reading of the Bible.* Cambridge: Cambridge University Press, 2009.

Dingle, Tony. *Settling. The Victorians.* Sydney: Fairfax, Syme and Wheldon Associates, 1984.

Ellul, Jacques. *Money and Power.* Illinois: IVP, 1984.

Gollan, Robin. *Radical and Working-Class Politics: A Study of Eastern Australia, 1850–910.* Melbourne: Melbourne University Press, 1960.

Hamilton, Clive. *Overconsumption in Australia: The Rise of the Middle-Class Battler.* Canberra: The Australia Institute, 2002.

Hamilton, Clive, and Richard Dennis. *Affluenza: When Too Much Is Never Enough.* Sydney: Allen and Unwin, 2005.

Hammond, J. L., and Barbara Hammond. *The Village Labourer 1760–832: A Study in the Government of England before the Reform Bill.* New York: Augustus M. Kelley, 1917 (1967).

Hays, Richard B. *The Moral Vision of the New Testament: Community, Cross, New Creation. A Contemporary Introduction to New Testament Ethics.* San Francisco: Harper Collins, 1996.

Holland, Tom. *Dominion: The Making of the Western Mind.* London: Little Brown, 2019.

Horne, Donald. *Money Made Us.* Melbourne: Penguin, 1976.

Horsley, Richard. *Covenantal Economics: A Biblical Vision of Justice for All.* Louisville: Westminster John Knox, 2009.

Howard-Brook, Wes. *"Come Out My People!": God's Call Out of Empire in the Bible and Beyond.* Maryknoll: Orbis, 2010.

Kocka, Jurgen. *Capitalism: A Short History.* Princeton: Princeton University Press, 2016.

Lake, Meredith. *The Bible in Australia: A Cultural History.* Updated Edition. Sydney: NewSouth, 2020.

Layard, Richard. "Income and Happiness: Rethinking economic policy." In Lionel Robbins Memorial Lectures 2002/3. London School of Economics, 2003.

Mackay, Hugh. *Australia Reimagined: Towards a More Compassionate, Less Anxious Society*. Sydney: Pan Macmillan Australia, 2018.

Massy, Charles. *The Call of the Reed Warbler: A New Agriculture, A New Earth*. Brisbane: University of Queensland Press, 2017.

McCarraher, Eugene. *The Enchantments of Mammon: How Capitalism Became the Religion of Modernity*. Cambridge: Belknap, 2019.

McCrindle. *Faith and Belief in Australia: A national study on religion, spirituality and worldview trends*. Sydney: McCrindle, 2017.

McLean, Ian. *Why Australia Prospered: The Shifting Sources of Economic Growth*. Princeton: Princeton University Press, 2012.

McMichael, Philip. *Settlers and the Agrarian Question: Capitalism in Colonial Australia*. Cambridge: Cambridge University Press, 1884.

Milbank, John. "The Body By Love Possessed: Christianity and Late Capitalism in Britain." *Modern Theology* 3 (1986) 35–65.

Myers, Ched. *The Biblical Vision of Sabbath Economics*. Washington: Tell the Word, Church of the Saviour, 2002.

Oslington, Paul. "Christianity's Post-Enlightenment Contribution to Economic Thought." In *Christian Theology and Market Economics*, edited by I. R. L. Harper and S. Gregg, 60–73. Cheltenham: Edward Elgar, 2008.

Piggin, Stuart, and Robert Dean Linder. *The Fountain of Public Prosperity: Evangelical Christians in Australian History, 1740–914*. Melbourne: Monash University Publishing, 2018.

Stanley, Fiona. "Address to the National Press Club." Canberra, 6 August 2003.

Tawney, R. H. *The Acquisitive Society*. Brighton: Wheatsheaf, 1921.

———. *Religion and the Rise of Capitalism*. London: Verso, 1926 (1938).

Wallerstein, Immanuel. *Historical Capitalism*. London: Verso, 2014.

———. *The Modern World-System II: Mercantilism and the Consolidation of the European World-Economy, 1600–1750*. New York: Academic, 1980.

Waterman, Anthony. *Political Economy and Christian Theology Since the Enlightenment: Essays in Intellectual History*. London: Palgrave Macmillan, 2004.

Weber, Max. *The Protestant Ethic and the Spirit of Capitalism*. New York: Taylor & Francis, 2005.

White, Lynn. "The Historical Roots of the Ecological Crisis." *Science* 155/3766 (1967) 1203–7.

Wink, Walter. *Naming the Powers: The Language of Power in the New Testament*. Philadelphia: Fortress, 1984.

Wright, Christopher J. *The Mission of God: Unlocking the Bible's Grand Narrative*. Downers Grove: IVP Academic, 2006.

Wright, N. T. *The New Testament and the People of God: Christian Origins and the Question of God*. London: SPCK, 2013.

Yoder, John Howard. *The Politics of Jesus*. Grand Rapids: Eerdmans, 1972.

"The Rust in the Wheat and the Dearth of the Dry Season"

Ned Kelly's Victorian Apocalypse

Glen O'Brien

Ned Kelly (1854–1880) may seem an unlikely subject through which to elucidate Australia's religious history. As an Irish Catholic living in colonial Victoria, he can be situated within the well-known theme of the "sectarian strand" which has seen Australian religious history primarily through the lens of conflict between Catholic and Protestant churches.[1] Beyond this, however, Kelly exhibited genuinely religious instincts at key points in his life, so that, while his life cannot be read as a saint's life, it can certainly be read as a Christian life.[2] Born in December 1854, in the shadow of an extinct volcano, Mt. Fraser, which overlooked the Victorian town of Beveridge, Kelly was baptized by Father Charles O'Hea. Father O'Hea would reappear at key points in Kelly's life, including during imprisonment in Pentridge in 1873 and at his execution in 1880. In the account he gave of his arrest for riotous behavior in Beechworth, in September 1877, Kelly expressed a sense of divine providence determining the boundaries of his life. Constable Thomas Lonigan "caught me by the privates and would have sent me to Kingdom

---

1. Hogan, *Sectarian Strand*.

2. The literature on Kelly is voluminous and continues to expand. Important works include Jones, *Ned Kelly*; McQuilton, *The Kelly Outbreak*; Clune, *The Kelly Hunters*; Corfield, *The Ned Kelly Encyclopedia*. The general trend in revisionist histories in recent decades has been to challenge earlier heroic accounts and rehabilitate the role of the police. These include Dufty, *Nabbing Ned Kelly,* and Kennedy, *Black Snake*. For the religious dimensions of Kelly's life, see O'Brien, "Seeing the Clouds through the Aperture of the Helmet" and "Have Pity on an Intelligent Young Man in an Awful Position."

come only I was not ready. . ."³ The phrase, "I was not ready" suggests that Kelly considered himself immortal until God decided otherwise. Lonigan would die at Stringybark Creek by Kelly's hand two years later.

As Kelly lay wounded in the station master's office after the Glenrowan siege of June 1880, he asked Dean Matthew Gibney to administer last rites. There followed an hour-long conversation including the hearing of confession. Gibney urged Kelly, "My son, say 'Oh, Jesus have mercy on me', and pray for forgiveness," to which Kelly responded that he had long since prayed such words. Gibney was struck by Kelly's calm frame of mind and even drew a reference to the Passion of Christ, observing the wounds in the outlaw's hands and feet.[4] This Catholic encounter is matched by an equally compelling Protestant one, in the death row visits to Kelly undertaken by the Wesleyan preacher, John Cowley Coles, in September and October of that year.[5] After hearing Coles preach in the prison chapel, Kelly told him, "I have heard all that you said this morning . . . I believe it all. Although I have been bushranging I have always believed that when I die I have a God to meet . . . When I was in the bank at Jerilderie, taking the money, the thought came into my mind, if I am shot down this moment how can I meet God?"[6] Coles and Kelly then knelt together and prayed, Kelly crossing himself and thanking the preacher for his ministry. As he stood before Judge Redmond Barry to receive his sentence in October 1880, Kelly assured the judge that he was ready to stand before a higher court, one to which Barry would also have to give an account.[7]

Each of these incidents demonstrate the religious instincts of Kelly at key moments in his life. What little education he received he received from the church and its book, which together (along with his solidarity with the oppressed Irish) formed part of the social imaginary he inhabited and informed his attitudes and actions.[8] His moral conscience was shaped by

3. Kelly, *Jerilderie Letter*, 48–49.

4. Jones, *Ned Kelly*, 327. Deborah Bird Rose argued in a 1994 article that Indigenous stories of Ned Kelly formed part of Aboriginal peoples' "search for a moral European" and suggests the possibility that through an awareness of these stories, "coloniser and colonised [might] share a moral history and thus fashion a just society." Rose, "Ned Kelly Died for Our Sins."

5. Coles, *Life and Christian Experience*, 136–38. Another Protestant who claims to have visited Kelly in prison was the medical doctor and philanthropist, John Singleton (1808–1891), one of the founders of the Melbourne City Mission. See Lynn and Armstrong, *From Pentonville to Pentridge*, 97, cited in Piggin and Linder, *The Fountain of Public Prosperity*, 383.

6. Coles, *Life and Christian Experience*, entry for 20 October 1880, 137.

7. Hirst, *The Australians*, 31–33.

8. The term "social imaginary" is drawn from the work of Charles Taylor who

an awareness of the existence of an afterlife, accountability toward God as judge, and an acute sense of the plight of the poor suffering under corrupt authority. While imprisoned at Pentridge in 1873, Kelly was given a hood to wear (possibly as a punitive measure), with two slits for the eyes, through which he gazed out at the exercise yard and the walls that confined him. Seven years later, at Glenrowan, he would gaze out through the aperture of an iron helmet, once again confined by an inescapable fate that not even his flash outlawry and dramatic cosplay could prevent. Sidney Nolan was interested in painting Ned Kelly in such a way that "the clouds could be seen through the aperture of the helmet." How was the world that Kelly saw through that aperture shaped by his reading of the Bible? It is impossible to know with any certainty, but this chapter will identify echoes of biblical themes in Ned Kelly's *Jerilderie Letter* of 1879. It will argue that Kelly was buoyed up by his success as a bandit to the point where he took the posture, not of a republican revolutionary, but of a divine Avenger announcing an impending apocalypse for colonial powers who resisted his right to roam the country and redistribute its wealth at his own whim. Without any sophisticated interpretive skills or theological education such a stance was nonetheless informed by Kelly's Christian faith and reading of the Bible.

Kelly's Catholic Bible

Kelly had limited formal education but was a person of quick intellect who enjoyed reading. Scots-Baptist James Ingram's bookstore would become one of Ned's favorite haunts in Beechworth.[9] While an inmate at Pentridge prison, Kelly read the Douay (Douay-Rheims) Bible, in the pastoral care of prison chaplain Charles O'Hea who had baptized both Ned and Dan Kelly.[10] This translation of the Bible was officially recognized by the Roman Catholic Church but not by Protestants. It served as a cultural marker between the Catholic Irish and their Protestant neighbors who, if they read the Bible at all, would have read the Authorized (King James) Version of 1611.[11] According to Ian Jones, O'Hea was "the greatest single influence on Kelly in his

---

defined it as referring to "the ways people imagine their social existence, how they fit together with others, how things go on between them and their fellow, the expectations that are normally met, and the deeper normative notions and images that underlie their expectations." See Taylor, *Modern Social Imaginaries*, 23.

9. Jones, *Ned Kelly*, 102.

10. Jones, *Ned Kelly*, 91.

11. The KJV New Testament would be revised for the first time in 1881, a year after Kelly's execution.

convict years."[12] O'Hea would later accompany Kelly to the gallows, indicating the cradle-to-the-grave role that the Catholic Church had in Kelly's life.

The Douay-Rheims Bible was an English translation of the Latin Vulgate whose New Testament portion first appeared in 1582, with the Old Testament completed by 1610.[13] It is named after the English College at Douai founded by William Allen (1532–1594) in Flanders which was relocated to Rheims in 1578 and then finally returned to Douai in 1593, hence the persistent hyphenation.[14] The idea behind the college was to train English speaking Catholic missionaries who would return to England in hopes of its reconversion. The translation team at Rheims was led by Gregory Martin (1542–1582), formerly of St John's College, Oxford, at the rate of two chapters a day. In that the Douay Bible relied on the Latin and not the original Greek and Hebrew it stands in the tradition of Wycliff rather than the Protestant tradition of Tyndale which privileged the original languages.[15] It included the Apocryphal books which the KJV omitted, and which most Protestants rejected, though the Church of England assigned them a deutero-canonical status, which saw them declared profitable and approved for public reading, but not for establishing doctrine.[16]

The English Catholic Bishop, Richard Challoner produced a revision between 1749 and 1752 which relied on the King James Version and removed the many Latinisms that had been rendered unintelligible by the earlier overly literal translation. Even then, this translation was at times impenetrable, especially the Psalms, which did not rely on Jerome's Vulgate but on the Greek Septuagint and the Gallican Psalter. F. F. Bruce discusses several of the oddities of translation.[17] As one example, consider the Douay-Rheims rendering of Psalm 67:13 (68:12 in Protestant Bibles), "The king of hostes, the beloved of the beloved; and to the beauty of the house, to divide the spoils." Challoner rendered this in a manner that only marginally improved its readability, "The king of powers is of the beloved; and the beauty of the house shall divide spoils." The Authorized Version of 1611, relying on the Hebrew text, rendered the verse, "Kings of armies did flee apace, and she that tarries at home divided the spoils."

12. Jones, *Ned Kelly*, 91.
13. "Douai" is a variant spelling.
14. Allen was a fellow of Oriel College, Oxford, who later became a cardinal.
15. Bruce, *History of the Bible in English*, 113.
16. See Article 6 of The Thirty-Nine Articles (1571), in Bray, *Documents of the English Reformation*, 288.
17. Bruce, *History of the Bible in English*, 116–17.

Certain Latinisms convey to today's reader a suggestion of Catholic theological terms. For example, in Matthew's version of the Lord's Prayer (Matt 6:9–13) we are asked to pray, not for our "daily" but for our "supersubstantial" bread, and the Good Samaritan tells the innkeeper that he will repay him "whatsoever thou shalt supererogate." This simply takes the Latin verb straightforwardly into English but might raise for a Protestant reader the specter of the doctrine of supererogation whereby the devout Christian does more than is required by God in order to gain additional merit. Both John the Baptist and Jesus call upon their hearers not to "repent" but to "doe penance" (Matt 3:2; 4:17) and when Jesus prays in Gethsemane, he asks for "this chalice" to pass (Matt 26:39). Paul and Barnabas "ordain priests" in Acts 14:23, though, interestingly, 1 Pet 5:1 urges respect for "seniors" rather than "presbyters" or "elders."

Challoner's New Testament text was revised by the Irish Catholic priest, Bernard MacMahon (c.1736–1816) in Dublin editions between 1783 and 1810, and these formed the basis of most nineteenth-century editions. From the 1830s, editions of the Douay-Rheims Bible were distributed from parish offices and bookshops in the Australian colonies. These included warnings about the heretical views to be found in non-Catholic versions of the Bible.[18] It is likely to have been one of these editions that Kelly encountered at Pentridge. Of course, it is impossible to know what passages he might have read, much less what he made of them. The Douay-Rheims Bible was a product of the Catholic Reformation produced at a time when English Catholics lived a clandestine existence under a Protestant hegemony. It remained part of that social imaginary which continued to operate among Irish Catholics in colonial Victoria where, if not illegal, they remained part of a despised underclass. At the time Kelly was reading the Bible in Pentridge in 1873, Catholics were embroiled in disputes with Protestants over the Bible in schools brought on by the Education Act of 1872.[19] Archbishop Roger Vaughan (1834–1883) positioned the secular education system in Australia as part of a global conspiracy against the Catholic faith. "If we take the papal Chair as a center, and cast our eyes around the world, we shall find that the Catholic Church is engaged in almost every country in a heavy conflict with her enemies."[20]

Patrick O'Farrell highlighted how such attitudes were deeply rooted in the history of English-Irish relations, and often justified the colonial

---

18. Lake, *Bible in Australia*, 117.
19. Bourke, *History of the Catholic Church in Victoria*, 95–103.
20. Quoted in O'Farrell, *Catholic Church in Australia*, 131.

subjection of Roman Catholics by a Protestant hegemony.[21] Mark Lyons has taken the view that the strength of anti-Catholic bigotry in colonial Australia has been overstated, arguing that it was the conservative nature of the Catholic Church and its opposition to liberal ideals which brought upon itself an opposition often experienced by Catholics as a persecution complex.[22] On this view, it was not only Protestant bigotry that led to a fortress mentality, but an internal Catholic impetus that sought separation and difference. John Molony's 1969 work *The Roman Mould of the Australian Catholic Church* showed how the anti-modernist, anti-Protestant ethos of The First Vatican Council (1870), characterized by Marian piety and the doctrine of papal infallibility, shaped the Australian Catholic Church.[23] As we will see, Ned Kelly's *Jerilderie Letter* reflects a knowledge of the history of Protestant persecution of Catholics and an (overinflated) sense of waging a war against colonial powers, not only as a beleaguered Catholic but as one who saw himself as an agent of vengeance.

The Jerilderie Letter (1879)

The Jerilderie Letter was dictated by Kelly to his fellow gang member, Joe Byrne, as they were robbing a bank and holding hostages in the New South Wales town of Jerilderie in 1879.[24] As a dictated letter, it bears marks of oral discourse that are akin to preaching. One who was present on the occasion and who might well have recognized the style of oratory was the Congregationalist missionary, the Rev. John Brown Gribble (formerly a minister of the United Methodist Free Church), who recalled how Kelly warned that the town would swim in its own blood.[25]

In his penetrating essay, "The Apocalyptic Chant of Ned Kelly," Alex McDermott describes the letter as providing "the emotional blueprint that was to guide the trajectory of Kelly's outlawry."[26] McDermott argues that the letter discloses Kelly's violent social pathology and is the work of somebody mentally unhinged by a sense of unjust persecution. For the most part, it

21. O'Farrell, "Bigotry and Religion in Australia, 1865–1950"; Breward, *History of the Churches in Australasia*, 11.

22. Lyons, "Sectarianism." See also Waldersee, *Catholic Society in New South Wales*.

23. Molony, *The Roman Mould of the Australian Catholic Church*.

24. David Dufty argues that the letter was probably written by James Wallace, a King Valley school teacher, postmaster, and friend of Byrne. Dufty, *Nabbing Ned Kelly*, 355.

25. McDermott, "Apocalyptic Chant," xxv.

26. McDermott, "Apocalyptic Chant," xxxiii.

is a rather tedious eight thousand-word recitation of Kelly's side of various incidents that had led to his criminal convictions over the years. There is an admission of horse stealing but a minimizing of such activity as not particularly serious crimes when compared to corruption in the Victorian police force. Driven by an exaggerated sense of Kelly's own importance, it swells in its later section toward a final apocalyptic denunciation in the style of an Old Testament prophet.

> I give fair warning to all those who has [sic]reason to fear me to sell out and give £10 out of every hundred towards the widow and orphan fund and do not attempt to reside in Victoria, but as short a time as possible after reading this notice, neglect this and abide by the consequences, which shall be worse than the rust in the wheat in Victoria or the druth [sic] of a dry season to the grasshoppers in New South Wales I do not wish to give the order full force without giving timely warning, but I am a widow's son outlawed and my orders must be obeyed.[27]

New Testament scholar, Richard B. Hayes proposed that there are "echoes" (technically, metalepses) of the Hebrew Scriptures in the New Testament. Rather than direct quotations, these are allusions which open up a mode of intertextuality between two or more texts.[28] "When a literary echo links the text in which it occurs to an earlier text, the figurative effect of the echo can lie in the unstated or suppressed (transumed) points of resonance between the two texts."[29] He found in his study of Paul's letters, "that the most significant elements of intertextual correspondence between old context and new can be implicit rather than voiced, perceptible only within the silent space framed by the juncture of two texts. If meaning is the product of such intertextual relations, then it is—to alter the figure—not so much like a relic excavated from an ancient text as it is like the spark struck by a shovel hitting rock."[30] Similarly, while there is no direct quotation of Scripture in the *Jerilderie Letter*, one may hear in it the echoes of many of the themes found in the Hebrew Scriptures—the tithe for the poor, concern for widows and orphans, ecological devastation and plagues of locusts as instrument of divine vengeance. Kelly grew up in poverty, trying to eke out a living from the hard ground of the Victorian bush. He saw his mother, Ellen (Quinn) (1832–1923), sentenced in 1878 to three years in prison on charges

---

27. Kelly, *Jerilderie Letter*, 83. The word "druth" is most likely a misspelling of "dearth."

28. Hayes, *Echoes of Scripture*; *Reading Backwards*; *Conversion of the Imagination*.

29. Hayes, *Echoes of Scripture*, 20.

30. Hayes, *Echoes of Scripture*, 155.

of the attempted murder of police constable Alexander Fitzpatrick. Given this background, it is unsurprising that Kelly would describe himself in the *Jerilderie Letter* as a widow's son outlawed whose orders must be obeyed.[31] His redistribution of the proceeds of his criminality to neighboring farmers and the destruction of selectors' mortgage notices might also have been a conscious (albeit misguided) appropriation of such biblical themes.

The theme of ecological devastation as an act of divine retribution against those who had taken advantage of or otherwise despised the poor is commonly found in the Hebrew Scriptures, particularly in the prophetic literature. In the ordering of the Catholic Bible, the prophetic books number eighteen (with the inclusion of Baruch) and date from the eighth to the fifth centuries BCE. The "major prophets" include Isaiah, Jeremiah, Ezekiel and Daniel, and the twelve so-called "minor prophets" (minor because shorter in length) include Joel, Amos, Hosea and Malachi.[32] Though they probably have their origins in the ideas of the actual prophets after whom they are named, they are the literary product of a series of unknown editors from Israel's exilic and post-exilic periods. The prophetic literature often includes threats of ecological devastation as an expression of Yahweh's anger toward both Israel and Judah for abandoning the covenant.[33] The book of Joel laments, "the husbandmen are ashamed, the vinedressers have howled for the wheat and for the barley, because the harvest of the field is perished" (Joel 1:11).[34] Only with repentance, mourning, and fasting, would the LORD restore the fortunes of the people so that once again "the floors shall be filled with wheat, and the presses shall overflow with wine and oil" (Joel 2:12–24). Amos decried the manner in which the wealthy "robbed the poor, and took the choice prey from him," warning that they shall "build houses with square stone, and shall not dwell in them [and] plant most delightful vineyards and shall not drink the wine of them" (Amos 5:11). For such, "the day of the Lord" would be darkness and not light (Amos 5:18–20). Similarly, Jeremiah warned the inhabitants of Judah who had sown wheat that they would reap thorns and be ashamed of your fruits, facing only "the fierce wrath of the Lord" (Jer. 12:13). In a similar rhetorical move, Kelly urges

---

31. Kelly, *Jerilderie Letter*, 83.

32. Joshua, Judges, I and II Samuel, and I and II Kings, largely narrative books, are designated the "former prophets" in Jewish tradition but included among the "historical books" in the Christian Bible.

33. "The fate of the land as a sign of YHWH's pleasure or displeasure represents a recurring motif running through the Twelve." Nogalski, *Introduction to the Hebrew Prophets*, 189.

34. All Scripture quotations are from the Douay-Rheims translation unless otherwise indicated.

those who joined the stock protection society to "with-draw their money and give it and as much more to the widows and orphans and poor of Greta district wher[e] I spent and will again spend many a happy day fearless free and bold." He advises that "it will always pay a rich man to be liberal with the poor and make as little enemies as he can as he shall find if the poor is on his side he shall loose [sic] nothing by it."[35] In the *Jerilderie Letter*, it is Kelly himself who takes the stance of the deity, ready to mete out the just punishments due to the wicked.

One of Sidney Nolan's celebrated Kelly paintings (now held at the Canberra Museum and Gallery) depicts Kelly as a massive, monstrous figure, looming over the landscape emerging from behind a mountain like an antipodean Godzilla, the stuff of nightmares.[36] "Kelly isn't only Kelly to me," Nolan said in 1964, "He's a symbol—the thing in the bush if you like."[37] Kelly has always loomed large in the Australian imagination meaning different things to different people. He cast himself, however, in the role of friend to the poor appearing suddenly out of the bush, "fearless, free and bold," to rain down judgment on their oppressors.

The threats of crop devastation and drought were very real in late nineteenth-century Australia. An epidemic of stem rust occurred in South Australia in 1889 which led, in an attempt to address the problem, to a series of intercolonial Rust in Wheat Conferences in the 1890s. Wheat breeding pioneer William Farrar could find no really effective means of resistance other than to develop breeds that did better in less rust-prone areas.[38] Stem rust was only one of several crops diseases that could decimate wheat production. Coupled with drought the results could indeed be apocalyptic. Drought, the monstrous "thing in the bush," could emerge at any time to upturn and annihilate the breadbasket of the colony. While First Nations people had developed sustainable ways of living with such conditions and were skilled at harvesting a wider range of food sources,[39] Europeans with their dependence on crops and livestock for their food economy were deeply vulnerable to such ecological "plagues." Reliable meteorological data on periods of drought is only available from the 1860s but there were severe drought conditions in Victoria between 1864 and 1866 and again in 1868 and 1877. Kelly's threat to bring a vengeance that was worse than the rust in the wheat or the dearth of a dry season, even if a vain boast, was likely

35. Kelly, *Jerilderie Letter*, 81–82.
36. Nolan, *Ned Kelly*.
37. Underhill, *Sidney Nolan*, 16.
38. Wallwork, "Role of Minimal Disease Resistance Standards," 588–92.
39. Pascoe, *Dark Emu*.

to have resonated with some power among the bush populations who had lived through such conditions.

The knowledge of church history that any reasonably well-taught Catholic might exhibit comes through in Kelly's view that any Irishman who joined the Victorian police would be "a disgrace" to "the mother that suckled him" as well as "a traitor to his country ancestors and religion as they were catholics [sic] before the Saxons and Cranmore [sic] yoke held sway since then they were persecuted and massacred thrown into martyrdom and tortured beyond the ideas of the present generation."[40] Here the experience of the Irish in colonial Victoria is placed into the longer narrative of sectarian conflict in Britain and Ireland. The "Cranmore yoke" may well be a reference to Archbishop Thomas Cranmer, the architect of the English Reformation, and thus, in Kelly's view responsible for the ensuing Protestant subjugation of the Catholic Irish. Kelly reaches even further back in history to invoke Saint Patrick as his progenitor.

> It will pay Government to give those people who are suffering innocence, justice and liberty. [I]f not I will be compelled to show some colonial stratagem which will open the eyes of not only the Victorian Police and inhabitants but also the whole British army... and that Fitzpatrick will be the cause of greater slaughter to the Union Jack than Saint Patrick was to the snakes and toads in Ireland.[41]

Kelly's hatred of the police and his animosity toward other agents of the crown are often seen as representing a politically republican stance and, along with the Eureka uprising at Ballarat in 1854, Kelly has become a heroic figure in the history of the worker's movement. This appropriation of Kelly should be met with some degree of scepticism as it is based on very little evidence of any organized plan of rebellion. A more personal, rather than political, set of beliefs appear to have been significant motivating factors in what came to be known as "the Kelly Outbreak." A brief exploration of the positioning of Kelly as a nationalist hero and an icon of the republican movement will be given here, since this is such a large part of his reception history. It will be argued, however, that the final flaring up of his banditry, leading to the siege at Glenrowan and his subsequent arrest and execution, were not driven by any political theory. They are better seen, rather, as the logical outcome of his experience as an Irish Catholic in colonial Victoria,

---

40. Ned Kelly, *Jerilderie Letter*, 64–65.

41. Ned Kelly, *Jerilderie Letter*, 27–28. "Fitzpatrick" was Alexander Fitzpatrick, the police constable whose actions toward the Kelly family are often considered the precipitating factor in the "Kelly Outbreak."

and in keeping with the religious dimensions of his life, which included a Messiah complex informed at least in part by his reading of the Bible and his knowledge of the long history of Protestant subjugation of the Catholic Irish.

Kelly a Revolutionary?

Ned Kelly's threats aimed at "the British Army and the Union Jack" have suggested to many a revolutionary sentiment and, indeed, the idea that Ned Kelly was planning a republican rebellion has firmly entered the Kelly legend, in spite of the nearly total lack of evidence to support the idea. The claim that when Kelly was arrested at Glenrowan, he had in his possession a draft constitution of a "Republic of North-Eastern Victoria" has gained considerable credence since it first appeared in Max Brown's *Australian Son* in 1948.[42] The claim is made that an article in *The Irish Times* in the late 1920s mentions this, though extensive searches of the *Times* archives have never uncovered the article. Then, in 1967, respected Kelly scholar and biographer Ian Jones presented a paper, "A New View of Ned Kelly," in which he raised the possibility of a Republican movement in the region during Kelly's lifetime. Melbourne journalist Leonard Radic told Jones that he had seen a copy of the rumored document in the Public Records Office in London in 1962, written in "quaint, mock, legalistic language."[43] However, again, this document has never been discovered even after extensive searching. In spite of the lack of documentary evidence for a declaration, Kelly scholars including John McQuilton and John Molony have taken the idea of the declaration of a republic seriously.[44]

The evidence for the existence of a republican movement in Victoria in the 1870s and 1880s is quite strong. Such a movement would of course have been an act of high treason and Phillips suggests that this may be the reason why no documentary evidence exists,[45] but this surely is arguing from silence. Though we usually think of Kelly's distinctive armor as the idiosyncratic and emblematic garb of a single individual, the fact that other members of the Kelly gang also wore makeshift armor, suggests to Phillips that they may have seen themselves as the avant-garde of a larger contingent of armed rebels. One eyewitness testified that Kelly had slipped away from the Glenrowan siege to address one hundred and fifty armed men on

---

42. Brown, *Australian Son*.
43. Phillips, "Ned Kelly and the North-East Victorian Republican Movement," para 3.
44. McQuilton, *Kelly Outbreak*; Molony, *I Am Ned Kelly*.
45. Phillips, "Ned Kelly and the North-East Victorian Republican Movement."

a nearby hilltop equipped with gunpowder and another that rocket flares were set off to signal to these men.[46] According to Police Constable Bracken (one of Kelly's hostages at Glenrowan), Kelly had declared that the people of the region were "damned fools to bother their heads about parliament" and "this is our country."[47] Phillips suggests that the murder of Aaron Sherritt and the attempted derailing of the train as it headed for Glenrowan with police reinforcements may be seen as pre-emptive strikes against the police in the lead up to the declaration of a republic.[48]

There are precedents, of course, for this kind of seditious declaration. A Declaration of Independence was drawn up during the Eureka miners' rebellion at Ballarat in 1854. The Presbyterian firebrand and passionate republican Rev. John Dunmore Lang published a draft Declaration of Independence for Victoria. "We the people of the province of Victoria in Eastern Australia, being both able and willing to govern ourselves, hereby solemnly declare, in the presence of almighty God, from whom alone we derive our political rights, and in the sight of the whole civilized world, which we call to witness this our act and deed, that we are henceforth free and independent."[49] Parliamentarian, James McPherson Grant, argued for a "Republic of Victoria" in the pages of *The Age* newspaper, which he conceived rather grandiloquently as, "a great, free and independent Republic—the hope and salvation of the world."[50] After four hundred to five hundred people gathered in Portland in the western part of Victoria in 1861, a separation league was formed which presented a petition to the House of Lords and the Governor of Victoria for the western part of the colony to secede and be renamed "Princeland." Perhaps not surprisingly, the crown rejected the proposal.

Certainly, the social unrest, economic hardships, land wars between squatters and selectors, poorly administered land acts, and police brutality and corruption in North-East Victoria in the 1870s could be seen as providing a context for republican sentiment to emerge and bubble over into armed resistance. It is just this kind of narrative that has become a popular part of the Kelly legend. The problem, again, is lack of evidence. Stuart E. Dawson, adjunct research fellow in the department of history at Monash University, has debunked the entire story of a Kelly-led republican movement as "a complex historical fiction" built more on wish fulfilment

46. Phillips, "Ned Kelly and the North-East."
47. Phillips, "Ned Kelly and the North-East."
48. Phillips, "Ned Kelly and the North-East."
49. Phillips, "Ned Kelly and the North-East."
50. Phillips, "Ned Kelly and the North-East."

than any reliable evidence.[51] The fact that neither Ned Kelly nor any of his supporters, nor the informers who gave information to the police, ever said a single word about a republic surely counts strongly against the theory.

Rather than any planned political insurrection, it is more likely that Kelly was acting out of an opportunistic banditry that, coupled with his misplaced sense of self-importance, led him to adopt the guise of a figure of vengeance, a biblical prophet, or even an avenging deity, advocating for the poor and threatening a swift vengeance for those who opposed him. While the idea of Kelly as a revolutionary republican has gained considerable traction in spite of the complete absence of historical evidence, the extent to which Kelly's Catholic identity motivated his actions and the impact of his religious instincts on his actions remain uncharted territory. And yet the religious aspects of his life are clearly available in the sources ready to be drawn out and investigated and there is a mythic quality to his place in Australian culture that often carries with it an almost religious fervor. It is in the combination of Kelly's violent disposition, his lifelong criminality, and the exaggerated sense of the role he would personally play in establishing a biblical justice in Queen Victoria's colony, not in any organized political charter, that we find an explanation of Kelly's dramatic posturing and flamboyant outlawry.

Conclusion

The Bible is a multivalent collection of texts whose meaning is not easily determined as something stable or fixed. The context in which it is read and applied determines its impact as much as (perhaps more than) any explanation of its divine origin or authority. As Shakespeare's Bossanio asks Portia in *The Merchant of Venice*, "In religion, what damned error but some sober brow will bless it, and approve it with a text, hiding the grossness with fair ornament?"[52] While the prophetic tradition in the Hebrew Scriptures may inspire advocacy for the poor and a commitment to social justice it may also provide the vocabulary that supports violence, subjugation, and exclusion. In the political sphere, parties across the spectrum have found ways to appeal to the Bible to support often incommensurable policy positions, and every competing form of Christian religion makes an appeal to the Bible to justify its beliefs no matter how divergent those beliefs may be. So, while biblically inspired social imaginaries might motivate action today, it is no easy thing to be sure that such actions will always have positive outcomes.

51. Dawson, *Ned Kelly and the Myth of a Republic*.
52. Shakespeare, *Merchant of Venice* act 3, sc. 2, l. 73.

I have argued here that Ned Kelly's religious instincts were genuine and were informed by his reading of Scripture and his membership of the Catholic Church. If religious identity is to be determined by such things as rites of initiation, open profession, and guidance from sacred texts, Kelly's cradle-to-the grave Catholicism makes it clear that he was a Christian. Not a saint, by any means, but a Christian, and a reasonably literate one at that. His life was shaped by poverty, criminality, and violence but at the same time punctuated by instances of pastoral care, grateful reception of the sacraments, a quickened conscience, repentance, and an awareness that beyond death there lay a "Great Assize" which all must undergo. Only God could finally judge anyone's life and motives and Kelly died seemingly ready to undergo that final assessment. Whether that confidence was based on a deluded hubris or a solid faith, we can probably never know. Nor can we know with certainty to what extent the echoes of the Hebrew Scriptures found in *The Jerilderie Letter* should be attributed to Kelly's close engagement with the Bible or simply reflect late nineteenth-century cultural familiarity with biblical themes. The long-standing debate over whether Kelly should be seen as a hero or a brute would be informed, however, by a deeper investigation into the religious aspects of his life.

In September 2011, scientists from the Victorian Institute of Forensic Medicine, conclusively determined that the remains exhumed two years earlier from the site of the former Pentridge Prison were those of Ned Kelly. Australia's most celebrated bushranger was then finally granted his dying request when he was buried, on 18 January 2013, near his mother Ellen and brother Dan, in the tiny Victorian town of Greta.[53] Prior to the burial, Monsignor John White said a Requiem Mass over the mortal remains of Kelly at St. Patrick's Catholic Church, Wangaratta, in the heart of what has come to be known as "Kelly Country." It was a fitting end for Kelly, a child of the church, who was not the first nor the last to read the Bible with ambivalent results.

---

53. Flanagan, "Saint or Sinner." For a biography of Ellen Kelly, see Kieza, *Mrs Kelly*. For Ned's sister, Kate Kelly, see Wilson, *Kate Kelly*.

Bibliography

Bourke, Father D. F. *A History of the Catholic Church in Victoria*. Melbourne: Catholic Bishops of Victoria, 1988.
Bray, Gerald, ed. *Documents of the English Reformation*. Minneapolis: Fortress, 1994.
Breward, Ian. *A History of the Churches in Australasia*. Oxford: Oxford University Press, 2001.
Brown, Max. *Australian Son: The Story of Ned Kelly*. Melbourne: Georgian House, 1948.
Bruce, F. F. *History of the Bible in English: From the Earliest Versions*. Third Edition. New York: Oxford University Press, 1978.
Clune, Frank. *The Kelly Hunters: The Authentic, Impartial History of the Life and Times of Edward Kelly, the Ironclad Outlaw*. Sydney: Angus and Robertson, 1955.
Coles, John Cowley. *The Life and Christian Experience of John Cowley Coles*. Melbourne: M. L. Hutchinson, 1893.
Corfield, Justin, ed. *The Ned Kelly Encyclopedia*. South Melbourne: Lothian, 2007.
Dawson, Stuart E. *Ned Kelly and the Myth of a Republic of North-East Victoria*. Creative Commons Attribution, June 2018.
Dufty, David. *Nabbing Ned Kelly: The extraordinary true story of the men who brought Australia's notorious outlaw to justice*. Sydney: Allen and Unwin, 2022.
Flanagan, Martin. "Saint or Sinner, Kelly's Bones are Laid to Rest." *The Age*, 19 January 2013. https://www.theage.com.au/national/victoria/saint-or-sinner-kellys-bones-are-laid-to-rest-20130118-2cyqz.html.
Hayes, Richard B. *The Conversion of the Imagination: Paul as Interpreter of Israel's Scripture*. Grand Rapids: Eerdmans, 2005.
———. *Echoes of Scripture in the Letters of Paul*. New Haven: Yale University Press, 1993.
———. *Reading Backwards: Figural Christology and the Fourfold Gospel Witness*. Waco: Baylor University Press, 2014.
Hirst, John. *The Australians: Insiders and Outsiders on the National Character since 1770*. Melbourne: Black Inc., 2010.
Hogan, Michael. *The Sectarian Strand: Religion in Australian History*. Ringwood: Penguin, 1987.
Jones, Ian. *Ned Kelly: A Short Life*. Sydney: Hachette, 2003.
Kelly, Ned. *The Jerilderie Letter*. Melbourne: Text, 2001.
Kennedy, Leo with Mic Looby. *Black Snake: The Real Story of Ned Kelly*. South Melbourne: Affirm 2018.
Lake, Meredith. *The Bible in Australia*. Sydney: NewSouth, 2018.
Lynn, Peter and George Armstrong. *From Pentonville to Pentridge: A History of Prisons in Victoria*. Melbourne: State Library of Victoria, 1996.
Lyons, Mark. 'Sectarianism.' In *Oxford Companion to Australian History*, edited by Graeme Davison, John Hirst and Stuart Macintyre, 583–84. Melbourne: Oxford University Press, 1998.
McQuilton, John. *The Kelly Outbreak 1887–1880: The Geographical Dimensions of Social Banditry*. Melbourne: Melbourne University Publishing, 1979.
Molony, John. *I Am Ned Kelly*. Melbourne: Allen Lane, 1980.
———. *The Roman Mould of the Australian Catholic Church*. Melbourne: Melbourne University Press, 1969.
Nogalski, James D. *Introduction to the Hebrew Prophets*. Nashville: Abingdon, 2018.

Nolan, Sidney. *Ned Kelly*, enamel paint on composition board, 1946, National Gallery of Australia, Canberra. https://nga.gov.au/exhibitions/ned-kelly/.

O'Brien, Glen. "'Have Pity on an Intelligent Young Man in an Awful Position': Two Colonial Clergy Responses to Ned Kelly." *Ethos Centre for Christianity and Society*, 4 Feb 2013. http://www.ethos.org.au/online-resources/engage-mail/intelligent-young-man-awful-position-ned-kelly.

———. "'Seeing the Clouds through the Aperture of the Helmet': Reading Ned Kelly's Life as a Christian Life." In *Finding a Home in the Uniting Church*, edited by Robert Renton, 256–71. Melbourne: Uniting Church National History Society, 2020.

O'Farrell, Patrick. "Bigotry and Religion in Australia, 1865–1950." *Humanities Research* 12/1 (2005). https://press-files.anu.edu.au/downloads/press/p13661/pdf/hrj-ch01.pdf.

———. *The Catholic Church in Australia: A Short History 1788–1967*. London: Geoffrey Chapman, 1969.

Pascoe, Bruce. *Dark Emu: Aboriginal Australia and the Birth of Agriculture*. Broome: Magabala Books, 2018.

Phillips, John Harber. "Ned Kelly and the North-East Victorian Republican Movement." *Independent Australia*, 19 Dec 2011. https://independentaustralia.net/australia/australia-display/ned-kelly-and-the-north-eastern-victorian-republican-movement,3843.

Piggin, Stuart and Robert D. Linder. *The Fountain of Public Prosperity*. Melbourne: Monash University Press, 2018.

Rose, Deborah Bird. "Ned Kelly Died for Our Sins." *Oceania* 65/2 (1994) 175–86.

"Sidney Nolan and his Ned Kelly Paintings." https://artsandculture.google.com/story/sidney-nolan-and-his-ned-kelly-paintings/BwXx5sON4e5sKA?hl=en.

Shakespeare, William. *The Merchant of Venice* (1596–98).

Taylor, Charles. *Modern Social Imaginaries*. New York: Duke University Press, 2004.

Underhill, Nancy. *Sidney Nolan: A Life*. Sydney: NewSouth, 2015.

Waldersee, James. *Catholic Society in New South Wales 1788–1860*. Sydney: Sydney University Press, 1974.

Wallwork, Hugh. "The Role of Minimal Disease Resistance Standards for the Control of Cereal Diseases." *Australian Journal of Agricultural Research* 58 (2007) 588–92.

Wilson, Rebecca. *Kate Kelly: The True Story of Ned Kelly's Little Sister*. Sydney: Allen and Unwin, 2021.

Part IV

Political and Personal Readings

The "Free Enterprise Parable"?
Contesting John Howard's Appropriation of a Story Told by Jesus

Deborah R. Storie

EXPLICIT BIBLICAL REFERENCES RARELY feature in Australian political and economic discourse. This makes then Prime Minister John Howard's use of the Parable of the Talents (Matt 25:14–30) in the lead-up to the 2007 federal election particularly interesting. According to Howard, this is "the free enterprise parable . . . that tells us that we have a responsibility if we are given assets to add to those assets."[1]

Howard, elected Member for Bennelong in 1974, is Australia's second-longest serving Prime Minister (1996–2007). His influence on the economic life and aspirations of the nation continues through legislation passed and policies implemented by governments in which he served, the careers of his admirers and mentees, and the seeming reluctance of subsequent governments to pursue objectives that do not enable the accumulation of private wealth by those already relatively well-endowed.

Despite his frequent celebration of settler Australia's Judeo-Christian foundations and appeal to Christian values, Howard is reticent about matters of personal faith and belief.[2] In his own words:

> The fundamentals of Christian belief and practice learned at the Earlwood Methodist Church have stayed with me to this

---

1. I accessed the full transcript of Howard's address through https://www.acl.org.au. Excerpts used in this chapter are cited in references listed in footnote 9.

2. Maddox, "Howard's Methodism"; Warhurst, "Beliefs of Australia's Prime Ministers."

> day, although I would not pretend to be other than an imperfect adherent to them. I now attend a local Anglican Church, denominational labels within Christianity meaning nothing to me. Any religious belief requires a large act of faith. To many people, believing in something that cannot be proved is simply a step too far. To me, by contrast, human life seems so complex and hard to explain yet so extraordinary that the existence of God has always seemed to offer a better explanation of its meaning than any other.[3]

This autobiographical self-disclosure reveals only that Howard respects "the fundamentals of Christian belief and practice" as he understands them, and that his perspective is theistic rather than atheistic. Does he seek to follow Jesus' teaching? Only Howard knows!

Given this dearth of information, it would be futile to speculate about whether Howard's understanding of the Parable of the Talents shaped his political practice. A more fruitful avenue of inquiry may be to explore the broader implications of his construal of Matt 25:14–30 as "the free enterprise parable." To what extent is it reflected in the economic policies pursued by the governments Howard led? How might it have influenced the attitudes of Australians who identify as Christians to wealth accumulation and the policies and practices that enable it? How might it have influenced assumptions among Australians who do not identify as Christian about what the Bible teaches regarding the economic dimensions of life?

These and related questions preoccupy me. As a follower of Jesus for whom the Bible is authoritative, I seek to read and respond to biblical texts in ways that love our neighbors and care for creation.[4] I am convinced that the Bible *can* be read, *should* be read, and *is meant to* be read, in ways that promote ecological and human wellbeing.[5] This is not, of course, how the Bible is invariably read.

These questions will, I hope, interest other Australians concerned about the well-being of our society and world. The Bible and how it is read matter. Biblical interpretation has shaped and will, in all likelihood, continue to shape, our culture, nation, and world.

John Howard's use of the Parable of the Talents provides the starting point for this chapter. I describe the relevant political discourse, as I

---

3. Howard, *Lazarus Rising*, 15.

4. I describe this reading framework in "Learning Our Limits" and "Reading Between Places."

5. Note previous calls for more responsible/ethical Bible reading in other contexts: Gutiérrez, *Theology of Liberation*; Okure, "Gospel-Based Biblical Hermeneutics"; Schottroff, *Parables*; Wink, *Bible and Human Transformation*.

experienced it, and review the public response provoked. I then share a translation of the parable's Greek text, and locate the parable within Matthew's Gospel and the historical context in which it was first told. Turning to my own story, I describe my teenage and young adult encounters with the Parable of the Talents, and how I came to read it differently while living among those ill-served by current economic arrangements. Both Howard's use of the parable and my inherited reading are consistent with the dominant tradition of its interpretation. The way I now understand the parable belongs to an alternative tradition that aligns with Jesus' other teaching about money, poverty, and riches, and takes seriously the economic and social dimensions of first-century and contemporary worlds. To provide a broader view of this alternative interpretive tradition, I invite readers to "listen in" as the parable is discussed in two contexts of struggle and suffering and introduce insights from two of its scholarly proponents. In conclusion, I urge Australians not to take references to biblical traditions in political discourse at face value, and suggest that more self-critical, nuanced, and historically and contextually informed reading practices might better equip us to contest and counter the public misuse of biblical texts.

John Howard's "free enterprise parable"

Thursday 9 August 2007. Along with several hundred other congregants at St Hilary's Anglican Church, Kew, I watched John Howard and Kevin Rudd address churches around Australia live stream from the National Press Club, Canberra. Howard referred to Matt 25:14–30:

> The Parable of the Talents has always seemed to me to be the free-enterprise parable—the parable that tells us that we have a responsibility if we are given assets to add to those assets.

When questioned about growing inequality, Howard conflated inequality and unemployment:

> I don't deny the rich have got richer . . . but they have not got rich at the expense of the poor getting poorer . . . . The first and most important thing we can do is to continue to run a strong economy. You've got to have a strong economy before you can have families in work.

He defended his party against perceptions of class bias:

> That we're indifferent to the vulnerable, we're only interested in the prosperous middle class and we really don't care very much

about others and we're pretty indifferent to the poor in our society—that's a charge that I not only take keenly but I fairly vigorously reject.

As evidence of his party's concern for the vulnerable, Howard cited Official Development Assistance (which his government reduced significantly although not as savagely as subsequent coalition governments)[6] and the Northern Territory Emergency Response (initiated June 2007).[7]

Appalled by the Prime Minister's appropriation of Jesus' teaching, I recalled a more personal encounter during the previous federal election campaign in 2004. Arriving at a public meeting in Launceston, Howard spoke briefly about parental choice in education before mingling with the crowd, shaking hands, exchanging a sentence or two, and moving on. "Pleased to meet you, Deborah." "Good evening, Mr Howard. I'm concerned about poverty, globally and within Australia. How will your government support the Millennium Development Goals?" "Millennium Development Goals . . . Remind me." "Eight goals to halve extreme poverty, hunger, maternal and infant mortality, improve access to education, and protect the environment by 2015. Your government is a signatory." "Yes, yes. The Millennium Development Goals. Very important." Howard went to move on but my grip on his hand was firm. "Prime Minister, during my lifetime, Australia has gone from being one of the most to one of the least economically equal societies." "I don't know what statistics you are using, Deborah, but I do not see wealth creation as a problem: the wealthier people become, the more generously they can give to the poor."[8]

Public Response

The 2007 "Address to the Churches" was rebroadcast for a national audience and received extensive commentary.[9] Despite featuring on television and

---

6. Official Development Assistance (ODA) is government aid that promotes the economic development and welfare of developing countries. Clare, "Australia's Foreign Aid Budget," graphs the ratio of Australian ODA to Gross National Income from 1973 to 2021.

7. The Northern Territory Emergency Response was a suite of measures introduced by the Howard Government in response to allegations of child sexual abuse in Aboriginal communities.

8. John Howard, personal communication.

9. Broadcast: Cleary, "Talkback." See, for example, Donald, Iggulden, and staff reporters, "Howard, Rudd Woo Christians Online"; Davis, "Arch-Rivals"; Iggulden, "Christian Community Hears from Howard, Rudd"; Adams, "Politics: Howard and Rudd Address Christians"; Shanahan and Rowbotham, "Howard's Net Porn Crusade."

radio and verbatim citations in newspapers, Howard's use of the Parables of the Talents provoked little public debate. Nicole Anderson from Smithton Tasmania accused Howard of "ludicrous . . . blatant misuse of scripture" and bemoaned the "gullibility" of Christians persuaded by "the leader who can quote glib Bible verses and spruik the ethically suspect prosperity doctrine."[10] An unidentified member of Ringwood Uniting Church contested Howard's reading by posting a sermon transcript that identified the noncompliant "whistleblowing" slave as the hero of the parable.[11]

Some years later, Holly Randell-Moon considered Howard's treatment of the Parable of the Talents within a wider discussion of his "discursive promotion of a Christian nationalism as consistent with neo-liberal ideals of individual freedom and wealth creation" to justify the retraction and privatization of public welfare services by appeal to "Christian values" thus construed.[12] On her analysis, individualistic assumptions and a conviction that accumulating private wealth is a moral good appear to drive Howard's reading of Christianity and the Bible. An "anti-wealth reading of Christianity, Randell-Moon notes, "is also possible for those with different political ideals."

Why did John Howard's construal of Matt 25:14–30 as "the free enterprise" parable" provoke so little public reaction? Of the likely contributing factors, I mention four. First, Australians may have little interest in the Bible and how it is used. That said, the protest that erupted following then Leader of the Opposition Tony Abbott's misuse of Jesus' words, "The poor you will always have with you" (Matt 26:11), indicates that some Australians are *very* interested in how the Bible is used and to what ends.[13]

Second, Howard is not alone in understanding the parable this way. Other parliamentarians have recruited it for similar purposes.[14] Although unusually frank in harnessing the parable to promote the accumulation of private "assets," Howard's application is a logical outcome of the dominant tradition of its interpretation (on which see below). To be sure, several leading commentators insist that the parable *should not* be used, as indeed it *has been* used, to endorse free enterprise and free market policies and practices

---

10. Anderson, "Howard's No Theologian."

11. John Mark Ministries, "Howard wrong."

12. Randell-Moon, "John Howard's Australia," citations here and following from 205, 207–8, and 204n5.

13. See, for example, Perusco, "Bible Bashing the Homeless"; Eltham, "Poor Will Always Be with Us."

14. Ross Cameron, Member for Paramatta 1996–2004, for example, claims that the parables of Matt 20:2–11 and 25:14–30 refute the notion that extreme profits might be morally suspect. Maddox, *God Under Howard*, 288, provides details.

or otherwise afford "spiritual legitimation" for the pursuit of wealth and the exploitation that so often accompanies it.[15] Yet, as some of these scholars acknowledge, the parable—*as they interpret it!*—provides the foundations on which such applications are based.[16]

Third, Australians who have heard of the Parable of the Talents may assume that it endorses wealth accumulation whether or not they have read it themselves. Phillip Adams, host of Radio National's *Late Night Live* (1991 to present), refers to this parable upon occasion.[17] His short-hand references imply that he expects his listeners and conversation partners to understand that the parable is often claimed as a biblical warrant for private wealth accumulation and inequality. Adams has not, so far as I know, revealed whether he has read the parable nor his views on how it *should* be interpreted.

Fourth, the lack of public reaction may reflect the degree to which Australian Christians share Howard's individualist assumptions and materialist convictions and aspirations. The parable, as he reads it, says what at least some of us *want* it to say.

Relocating the Parable

The Gospel according to Matthew is the first but not the earliest of the four New Testament Gospels.[18] Composed by an unknown author between 75 and 95 CE, it tells the story of Jesus for a predominately Jewish Greek-speaking audience well-versed in the Scriptures of Israel. Matthew drew heavily on the Gospel of Mark, dated around 70 CE, on oral traditions about Jesus, and on traditions also known to Luke. Matthew probably adapted the Parable of the Talents from oral tradition.[19]

Neither Jesus nor the narrator identify the story of Matt 25:14–30 as a parable. Elsewhere in the Gospels, the term (*parabole*: *para*, alongside

---

15. See, for example, Luz, *Matthew 21–28*, 250–51, 261–62; Collins, *Wealth, Wages, and the Wealthy*, 127. Citation from Luz, *Matthew 21–28*, 261.

16. Luz, *Matthew 21–28*, 261: "The parable itself invites misunderstanding." Australian Jesuit Brendan Byrne, *Lifting the Burden*, 189, is concerned that the parable "appears to endorse a highly capitalist mode of proceeding in regard to the use of wealth which sits ill with Jesus' instruction on the use of money elsewhere."

17. See, for example, Adams, "Myths About American Poverty."

18. While respecting the anonymity of the Gospel writers, I use the traditional names to refer to both the Gospels and their human authors.

19. Some scholars claim that the parables of Matt 25:14–30 and Luke 19:12–27 are amendments of a written tradition known to both Matthew and Luke. See, for example, Luz, *Matthew 21–28*, 248–58. I think otherwise.

+ *balo*, to throw) is used to designate indirect communication of various kinds: short fictional narratives, aphorisms, puzzles, metaphors, and other forms of figurative speech. This reflects its usage in the Septuagint (the Greek translation of the Hebrew Bible) where it is also used of non-verbal communicative acts.[20]

The text of Matt 25:14–30 translates as follows:[21]

> [14] For it is as if someone, as he was leaving, summoned his slaves and gave over his property to them. [15] And to one he gave over five talents, to another two, to another one, to each according to their ability/power. And he left immediately. [16] The one who had received the five talents went and worked with them and gained another five. [17] In the same way, the one with two gained another two. [18] But the one who had received the one talent went and dug the ground and hid his lord's silver. [19] After a long time the lord of those slaves came and settled accounts with them. [20] And the one who had received the five talents came forward, bringing another five talents, saying, 'Lord, you gave over to me five talents. Behold, I gained another five talents' [21] His lord said to him, 'Well done, good and faithful slave; you have been faithful in a little, I will set you over much; enter the joy of your lord.' [22] And the one with two talents came forward, saying, 'Lord, you gave over to me two talents. Behold, I gained another two talents' [23] His lord said to him, 'Well done, good and faithful slave; you have been faithful in a little, I will set you over much; enter into the joy of your lord' [24] But the one who had received the one talent came forward, saying, 'Lord, I knew that you were a harsh/hard/dried up person, reaping where you did not sow, and gathering where you did not scatter. [25] And I feared. And I went and hid your talent in the ground. Behold, have what is yours.' [26] But his lord replied, 'You evil slave and hesitant/timid! You knew, did you, that I reap where I did not sow, and gather where I did not scatter? [27] Then you ought to have put my silver on the [moneylenders'] tables and on my return I would have collected what was mine with interest. [28] So take up the talent from him and give it to the one with the ten talents. [29] For to all those who have, more will be given, and they will have an abundance; but from those who have not, even what they have will be taken up from them. [30] And this worthless/unprofitable

---

20. *Mashal* carries a similar range of meanings in the Hebrew Bible.

21. In translating the text, I attempt to retain its story-telling features and juxtapose English words to reflect connotations conveyed by the Greek.

slave, throw him out into the outer darkness where there will be weeping and gnashing of teeth'

According to Matthew, Jesus told this parable to his closest disciples two days before Passover on the Mount of Olives. The disciples had asked Jesus privately, "What will be the sign of your coming and of the end of the age?" (24:3). Jesus concludes his lengthy response (24:4—25:46) with four stories told one after the other (24:45-51; 25:1-13; 25:14-30; 25:31-46). The Parable of the Talents precedes the final story that describes the judgment of "all the nations" at "the end of the age."

"The age" whose "end" the disciples anticipated (24:3) was highly unequal. A Roman procurator governed Judea in collaboration with the ruling priesthood and temple establishment. Rome ruled Galilee, Idumaea, and Peraea through client kings, the Herods. In Palestine as elsewhere, a small governing elite controlled most land, labor, and other resources through a slightly larger retainer class of priests, scribes, administrators, and soldiers. The vast majority of the population lived at subsistence or sub-subsistence levels.[22] Narrow livelihood margins, together with heavy taxes, other obligations, and military incursions, meant that injury, crop failure, unemployment, or misadventure led to debt and, via debt, to loss of ancestral lands, bonded labor, imprisonment, slavery, or starvation.

Herodian, ruling priestly and other wealthy families used slaves to administer their kingdoms, households, and estates. Large numbers of Jews had been enslaved during the military campaigns of 63 and 53-48 BCE and following the revolts of 4 BCE and 6 CE.[23] One way or another, most people used the products of slave labour, were subject to impositions mediated by slaves, and accessed services provided by slaves. For their part, slaves had no choice but to negotiate situations in which their survival depended on serving the system that enslaved them.

The cumulative effect of these political and economic arrangements was to give more to those who had already taken too much and to take from the dispossessed the little they still had. No wonder Jesus and his disciples anticipated "the end of the age."[24]

---

22. Here and following, Oakman, *Economic Questions*, 75; Arlandson, *Women, Class and Society*, 18-98.

23. Here and following, Glancy, *Slavery*; Arlandson, *Women, Class and Society*, 99-101.

24. Wright, *New Testament*, 157-201, describes how longing for liberation and widespread resistance to Roman and Herodian rule constantly simmered.

Taking It Personally—Learning to Listen

My earliest memories of the Parable of the Talents are from when our teenage Bible Class explored our "talents" (things we excelled at and enjoyed) in order to choose careers in which we might succeed and glorify God. Since then, I've most often heard the parable expounded allegorically to support prosperity or stewardship teaching. The person going on a journey represents God or Jesus; the first two servants [sic] represent exemplary disciples; the third serves as a warning. Until Jesus returns, we should use the resources "with which God has blessed us" and the opportunities "God brings our way" wisely, tithing 10 percent before providing for our families, preparing for retirement, and insuring against misfortune. In none of this was the parable related to Jesus' teaching elsewhere in Matthew, other biblical traditions, or the socio-economic realities of first-century Palestine and twenty-first-century Australia. In effect, the Parable of the Talents was used to bolster an ethos of individual wealth acquisition tempered by charity, tithing, and random acts of kindness, readily accommodated within existing economic and political structures. The parable, as I inherited it, merged seamlessly with the individualistic middle-class aspirations of the culture to which I belonged.

Dominant scholarly and ecclesial traditions of interpreting the parables of Jesus begin with the predicate that parabolic lords and masters represent God or Jesus or are otherwise good.[25] This allegorical identification exerts a decisive influence on how other characters and their actions are judged, parables understood, and connections between parables and their narrative, historical, and reception contexts explained. In the case of Matt 25:14–30, the slave-owner (who stands for God) and everything he does, says and expects must, by definition, be good and just and true (as would be the case for God).[26] Divinizing this character requires other aspects of the parable to be allegorized, rendering the parable unable to speak about power, slavery, money and its use, imprisonment and torture. This interpretive tradition supports the individualized, decontextualized, and depoliticized reading that I inherited, and provides the foundations for the individualized, decontextualized, and re-politicized application promoted by Howard.

I began reading parables differently while living among the rural poor in a conflict-affected region of Central Asia. My neighbors taught me to see shadow sides of economic relations to which I had been previously

---

25. This predicate is defended by Gerhardsson, "Frames," and refuted by Schottroff, *Parables*, 88–114; Storie, "Matthew 20:1–15," 203–6.

26. Snodgrass, *Stories with Intent*, 528–42, reviews variants of the dominant tradition of interpreting Matt 25:14–30 and Luke 19:11–27.

oblivious. In their experience, free enterprise, free markets, and other incursions of national and global economies took away what little they had. Similarities between the world of the Gospels and the world around me brought the Gospels and daily life closer together so that, without any conscious intention, I began to imagine myself into Gospel narratives and to imagine their stories playing out around me. Hearing Jesus' parables *as if* among those to whom he first told them, I found myself ethically and existentially addressed: Were I in that situation, what would I do, and would I do rightly?

Jesus' disciples, like my neighbors, were peasants, fisherfolk, daily laborers, and petty officials. They knew what it was to be hungry, cold, and afraid, were inured to hardship, and alert to danger. They, like my neighbors, derived little benefit from prevailing economic and political arrangements. Unlike my Islamic neighbors, the disciples were Jews who knew their Scriptures and, knowing their Scriptures, lived in hope and with expectation, anticipating "the end of the age."

Under my neighbors' tutelage, I began to read the Parable of the Talents differently. Why, I wondered, had I previously assumed that the wealthy traveler/slave-owner/lord represented Jesus or God, an allegorical identification that neither Jesus nor the Gospel writer provide? Having relinquished that predicate, I could—and did!—question the slave-owner's perspective and probity, ethics and expectations; inquire into the methods through which his "good and faithful" slaves gained double the talents handed over to them; and weigh the credibility of his assessment of his non-compliant slave and that slave's assessment of his lord.

Listening *as if* among the disciples on the Mount of Olives, I knew about talents, who dealt with them, and the consequences of such dealings. A talent was the largest monetary unit of which Jesus could speak.[27] One talent of silver, equivalent to sixteen thousand *denarii*, was more than we disciples could hope to earn if we could find work, were able to work, and were paid for our work every day for seventeen years. While we disciples prayed for daily bread and freedom from debt (Matt 6:11–12), powerful elites dealt in talents, although their slaves did the actual dealing. The parable's "good

---

27. The *Shorter Oxford Dictionary* entry for "talent" lists three meanings: (i) a denomination of weight [between 30 and 40 kg] used by the Assyrian, Babylonian, Greek, and Roman empires; (ii) an inclination, disposition, propensity, will, wish, desire, state of mind; (iii) a power or ability of mind or body viewed as something divinely entrusted to a person for use and improvement. This third sense "originated in a figurative use of the first sense of the word taken from the Parable of the Talents." There is no evidence that talent meant anything other than a weight or an amount of money (measured by its weight in metal) in the first century.

and faithful" slaves do not reveal how they accumulated talents and their lord does not ask. Listening *as if* a disciple, I did not need it spelt out.[28]

Imagining myself into the story, I heard the parable in the light of all I had experienced as a surrogate member of the Gospel world. On the surface of things, neither Jesus nor Matthew indicates which characters act well and which badly, but I remembered Jesus' warning (6:19–21, 24):

> Do not store up for yourselves treasures on earth, where moth and rust consume and where thieves break in and steal . . . For where your treasure is, there your heart will be also. . . You cannot serve God and Mammon.

Listening *as if* among the disciples, I was familiar with scriptural traditions about interest (*tokos*), justice and injustice, and the fear of God. The Torah explicitly forbids taking *tokos* (Exod 22:25; Lev 25:36–37; Deut 23:19).[29] The Psalms, Proverbs, and prophets refer to taking *tokos* as a practice of the unrighteous/unjust (Psa 55:11; Prov 28:8; Ezek 22:12) from which the righteous/just refrain (Psa 15:5; Ezek 18:8, 13, 17). Leviticus 25:35–37 portrays taking *tokos* or otherwise profiting from human need as antithetical to the fear of God. The third slave's characterization of his owner (19:24), admission "I feared," and refusal to comply with his owner's unspoken wishes (19:25), together with his owner's rebuke for not putting the talent "on the money' lender's table" from whence he could have "collected what was [his] with *tokos*" (19:27), reverberate against the Scriptures.[30] Fear God or take interest; you cannot do both.

Imagining myself among the disciples, I continued listening as Jesus segued from one story to the next:

> When the Son of Humanity comes in his glory, and all the angels with him, he will sit on the throne of his glory. And all the nations will be gathered before him. And he will separate them one from another, as a shepherd separates the sheep from the goats . . . (25:31–32).

The contrast between the economic outcomes the parabolic slave-owner rewards and those affirmed by the Son of Humanity (25:34–40) is stark. Echoes of Ezekiel 34 amplify the dissonance between the economic practices

---

28. Similarly, Ukpong, "Parable of the Talents," 197.

29. *Tokos* occurs in the Gospels only here and at Luke 19:23. Many English versions soften biblical prohibitions against and condemnations of taking *tokos* with qualifiers such as "excessive" or "exorbitant" not found in the Hebrew and Greek manuscripts.

30. Similarly, Ukpong, "Parable of the Talents," 198.

and vision of the kingdoms of this world with those of God's kingdom.[31] Like John, Jesus, and the prophets before them, the third slave of the Parable of the Talents refuses to participate in exploitative schemes, speaks truth to power, and suffers for justice's sake (Matt 5:11). But *that*, the Son of Humanity declares, is *not* the end of the story.

Listening In

As I later discovered, this realistic reading of Matt 25:14–30 was neither innovative nor radical. What scant evidence we have suggests that it may reflect how early gatherings of believers understood the parable before the Church gave interpretive authority to those well served by prevailing political and economic arrangements.[32] Centuries later, this now-alternative tradition is intuitively forged by those whose contexts and life experiences are somewhat analogous to those of Jesus and his earliest followers. The lived experiences of a *campesino* congregation in Nicaragua and of a maximum-security prisoner in the United States of America illuminate the parable.

A *Campesino* Reading: scattering money multiplies love

Ernesto Cardenal served as a priest at Solentiname, Nicaragua, during the cold war and its aftermath. Rather than give a homily each Sunday, Cardenal invited the congregation to discuss the lectionary reading. The *campesinos'* readings were directly informed by their experience of being dispossessed through debt, commercial land acquisitions, and armed conflict.

On first hearing, the parable of Matt 25:14–30 polarized the congregation.[33] William declared it "a lousy parable" about "speculating with money." Cardenal agreed that it was "a very ugly example" of "exploitation." Pancho wondered whether the parable was about money at all. As conversation continued, the congregation debated whether to interpret the parable realistically or allegorically.

> Oscar: That man had to go away and he wanted his money to increase. And he looked for others who were

---

31. Ezekiel 34, an oracle against "the Shepherds of Israel," anticipates divine judgment of the "strong" and "fat" who push aside and prey upon the "thin," "weak" and "injured."

32. On which, see DeBode and Myers, "Towering Trees and 'Talented' Slaves"; Kitchen, "Rereading."

33. For the full transcript see Cardenal, *Gospel in Solentiname*, 78–81.

>   exploiters like him, and he gave them money so
>   they'd exploit the people and earn more and get
>   double what he was leaving them ... But the guy
>   that didn't get much, he didn't cooperate ... He was
>   conscientious because he didn't have the strength
>   to exploit his brothers and sisters ... Then the boss
>   got sore when he comes and hands back the same as
>   what he'd been given.
>
> Priest: See, Oscar, here Christ gives the example of an ex-
>   ploiter, and his employees were exploiters too; and
>   he wants them to multiply his money. And Christ
>   says that's the way God acts with us.
>
> Oscar: What God wants us to multiply is love! ... That's
>   what this Gospel is saying, but maybe the rich
>   don't understand it, and then what they do is screw
>   you ... Christ says that just as exploiters multiply
>   money; so we ... must multiply love.
>
> William: And love is money; love is wealth well-distributed;
>   the two things are related ... But the bad servant
>   accuses [the master] of harvesting where he didn't
>   sow. He makes him out a monster.
>
> Priest: As a miser is relentless in demanding with money;
>   so God is relentless with love.... Those who have
>   the most love will become richer and those who have
>   very little are going to be left poorer, says Christ.
>
> Oscar: In that sense the thing is fine ... But the truth is that
>   this Gospel is a little involved with the question of
>   money ...

The *campesinos* eventually interpreted the parable in a double sense, adroitly combining a realistic reading (that spoke of and into their lived experience) with the allegorical reading (that Cardenal preferred). This compromise did nothing to assuage anxieties about the likely consequences of the parable when read by wealthy people. Oscar articulated the problem:

> If, unfortunately, somebody comes along who is quite ... inter-
> ested in money and, unfortunately, he starts to read this Gospel,
> and understands it in his own way, these words are going to
> make him worse than before.... If, unfortunately, [rich people]
> read it, they'll think it's a defense of them.

The *campesinos* expected rich readers to miss the point.

A Maximum-Security Reading: The Gospel according to Smitty

Inmates of a maximum-security prison in the United States read the Bible with a visiting chaplain.[34] One week, the prisoners chose to read the Parable of the Talents only to declare it "boring." They assumed that the parable taught about "talents God gave us" and "how we should use them" and initially rejected the chaplain's suggestion that the rich man might *not* be God. Even after learning that "talents" were money and the "servants" were slaves, the prisoners struggled to engage until their chaplain suggested they imagine themselves into the story.

> Fortna: Which of those three slaves in the story do you like the best?
>
> Smitty: I kinda dig that third dude.
>
> Fotna: Let's say you're that guy.... A single talent was worth about fifteen years' wages for a poor laborer.
>
> Smitty: You mean, we talking big money.
>
> Fortna: So, Smitty, how do you feel about the boss who left you with all this money to invest for him?
>
> Smitty (after a pause and then very slowly): Why that son-of-a-bitch!
>
> Fortna: Why?
>
> Smitty: He just part of the System. He tryin' to use me to make his money for him ... He gets the cash. I gets the rap. He exploitin' me man!
>
> Fortna: So is he God?
>
> Smitty: Course not. Who sayin' that?

Imagining himself into the parable *as if* the third slave, Smitty escaped the constraints of the dominant tradition to read the parable in the light of his own experiences of power, "big money," and exploitation.

The Alternative Tradition in Biblical Scholarship

The alternative tradition of interpreting the Parable of the Talents is somewhat resurgent within ecclesial and scholarly contexts. William Herzog and Richard Rohrbaugh pioneered this tradition by applying the pedagogical

---

34. The story is told by Fortna, "Jesus' Parable of the Talents through Underclass Eyes."

methods of Paulo Freire and insights from cultural anthropology respectively.³⁵ Unfortunately, the decision to conflate the parables of Matt 25:14–30 and Luke 19:11–27 and interpret "reconstructed" parables of their own devising compromised their contributions. Two more recent scholars interpret the parable as related by Matthew. Both pay careful attention to the parable's socio-historical, literary, and canonical contexts, and to the contemporary contexts from which they read.

A Nigerian Non-Elite Perspective

Justin Ukpong interprets the Parable of the Talents from "a non-elite perspective" informed by "the local money-lending business in Nigeria."³⁶ Listening to what the parable and its protagonists do and do not reveal, he explores aspects of the parable not explicitly explained through reference to its socio-historical and narrative contexts.

The Parable of the Talents,

> opens a window to a social world of exploitation of the poor by the rich, a 'kingdom' in which only those that participate in the exploitation that makes the rich stay rich share in the 'joy' of the rich while those who fear God and refuse to participate are made to suffer. This is diametrically opposed to the 'kingdom of heaven' which, for Matthew, belongs to the poor in spirit, the meek and those that suffer for being upright (Matt 5:3, 5, 10). The master and the servants [sic] that amassed wealth for him are exploiters that stand condemned at the last judgment. The third servant [sic] that criticized the master represents the 'prophetic' voice of the gospel and is the role model for Christians.

Ukpong thus interprets the parable as a critique of "the exploitation of the poor by the rich through their agents that was going on in the society in Jesus' time" and "by extension of exploitation in our own time."

Ukpong maintains that the parables of Jesus' farewell discourse (24:45–51; 25:1–13, 14–30) speak of the suffering that will continue until Jesus returns to judge the nations.³⁷ This judgment pertains not only to how the nations respond to human need, "but also and more especially" to their responsibility for "socio-economic structures of exploitation and oppression."

---

35. Herzog, *Subversive Speech*, 158–67; Rohrbaugh, "Peasant Reading."
36. Here and following, Ukpong, "Parable of the Talents," 190–91, 197–99.
37. Here and following, Ukpong, "Parable of the Talents," 201–5.

A Middle-Class German Perspective

Luise Schottroff struggled to reconcile the dominant traditions of interpreting parables with the teaching and ethics of Jesus until Herzog's work convinced her that parabolic masters and lords do not necessarily represent God or Jesus. She now reads parables "at face value" as "stylized fictional but realistic accounts of daily life including social structures and related violence and injustice."[38] Schottroff approaches the parables as "a beneficiary of Western wealth" living "under conditions of growing militarism and intensifying economic imperialism in the dominant Western world."[39] Wary of "Christian strategies to silence the poor," she seeks to interpret Jesus' parables in ways that "do good" and "keep the Torah."[40]

Of the Parable of the Talents, she writes:

> For centuries this story was read as a story about a God who punishes his lazy slave, the believer who does not obey God's commandments. . . A horror story about a violent and extremely wealthy slave owner is by interpretation converted into something declared to be the gospel. This gospel makes people who do not identify with the rich man or the successful slaves, but with the critical slave, feel cold and uneasy. Is not the third slave speaking the truth about his master?[41]

It is, she insists, possible to maintain the dominant tradition of interpretation only "if the imagery of the parable is read without any reference to human life."[42]

The parable, as Schottroff reads it, is interpreted by the following story (Matt 25:31–46) and Jesus' earlier teaching: "The third slave has acted as Jesus taught in the Sermon on the Mount. He has not served mammon (Matt 6:24)." Heard together, these texts "confront us with God's justice" and "demand" that we "practice the repentance of the rich."

Reading the Parable of the Talents in Australia

After returning to Australia, the ethical and existential questions with which the Parable of the Talents confronted me grew more acute. I could no longer

---

38. Schottroff, *Parables*, 29–37.
39. Schottroff, "Kingdom of God," 171; *Parables*, 2.
40. Schottroff, *Parables*, 225.
41. Schottroff, "Kingdom of God," 170.
42. Here and following, Schottroff, *Parables*, 223–24.

accept bank statements and superannuation reports at face value: What lay behind interest accrued and value gained? Was I reaping where I hadn't sown and gathering where I hadn't scattered? I questioned the prices of products I used: Who paid the real cost of my comfort and convenience? No longer content to work to the best of my ability, I interrogated the ecological and other consequences of small animal veterinary practice: To what future were we contributing? The parable no longer asked: *Were* I in that situation, what would I do, and would I do rightly? It confronted me: You *are* in an analogous situation . . . What *will* you do, and will you do *rightly*? What consequences might ensue from what you *do* and *do not* do?

Newly estranged from the individualistic assumptions and aspirations of my native culture, Matthew's parables pushed me to probe Australia's present and past. "The age" in which we live is highly unequal. The (relative) power and privilege enjoyed by most settler and immigrant Australians is not "a blessing from God," but the legacy of colonization and slavery: stolen lands and peoples, extractive industry, exploitative trade, extravagant expectations. Our politics and culture normalize destructive commercial-industrial practices and promote irresponsible patterns of consumption. The client kings of global capitalism deal in vast sums, channeling ever more resources to produce products and services for those who can pay.[43] And yet, despite mounting evidence to the contrary, many people still assume that capitalism can, in principle at least, expand indefinitely to provide opportunities for all, alleviating poverty and improving living standards for most of the world's inhabitants.[44] Now that we have exceeded the absolute limits of the earth's resources, the reality is that supply can no longer rise to meet demand—when some take more, others have less. Creation groans (Rom 8:22).

Howard's appropriation of Matt 25:14–30 as "the free enterprise parable" is part of this picture, as are the economic agendas pursued by the governments he led. Yes, the pursuit of wealth has been a defining trait of non-Indigenous Australian society since white settlement.[45] And yes, many of the economic reforms Howard celebrated and extended were initiated by Labor governments (1983–96). But Hawke and Keating retained the egalitarian ideals of governments since World War II and were, therefore, willing to intervene to moderate the extremes that would otherwise have arisen.[46]

---

43. WWF, *Living Planet Report 2014*, 38–39; Chancel et al., eds., *World Inequality Report*, 182–83; UNDP, *Human Development Report 2016*; Hoogvelt, *Globalization*.

44. Here and following, Hoogvelt, *Globalization*.

45. On which see Cornford, "Money Made Us," in this volume.

46. Here and following, Hogg, "Myths and Markets, 239–41.

Howard, in contrast, reshaped Australia's economy and society around the imperative of profit maximization, progressively dismantled safeguards against inequality, and used "the cover of egalitarian rhetoric" to move our "political culture towards the aspirational end of the spectrum."[47] Under Howard, the individualistic capitalistic ethic of profit maximization became the ultimate ethic on which the economy depended and to which all other ethical considerations must give way.

Since Howard, both sides of politics have reinforced this hegemonic ideology by operating as if no valid alternative to capitalism were possible.[48] If the conviction that governments should facilitate the accumulation of private assets was a constant of Howard's political career, his appropriation of the Parable of the Talents as "the free enterprise parable" presented that conviction as a divine imperative and a Christian obligation that responsible governments must enable. Under Howard, the vice of greed became the virtue of aspiration.

Parables do not interpret themselves. When isolated from the narrative, canonical, and historical contexts to which it belongs, the Parable of the Talents can be—and has been—deployed for a wide range of purposes. But, as I have argued, the parable points in other directions when these contexts are retained.

Matthew 25:14–30 is not "the free enterprise parable" as Howard would claim. When read allegorically, the parable does not speak about money and its accumulation, except in so far as that those "rich in love" distribute wealth and do not accumulate assets. When read as a fictional, abstract yet realistic story, the parable critiques wealth accumulation and the values, ambitions, and structures that promote it. Heard *as if* in its narrative and historical contexts, the parable challenges contemporary readers ethically and existentially: We *are* in somewhat analogous situations: What

---

47. Kelly, "The Politics of Economic Change," 229.

48. The success of Howard's "ideological repositioning of Australian society" is evident in the reluctance of subsequent governments to pursue policy objectives through strategies that do not conform to the assumptions and methods of capitalism, Labor's retreat from the economic policies it took to the 2019 election, and the limits of the 2019 *Royal Commission into Misconduct in the Banking, Superannuation and Financial Services Industry*. As found by Bottomley, Byrne and Flett, *Tempered Justice*, 7–8: The Letters Patent under which the Royal Commission operated prevented it from recommending "any changes that would fundamentally challenge the assumptions of capitalist ethics underpinning the Australian economy." The Commission's inability to interrogate the legislative framework within which financial institutions and much of the economy operate rendered it unable to identify or redress the root causes of misconduct.

will we do and will we do *rightly*? What consequences might ensue from what we *do* and do *not* do?

How might the public misuse of this and other biblical texts be more effectively contested? Meredith Lake observed that "a degree of biblical literacy—along with critical skill in evaluating how the Bible has been taken up and interpreted in our history—can only help Australians grapple well with the choices Australia faces."[49] Without greater biblical literacy we cannot hope to distinguish between the teachings of Jesus and what politicians and others take them to mean.

Reading the Bible "wasn't meant to be easy."[50] The cultural challenges are formidable, particularly for those who, habituated to power, are culturally conditioned not to see those dimensions and implications of biblical texts that challenge individualistic materialistic assumptions and aspirations.[51] Are we ready to learn from those ill-served by current economic and political arrangements? Are we brave enough to prioritize and amplify non-elite perspectives?

For those who read the Bible theologically (as the word of God), there are further questions to be asked. Are we willing to cultivate a degree of hermeneutic and existential humility, develop self-critical reading practices, and attend to the economic, social, and ecological dimensions of biblical and contemporary worlds? Confronted by God's justice, will we resist the ideologies and structures that enable those already in possession of assets to add to those assets no-questions-asked?

---

49. Lake, *Bible in Australia*, 428.

50. I play here on a saying associated with Australia's third-longest serving Prime Minister, Malcolm Fraser. On which, see Wilkes, "Life wasn't meant to be easy."

51. Note points of connection with Nthla, "A Black View" and Schottroff, *Parables*, 81–89. Nthla's account of how individualized and personalized notions of sin, guilt, and salvation prevented many white Christians from joining the struggle against apartheid in South Africa traces the intersections of faith, dominant cultural assumptions, and political ideologies.

Bibliography

Adams, David. "Politics: Howard and Rudd Address Christians Across the Nation." *Sight Magazine*, 10 August 2010. https://www.sightmagazine.com.au/features/2728-politics-howa-a-rudd-address-christians-across-the-nation-2.

Adams, Phillip. "The Myths About American Poverty." *Late Night Live*, Radio National, 18 March 2021.

Anderson, Nicole. "Howard's No Theologian." *ABC News*, 13 August 2007. https://www.abc.net.au/news/2007-8-13/howards-no-theologian/638664.

Arlandson, James Malcolm. *Women, Class and Society in Early Christianity: Models from Luke-Acts*. Peabody, KS: Hendrickson, 1997.

Bottomley, John, Brendan Byrne, and John Flett. *Justice Tempered: A Report for the Financial Sector Union*. Melbourne: University of Divinity, 2020.

Brown, Lesley, ed. *The New Shorter Oxford Dictionary*. Oxford: Oxford University Press, 1993.

Byrne, Brendan. *Lifting the Burden: Reading Matthew's Gospel in the Church Today*. Collegeville, MN: Liturgical Press, 2004.

Campbell, Roshena. Concession Speech. *7 pm ABC VIC News*, 2 April 2023.

Cardenal, Ernesto. *The Gospel in Solentiname*. Translated by Donald D. Walsh. Vol. 4. Maryknoll: Orbis, 1982 [1977].

Chancel, Lucas, Thomas Piketty, Emmanuel Saez, and Gabriel Zucman, eds. *The World Inequality Report*. World Inequality Lab, 2022. https://wir2022.wid.world/www-site/uploads/2021/12/WorldInequalityReport2022_Full_Report.pdf.

Clare, Angela. "Australia's Foreign Aid Budget 2020–21." *Budget Review 2020–21*. Parliament of Australia, 2021. https://www.aph.gov.au/About_Parliament/Parliamentary_Departments/Parliamentary_Library/pubs/rp/BudgetReview202021/AustraliasForeignAidBudget.

Cleary, John. "Talkback: John Howard and Kevin Rudd Address the Australian Christian Lobby." *Sunday Nights*, Radio National, 12 August 2007. https://www.abc.net.au/radio/programs/sundaynights/talkback-john-howard-and-kevin-rudd-address-the-australian-chris/7743850.

Collins, Raymond E. *Wealth, Wages, and the Wealthy: New Testament Insight for Preachers and Teachers*. Collegeville: Liturgical, 2018.

Davis, Mark. "Arch-Rivals Spread Own Kind of Word." *Sydney Morning Herald*, 10 August 2007. https://www.smh.com.au/national/arch-rivals-spread-own-kind-of-word-20070810-gdqtp3.html.

DeBode, Eric, and Ched Myers. "Towering Trees and 'Talented' Slaves." *The Other Side* 35 (1999).

Donald, Peta, Tom Iggulden, and staff reporters. "Howard, Rudd Woo Christians Online." *ABC News*, 9 August 2007. https://www.abc.net.au/news/2007-8-10/howard-rudd-woo-christians-online/636110.

Eltham, Ben. "The Poor Will Always Be with Us: So Says the Book of Matthew (and Tony)." *The New Matilda*, 10 October 2014. https://newmatilda.com/2014/10/14/poor-will-always-be-us-so-says-book-matthew-and-tony/.

Fortna, Robert T. "Reading Jesus' Parable of the Talents through Underclass Eyes." *Forum* 8 (1992) 211–28.

Gerhardsson, Birger. "If We Do Not Cut the Parables out of Their Frames." *New Testament Studies* 37 (1991) 321–25.

Glancy, Jennifer A. *Slavery in Early Christianity*. Oxford: Oxford University Press, 2002.
Gutiérrez, Gustavo. *A Theology of Liberation: History, Politics and Salvation*. London: SCM, 1974.
Hayne, Kenneth M. *Report of the Royal Commission into Misconduct in the Banking, Superannuation and Financial Services Industry*. Commonwealth of Australia, 2019.
Herzog, William R. II. *Parables as Subversive Speech: Jesus as Pedagogue of the Oppressed*. Louisville, KY: Westminster/John Knox, 1994.
Hogg, Robert. "Myths and Markets: Australian Culture and Economic Doctrine." *Journal of Australian Studies* 26/72 (2002) 235–41.
Hoogvelt, Ankie. *Globalization and the Postcolonial World: The New Political Economy of Development*. London: Palgrave, 2001.
Howard, John. *Lazarus Rising: A Personal and Political Autobiography*. Pymble, NSW: Harper Collins, 2010.
Iggulden, Tom. "Christian Community Hears from Howard, Rudd." *Lateline*, 9 August 2007. http://www.abc.net.au/lateline/content/2007/s2001192.htm.
John Mark Ministries. "Howard Wrong on the Parable of the Talents." Sermon transcript from 22 April 2007. http://www.jmm.org.au/articles/19982.htm.
Kelly, Paul. "The Politics of Economic Change in Australia in the 1980s and 1990s." In *The Australian Economy in the 1990s*, edited by David Gruen and Sona Shrestha, 222–34. Kirribilli: Economics Group, Reserve Bank of Australia, 2000.
Kitchen, Merrill. "Rereading the Parable of the Pounds: A Social and Narrative Analysis of Luke 19.11–28." In *Prophecy and Passion: Essays in Honor of Athol Gill*, edited by David Neville, 227–46. Adelaide: ATF, 2002.
Lake, Meredith, *The Bible in Australia: A Cultural History*. Sydney: NewSouth, 2020.
Luz, Ulrich. *Matthew 21–28*. Minneapolis, MN: Fortress, 2005.
Maddox, Marion. *God under Howard: The Rise of the Religious Right in Australian Politics*. Crows Nest, NSW: Allen & Unwin, 2005.
———. "Howard's Methodism: How Convenient?!" *Journal of Australian Studies* 28/83 (2004) 1–11.
Murray, Kim. "John Howard's Policies: Formed over a Lifetime, So Why Were We Surprised?" Paper presented at The Howard Decade Conference, University of Canberra, 2006. https://parlinfo.aph.gov.au/parlInfo/download/media/pressrel/2YZI6/upload_binary/2yzi66.pdf;fileType=application%2Fpdf#search=%22media/pressrel/2YZI6%22.
Nthla, Moss. "A Black View of White Christianity." *Working Together* 3 (1999) 1–5.
Oakman, Douglas E. *Jesus and the Economic Questions of His Day*. Lewiston, NY: Edwin Mellen, 1986.
Okure, Teresa. "'I Will Open My Mouth in Parables' (Matt 13:35): A Case for a Gospel-Based Biblical Hermeneutics." *New Testament Studies* 46/3 (2000) 445–63.
Perusco, Michael. "Bible Bashing the Homeless, Abbott Style." *The Age*, 16 February 2010. http://www.theage.com.au/opinion/bible-bashing-the-homeless-abbott-style-20100215-02tj.html#ixzz1XdpDFMqz.
Randell-Moon, Holly. "Social Security with a Christian Twist in John Howard's Australia." In *Mediating Faiths: Religion and Socio-Cultural Change in the Twenty-First Century*, edited by Guy Redden and Michael Bailey, 203–15. London: Routledge, 2011.

Rohrbaugh, Richard. "A Peasant Reading of the Parable of the Talents/Pounds: A Text of Terror?" *Biblical Theology Bulletin* 23 (1993) 32–39.

Schottroff, Luise. "The Kingdom of God Is Not Like You Were Made to Believe: Reading Parables in the Context of Germany and Western Europe." In *The Bible and the Hermeneutics of Liberation*, edited by Alejandro F. Botta and Pablo R. Andriñach, 169–79. Atlanta, GA: SBL, 2009.

———. *The Parables of Jesus*. Minneapolis, MN: Fortress, 2006.

Shanahan, Dennis, and Jill Rowbotham. "Howard's Net Porn Crusade." *The Australian*, 10 August 2007.

Shorrocks, Anthony, James Davies, and Rodrigo Lluberas. *Global Wealth Data Book*. Zurich: Credit Suisse Research Institute, 2019.

Snodgrass, Klyne R. *Stories with Intent: A Comprehensive Guide to the Parables of Jesus*. Grand Rapids, MI: Eerdmans, 2008.

Storie, Deborah. "Learning Our Limits: Challenges to Faith and Imagination." *Working Together* 4 (2004) 1–2, 14–16.

———. "Matthew 20:1–15: The 'Parable of the Workers in the Vineyard' or 'of a Manager-Disciple?'" In *Encountering the Parables in Contexts Old and New*, edited by Thomas E. Goud and Robert Cousland, 196–222. London: Bloomsbury T&T Clark, 2023.

———. "Reading between Places: Participatory Interpretive Praxis." *Pacifica* 18 (2005) 281–301.

Ukpong, Justin. "The Parable of the Talents (Matt 25:14–39): Commendation or Critique of Exploitation? A Socio-Historical and Theological Reading." *Neotestamentica* 46 (2012) 190–207.

UNDP. *Human Development Report: Human Development for Everyone*. New York: UNDP, 2016.

Warhurst, John. "The Beliefs of Australia's Prime Ministers." *Eureka Street*, 11 November 2010.

Wilkes, Gerald A. "Life wasn't meant to be easy." In *Stunned Mullets & Two Pot Screamers: A Dictionary of Australian Colloquialisms*. South Melbourne: Oxford University Press, 2008. https://www-oxfordreference-com.ezproxy.slv.vic.gov.au/view/10.1093/acref/9780195563160.001.0001/acref-9780195563160-e-1835.

Wink, Walter. *The Bible and Human Transformation: Towards a New Paradigm for Biblical Study*. Philadelphia, PA: Fortress, 1973.

Wright, N. T. *The New Testament and the People of God: Christian Origins and the Question of God*. London: SPCK, 1992.

WWF. *Living Planet Report 2014*. Gland, Switzerland: WWF, 2014.

Truth Within the Public Square
Morality, Rhetoric, and the Australian Christian Lobby[1]

Michelle Eastwood

> Justice is turned back,
> and righteousness stands far away;
> for truth has stumbled in the public squares,
> and uprightness cannot enter.
> Truth is lacking,
> and he who departs from evil makes himself a prey.
> The Lord saw it, and it displeased him
> that there was no justice.
> He saw that there was no man,
> and wondered that there was no one to intercede.
>
> Isaiah 59:14–16a (ESV)

The Australian Christian Lobby (ACL) is a group that claims to be "a voice for God's truth in the public square."[2] ACL rhetoric frames the public square as incorporating politics, business and social relations, and presents

---

1. The NRSVUE translation will be used throughout this article, unless otherwise stated.
2. Australian Christian Lobby, "Truth Made Public," para 11.

God's truth as synonymous with a form of conservative Christianity that is perceived to be under attack in contemporary Australian society.[3] The mandate to be a voice for God's truth is derived from a reading of Isa 59:14–16a which speaks of a lack of truth, justice and righteousness in the public square. The ACL presents this text as being analogous to contemporary social and political conditions in Australia, claiming that Christianity is "being pathologized and blamed for significant harms."[4] Within the rhetoric of the ACL is the implication that there is one true singular Christian perspective, particularly on issues of gender and sexuality.

In contrast, John Warhurst, Emeritus Professor of Political Science at Australian National University, states that "the first thing that must never be forgotten about Christianity in Australia is that it is amazingly diverse. No one can ever claim to speak on its behalf."[5] He suggests that the Christian churches in Australia are more progressive than society in general, and broadly agree on issues such as education, welfare, and aged care. Warhurst notes that the main exception to this progressivism is in the area of sexual mores. Sexual mores in this context are often connected to the rights and recognition of queer people, particularly with regards to marriage equality. More recently conservative Christian opposition has been evident in public discourse because of legal moves to ban conversion practices and public debates about the legitimacy of transgender identities.

Even though Christians in Australia may hold attitudes that are broadly more conservative toward sexuality and gender identity than the general population, this does not mean that all Australian Christians support a hard-line anti-LGBTIQA+ stance. A 2017 Galaxy Research poll at the time of the marriage equality debate found that 54 percent of Christians supported marriage equality and "61 percent do not like having conservative religious groups presenting their views on same-gender marriage as

---

3. The ACL claims that "classical Christianity" is the "greatest stronghold of truth," although this is not aligned with any specific denomination. "Truth Made Public". Robert E. Webber claims that classical Christianity is to be "orthodox, evangelical and ecumenical." He further notes that the canon, Apostle's creed, doctrine of the trinity, and affirmation of Jesus as both fully human and fully divine is core to an understanding of classical Christianity. *Ancient-Future Faith*, 28–29. This is interesting given the ACL's support for Israel Folau who reportedly rejects a trinitarian understanding of God. It is for this reason that biblical scholar Mark Jennings describes the ACL's position as a "new and strange kind of orthodoxy" that prioritises anti-LGBTIQA+ sentiment over traditional Christian understandings. Maddox, "Why is the Australian Christian Lobby waging a culture war?" para 23.

4. Australian Christian Lobby, "Truth Made Public."

5. Warhurst, "Australia's Christians," para 9.

though they are speaking for all Christians in the country."[6] Indeed, the Uniting Church of Australia has accepted openly gay clergy since 2003 and in 2018 began allowing same-gender marriages in their congregations.[7] More recently there have been moves within the Anglican Church of Australia to bless same-gender marriages.[8] It should be noted, however, that the acceptance of marriage equality in both these churches has led to acrimonious internal debates and threats of potential schism.[9] These are just two examples demonstrating explicit moves toward LGBTIQA+ inclusion and its consequences in Australian churches.

There are many Christians in Australia who reject the stance of the ACL, as evidenced by *#acldoesntspeakforme*, which began trending during the marriage equality debate. I am one of the people who has used this hashtag to distance myself from the claims of the ACL, and to illustrate that there are a range of views held by Australian Christians on any given topic. Given the continued dominance of the ACL in the media, and its disproportionately loud voice within Australian politics, it is important to evaluate the claims the ACL is making. In this chapter, I will consider the formation and claims of the ACL; explore Isa 59:14–16 within the context of the broader text; and evaluate the ACL's use of this passage in their messaging. The ACL's rhetoric on gender and sexuality as a key symbol of morality will provide the main focus of the chapter because this is an area where the ACL is frequently quoted in the media, as well as being a consistent theme in their videos and publications. I suggest that the ACL's lack of sophisticated theological and biblical literacy allows a surface level interaction with the text that is rhetorically shrewd, but that ultimately is undermined by a close reading of the text.

---

6. Hutchens, "Most Christians in Australia," para 3.

7. The Uniting Church of Australia adopted two understandings of marriage: marriage is the union of a man and a woman; marriage is the union of two people. Congregations and clergy are free to adopt either understanding. Uniting Church of Australia, "15th Assembly Decision on Marriage."

8. In 2020, the Anglican Appellate Tribunal ruled that a service of blessing for civil marriages, including same-gender couples, was valid. Anglican Communion News Service, "Wangaratta's same-sex wedding blessing 'valid,' Australia's highest Church court rules."

9. In the Uniting Church this can be seen through the development of the Assembly of Confessing Congregations. Tronson, "Assembly Confessing Congregations."

The GAFCON (Global Anglican Future Conference) movement within the Anglican Church of Australia has also threatened disaffiliation. Douglas, "GAFCON Australia."

History of the Australian Christian Lobby

The main purpose of the ACL, as stated on their website, is to argue for Christian values and rights within the Australian political and legal spheres. The ACL is not a church and claims no affiliation to any specific denomination which means that the ACL is free to choose which issues to pursue or ignore without being beholden to or constrained by any institutional church doctrinal stance or structure.[10] The ACL, in its capacity as a lobby group, is often called upon by the media to give a "Christian" perspective on key issues. Indeed, Marion Maddox describes the Australian Christian Lobby (ACL) as the "peak Christian lobby group" in Australia.[11] The ACL is not the only Christian lobby group in Australia, although it is probably the loudest.[12]

The ACL was formed in 1995 by evangelical businessman John Gagliardi and retired Baptist minister John McNicoll.[13] Originally called the Australian Christian Coalition, it was modelled on the Christian Coalition of America, a conservative "pro-family" lobby group who see their main work as "voter education."[14] Timothy Jones suggests that a similar "conservative morality campaign" from Britain—the Australian Festival of Light, which began in the 1970s—paved the way for the development of the New Christian Right which he describes as based on "anti-permissive, anti-feminist and anti-LGBTA politics."[15] Jones convincingly argues that the New Christian Right, of which the ACL is an example, "was founded not on a common faith but on a common conservative sexual ideology."[16] This would seem to be true of the ACL which, from the beginning, has been

---

10. Marion Maddox points out that the term "non-denominational," as distinct from ecumenical or inter-denominational, reflects an ecclesiology connected to the mega-church movement which relies on "divine appointment" and charismatic leadership, rather than structures with more accountability. "Right-wing Christian intervention," 134. Iles grew up within the Brethren tradition, but reportedly calls himself "denominationally confused." Napier-Raman, "Martyn Iles, the youthful face," para 4.

11. Maddox, "Right-wing Christian intervention," 134.

12. Other notable lobby groups in Australia are the National Council of Churches in Australia, Love Makes a Way, and Australians for Marriage Equality. Micah Australia is a group that assists people to develop their advocacy skills, and the Centre for Public Christianity is a media company that offers Christian perspectives on contemporary issues. Hillsong Church frequently invites key politicians to participate in their annual conference, although doesn't identify as a lobby group.

13. Ireland, "Who are the Australian Christian Lobby?" para 11.

14. Christian Coalition of America. "We are the Christian Coalition of America," para 2.

15. Jones, "Australian Secularism," 330.

16. Jones, "Australian Secularism," 330.

predominantly focused on opposing any sexual expression outside of a heteronormative, nuclear family.

In 2001, under the leadership of Jim Wallace, a former brigadier in the SAS and Special Forces, the Australian Christian Coalition changed its name to the Australian Christian Lobby in order to distance itself from the associated American model. In 2013, Lyle Shelton, a Pentecostal youth pastor, became Managing Director of ACL and remained in this role until 2018. Shelton resigned in order to run for a senate seat in Queensland as part of Cory Bernardi's Australian Conservative Party.[17] Shelton was succeeded by Martin Iles, a relatively young law graduate, as the face of the ACL from 2008 to March 2023. Iles was abruptly terminated from this position at the start of March 2023.[18] The ACL has appointed Michelle Pearse (CEO) as Iles' successor, however this chapter was written while Iles was still ACL's Managing Director and, therefore, will concentrate on his tenure and influence in this position.

In terms of governance, the ACL is a company registered as a not-for-profit organization. It relies on donations from members and others to support its work and pay staff wages.[19] It is unclear how many members the ACL has, although the website claims that "over 220,000 individuals share their vision."[20] ACL describes itself as a grassroots organization and it has no clear connection to any specific church or denomination. Maddox reports that there is no mechanism for churches or individual members to contribute to policy decisions.[21] Rather, the ACL position reflects that of the Managing Director and the ACL board.

The ACL board consists of seven white male directors including former Managing Director, Jim Wallace. The board members are connected

17. Cory Bernardi's Australian Conservative Party was voluntarily deregistered after the 2018 election after attracting less than 1 percent of the vote. See Withers, "The Spectacular Failure."

18. Iles departure was announced on his personal facebook page, with Iles reporting that the board had decided to move in a different strategic direction. Segaert, "Inside the Australian Christian Lobby's identity crisis," para 1. Iles has since been appointed as Chief Ministry Officer at Answers in Genesis, which Iles described as a "large Christian apologetics and education ministry." Ham, "Special Ministry Announcement from Ken Ham," para 2.

19. The ACNC reports that the ACL has 2,000 volunteers and 24 staff.

20. The ACL website, as of January 31, 2022, claimed that over two hundred and twenty thousand individuals share their vision. On this same date the Worldometer, based on United Nations data reported Australia's population as 25.97 million ("Australia Population," This places the ACL's number of supporters at less than 1 percent of the population, and perhaps 2 percent of individuals who identify as Christian in Australian.

21. Maddox, "Right-wing Christian Intervention," 134.

to a range of business and corporate entities.[22] Only one board member, Ric Benson, is a church minister and it is unclear the level of theological training that any of the board or the Managing Director, Martin Iles, have undertaken. This is not to suggest that individuals who choose to lobby for Christian issues must have specific theological training. However, ACL claims to be speaking as a voice for God's truth are predicated on the notion of biblical truths, therefore there is an imperative to deal responsibly and thoughtfully with the text so that this witness does not further undermine the integrity and broader public standing of Christianity in this country.

Martin Iles and the "Truth of It"

Martin Iles, as the face of the ACL, often makes claims about biblical texts and *the truth* they contain. In an interview with Eternity News, Iles decried "a lack of understanding of the beliefs that we have, what Scripture actually says about the times we live in, particularly in a way that is well applied and robustly understood."[23] Arguments about *what Scripture actually says* can be fraught. Even biblical scholars and theologians do not always agree on what a passage means or its concrete application to specific contemporary issues, as evidenced throughout this volume. Any claim to know what the Bible *really* says is debatable at best. Biblical scholars do, however, agree broadly on guiding principles that assist us to read the Scriptures in responsible and trustworthy manners.

A key principle for interpreting the biblical text responsibly is to acknowledge the diversity it contains.[24] The Bible is a collection of books that reflect different theologies, socio-cultural contexts and perspectives, some of which seem to contradict each other. It was written across hundreds of years, predominantly in Hebrew and Greek, within cultures and contexts fundamentally different to those of twenty-first century Australia. This means that there is a range of theologies and understandings of God contained within the Bible, thereby resisting any singular explanation.

---

22. One board member is Graham Packer, Chairman of Citipointe Christian College. Citipointe Christian College recently faced a media and public backlash when a contract was made public that parents and staff were required to sign endorsing only heteronormative, monogamous unions and a "biological" understanding of sex. Smee, "Citipointe Christian College teachers ," para 5.

23. Delbridge "Meet the New Managing Director," para 42.

24. Anthony C. Thiselton describes a "responsible plurality" that allows for differing interpretations guided by sound scholarly principles. "Future of Biblical Interpretation," 11–28.

Another principle is to read texts within their narrative and, as far as possible, historical context. Each book is informed by the cultural and cultic context within which it was written. Customs and ideas that were understood by the writers and their historical audience do not translate directly onto customs within contemporary contexts. Readers must "mind the gap" when interpreting the Bible in light of the current Australian context, both the language gap and the cultural gap.

Interestingly, Iles' vlog, "The Truth of It," and other ACL presentations contain very few explicit references to the Bible. Meredith Lake notes that Australia has a "culture wary of Bible bashers"[25] which may partially explain this reticence. Alternatively, it could be suggested that Iles excludes direct references to the Bible to avoid alienating potential supporters who share the ACL's morally conservative stance but are not themselves Christian. The lack of biblical references allows non-Christians to comfortably agree with most of the ACL's claims, while the infrequent and vaguely explained biblical allusions serve to reassure supporters for whom the Bible is authoritative. Avoiding direct references to specific biblical texts is also a savvy rhetorical strategy which allows Iles to distance himself and the ACL from engagement with critical readings of the biblical text which could undermine his insistence on a singular understanding of truth and God's word.

Iles is very selective in his use of biblical texts, choosing snippets that appear to support his overarching contention, a method often known as proof-texting. In a video running more than fifty minutes long and addressing the Federal Government's Religious Discrimination Bill 2021, Iles explicitly references just three Bible texts: Romans 13, the Sermon on the Mount (Matt 5:3–12) and Isaiah 59.[26] Romans 13 begins with the exhortation to obey governing authorities, and Iles uses this as justification for the need for Christian political leadership and influence, despite the fact that this passage is referring to obeying Roman leadership rather than a Christian or even Jewish authority. Iles uses the Sermon on the Mount to explain that Christians must expect to be opposed and persecuted (vv. 10–2) while he avoids the social justice themes central to the rest of the Sermon. And,

---

25. Lake, *Bible in Australia*, 358.

26. Australian Christian Lobby, "The Truth of it S6E6." The Religious Discrimination Bill 2021 was introduced as a direct result of the marriage equality result. Prime Minister Scott Morrison and Attorney-General, Christian Porter sponsored the Religious Freedom Review, a report developed by an expert panel chaired by Phillip Ruddock. The panel was convened to appease conservative anger over the marriage-equality plebiscite result. Australian Government, Attorney General's Department, "Religious Discrimination."

as noted, he uses Isaiah 59 as an argument for speaking "truth" loudly into the public square.

Rhetoric from the ACL frequently alludes to *the truth*. The use of the definite article (i.e. *the* truth) implies that there is a singular Christian understanding of truth and a widely accepted set of Christian principles and ethics. This truth is not articulated or explained. Rather it carries an assumed meaning and message that can be understood by "real" Christians. This ambiguity is probably intentional, allowing a broad group of individuals who identify as Christian to join under the same banner to become "us" with the ACL. In contrast is "them" who can be viewed as anyone who opposes the Christian individual or Christian institution. In this way, the use of the phrase *the truth* conveys a claim to divine Christian authority that stands in direct opposition to secular worldly knowledge. There is also a demarcation in Iles' rhetoric between "real" Christians, who accurately follow the ancient traditions, and other post-modern, heterodox forms of Christianity.[27]

On the ACL "About" page, truth is mentioned eight times in a blurb less than four hundred words long.[28] *The Truth of it* is also the name of the vlog presented by Iles, and the name of his travelling show. It is claimed that, in his presentations, Iles "cut[s] through the fake news and delivers the truth of it."[29] For Christians, usage of the phrase *the truth* may be heard as an allusion to the statement in John's gospel that Jesus is "the way, the truth and the life" (14:6), or a reference to "the Spirit of truth" (16:13), as well as the claim that "you will know the truth and the truth will set you free" (8:32). Indeed, truth is a frequently occurring theme across the breadth of the books of the Bible. When Iles speaks about truth, his rhetoric resonates with Christian audiences familiar with the rhetoric of truth and also these well-known passages. In this way, Iles employs specific biblical imagery and language to convey that the ACL shares a common understanding with everyday Christians. This reinforces the notion that the ACL is able to speak with biblical authority into Australian public and political discourses.

The ACL claims that Christians in Australia are being persecuted for speaking the truth. This rhetoric of oppression has increased in response to

---

27. In an interview with *Eternity News*, Iles connects postmodern ideology with the denigration of truth and suggests it is the equivalent of cultural Marxism. Delbridge, "Meet the New Managing Director" para 50. This is a clear example of the way Iles employs conservative rhetoric and jargon to disparage anyone he classifies as socially liberal.

28. Australian Christian Lobby, "Truth Made Public." Following a link titled "Who We Are," hidden at the bottom of the ACL website takes the interested individual to the ACL "About" page. The page bears the title "Truth made public" and contains an outline of the ACL ethos.

29. "The Truth of It," Australian Christian Lobby, para 1.

the recent introduction of laws banning conversion practices in Victoria.[30] Iles speaks of "soft persecution"[31] of Christians and states that Christians in Australia are being "blamed for significant harms."[32] This creates the impression that Christians and Christian institutions are the vulnerable victims of attacks and suppression of their rights. The harms are left unstated, allowing the reader to interpose their own understanding of "significant harms" into this claim. This promotes the identification of a vulnerable Christian in-group which is contrasted with the aggressive, non-Christian, other.

To some extent, it is probably accurate to suggest that Christianity in Australia is being blamed for significant harms. On one end of the spectrum, the harms may be understood as complicity in the sexual abuse crisis. On the other end, significant harm may be understood as no longer being able to assume Christian dominance and unchallenged Christian social and cultural norms. Kishor Napier-Raman suggests that this persecution or blame is little more than "simply being made to follow the law."[33] Iles audience will likely hear a reference to their own experience of resistance to assumed Christian norms, perhaps failing to see the connection between the revelations from the Royal Commission, negative treatment of LGBTIQA+ people by the church along with other perceived harms and the rise in antagonism to church, Christianity, and Christians.

Iles leverages his followers' experience of social resistance to Christianity alongside rhetorical tools such as biblical language and allusion, a lack of specificity, and a positioning of Christians and Christianity as underdogs and scapegoats in Australian society, to promote the idea that Christianity in Australia is under threat. This positions the ACL as a valiant warrior fighting against contemporary culture wars.[34]

---

30. Conversion practices, also known as "conversion therapy," are behaviors intended to change a person's sexuality and gender orientation to cis-straight. It has been linked to a variety of harms including depression, anxiety, and suicide. It is gradually being banned in many jurisdictions across the world, including in the state of Victoria. Victorian Government, "LGBTQ+ Change and Suppression Practices Fact Sheet." Despite the evidence that conversion practices do not work and are linked to real and ongoing harms, Iles has spoken out against the laws and used them as evidence of the potential persecution of Christians who continue to enact these behaviors. Australian Christian Lobby, "Vic Conversion Therapy Bill Walk-Through," para 1, 42, 46.

31. Delbridge, "Meet the New Managing Director," para 20.

32. Australian Christian Lobby, "Truth Made Public," para 2.

33. Napier-Raman, "Martyn Iles, the youthful ," para 6.

34. In an interview with Nick Carter, Iles states that the political left have declared war on ideas, thought, belief, and opinion. ACL, "Culture Wars and The Silencing of the Faith" (32:36). In another video, Iles speaks of building a war chest to oppose moderate liberals who "will cross the floor to create this disaster." In this case, the disaster is requiring Christian schools to comply with anti-discrimination laws that apply to other

Isaiah 59 (and 58)

The "Who We Are" page on the ACL website contains two biblical references: Prov 13:34 and Isa 59:14–16a. The analysis here will be limited to the Isaiah passage because of its inclusion of the word "truth" which the ACL frequently uses within their rhetoric.

Isaiah sits within the prophetic corpus, books which contain collections of oracles and words spoken to the Israelites to remind them of what God desired. The book of Isaiah is one of the largest biblical prophetic texts and records ancient Israelite theologizing about the destruction of the temple and the exile of the Israelites to a foreign land.[35] The traumatic experience of being conquered and exiled from the Promised Land led the ancient Israelites to wrestle with the idea that YHWH had abandoned God's chosen people, and what might be done to avoid similar calamities in future.

Chapter 59 of Isaiah is within the section of this book sometimes referred to as Third or Trito-Isaiah and is commonly thought to have been composed during the post-exilic or restoration period.[36] Schuele suggests that, even within this later section of Isaiah, two distinct theological explanations exist. The exile was a result of Israel's failures and inadequacies, as represented by Isaiah 58 and 59. Alternatively, an eschatological explanation means that the exile is the precursor to Israel "receiv[ing] its place at the top of the political world" (Isa 60–62).[37] Schuele notes that the redactors of Trito-Isaiah did not see the need to remove or harmonise these two competing theologies.

---

businesses. ACL, "Martyn Iles—Today," (6:29).

35. The exile was completed over a series of deportations and did not include the whole Israelite people. Norman K. Gottwald notes that it is the "leadership of the state and of the cult" as well as upper-class Judahites who were killed or deported to Babylon. He suggests that the post-exilic "reconstructed community of Judah" centered on Jerusalem in communication with many diasporic Jewish communities. Gottwald also notes that during this period many Jews fled to neighboring countries, therefore he suggests the terms dispersion and restoration as more accurate than exilic and post-exilic. *Hebrew Bible*, 420–23.

36. The division of Isaiah into three parts, Proto- (1–39), Deutero- (40–55), and Trito- (56–66) is associated with Bernhard Duhm (1847–1928), although divisions in the book were observed before then. Current scholarship has focused more on the compilation of the book as a literary whole through the lens of redaction criticism and composition history. Becker, "The Book of Isaiah," 39–44. Andreas Schuele states that the majority of scholars places the writing of Isaiah as contemporaneous with Ezra and Nehemiah's restoration of Israel. However, there are indications in the text that might suggest a later dating. "Who is the True Israel?" 180.

37. Schuele, "Who is the True Israel?" 181.

On the exiles' return, the Israelite nation struggled with the reintegration of the community. In particular, the exiles fitting in with communities of people who had stayed on the land.[38] The return to the land also meant a rebuilding of the temple, their cities, their communities, and their cultic and religious practices. One potential response to the challenge of reintegration is seen in the books of Ezra-Nehemiah where some Israelite leaders are shown as focusing on strict racial and religious purity which, they claim, conforms to their interpretation of YHWH's law (*torah*).[39] In this understanding, by strictly obeying *torah*, the Israelites will be able to maintain a community of righteousness and YHWH would have no reason to destroy or send the Israelites into exile again. However, a number of the prophetic texts, including Isaiah 58–59, link piety and worship with a vision of justice for all members of the community. In this reading, religious purity is meaningless if there are members of the community who are marginalised and oppressed. It is against this historical background that this passage from Isaiah can be understood.

Isaiah 59 can be divided into three main sections. The first section (vv. 1–8) is a litany of wrongs and evils that "you" have committed. The audience that comprises the "you" is not defined or clarified within this passage. It can be understood, however, as the Israelites identified in the previous chapter which is part of this same rhetorical sequence.[40] Verse 9 begins the second section (vv. 9–15a) with the words "therefore," the perspective changing to the first-person plural indicated by repeated use of the terms "we" and "us." "We" are blind and stumble (v. 10), "we" moan and look for justice (v. 11), "we" acknowledge our iniquities (v. 12). These actions show Isaiah taking responsibility on behalf of the Israelites for the lamentable situation described in vv. 14–15b. The message of the first two sections is that *you* have done wrong, and the consequences are that *we* bear the pain and misery. Verse 14 begins with a conjunction, left out of the NRSV and ESV translations and the translation included on the ACL website. The NIV more accurately translates this as "*so* justice is turned back," indicating that these verses are an outcome of what has been said in the preceding verses.

---

38. Nissim Amzallag makes a distinction between the "sons of exile" and the "peoples of the land," the former who are returnees while the latter are those who have remained in Judea. "The Authorship of Ezra and Nehemiah," 275.

39. This can be seen in Ezra 9 where the people of the land are described as "unclean" and "pollution" (v. 11), and in Ezra 10 which contains a list of the descendants of priests who had married foreign women. In Neh 13:3, in a response to reading "from the book of Moses," there is a separation between Israel and "all those of foreign descent."

40. Isaiah 58:1 identifies this as an oracle directed at the "house of Jacob," an alternative name for Israel, to announce their rebellion and identify their sins.

Justice is turned back *because* of the sins and injustices outlined in verses 1–9. These include lips that have spoken lies (v. 3) and an absence of calls for justice, a lack of integrity, and evil plots (v. 4). None of the sins and injustices identified in Isaiah 59 concern questions of sexuality, gender, or a general assumed morality on which the ACL is so focused.

Section 1—59:1–8	*Litany of wrongs "you" have committed*
Section 2—59:9–15a	*"We" take responsibility*
Section 3—59:15b–21	*YHWH's response*

Outline of Isaiah 59

The third section of Isaiah 59 (vv. 15–21) outlines YHWH's wrath, retaliation, and vengeance which will be visited on those in the west and east (v. 19), which Walter Brueggemann describes as "rhetorical overkill."[41] However, for the Israelites who repent, YHWH will be a redeemer (v. 20).[42] According to Lev 25:25, the redeemer is a person who settles the debts of a fellow Israelite, saving them from financial distress. It is not about having political or cultural dominance or sway. Within Isaiah 59 there is no explicit reference to financial difficulties or debts and so the question arises: what does redemption look like in this context?

An answer can be found in Isaiah 58. This chapter begins with the question of what YHWH requires of the people. YHWH requires that the oppressed go free (v. 6), injustice is addressed (v. 6), the hungry are fed (vv. 7, 10), the homeless are housed (v. 7), the naked are clothed (v. 7), and the needs of the afflicted are met (v. 10). Niskanen notes that the redeemer (Isa 58:4; 59:20) restores the inheritance, including ancestral land and fortunes.[43] Goldingay also notes the connotations of economic oppression in this chapter that is visited on servants and slaves.[44] He suggests that these offenses against another person results in injuring the relationship, which is the sin being condemned in this passage.

Interestingly, among these instructions encouraging social justice, chapter 58 contains an explicit instruction to "remove the pointing of the finger, the speaking of evil" (v. 9) as well as instructions for observing the Sabbath (v. 13). Sabbath observances are intrinsically related to not harming another and, like fasting, are "designed to lead us to lives not dominated by

---

41. Brueggemann, *Isaiah 40–66*, 201.
42. Williamson, "Ruth," 33–68.
43. Niskanen, *Isaiah 56–66*, 20.
44. Goldingay, *Isaiah 56–66*, 169.

self-interest but rather centered in YHWH's desires and filled with acts of mercy and compassion towards others."[45] Redemption is connected to alleviating poverty and other injustices that are connected to marginalization and oppression.[46] It is a lack of concern about these things that leaves the Israelites' hands defiled with blood (59:3). Brueggemann explains the reference to blood as "any action that diminishes or harms other members of the community," and notes that both action and speech are means of hurting others and violating Yahweh's expectations.[47] With this background in mind, I will now consider the ACL's use of Isa 59:14–16a.

Truth is Lacking (Isa 59:14–16a)

Given the ACL's rhetorical use of the notion of truth, it is understandable that they have chosen these specific verses from Isaiah as a call to action and a justification for their various programs. Taken in isolation, this short excerpt can be seen to communicate that God is unhappy because truth is lacking and there is no person willing to defend it. This lack of willingness provides a lacuna for Martin Iles and the ACL to fill. However, a closer inspection of these verses within their biblical context undermines the reading presented by the ACL.

The ACL exists to promote Christian issues within Australian society. It must be noted however, that just as Iles misconstrues the structure of public life in Romans, so too does he simplistically equate the public square of the Israelites in Isaiah as analogous to the wider contemporary Australian society. In Isa 59:14, we are presented with a public square where the actions of Israelite society are visible for all to see. Two pairs of figures are presented (justice and righteousness; truth and uprightness) as personified images that are turned away, standing at a distance, stumbling, and blocked from entry. John Goldingay notes that the public square is "the place where trade is carried out and therefore dishonesty is practiced."[48] He also notes that it is the place where the elders meet to deal with disputes within the community.[49] It is within these practices of legal processes that truthfulness has collapsed and justice is denied.

---

45. Niskanen, *Isaiah 56–66*, 25.

46. Goldingay observes that alleviating poverty is conceptualised in the text as the "neglect of a minority of people who lack food, homes and clothing" and that this neglect comes at the hands of members of their community. *Isaiah 56–66*, 203.

47. Brueggemann, *Isaiah 40–66*, 196.

48. Goldingay, *Isaiah 56–66*, 217.

49. Childs also draws attention to the legal context of this passage. *Isaiah*, 487.

The first half of verse 14 suggests a rejection by the community, while the second half broadens the image into a wider public witness visible for all to see. It presents a picture of a society that has rejected God's way and actively creates barriers to truth and justice. In a similar way, the ACL's rhetoric suggests that Australian society has rejected the truth and willingly works against justice, particularly for Christians.

This idea is reinforced by verse 15 that reiterates the lack of truth, and further notes that those who refuse to participate in evil become "prey." The one (literally "he") who stands for truth makes themself vulnerable, presumably to those who oppose truth, justice, and righteousness. This is the crux of the rhetoric that the ACL employs, positioning themselves as the righteous and moral individual who is bravely speaking into the hostile public square on behalf of Australian Christians.

The second half of verse 15 reveals that it is not just the public who has witnessed the injustice, but YHWH has also seen and is displeased, with verse 16a elaborating that there is no man (Hebrew, *ish*) to witness the horror and who is able to intercede. The explicit use of *ish* to connote a human here, stands in contrast to the earlier personified and perhaps divine characters of wisdom, righteousness, truth and uprightness.[50] The ACL urges Christians to be the *ish* ready to intercede in order that the claim that truth and justice is lacking in Australian society will be demonstrably false. The ACL, through its mouthpiece, Martin Iles, purports to loudly speak the truth in the public to encourage others, as well as to influence the social, cultural, and political milieu of contemporary Australia so that it does not resemble the public square described in verses 14–16a. The ACL has chosen not to include the second half of verse 16 (or the rest of chapter 59) that says that, because of this situation, it is God who will intervene with God's own righteousness. There are a number of problems associated with this reading.

Firstly, the choice to stop the quote at v. 16a presents this passage as a call to arms against the stumbling of truth, justice, and righteousness outlined in vv. 14–15. However, when read within the context of the whole chapter, this section no longer reads as a provocation to correct societies' missteps. Rather, it is a call to repentance.

Noted biblical scholar, Brevard S. Childs notes that the three sections of this chapter "probe theologically the nature of God's righteousness, the response of faith as repentance and the demand for God's sole eschatological intervention."[51] He notes that the faithful of Israel recognize that they too

---

50. Uprightness here is perhaps better understood as honesty and integrity. Friesen, *Isaiah*, 423.

51. Childs, *Isaiah*, 489.

are enmeshed within the self-destructive culture and share Israel's guilt. This leads to them to "throw themselves completely on God's mercy without offering any mitigating excuses." In response, it is "God alone [who] can shatter the power of sin and bring justice and salvation to suffering Zion."[52] In this way, ACL's reading of this passage places themselves in the position of God, rather than recognizing their own complicity in societal guilt and failings.

Secondly, Isaiah 58 and 59 are directed to "my people," which is to say, the Israelites. Hanson notes that ancient Israel was a somewhat homogenous society which is in stark contrast to the "modern pluralistic society" that we live in.[53] While the prophet was addressing a group all practising basically the same religion, the ACL is directing their speech towards a society comprised of people of many faiths and of none. Their rhetoric is aimed at transforming not just the laws that pertain to Christians, but to all Australians. This would seem to be an over-reach and ignores the passage in the Gospel of Matthew (22:21)[54] which suggests Jesus endorses, or at the very least can be seen to acknowledge, the separation between religion and state.

Thirdly, the references to lying lips, a muttering tongue (v. 3), and "empty arguments" (v. 4) draw attention to the idea that rhetoric can be just as harmful—and therefore just as sinful—as physical violence, which is also decried within these chapters. Bruggeman notes that the "hands of Israel are 'defiled' by blood," and that this accusation refers not just to physical violence, "but to any action that diminishes or harms other members of the community."[55] In a similar way, rhetoric that harms LGBTIQA+ Australian Christians may be conceptualized as defiling those who perpetuate this violence.

One concrete example of harms toward LGBTIQA+ individuals by Australian churches are sexual and gender orientation change efforts, previously known as conversion therapy. Jones et al. note that significant harms are associated with sexual and gender orientation change efforts, and impacted individuals are "significantly more likely to come from religious backgrounds or be religious."[56] Iles not only denies these harms have occurred in Australia, he has been very vocal in his opposition to laws

---

52. Childs, *Isaiah*, 490.

53. Hanson, *Isaiah 40–66*, 216.

54. Matthew 22:21 reads: "They answered, 'Caesar's.' Then he said to them, 'Give therefore to Caesar the things that are Caesar's and to God the things that are God's.'"

55. Brueggemann, *Isaiah 40–66*, 196.

56. Sexual and gender orientation change efforts are not restricted to Christianity in Australia but are observed within a range of religious contexts. Jones et al. note that one of the barriers to healing is the idea that LGBTQIA+ people are not Christian. Jones et al., "Supporting LGBTQA+ peoples' recovery," 368.

protecting LGBTIQA+ individuals from these types of practices.[57] He rejects the evidence of harm and construes conservative Australian Christians as the real victims.[58] This rhetoric perpetuates harms against the LGBTIQA+ community who are already some of the most vulnerable members of Australian society. It also stands in direct contrast to the claims of truth and justice that are referred to in Isa 59:14–16b.

Iles, on behalf of the ACL, dismisses any criticisms of their work by claiming that the critique is grounded in liberal or progressive misunderstandings of the Bible and Christianity that misrepresent truth. Iles says:

> One of the fundamentals that I know and have known since reading my Bible is that people will respond differently to the truth. Some people love it, and love you for it, and some people hate it, and hate you for it.[59]

Iles here does not distinguish between truth, the public reception of the Bible, and his own interpretation of the biblical text. Any response, either positive or negative, confirms Iles' prior convictions and places the respondent within the "us" or "them" category. It has little to do with righteousness or justice, but rather reflects Iles'—and presumably the ACL's—understanding of truth, morality, and Christianity.

The ACL uses the rhetoric of truth, justice, and righteousness to substantiate their argument for Christian rights and values in the Australian public square. The rights that the ACL focuses on are predominantly the right to discriminate against LGBTIQA+ people, the right to deny people access to voluntary assisted dying and women access to abortions, and the right to religious freedom in the face of a perceived discrimination, none of which are mentioned or even alluded to in this section of Isaiah. The ACL is less concerned about the rights of LGBTIQA+ people to live in safety, the rights of Indigenous people, or the rights of asylum seekers and refugees to access protection,[60] all of whom are vulnerable, marginalized and would benefit from voices speaking about the injustice they face within Australian society.

---

57. See: Australian Christian Lobby, "The Truth of It, Ep 24"; Australian Christian Lobby, "Now what? How should we live with bad laws?"; and Martin Iles, "Conversion Therapy Ruse."

58. Iles describes a report from the Tasmanian Law Reform Institute as "a kind of vilification" (9:00) that "incites contempt and hatred towards faith communities on completely baseless grounds."(4:00) Australian Christian Lobby, "The truth about new conversion therapy plans, The Truth of It, Ep. 94."

59. Delbridge, "Meet the New Managing Director," para 55.

60. The ACL has shown some concern for refugees including "cautious" support of the Medevac Bill in 2019, although this is often connected to persecution of Christians around the world.

Conclusion

The ACL, through their Managing Director Martin Iles, often draws on the Bible as a source of authority for their claims and actions. This reflects a wider use of the Bible throughout the history of white Australia to claim moral and ethical authority that has been used to inform political and legal decisions. Indeed, as Meredith Lake points out, the Bible "has been a substantial source of political rhetoric and imagination"[61] and "has had social, cultural and institutional impacts that we continue to live with today."[62] University of Sydney Associate Professor David Smith, who studies religion and politics, notes that despite a long period of conservative federal government with explicit links to Christianity, there is not "a widespread sense of Australia as a 'Christian nation.'"[63] Smith points out that religious organizations in secular nations have political power only when they are seen to have moral authority

While Christianity and the church may have had moral authority in the past, the National Church Life Survey results show a decline in trust of the Christian churches in Australia linked to the Royal Commission into Institutional Child Abuse.[64] Lake observes that "a familiarity with the Scriptures did not, in itself, prevent them [Christians] from inflicting deep and lasting harm on vulnerable people."[65] The revelations from the Royal Commission, particularly the sexual nature of much of the abuse, has contributed to a decline in the perceived moral authority of the church and of other Christian institutions in Australia. Truth has stumbled, not because of misinformation from outside, but because many of those with power inside Christian communities have spread untruths and been willing for the truth to be supressed.

Rather than suggesting that this passage critiques contemporary Australian society as whole, Isaiah 58 and 59 may serve as a reminder to the church of their responsibility to challenge injustice, support the oppressed, and be a voice for social justice within broader society. Christian lobby group Love Makes A Way demonstrates one way that this can be achieved through their nonviolent demonstrations and visible prayer for those impacted by the treatment of refugees and asylum seekers in Australia.[66]

61. Lake, *Bible in Australia*, 246–47.
62. Lake, *Bible in Australia*, 365.
63. Smith, "No longer a 'Christian nation,'" 231.
64. Pepper and Powell, *Religion, Spirituality and Connections*," 10.
65. Lake, *Bible in Australia*, 348.
66. For more information see: https://actionnetwork.org/groups/love-makes-a-way-australia.

Micah Australia trains Christians to advocate against poverty, climate change, and rising global conflicts, all of which disproportionately impact marginalized people.[67] The National Council of Churches is an ecumenical group which advocates for Indigenous people, works to build interfaith relationships, and provides resources to make churches safer. These actions to address matters of concern for vulnerable people are likely to contribute positively to the moral authority of Christianity in Australia, if that is the desired outcome, rather than using the law or political systems to discriminate against minorities and those who are already marginalized within the wider Australian community.

In truth, the ACL's rhetoric is limited to promoting the interests of a select group of Christians that are not necessarily representative of wider Christian attitudes in Australia. They are predominantly focused on policing morality, which in the ACL's communications is too often reduced to sexuality and gender identity. The witness of the ACL can then be perceived as continuing to support small interest groups while harming vulnerable people. This brings the validity of all Christian claims about justice and truth into question. For this reason, one hopes that the wider public may understand that the ACL does not speak for all Australian Christians, including me.

Bibliography

Action Network. "Love Makes a Way Australia." https://actionnetwork.org/groups/love-makes-a-way-australia.

Amzallag, Nissim. "The Authorship of Ezra and Nehemiah in Light of Differences in Their Ideological Background." *Journal of Biblical Literature* 137/2 (2018) 271–97.

Anglican Communion News Service. "Wangaratta's same-sex wedding blessing 'valid,' Australia's highest Church court rules." November 12, 2020. https://www.anglicannews.org/news/2020/11/wangarattas-same-sex-wedding-blessing-valid-australias-highest-church-court-rules.aspx.

Australian Christian Lobby, "The truth about new conversion therapy plans, The Truth of It, Ep. 94" 16 June 2022. https://www.youtube.com/watch?v=XxDvmy7tpMw.

———. "Culture Wars and The Silencing of the Faith—Martyn Iles Interview." 2 December 2020. https://www.youtube.com/watch?v=EpJ5vmWjyNk.

———. "Martyn Iles—Today was nearly the end of Christian schooling in Australia." 10 February 2022. https://www.youtube.com/watch?v=Vh7TqRK6uFc.

———. "Now what? How should we live with bad laws?" 5 February 2021. https://www.facebook.com/ACLobby/videos/274827987309080.

———. "The Truth of It, Ep 24." 7 November 2019. https://www.youtube.com/watch?v=s9FLLD0TMio.

———. "The Truth of It." www.acl.org.au/thetruthofit.

---

67. For more information, see: https://www.micahaustralia.org/about-us/.

———. "The Truth of it S6E6: Religious discrimination Bill." 14 May 2020. https://www.facebook.com/ACLobby/videos/577109009603673/.
———. "Truth Made Public." https://www.acl.org.au/about.
———. "Vic Conversion Therapy Bill Walk-Through." 8 December 2020. https://www.acl.org.au/blog_vic_conversiontherapybillwalkthrough.
Australian Government, Attorney General's Department. "Religious Discrimination." https://www.ag.gov.au/rights-and-protections/human-rights-and-anti-discrimination/freedom-religion.
Becker, Uwe. "The Book of Isaiah: Its Composition History." In *The Oxford Handbook of Isaiah*, edited by Lena Sofia Tiemeyer, 37-56. New York, NY: Oxford University Press, 2020.
Brueggemann, Walter. *Isaiah 40–66*. Louisville, KY: Westminster John Knox, 1998.
Childs, Brevard S. *Isaiah*. Lousiville, KY: Westminster John Knox, 2001.
Christian Coalition of America. "We are the Christian Coalition of America." https://cc.org/about-us/.
Delbridge Tess. "Meet the New Managing Director of the Australian Christian Lobby." *Eternity News*, 8 February 2018. https://www.eternitynews.com.au/australia/who-is-martyn-iles/.
Douglas, Robyn. "GAFCON Australia Threatens Disaffiliation." *The Living Church*, 14 December 2020. https://livingchurch.org/2020/12/14/gafcon-australia-threatens-disaffiliation-for-same-sex-ruling/.
Friesen, Ivan. *Isaiah*. Harrisonburg, VA: MennoMedia, 2009.
Goldingay, John. *Isaiah 56–66*. London: Bloomsbury, 2014.
Gottwald, Norman K. *The Hebrew Bible: A Socio-Literary Introduction*. Philadelphia, PA: Fortress, 1985.
Ham, Ken. "Special Ministry Announcement from Ken Ham." *Answers in Genesis*, 12 May 2023. https://answersingenesis.org/ministry-news/core-ministry/special-ministry-announcement-ken-ham/.
Hanson, Paul D. *Isaiah 40–66*. Louisville, KT: Westminster John Knox, 2012.
Hutchens, Gareth. "Most Christians in Australia support marriage equality and want a free vote." *The Guardian*, 21 July 2017. https://www.theguardian.com/australia-news/2017/jul/21/most-christians-in-australia-support-marriage-equality-and-want-a-free-vote.
Iles, Martin. "Conversion Therapy Ruse." 24 November 2020. https://www.acl.org.au/blog_ml_conversion_therapy_ruse.
Ireland, Judith. "Who are the Australian Christian Lobby?" *Sydney Morning Herald*, 19 February 2016. https://www.smh.com.au/politics/federal/who-are-the-australian-christian-lobby-20160219-gmy67y.html.
Jones, Tiffany, Jennifer Power, Timothy Willem Jones, Maria Pallotta-Chiarolli and Nathan Despott. "Supporting LGBTQA+ peoples' recovery from sexual orientation and gender identity and expression change efforts." *Australian Psychologist* 57/6 (2022) 359–72.
Jones, Timothy Willem. "Australian Secularism, the Sexual Revolution and the Making of the New Christian Right." *Australian Historical Studies* 52/3 (2021) 317–30.
Lake, Meredith. *The Bible in Australia*. Sydney: NewSouth, 2020.
Maddox, Marion. "Right-wing Christian intervention in a naïve polity: the Australian Christian Lobby." *Political Theology* 15/2 (2014) 132–150.

———. "Why is the Australian Christian Lobby waging a culture war over LGBTQ issues?" *The Conversation*, 4 February 2021. https://theconversation.com/why-is-the-australian-christian-lobby-waging-a-culture-war-over-lgbtq-issues-127805.

Micah Australia. "About Us." https://www.micahaustralia.org/about-us/.

Napier-Raman, Kishor. "Martyn Iles, the youthful face of the Christian right." *Crikey*, 26 June 2019. https://www.crikey.com.au/2019/06/26/martyn-iles-the-youthful-face-of-the-christian-right/.

Niskanen, Paul V. *Isaiah 56–66*. Collegeville, MN: Liturgical, 2014.

Pepper Miriam and Ruth Powell. *Religion, spirituality and connections with churches: results from the 2018 Australian Community Survey*. Sydney: NCLS Research, 2018.

Schuele, Andreas. "Who is the True Israel? Community, Identity, and Religious Commitment in Third Isaiah (Isaiah 56–66)." *Interpretation* 73/2 (2019) 174–84.

Segaert, Anthony. "Inside the Australian Christian Lobby's identity crisis." *The Sydney Morning Herald*, 4 March 2023. https://www.smh.com.au/politics/federal/inside-the-australian-christian-lobby-s-identity-crisis-20230228-p5co7y.html.

Smee, Ben. "Citipointe Christian College teachers threatened with dismissal for expressing homosexuality." *The Guardian*, 21 March 2022. https://www.theguardian.com/australia-news/2022/mar/21/citipointe-christian-college-teachers-threatened-with-dismissal-for-expressing-homosexuality.

Smith, David T. "No longer a 'Christian nation': why Australia's Christian Right loses policy battles even when it wins elections." *Religion, State & Society* 49/3 (2021) 231–47.

Thisleton, Anthony C. "The Future of Biblical Interpretation and Responsible Plurality in Hermeneutics." In *The Future of Biblical Interpretation: Responsible Plurality in Biblical Hermeneutics*, edited by Stanley E. Porter Jr and Matthew R. Malcolm, 11–28. Westmont, IL: IVP, 2013.

Tronson, Mark. "Assembly Confessing Congregations—Uniting Church." *Christian Today*, 14 September 2023. https://christiantoday.com.au/news/assembly-confessing-congregations-uniting-church.html.

Uniting Church of Australia. "15th Assembly Decision on Marriage Frequently Asked Questions." August 2018. https://ucaassembly.recollect.net.au/nodes/view/389.

Victorian Government. "LGBTQ+ Change and Suppression Practices Fact Sheet." November 2020. https://www.vic.gov.au/lgbtq-change-and-suppression-practices-fact-sheet.

Warhurst, John. "Australia's Christians form a broader political church that most realise." *Sydney Morning Herald*, 19 April 2017. https://www.smh.com.au/opinion/australias-christians-form-a-broader-political-church-that-most-realise-20170419-gvnoac.html.

Webber, Robert E. *Ancient-Future Faith: Rethinking Evangelicalism for a Postmodern World*. Grand Rapids, MI: Baker, 1999.

Williamson, Robert. *The Forgotten Books of the Bible: Recovering the Five Scrolls for Today*. Minneapolis, MN: Fortress, 2018.

Withers, Rachel. "The spectacular failure of the Australian Conservatives." *Crikey*, 24 June 2019. https://www.crikey.com.au/2019/06/24/cory-bernardi-australian-conservatives/.

Worldometer. "Australia Population." Accessed 31 January 2022. https://www.worldometers.info/world-population/australia-population/.

Solid Rock, Sacred Ground

Reading the Hebrew Bible within
a Five Kilometer Radius

MEGAN TURTON

> Our age is retrospective. It builds the sepulchers of the fathers. It writes biographies, histories and criticism. The foregoing generations beheld God and nature face to face; we, through their eyes. Why should we not also enjoy an original relation to the universe? Why should we not have . . . a religion by revelation to us, and not a history to theirs?
>
> RALPH WALDO EMERSON[1]

WITHIN THE SECOND EDITION of *The Bible in Australia*, Meredith Lake acknowledges that she is writing the preface "under something like a lockdown" while the world is grappling with a pandemic.[2] Lake is writing in Winter 2020, presumably in Sydney where she resides. Melbourne, meanwhile, was experiencing its own lockdown, the second of six that would be imposed throughout 2020–2021 in order to curb the spread of COVID-19. From the ninth of July to the second of August, Metropolitan Melbourne and Mitchell Shire were put under stage three restrictions. People could only leave their homes for four reasons: shopping for food and essential items; exercise;

---

1. Emerson, *Nature*, 1.
2. Lake, *Bible in Australia*, xxii.

medical care; and, work (if unable to work from home).³ From the second of August, Victoria initiated a State of Disaster—alongside the existing State of Emergency—and imposed stage four restrictions on Metropolitan Melbourne for a further six weeks, under which Melburnians could only exercise for one hour outside per day, no further than a five kilometer radius from their homes.⁴ The second lockdown would last one hundred and eleven days and, in all, Melbourne would go on to experience over two hundred and sixty-two days of lockdown since the pandemic began, one of the longest periods of lockdown in the world.⁵

Back in the winter of 2020, Lake wondered "how the pandemic will reshape the Bible's place in contemporary Australian life."⁶ She noted that there were already indications of change among the regular readers of the Bible "in the contours of devotional life." Over lockdown, churches suspended their regular services and moved their meetings online, disrupting the way believers corporately encountered and experienced the Bible. She contemplated the forging of new forms of worship in digital and domestic spaces, still "nourished by Scripture," and invoked the hopeful words of human rights lawyer Nyadol Nyoun, that we may make something of this "sacred pause."⁷ Referencing Constant Mews, a historian on medieval religion and thought, Lake anticipated that, if past pandemics are any guide, we might expect a "mystical, inward turn to spiritual life."⁸ Indeed, Mews contemplates the acceleration of "de-institutionalization from formal religious belonging" and a greater "multiplicity in forms of worship."⁹

A question that Lake could not then have addressed is whether and how Melbourne's experiences of COVID-19 and one of the world's longest lockdowns might further redefine the city's relationship with urban greenspaces. Lockdown restrictions required the closure of institutional sacred places and the capacity for people to congregate was severely limited.¹⁰ With human movement restricted to five kilometers, local urban parklands assumed a level of importance that was possibly unprecedented since the beginning of Melbourne's colonial history. People flocked to whatever parkland they could during the limited time they were allowed outside, supporting the

3. ABC, "Victoria Reimposes."
4. Victorian State Government, "Premier's Statement."
5. Zhuang, "Melbourne."
6. Lake, *Bible in Australia*, xxiii–xxiv.
7. Nyoun, "From the Wreck," para 14.
8. Nyoun, "From the Wreck," para 14.
9. Mews, "Coronavirus."
10. See Brett and Gilmour, "Worship."

ever-growing evidence that nature and greenspaces are vital for human wellbeing. The lockdown exposed geographical inequalities, as some Melburnians found they had little or no parkland within five kilometers of their home.[11] In some cases, previously privatized greenspaces like the Northcote Golf Course were overrun by residents, prompting new conversations on whether these should be made available to the public post-COVID.[12] In a world in which opportunities for spiritual nourishment became severely curtailed, local "wildernesses" assumed a new aura of magic, of "holiness."[13]

The sanctity of land and nature, "Country," is something that has been known and maintained by the Indigenous peoples of what is now called Australia since time immemorial. One of the foundational principles of Aboriginal and Torres Strait Islander cultures, spiritualities and theologies is the intimate relationship between the original owners and the land of their ancestors.[14] Land is not an object but is inhabited by spirit, the creator-ancestors, that sustains the First Peoples who, in turn, look after the land their kin.[15] This relationship continues despite the ongoing realities of colonial dispossession and struggles for native title recognition. In contrast, much Western theology has "de-sanctified" nature under the influence of the modern philosophies of Europe that drew sharp distinctions between mind and matter, rendering nature inert and inanimate, mere material to be exploited for human use. Biblical passages, like the injunction to "subdue" the earth (Gen 1:28), were (mis)used by colonizers and imperialists to sanction an instrumentalist view of nature and the displacement of Indigenous peoples from their ancestral lands.[16] These ideologies have contributed to the catastrophic consequences that we now face as human-induced climate change and global warming threaten the longevity of all life on earth.

All of this raises the question: in light of the pandemic, and a renewed sense that human wellbeing is interconnected with the wellbeing of the greater ecosystems of which we are a part, how might we reconceptualize

11. Lakhani et al., "340,000 Melburnians."

12. Davey, "Fair Way?"

13. In modern ecological discussion, "wilderness" refers to natural habitat that is not manipulated or managed by humans. I use the term, somewhat incorrectly, throughout this paper to evoke the sense in which "wildness" and "otherness" can persist in lands (and waters) under human control or influence. I am informed by Bauckham, *Bible and Ecology*, 103–40.

14. See. e.g., Champion and Dewerse, *Yarta Wandatha*; Gondarra, *Reflections*, 29–55; Pattel-Gray, "Black Truth"; Deverell, *Gondwana*, esp. 9–35; Paulson and Brett, "Five Smooth Stones,"; Bowden, "Searching Altyerre," esp. 1–28, and the contributors to *Spirituality of Catholic Aborigines*.

15. Deverell, *Gondwana*, 9–15.

16. See Brett, *Decolonizing God*, 7–43, and the literature cited, 20n38.

the wildernesses at our doorsteps—how might those from within the modern West go about "re-sanctifying" the land?[17] I propose that we read our local landscapes with and through passages in the Hebrew Bible that reveal tree and soil, stone and water, wind and bird, are capable of the state of holiness and of holding the divine presence.[18]

Jewish biblical scholar Benjamin Sommer contends that parts of the Hebrew Bible articulate an understanding of "fluid divine selfhood."[19] According to Sommer, the "deity can produce many small-scale manifestations that enjoy some degree of independence, without becoming separate deities."[20] That is, the Israelite God Yahweh could materialize in a number of geographical locations without challenging a monotheistic worldview. These manifestations "were part of God but not all of God."[21] A corollary of the notion of fluid divine selfhood is that God is capable of a multiplicity of divine embodiments, particularly within nature and natural materials.[22]

Within this paper, I read these texts of the Hebrew Bible through my own experiences of the greenspaces in Melbourne's Northeast along the Birrarung (The Yarra River) and Merri Merri (Merri Creek) that I grew to revere during the extensive lockdowns. I acknowledge my privilege in being able to live within five kilometers of these special places on the Country of the Wurundjeri people of the Kulin nations.[23] As a non-Indigenous

---

17. This parallels the thesis of David Tacey that Australians need to recover a sense of the sacred—a process he calls "re-enchantment"—in land, place, and the ordinary. I differ from Tacey in his suspicion that this kind of worldview is "'unrecognizable' from the point of view of the old Judeo-Christian dispensation." Tacey, *Re-enchantment*, 93–122, 163–85, quote at 98.

18. From the native Israelite point of view, the chief determinant for sanctity, for holiness, is the presence of the deity. See Wright, "Holiness," 307.

19. Sommer, *Bodies*, 38–44, 54–75.

20. Sommer, *Bodies*, 38.

21. Sommer, *Bodies*, 54.

22. Sommer, *Bodies*, 44–54. By using Sommer's model, I do not directly address whether the Israelite's worldview or my own interpretation of that worldview is panentheistic or animistic, although I acknowledge that there is some overlap between these belief systems and Sommer's model of fluid divine selfhood. For discussion, see Sommer, *Bodies*, 140–43; Bauckham, *Bible and Ecology*, 86–87; Joerstad, "Animism"; Wallace, *God*, 610. Partially inspired by Mark I. Wallace, I use the poetic language "God *was/is* [natural phenomenon]," without claiming that there is no difference between God *and* [natural phenomenon]. See Wallace, *God*, 13–16. This phraseology, whether it be figurative, literal, or both, is preserved in the Hebrew Bible (see examples below), alongside traditions that oppose the idea that Yahweh could have many bodies or could be identified, even momentarily, with natural phenomena. On the contributions of this dialectic to contemporary Jewish and Christian theology, see Sommer, *Bodies*, 124–43.

23. See further, Eidelson, *Melbourne Dreaming*.

Australian, I cannot understand and experience the land in the same way as the traditional owners. I draw upon ecological hermeneutics—a biblical interpretive stance that has, fittingly, largely developed within the context of Australia.[24] I take for granted that the "Earth" and "Earth community" have a voice, a voice that can be retrieved from the biblical text and also experienced as "original revelation" that illuminates the text's ongoing meanings and significances within a particular location.[25] I read the biblical texts and Melburnian landscape alongside local histories, geology, ecology, and Australian writings that explore the sanctity of place and nature.

When God Was a Tree and the Soil: The Yarra Flats

A remnant of ancient river red gums clusters along the Birrarung as it winds through a section of preserved wetlands known as the "Yarra Flats" in the suburbs of Ivanhoe East and Eaglemont. Once endemic to the open woodlands of the land we now call Melbourne, river red gums were felled in large numbers as the settlement expanded. From 1863, the gums were commercially harvested. Most of Melbourne's significant older trees, the ones that pre-dated white settlement, are river red gums—*Eucalyptus camaldulensis*. These veterans are anything from four hundred to eight hundred years old.[26] Historian James Boyce comments that it is nothing short of "a miracle that such stupendous living connections with the Yarra of 1835 have survived."[27]

In order to approach the old trees in the Yarra Flats, you have to veer off the main concreted path of the Yarra Trail. This less visible track, which more faithfully follows the loops and whirls of the river, becomes earthen and narrow and the vegetation on either side presses back into the pathway. The first time I walked this path, I did not know that the trees were there. I first noticed that I felt more enclosed, the world had become darker and cooler. Then, as I rounded a corner and the path sloped downwards, I had the distinct impression of being *watched* and of being in *the presence*. There is a surge of reverence that is provoked by looking up into an age-old river red gum that is so wide three people cannot link their arms around it, and is so tall that the eyes cannot take it in in one view. It was not an entirely comfortable

---

24. Habel, "Earth Bible."

25. Habel, "Ecological," 1–8. "Original revelation" echoes the phrasing used by Ralph Waldo Emerson, quoted at the beginning of this paper.

26. Cunningham, *City*, 214, 218.

27. Boyce, *1835*, 211.

encounter. I felt an irrepressible urge to silently tiptoe past the convocation without making a noise, lest I disturb something profound and unknown.

I am not alone in experiencing awe in the presence of great trees. The Melbourne writer Sophie Cunningham, after meeting a particularly impressive river red gum in St Kilda, struggles to describe the experience, "It is hard to convey the intensity that this particular tree emanates as it stands, like a sentinel or an ancient god, looking across the land, without sounding slightly crazy."[28] On Melbourne's old river gums, Boyce reflects, "I return to them often in my imagination because their roots, endurance, graceful hospitality, silent majesty and very survival seem to testify that . . . there is some force greater than us."[29] Within his memoir and ode to the Australian landscape, Don Watson regards a tree:

> Its power quickly comes apparent: the height, the mass, the form, the force, tenacity, grace or agelessness it expresses. The color, light, movement and sound it generates; the vigor, strength, fecundity, the life force. The moods, the terror, the terror and the wonder it excites.[30]

These arboreal encounters of sentience, of awe, terror, and wonder, should be recognizable to anyone with some familiarly with the Hebrew Bible. The ancestors and founders of the Israelite nation viewed their God as frequently becoming manifest in or around sacred trees.[31] Remarkably, these encounters are retained with the Pentateuch and elsewhere, despite the laws within Deuteronomy that mandate that valid worship must be performed within a single, centralized sacred place, *maqom* (Deut 12), and not under any green tree (Deut 12:2) or with the *'asherah* (Deut 7:5; 12:3; 16:21).[32] The latter was likely a live tree, tree stump, or wooden pole that, although once associated with the cult of the Northwest Semitic goddess Asherah, became incorporated as a legitimate cultic object in ancient forms of Yahweh worship.[33]

The famous story of God's self-disclosure to Moses in Exodus 3–4 has Yahweh present in the form of a burning bush. Exodus 3:2 provides that a *mal'akh*, a messenger or angel of Yahweh, appeared to Moses in a flame of fire out of the bush. Within verse four, however, it is God who calls out to Moses out of the bush, "Moses, Moses!" The ancient poem in Deuteronomy

28. Cunningham, *City*, 219.

29. James Boyce, *1835*, 212.

30. Watson, *Bush*, 188.

31. Sommer, *Bodies*, 44–49; Bauks, "Sacred Trees," esp. 280–82.

32. Translations are generally based on the NRSV, unless they are my own, as is the case here.

33. Olyan, *Asherah*; Hadley, *Cult*, 77–83.

33 refers to Yahweh as "the one who dwells in a bush" (v.16). The term "angel," therefore, is used here to signify "a manifestation or small-scale embodiment of part of Yahweh."[34]

There are many hints of sacred trees holding an incarnation of the Israelite God within the ancestral narratives. The oak of Moreh marks the sacred place, the *maqom* of Shechem at which Yahweh appears to Abram and Abram builds an altar (Gen 12:6–7, 35:4; Deut 11:29–30). Similarly, Abram built an altar by the oaks of Mamre at Hebron (Gen 13:18), where "Yahweh manifested" to him again as Abraham (Gen 18:1). Abraham plants a tamarisk tree in Beersheba to invoke there the name of Yahweh-El-Olam, "Yahweh, the Everlasting God" (Gen 21:33, 26:23–25).[35]

The survival of Israel's regional sacred trees within the Pentateuchal narrative, despite the forces of religious (and political) orthodoxy and centralization, is mirrored by a story about one of central Melbourne's last remaining giant red gums. The tree encroached onto Elizabeth Street, alongside St Francis' Church, projecting into the street through a gap left in the church fence. In the early 1840s it acted as a church belfry, the bell hanging from one of its massive branches. Eventually, the red gum was felled in 1878 when St Francis' was extended, but a remnant of it continues to stand in the sanctuary of St Patrick's Cathedral in the form of an episcopal chair that was carved from its trunk.[36] The symbolism is multivalent—is the living potency of the felled tree subdued by its reworking into religious paraphernalia or does the tree infect the enclosed space with its wild holiness?

One of the ways in which something of the divine might be known through ancient trees is by contemplating their relationship to life, death, and time. Cunningham observes that "death is a mutable thing in trees."[37] A tree's trunk and all its wood are comprised of dead cells; the life of a tree is in the thin sliver of living tissue on its outside. The final stage in a tree's life, the point when the rate of cell division falls behind the rate of cell death, is known as senescence. River red gums can exist in a state of senescence for more than a hundred years. New trees can sprout from old trees and, when a mature tree topples, up to seven young stems may grow from the parent.[38] Even dead, mature river red gums continue to serve an ecological purpose as "habitat" trees, because each tree, on average, supports an estimated

---

34. Sommer, *Bodies*, 41–42, quote at 48.
35. Sommer, *Bodies*, 40, 41–42, 48–49; Olyan, *Asherah*, 5n15.
36. Annear, *Bearbrass*, 39; Cunningham, *City*, 222.
37. Cunningham, *City*, 215.
38. Colloff, *Flooded Forest*, 13–14.

sixteen mammals, forty-four birds, and seven hundred insect species in their hollows.[39]

When you try and view time from the perspective of a river red gum, it stretches out into something like immortality. River red gums can live for generations, over five hundred years, a human lifespan is only a fraction of their lifetime. A subfossil, likely to be *Eucalyptus camaldulensis*, that was removed from nineteen meters below the Yarra River has been dated to 8,780 years before the present. A group of *Eucalyptus* species that contains the red gums evolved at least five million years ago.[40]

A further reason that "these trees are considered sacred, indeed *feel* sacred, is that their presence traces the history of the elements."[41] The roots of mature red gums can go down ten meters—think of the paths these roots take through the riverbanks and swamps, connecting and entwining with the primordial mud. This cool and private place is also sacred: does not God ask Moses as he approaches the burning the bush to remove his sandals, because he is standing on holy soil (*'admat-qodesh*) (Exod 3:5)? In the Exodus legal tradition, Yahweh instructs Moses to inform the Israelites that their local altars should be built from the earth (*'adamah*) and in these sacred places God promises to come and bless worshippers (Exod 20:24). Humankind (*'adam*), who is made in the image of God in the first creation story (Gen 1:27–28), is also made from the dust of the ground (*'adamah*) in the second creation story (Gen 2:7–8)—the same substance from which God makes the trees (v. 9). I must admit that in those wetlands of the Birrarung that smell of mud and limb and leaf and decay and life, I have felt an enormous peace knowing that I might one day lay down and return to the earth, that holy dirt.

When God was a Bird and the Wind: Wilson Reserve

It was September 30, 2020, that my obsession with birdwatching began. I know this because it was seeded by a single Facebook post by the CERES Community Environment Park, an urban farm located by the Merri Creek in Brunswick.[42] At this time, Melbourne was still in its second lockdown. The post heralded the return of the sacred kingfisher to the Merri Creek. Kingfishers winter in the warmer climate of the north and then return to the south in spring for breeding season. The sacred kingfisher went missing from the Merri for more than twenty years due to water pollution and

---

39. Cunningham, *City*, 215.
40. Colloff, *Flooded Forest*, 51–52.
41. Cunningham, *City*, 231.
42. CERES, "Sacred Kingfisher."

habitat destruction, but "miraculously returned" in 1993 after the creek was reclaimed and cleaned up by the local community. For the CERES community, the sacred kingfisher is a sign that "regeneration of land is possible, and life and fertility can return even when it seems hopeless." In response to the arrival of the first kingfisher in 2020, the community sent out a message of thanksgiving, "It is not given that the kingfisher will return each year... And we give our thanks for their blessing and bless them in return."[43]

Birds have an internal "clock-and-compass," a sense of where they should be and when.[44] From a biblical perspective, we might say that birds keep sacred time.[45] Of the birds of the Australian bush, poet Judith Wright writes, "Then at their time they come, timid or bold," and of the black cockatoos, "while other birds were quiet in prayer or fear, *these knew their hour*."[46] Coming out of a winter in lockdown, the return of the sacred kingfisher was a sign, an omen (in Hebrew, an *'ōt*), and I was determined to see one.[47] I did not have any luck along the Merri, but my research into birdwatching eventually led me to Wilson Reserve in Ivanhoe, a native woodland and wetland on the Birrarung. Not only did I eventually glimpse a sacred kingfisher, but I sighted the azure kingfisher, a bird rarely seen within such proximity to the city.

The first time I saw the kingfisher, Exod 24:10 came to mind, "And they saw the God of Israel. Under his feet was like a pavement of sapphire stone, like the very heaven for clearness."[48] The blue of the kingfisher is more beautiful than a sapphire; it shimmers and changes with the light like blue fire. When you see a kingfisher dive for food in a still pool and then return to its perch in a moment, the flash of blue is a revelation. The sky breaks open and a piece of the waters normally held up by the dome plunges into the water (Gen 1:6–8); an undoing and redoing of creation, as water reunites with water and then returns to the heavens again. Perhaps the kingfisher is related to the God of creation in Gen 1:12. The spirit, the wind of God (*ruah*

---

43. CERES, "Sacred Kingfisher."
44. See Ackerman, *Genius*, 227–76.
45. E.g., Gen 2:3; Exod 20:8–11.
46. Wright, "Black Cockatoos," in *Birds*, 46. My emphasis.

47. The origin of the name *Todiramphus sanctus* is complex. The epithet *sanctus* is first extant in John Latham's 1782 description of the species. Latham, citing Sydney Parkinson's journals, claimed that the "Respected Kingsfisher" of Tonga and the "Venerated Kingfisher" of the Society Islands—both now called collared kingfishers—and the "Sacred Kingsfisher" of the "South Seas" were held in veneration by the Indigenous peoples of the areas, "perhaps on account of their being frequently seen flying about *Marais* and *burial-places*." See Latham, *General Synopsis*, 621–24.

48. My translation.

'*Elohim*) that hovers over the face of the deep is described as moving like a bird (*merahefet*; cf. Deut 32:11).[49]

God's embodiment in bird-form, perhaps foreign to a modern Western worldview, is resonant with the avian imagery of God in the Hebrew Bible. Yahweh frequently takes winged form in the Psalms (17:8, 36:8, 57:2, 61:5, 63:8, 91:4), where the shadow of God's wings provide refuge. While it is tempting to dismiss this language as purely metaphorical or figurative, the literary imagery draws on iconographic motifs found in Syro-Palestinian art in which gods are depicted with wings.[50] This includes the Egyptian bird-God Horus who takes the form of a falcon, a falcon-headed man, and the winged disk.[51] Perhaps, in particular times and places, God's body is that of a bird on the wind, feather, beak, flesh and claw.[52]

When God Was Stone and Water: The Merri Merri

The Merri Creek flows about sixty kilometers from the Great Dividing Range north of Wallan, through Melbourne's northern suburbs to Abbotsford where it meets the Yarra River just above Dights Falls. Its geological story stretches back over four hundred million years, when the ocean left behind layers of sandstone and mudstone. From 4.6 to 0.8 million years ago, volcanoes erupted, sending lava on a journey through the ancestral valleys of the Merri and Darebin Creeks and into the basin of the Yarra, nearly as far as the present-day Central Business District. The modern-day Merri Creek was formed over many years by water carving through the surface of the lava.[53] The waterway is significant for the Wurundjeri-willan and other clans in and around Melbourne: the confluence of the Merri Merri and the Birrarung was a traditional meeting place. Following European settlement, the Merri Creek Aboriginal School, the Native Police Corps, and the Merri Creek Protectorate Station were located nearby.[54]

---

49. Wallace, *God*, 22–23. For a reading from an Aboriginal perspective, see Prentis, "Birds," 24–25.

50. LeMon, *Winged Form*.

51. LeMon, *Winged Form*, 31–34, 74–82, 150–51.

52. In his translation of Genesis 1 into Boonwurrung, even the colonist William Thomas, "though weighed down by the settler ideologies of the nineteenth century, envisaged the possibility of God embodied as an eagle." Thank you to Mark G. Brett for drawing this to my attention (private correspondence). See Thomas, "Succinct Sketch," 130–31.

53. Merri Creek Management Committee, "About Merri Creek."

54. Eidelson, *Melbourne Dreaming*, 52–55.

The creek is called the Merri Merri for reason—Merri is the Woiwurrung word for "rocky." The lava flows left behind basalt or bluestone in the creek corridor that was quarried from the 1850s after European settlement. Many of early Melbourne's buildings and roads, including Pentridge Prison, were built from the stones of the Merri. Some of the earliest quarries were in the section of the creek that I frequent, between CERES in Brunswick, and the Birrarung in Abbotsford.[55] Over time, many of the former bluestone quarries became municipal rubbish tips and the creek attracted industrial activity, becoming an urban gutter and wasteland. It was not until the 1970s that, through the coordinating efforts of local councils (Merri Creek Coordinating Committee) and community groups (Friends of Merri Creek), the creek and its environs were brought back to life as urban reaches were revegetated, native trees and shrubs were replanted, and the native birds returned to their homelands.[56]

The waters that I follow in Northcote and Clifton Hill laugh and dance over the paths of the river stones, rivulets shimmer and glitter in the sun. The blue cliff rockface rises high over the water, giving the impression of what local ecological philosopher Freya Mathews describes as "stone terraces and amphitheaters, steps and water gardens." Within the water, "shoals of shards and spheres [are] tossed together, like simple petrified souls."[57] Spherical stones, although formed by the natural force of water, bear the mark of artifacts, of intelligent intent. Their geometry is reminiscent of the celestial, the cosmological.[58] And these are not the only rocks of the Merri Creek to have a deiform presence. The rocky cliff faces of the Merri Gorge between St Georges Road and Dights Falls are formed by cooling lava, creating tall basalt columns. Due to weathering, columns have collapsed and tumbled into the stream over time.[59] Some of the vertical fractures at the top of the cliff appear to be leaning forward, watching over the ablutions of the river.

Biblical texts, particularly the stories of the ancestors, testify that divine embodiment was possible not only in wood but also in stone.[60] Given that Deuteronomy (7:5, 12:3, 16:22) prohibits the setting up of sacred stone pillars, the *matsebot*, the retention of these visitations within the Pentateuch is extraordinary. According to Genesis 28:10-22, Jacob, after experiencing

---

55. Merri Creek Management Committee, "Historical Heritage."

56. Merri Creek Management Committee, "Wastelands to Parklands"; Friends of Merri Creek; "From Waste to Parklands."

57. Mathews, *Journey*, 25.

58. Mathews, *Journey*, 17.

59. Merri Creek Management Committee, "Geological and Geomorphological."

60. Sommer, *Bodies*, 49–54; Zevit, *Religions*, 256–65; Olyan, *Asherah*, 5n15.

a divine visitation through a dream while sleeping in Bethel, took a stone from under his head. He set it up for a pillar, a *matsebah,* poured oil on it, and called the sacred place "House of God" *(bet-ʾel).* Similarly, in Genesis 35:13–15, Jacob sets up a *matsebah* where God had spoken with him, poured out a libation and oil on it, and called the sacred place the house of God *(bet-ʾel).* In these passages it appears that, upon anointing, the stone becomes a place appropriate for divine dwelling.[61] Within Gen 31:13, God appears to Jacob and announces "I am the God; a *bet-ʾel* that you anointed there; a pillar."[62] An early poem, Genesis 49:24, may recall the notion of Yahweh's embodiment in stelae or *bet-ʾels* when it refers to God as the "stone *(ʾeben)* of Israel."[63] Some texts may even suggest that God could be present in the stones of an altar. Genesis 33:20 reads, "There he erected an altar and called it *El-Elohe-Israel.*" In this verse, Jacob seems to call the altar itself by the name "El, God of Israel," the stone being identified with the deity.[64]

The Merri, making its own pace through the valley and attending so devoutly to its "fluvial business," perpetually anoints its ancient stony vessel. Water, one of the foundations of all life on earth, is also one the greatest agents of holiness within the Hebrew Bible, one of the mediums which can bring about a change in condition, consecrating people (Exod 19:10) and priests (Exod 29:4).[65] In select biblical texts, "the life-giving quality of water is attributed to supernatural agency, if not presented as having a divine substance itself."[66] The book of Jeremiah presents God as the "the fountain of living waters." The connotation of the "living waters" *(mayim hayyim)* is twofold: living water combines the life-giving quality with its origination from a natural source, as opposed to the water of an artificial cistern that is still-standing (Jer 2:13).[67] The source of "living waters" is frequently located in the temple of Jerusalem (Ps 45:6; Ezek 47:12), but from the divine sanctuary it flows to every part of the land, growing into a mighty stream that nourishes trees that bear fruit every month (Ezek 47:1–12).[68] This temple

---

61. Sommer, *Bodies,* 49–50.

62. My translation. On the grammatical issues, see Sommer, *Bodies,* 50, 207n74; Skinner, *Genesis,* 395.

63. Sommer, *Bodies,* 51.

64. Skinner, *Genesis,* 416; Sommer, *Bodies,* 51.

65. Ben Zvi, "Thinking of Water," in Ben Zvi and Levin, *Thinking of Water,* 25–26.

66. Nissinen, "Sacred Springs," in Ben Zvi and Levin, *Thinking of Water,* 30.

67. Nissinen, "Sacred Springs," 30.

68. Nissinen, "Sacred Springs," 31.

imagery is reminiscent of the sacred space of Eden, the source of the four cosmological rivers that watered the entire world (Gen 2:10–14).[69]

Although there is perhaps less evidence that Israel's God manifested in regional water shrines than in trees and stones, the patriarchal narratives depict pivotal moments of divine encounter at water sites. A *mal'akh* appears to Hagar by a water spring (*'en hammayim*) on the way to Shur and reveals to her the name of her son, Ishmael, and promises her a multitude of offspring (Gen 16:7–12). It is later revealed that it is none other than Yahweh who is speaking to her and from this experience the local deity *and* the well derive their name: *El-Roi* ("a God of Seeing") and *Beer-lahai-roi* ("Well of the Living One of Seeing") (vv. 13–14).[70]

Also at Beersheba ("Well of Seven" or "Well of the Oath"), a *mal'akh* of God promises Hagar to make a great nation out of her son and God opens her eyes to a well of water (*be'er-mayim*) (Gen 21:14–19). Later, Abraham plants the tamarisk tree in Beersheba and at the sacred well he calls on the name of *El-Olam*, "Eternal God" (Gen 21:33), presumably the name of a local *numen* who is linked in the narrative with Yahweh.[71] Yahweh also appears to Isaac at Beersheba, a place Isaac clearly designates as a site of worship by building an altar (Gen 26:23–25). Later again, Jacob offers sacrifices to the God (*El*) of his father Isaac at Beersheba and God speaks to Jacob in night visions (46:14).[72]

Watery encounters with the divine are not limited to the Israelite ancestors. Mathews, upon completing her pilgrimage to the source of the Merri north of Wallan, reflects upon the transformative experience using biblical language and imagery. The group's last morning before reaching their "sacred destination" dawns in "biblical radiance"; when Mathews returns it is like she has had vision from the other side of things, "I burned, bright as a biblical bush, with its afterlight."[73] Bathing in and drinking from the living waters is a sacrament.[74] In complete deference to her localized experience of encountering the "primal source," which is surrounded by wildflowers, she asks, "Could Eden itself, where the primal rivers rose, boast anything more holy than these tiny illuminations from the manuscripts of creation?"[75]

69. Stager, "Jerusalem," 38–39.
70. Skinner, *Genesis*, 287–89.
71. Skinner, *Genesis*, 324, 327.
72. Skinner, *Genesis*, 366, 491–92.
73. Mathews, *Journey*, 7, 10, 18, 41.
74. Mathews, *Journey*, 44, 47.
75. Mathews, *Journey*, 47.

Final Reflections

What role can the Bible have in reshaping our attitudes towards sacred spaces and nature in contemporary Australian life? In the wake of the pandemic, and its restrictions on human movement and religious congregation, the Hebrew Bible is a resource by which we might reconsider our relationship with and responsibility towards local ecosystems. Why should the Merri be considered any less numinous, any less holy, than the primal rivers of Eden? Within the Hebrew Bible, God is wood and earth, stone and water, feather and wind. The portrayal of divine embodiment in these texts, at particular times and particular places, invites us to consider: if these elements constitute God in the Bible, could not any of them hold God's living presence today? And, if all creation is potentially sacred, how might we "comport ourselves to the natural world with reverence and adulation to the enfleshment of God in the biosphere?"[76]

The Hebrew Bible suggests that visitors can encounter God in nature but standing on solid rock, sacred ground requires reverence and a willingness to ask, "*Who are you*?" This is perhaps the truest for our urban greenspaces which sustain us on a daily basis but, in so doing, become dangerously familiar and ordinary. Yet, as Mathews notes, "Do we have any choice, ultimately, but to turn back to the familiar, to the world we have so rapidly and hungrily made over to our own design? When we examine it again, won't we find cracks in its ordinariness, with strangeness, dangers and distance showing through?"[77] If we look for divinity in the wildernesses at our doorstops, we might find that humanity's own sanctification and ultimate redemption from destruction begins with the restoration of God the creek, the return of God the kingfisher, and the preservation of God the ancient tree.

---

76. Wallace, *God*, 24.
77. Mathews, *Journey*, 11–12, 45, quote at 11.

Bibliography

ABC. "Victoria Reimposes Coronavirus Stage 3 Lockdown on Metropolitan Melbourne and Mitchell Shire after Record Rise in Cases." *ABC News*, 7 July 2020, updated 8 July 2020. https://www.abc.net.au/news/2020-27-07/victoria-reimposes-lockdown-as-coronavirus-cases-rise/12429990.

Ackerman, Jennifer. *The Genius of Birds*. Brunswick, VIC: Scribe, 2016.

Annear, Robyn. *Bearbrass: Imagining Early Melbourne*. Port Melbourne, VIC: Mandarin, 1995.

Bauckham, Richard. *Bible and Ecology: Rediscovering the Community of Creation*. Waco, TX: Baylor University Press, 2010.

Bauks, Michaela. "Sacred Trees in the Garden of Eden and Their Ancient Near Eastern Precursors." *JAJ* 3 (2021) 267–301.

Ben Zvi, Ehud, and Christoph Levin, eds. *Thinking of Water in the Early Second Temple Period*. Berlin: De Gruyter, 2014.

Bowden, Michael. "Searching *Altyerre* to Reveal the Cosmic Christ: A Contribution to the Dialogue between the Ancient Arrernte Imaginary and Christianity." PhD diss. University of Divinity, 2019.

Boyce, James. *1835: The Founding of Melbourne and the Conquest of Australia*. Collingwood, VIC: Black Inc., 2012.

Brett, Mark G. *Decolonizing God: The Bible in the Tides of Empire*. Sheffield: Sheffield Phoenix, 2009.

———. *Locations of God: Political Theology in the Hebrew Bible*. New York: Oxford University Press, 2019.

Brett, Mark G., and Rachelle Gilmour. "Worship in Exile as an 'Essential Service.'" *ABC Religion & Ethics*, 30 March 2020. https://www.abc.net.au/religion/hebrew-bible-worship-in-exile-as-essential-service/12102306.

CERES Environment Park. "The Sacred Kingfisher Has Returned!" 30 September 2020. https://www.facebook.com/CERES.Environment.Park/posts/10158696693480818.

Champion, Denise, and Rosemary Dewerse. *Yarta Wandatha*. Salisbury, SA: Denise Champion, 2014.

Colloff, Matthew. *Flooded Forest and Desert Creek: Ecology and History of the River Red Gum*. Collingwood, VIC: CSIRO, 2014.

Cunningham, Sophie. *City of Trees: Essays on Life, Death and the Need for a Forest*. Melbourne: Text, 2019.

Davey, Melissa. "Fair way? Covid Turned a Melbourne Golf Course into a Public Park and Now No One Wants to Leave." *The Guardian Australia*, 17 October 2020. https://www.theguardian.com/australia-news/2020/oct/17/fair-way-covid-turned-a-melbourne-golf-course-into-a-public-park-and-now-no-one-wants-to-leave.

Deverell, Garry J. *Gondwana Theology: A Trawloolway Man Reflects on Christian Faith*. Reservoir, VIC: Morning Star, 2018.

Eidelson, Meyer. *Melbourne Dreaming: A Guide to Exploring*. Canberra: Aboriginal Studies, 2014.

Emerson, Ralph Waldo. *Nature*. London: Penguin Books, 2008.

Friends of Merri Creek. "From Waste to Parklands." https://www.friendsofmerricreek.org.au/index.cfm?display=1151334.

Gondarra, Djiniyini. *Series of Reflections of Aboriginal Theology: Four Reflections Based on Church Renewal, Christian Theology of the Land, Contextualization and Unity.* Darwin: Bethel Presbytery, Northern Synod of the Uniting Church in Australia, 1986.

Habel, Norman C. "The Earth Bible Project." *SBL Forum Archive*, July 2004. https://www.sbl-site.org/publications/article.aspx?ArticleId=291.

———. "Introducing Ecological Hermeneutics." In *Exploring Ecological Hermeneutics*, edited by Norman C. Habel and Peter C. Trudinger, 18. Atlanta, GA: SBL, 2008.

Hadley, Judith M. *The Cult of Asherah in Ancient Israel and Judah: Evidence for a Hebrew Goddess.* New York: Cambridge University Press, 2000.

Hendriks, Joan, and Gerry Hefferan, eds. *A Spirituality of Catholic Aborigines and the Struggle for Justice.* Kangaroo Point, QLD: Aborigines & Torres Strait Islander Apostolate, 1993.

Joerstad, Mari. "A Brief Account of Animism in Biblical Studies." *JSRNC* 14 (2020) 250–70.

Lake, Meredith. *The Bible in Australia: A Cultural History.* 2nd ed. Sydney: NewSouth, 2020.

Lakhani, Ali, et al. "340,000 Melburnians Have Little or No Parkland within 5km of Their Home." *The Conversation*, 12 August 2020. https://theconversation.com/340-00-melburnians-have-little-or-no-parkland-within-5km-of-their-home-144069.

Latham, John. *A General Synopsis of Birds.* Vol. 1, Part 2. London: Printed for Benj. White 1782.

LeMon, Joel M. *Yahweh's Winged Form in the Psalms: Exploring Congruent Iconography and Texts.* Fribourg: Academic, 2010.

Mathews, Freya. *Journey to the Source of the Merri.* Port Adelaide, SA: Ginninderra, 2003.

Merri Creek Management Committee. "About Merri Creek." https://www.mcmc.org.au/about-merri-creek.

———. "Merri Creek and Environs Strategy Chapter 1.2—Historical Heritage." https://www.mcmc.org.au/about-merri-creek/merri-ck-environs-strategy/merri-creek-strategy/272-mces-12-historical-heritage.

———. "The Merri Creek Sites of Geological and Geomorphological Significance Chapter 3." https://www.mcmc.org.au/about-merri-creek/geology-geomorphology/significant-sites.

———. "Merri Creek from Wastelands to Parklands." https://mcmc.org.au/images/MerriCreek_Exhibition_fronts.pdf.

Mews, Constant. "Coronavirus: Plagues, Pandemics, and Religious Ramifications through History." *Lens by Monash University*. https://lens.monash.edu/@politics-society/2020/04/08/1379920/coronavirus-plagues-pandemics-and-religious-ramifications-through-history.

Nyoun, Nyadol. "From the Wreck of the Pandemic We Can Salvage and Resurrect an Inner Life." *The Guardian Australia*, 9 August 2020. https://www.theguardian.com/australia-news/2020/aug/09/from-the-wreck-of-the-pandemic-we-can-salvage-and-resurrect-an-inner-life.

Olyan, Saul M. *Asherah and the Cult of Yahweh in Israel.* Atlanta, GA: Scholars Press, 1988.

Pattel-Gray, Anne. "Black Truth, White Fiction: The Recognition of Aboriginal Women's Rites." In *Feminist Poetics of the Sacred: Creative Suspicions*, edited by Frances Devlin-Glass and Lyn McCredden, 55–69. Oxford: Oxford University Press, 2001.

Paulson, Graham and Brett, Mark G. "Five Smooth Stones: Reading the Bible Through Aboriginal Eyes." *Colloquium* 45 (2013) 199–209.

Prentis, Brooke. "What Can the Birds of the Land Tell Us?" In *Grounded in the Body, in Time and Place, in Scripture: Papers by Australian Women Scholars in the Evangelical Tradition*, edited by Jill Firth and Denise Cooper-Clarke, 19–30. Eugene, OR: Wipf & Stock, 2021.

Skinner, John. *A Critical and Exegetical Commentary on Genesis*. Edinburgh: T & T Clark, 1930.

Sommer, Benjamin D. *The Bodies of God and the World of Ancient Israel*. Cambridge: Cambridge University Press, 2011.

Stager, Lawrence E. "Jerusalem as Eden." *BAR* 26/3 (2000) 36–47, 66.

Tacey, David J. *Re-Enchantment: The New Australian Spirituality*. Sydney: HarperCollins, 2000.

Thomas, William. "Succinct Sketch of the Aboriginal Language." In *The Aborigines of Victoria: With Notes Relating to the Habits of the Natives of Other Parts of Australia and Tasmania*, edited by R Brough Smyth, 118–33. Vol 2. Melbourne: John Ferres, Government Printer, 1878.

Victorian State Government, "Premier's Statement on Changes to Melbourne's Restrictions." 2 August 2020. https://www.dhhs.vic.gov.au/updates/coronavirus-covid-19/premiers-statement-changes-melbournes-restrictions-2-august-2020.

Wallace, Mark I. *When God Was a Bird: Christianity, Animism, and the Re-Enchantment of the World*. New York: Fordham University Press, 2018.

Watson, Don. *The Bush: Travels in the Heart of Australia*. Melbourne: Penguin Group Australia, 2014.

Wright, David P. "Holiness, Sex, and Death in the Garden of Eden." *Biblica* 77 (1996) 305–29.

Wright, Judith. *Birds: Poems by Judith Wright*. Canberra: National Library of Australia, 2003.

Zevit, Ziony. *The Religions of Ancient Israel: A Synthesis of Parallactic Approaches*. London: Continuum, 2001.

Zhuang, Yan. "Melbourne, after 262 Days in Lockdown, Celebrates a Reopening." *New York Times*, 22 October 2021. https://www.nytimes.com/2021/10/22/world/australia/melbourne-covid-lockdown-reopening.html.

Magnificat, Invasion, Reception, and the Call to Listen

Anne Elvey

A SONG OR POEM, the Magnificat is found toward the beginning of the Gospel of Luke, one of four canonical gospels in the Second (or New) Testament, also known as the Third Gospel because of its usual placement after the Gospels of Matthew and Mark. The Magnificat is one of several songs that punctuate what are called Luke's Infancy Narratives, the stories of the announcement, birth and early years of John the Baptist and Jesus. These songs (commonly known as Magnificat, Benedictus and Nunc Dimittis, from the opening words of their Latin translations) function to highlight the theology embedded in the stories of annunciation, visitation and birth, and the relation of G-d to the hopes of a people subject to Roman occupation.[1] The Magnificat, or Mary's song, comes at the end of an episode known as the Visitation. After the Annunciation in which the angel, Gabriel, announces to the Lukan Mary that she will become pregnant with the divinely-ordained child, Jesus, and she hears that her elderly relative Elizabeth is herself miraculously pregnant, Mary sets out in haste to visit her. The two women are the central and only speaking characters in the Visitation episode, a narrative heightened by references to a holy spirit (or sacred breath) and the inheritance of the purposeful resistance and activity

---

1. I use "G-d" without the vowel to unsettle the naming of the divine, both out of respect for many Jewish traditions and as a way of opening a space for unknowability in relation to the divine, including a calling into question of the gendering of G-d in binary terms.

of other biblical women, including Miriam, Deborah, Jael, and Hannah. Here is the *New Revised Standard Version* translation of Mary's song followed by my alternative translation, using non-binary pronouns for the divine and with an ear to the body and matter:

> And Mary said,
> "My soul magnifies the Lord,
>   and my spirit rejoices in God my Saviour,
> for he has looked with favour on the lowliness of his servant.
>   Surely, from now on all generations will call me blessed;
> for the Mighty One has done great things for me,
>   and holy is his name.
> His mercy is for those who fear him
>   from generation to generation.
> He has shown strength with his arm;
>   he has scattered the proud in the thoughts of their hearts.
> He has brought down the powerful from their thrones,
>   and lifted up the lowly;
> he has filled the hungry with good things,
>   and sent the rich away empty.
> He has helped his servant Israel,
>   in remembrance of his mercy,
> according to the promise he made to our ancestors,
>   to Abraham and to his descendants forever."
> (Luke 1:46–55 NRSV)

> And Mary said,
>
> "My whole bodied self amplifies the Name,*
> and my breath celebrates G-d my liberator,*
>
> for they noticed the humiliation of their enslaved woman.
> Observe, therefore, from now all generations
> will regard me as fortunate,
>
> for the powerful one has done great things for me.
> And their name is sacred,*
>
> and their mercy extends into generation and generation
> for those who respect them dearly.*
>
> G-d performed great deeds with their arm,
> they scattered and squandered the arrogant
> in the purposes of mind;

they took down the powerful in their sovereignty
and lifted up the shamed,

those who are hungry they filled with good things
and those who are rich they sent forth empty.

They supported Israel their child,
remembering mercy,

just as they spoke to our ancestors,
to Abraham and to Abraham's descendants into the ages."

(Luke 1:46–55, my translation)[2]

The Magnificat has many afterlives beyond the biblical text, most notably in choral music. My interest in the afterlives of the Magnificat began around 2014 with an exploration of its reception in creative writing in Australia from the early to mid-twentieth century, in particular a short story "Magnificat" by settler writer Henrietta Drake-Brockman published in *The West Australian* newspaper in January 1939.[3] My interest broadened to art and contemporary poetry, and the way these genres themselves are forms of biblical interpretation. I wanted to have a conversation between these various cultural receptions of the Magnificat, the Magnificat itself, and critical contemporary concerns, predominately ecological ones. As a settler writer, I also wanted to think about what it means to have this conversation on someone else's Country, Country that remains unceded and where I have lived with the privileges of the multiple thefts of First Nations lands, seas and

---

2. I have put an asterisk against a few aspects of my translation. In line 1, I note two things: (1) *psyche* which the NRSV translates as soul refers to the whole self—body, mind, spirit; (2) *kyrios* which the NRSV rightly translates "Lord" may refer to the unspoken divine name in the Jewish tradition of Luke's Mary, so rather than retain "Lord," I have simply put "the Name," in Hebrew *ha shem*, which can stand in for the divine name. Nonetheless, the parallel and contrast between *kyrios* ("Lord," "master," "owner of slaves," "ruler," even "sovereign") and Mary's self-designation as *doule* ("enslaved woman") needs to be kept in mind. In line 2 to emphasise the corporeal materiality of *pneuma*, in the NRSV translated "spirit," I have opted for *pneuma*'s alternative meaning "breath," which echoes the physicality of speaking/singing. In line 7 I have chosen "sacred" over "holy" for *hagios*, to shift the register of how we hear this word. In line 9 I have translated *tois phoboumenois*, which the NRSV has as "those who fear . . ." as "those who respect . . . dearly," to pick up on the idea of fear as awe but with a more contemporary nuance of "respect," adding "dearly" to do double service as both relational and costly.

3. As Nazi aggression towards Jews and the annexation/invasion of neighbouring states began to escalate, Drake-Brockman's story interwove the Magnificat with a vivid and poignant narrative of the horrors of war. H. Drake-Brockmann, "Magnificat," 5.

skies, in particular Ballardong Noongar Country, Dja Dja Wurrung Country, Wathaurung Country, Wurundjeri Country, Boon Wurrung Country and the traditional lands that make up Lutruwita (Tasmania), the places where my British and Irish (and possibly Scottish) ancestors arrived—some forcibly, some as migrants—from the 1840s onwards and the places where I have lived and worked.

While I was developing my project "Reading the Magnificat in Australia," I was excited to see the publication in 2018 of Meredith Lake's *The Bible in Australia*. I eagerly read it and enjoyed the historical narrative, especially its readability, analysis, and the focus on particular details such as the weight of Cook's Bible.[4] Coming from a complex of disciplines that include biblical studies, ecological theology and poetry, however, I was left a little dissatisfied by Lake's narrative. Perhaps it felt too settled.

The Bible in Australia has informed my work, especially when I was asking about the arrival of the Magnificat on Boon Wurrung Country where I live. But my purpose was and is different: I want to unsettle engagements with biblical texts from the perspective of biblical studies, and to do so through a creative reading practice. I wish to unsettle a discipline that gives insufficient regard to the way its focal texts—the book of books that make up our Bibles—arrived as material artefacts of colonial invasion and are themselves indebted to the materiality of the Earth community in their production and reproduction.[5] I felt that while Lake touched on this, her work did not go far enough. Neither does mine.

This essay draws on my work *Reading the Magnificat in Australia*, first with a focus on the arrival of the Magnificat on Boon Wurrung Country where I now live and work, then with a sketch of some settler responses to the Magnificat, and finally with a reading of the Magnificat in relation to Ballardong Noongar Country where my mother was born in 1925.[6] I believe the future of works like this and such as Lake's cultural history is collaboration with First Nations. While I am not there yet, through my creative engagement with the Magnificat as a settler who has lived most of her life on the lands of the Kulin nation, I suggest that the biblical song of Mary points away from itself, pressing settler readers to listen to First Nations and to listen again.

---

4. Lake, *Bible in Australia*, 21.

5. Rose, *Reports from a Wild Country*, 59–61; Boer, *Last Stop*; Brett, *Decolonizing God*; Elvey, *The Matter of the Text*, 28–43.

6. Elvey, *Reading the Magnificat*. This essay draws closely on material published in chapters 1 and 4 of Elvey 2020 with permission of the publisher Sheffield Phoenix Press.

The Lure of the Magnificat

When the Magnificat arrived in Australia with British colonizers, both as part of the Bible and, drawn from there, it came as a traditional daily prayer, prayed individually and communally. Not only was the Magnificat prayed and sung in homes, monasteries, convents, churches, concert halls, and recital centres, but it also became attached—as title or internal reference—to cultural expressions ranging from pious verse to abstract expressionist art.[7]

I am drawn to the Magnificat as the starting point for reading as an Australian settler scholar principally because of its complex relation to and resistance of colonial, imperial logic. Further, as a poet and biblical scholar, primarily working with the Gospel of Luke, I have become interested in the poetic texts—poems, songs, hymns—as they appear in the Lukan Infancy Narratives, as texts that have afterlives in the daily liturgy of the church, and beyond. The Lukan Magnificat is a song-poem sung-spoken in the voice of a woman and in the context of two women meeting. While some manuscripts attribute the song to the Lukan Elizabeth, I accept the tradition that it is Luke's Mary who sings it. As a woman's song, steeped in ancestral knowledge and resistance, the song can be understood not only as a song of praise but also as protest.[8] How did this protest song arrive on Boon Wurrung Country?

The Magnificat as Colonial Artefact

Meredith Lake proposes that the Bible arrived in Australia, mediated by European, specifically British, imperialism.[9] It arrived "thick" with British/European associations, and with its status as revealed divine Word, assuring "knowledge of salvation" and "ultimate truth," ripe for colonial imposition, in some cases benignly and oftentimes destructively, even at the same time.[10] Biblical songs, such as the Magnificat, carry this British/European imperial colonialist overlay. In their early contexts of oral performance and writing they would have been rooted in particular lands and their more-than-human interrelationships. By more-than-human, I mean to include humans, other animals, plants, rocks, waters, fungi, viruses, the whole created order of a diverse Earth community of beings. First Nations women understand kinship as something similar to more-than-human in

---

7. Elvey, *Reading the Magnificat*, chapters 1–4.
8. Elvey, *Reading the Magnificat*, 11.
9. Lake, *Bible in Australia*, 7.
10. Lake, *Bible in Australia*, 6; Rose, *Reports from a Wild Country*, 59–61, 149, 179; Boer, *Last Stop*.

the sense I am using the term.[11] More-than-human interrelationships are proper to Country. In an ecological context, relationships within habitats and ecosystems are more-than-human. As colonial imports, biblical songs' ancient ties to distant lands, seas, and skies are stretched thin if not entirely severed. In Australia, the Magnificat is separated from the habitats in which the song arose and differs in this way from First Nations songs proper to Country, so a tension may exist between this biblical song and First Nations cultures. Lake writes that "the Bible is not really indigenous to any one place or people" and points to its multiplicities: of authorship, languages, and cultures, even in the "biblical" lands from which it emerged.[12] She claims that the globalizing Bible is "a text that crosses cultures and reshapes cultural boundaries," citing, for instance, its use in "Indigenous rights movements" in Australia.[13]

Yet it is precisely the transgressive quality of the Bible that makes it problematic in a colonial context where the Bible has been and is still used as a weapon of contact against Indigenous cultural beliefs and practices.[14] Anne Brewster reports that in a mode of resistance to biblically-based undermining of Indigenous culture and the Bible's status as a material artefact of colonization, Oodgeroo Noonuccal saw "her writing as a material alternative to the Bible for her people, a translation of an oral Aboriginal voice in writing."[15] First Peoples negotiate relations between Indigenous culture and the Bible in Australia in multiple ways, but that is not my focus in this essay.[16] How might I read a biblical song, the Magnificat, on Boon Wurrung Country where I live and work? How might a reading of the Magnificat speak into the invasive occupation of Ballardong Country by my ancestors?

The Magnificat on Boon Wurrung Country

A "first" (and failed) attempt at British settlement on Boon Wurrung Country occurred at Sullivan Bay, Sorrento, beginning in October 1803. James Hingston Tuckey (1776–1816), an Irish-born British mariner wrote a diary

---

11. See, for example, Moreton-Robinson, *Talkin' Up to the White Woman*, 18–21.
12. Lake, *Bible in Australia*, 5.
13. Lake, *Bible in Australia*, 8.
14. Morgan, "Colonising Religion," 36–37; Rose, *Reports from a Wild Country*, 149–62; Elvey, *Matter of the Text*, 72–77.
15. Elvey, *Matter of the Text*, 74; Brewster, "Oodgeroo," 101.
16. See, for example, Paulson and Brett, "Five Smooth Stones," 199–214; Beckett, "Aboriginal Histories," 99; Burramurra and McIntosh, "Motj and the Nature of the Sacred," 11; Skye, *Kerygmatics*, 66.

of the voyage of the *Calcutta* that included a short attempt to establish a British colony in Victoria at Sullivan Bay, which is near the bayside town of Sorrento on the Mornington Peninsula, on Boon Wurrung Country.[17] His account exhibits the prevailing logic of white possession and the desire to extract from the land, as the invading group of convicts, soldiers and settlers, searched for coal and other mineable resources.[18] After what was supposed by Tuckey to be friendly contact with the local Boon Wurrung people, the people organized and resisted the invaders leading to two documented killings by the British.[19] Tuckey's account of contact suggests that the local people were already familiar with the violence of British guns and at least one bore the signs of the imported disease, small pox.[20] Tuckey remarks on his perceptions of the site as beautiful and inhospitable, where drinking water was hard to find and fish were scarce despite the evidence that Boon Wurrung people had access to water and seafood, and despite his seeing valleys luxuriant with grasses and "well-watered" grassy "meadows."[21]

The invading party's chaplain, an Anglican, Rev. Robert Knopwood, performed Sunday services, baptisms, weddings, funerals, and other official functions.[22] Relating the contact conflict that Tuckey also describes, Knopwood reports on the killing of two Indigenous people whom he stereotypes negatively in his diary entry for 23 October 1803.[23] The next entry for the same day, a Sunday, records "At 11 the whole of the camp assembled, and the Governor at the head of the Royal Marines, with officers, to hear divine service, which was performed in the square of the parade before all hands."[24] Here is a piercing juxtaposition of colonial invasive violence and Christian worship.[25]

17. Tuckey, *Account of a Voyage*, 153–204. Earlier in 1801, Lt James Grant had landed and set up camp on Churchill Island in Western Port Bay, as noted on an information board on Churchill Island.

18. Tuckey, *Account of a Voyage*, 165, 200.

19. Tuckey, *Account of a Voyage*, 154, 167–74, 200.

20. Tuckey, *Account of a Voyage*, 176.

21. Tuckey, *Account of a Voyage*, 157–59, 164, 196–98, 200.

22. See Knopwood, *Diary*, 23–39. On Knopwood and the conditions of the Sullivan Bay settlement, see further, Presland, *First People*, 22, 84–85; Cotter, *Boon Wurrung*, 23; Nepean Historical Society, "Collins 1803 Settlement;" Monks, "Knopwood."

23. Knopwood, *Diary*, 26.

24. Knopwood, *Diary*, 26.

25. A juxtaposition Valda Cole ignores in her discussion of the first settler prayer service on the Mornington Peninsula. "Settlers," 186. Cole's article begins with reference to the 1988 Bicentenary, celebrating the landing of the First Fleet in 1788. I read its tone as missing an understanding of the problematics of celebrating colonial invasion. Alongside this is my uneasiness with the article's interest in the celebration of the "first"

Reporting on his reflections at Port Phillip colony, Sullivan Bay, Sorrento, 1803, Tuckey imagined a new Roman empire:

> These thoughts naturally led to the contemplation of future possibilities. I beheld a second Rome, rising from a coalition of banditti. I beheld it giving laws to the world, and superlative in arms and in arts, looking down with proud superiority upon the barbarous nations of the northern hemisphere; thus running over the airy visions of empire, wealth, and glory, I wandered amidst the delusions of imagination.[26]

By early 1804, the 1803 British colony on the Mornington Peninsula had disbanded and moved to Tasmania, where Knopwood became the first chaplain. But the logic of empire would impact Boon Wurrung Country profoundly, as British invasion proceeded in years to come.

Beyond Tuckey's and Knopwood's reports of Indigenous engagement with and resistance toward the British arrivals in 1803, I cannot know what Boon Wurrung people made of this rag-tag settlement on Country, or of guns used for hunting kangaroos, and relations between soldiers and convicts, whether Boon Wurrung resistance was a factor influencing the colonists' departure, nor whether the people of the land listened as the Magnificat was read or sung by these strangers, if indeed it was. Mark Brett takes Luke 1:52, "He has brought down the mighty from their thrones and lifted up the lowly," as epigraph to the closing chapter of his *Decolonizing God*, entitled "Postcolonial Theology and Ethics."[27] British colonization of Australia created the conditions to which Brett's use of this stanza could be read as a response. The socio-political structuring of Indigenous communities was not on the model of empire, British or Roman, though Tuckey himself imagined the colony as a new Rome.[28] The Magnificat, as a song of protest, subverting imperial power, only becomes relevant (potentially) when that kind of power, in the form of the British empire, imposes itself on Indigenous people and Country. At the point of imperial invasion, the Magnificat arrives with church ceremony and Bible law as part of colonial cargo, and as one of many agents of colonization. This invasive process on Boon Wurrung Country led by the 1860s to a decimation of the population

---

and other early Christian services in Victoria, without critiquing their meaning for Boon Wurrung and other local First Nations.

26. Tuckey, *Account of a Voyage*, 191–92.
27. Brett, *Decolonizing God*, 178.
28. Tuckey, *Account of a Voyage*, 191–92.

on Country and the removal elsewhere of Boon Wurrung people, including through the abduction of Indigenous women by whalers.[29]

Possessive desire, translated into ownership, imposes settler will on land and its customary custodians, who are constructed as without will.[30] But to say that Boon Wurrung women, ancestors of contemporary Boon Wurrung people, were abducted does not deny their capacity for agency in order to survive in what were and are traumatic situations of invasion. In terms of the reversals of the Magnificat (1:51–53), the colonial imposition of will is an oppressive infliction of power epitomized in the occupation of the land. While the land is not mentioned directly, it is present in the song, through references to the ancestors and the divine promise (1:54–55).[31] In the context of first century Roman occupation of Judaea and the Galilee, the Magnificat is a protest song which Luke attributes to a young Jewish woman. Some scholars suggest that the speaker was humiliated by some form of sexual assault and, reading between the lines of the reversals, shamed as a daughter of Israel by the ongoing Roman occupation of her land.[32] In the mouth of the Lukan Mary, the song suggests that the colonized woman has a voice, and can call on her culture and ancestry to make her case. Women like the Lukan Mary exercise agency and negotiate their purposes in the midst of oppression.[33] The song is unsettling, perhaps violently so, for the beneficiaries of British dispossession of Boon Wurrung people, not only because it is a demand to recognise the truth of colonial land-theft. There is an appeal, also, to listen between the lines of both Mary's song and colonial history, to recognize the agency of Boon Wurrung women, and to hear a call to reconfigure the learned desires of the will of white possession.

Some Nineteenth and Twentieth Century Settler Uses of the Magnificat

Carrying the biblical and liturgical traditions of Christianity, and the European cultural tradition of choral composition and performance, the Magnificat arrived in Australia with the white possessive of British colonisation. In addition to the many references to nineteenth and twentieth-century performances of the Magnificat, Handel's or Bach's for example, the Magnificat

29. Briggs, *Journey Cycles*, 31.

30. Moreton-Robinson, *White Possessive*, 114.

31. See the discussion in Wenell, *Jesus and the Land*, 104–38. See also Trainor, *About Earth's Child*, 10–11.

32. See Fitzmyer, *Luke I–IX*, 367; Schaberg, *Illegitimacy*, 97–98; Bovon, *Luke 1*, 60.

33. Jacob, *Reading Mary*, 91–123.

is mentioned in the press as early as 1827.[34] One result of the 1788 British invasion of Australia was the introduction of Christianity to Indigenous peoples, and the congregational recitation or singing of the Magnificat was a material, embodied manifestation of colonization that would come to have multiple meanings.[35]

In the twentieth century, across the country, creative writings themed on the Magnificat were published from time to time. Arthur Symons's 1909 "Magnificat" in the *Quiz* (Adelaide), praises God for the speaker's erotic love of a woman.[36] A more pious version appears in an article on the Magnificat in 1915 in the *Prahran Chronicle*, shifting the subject of the song to its traditional speaker Mary, so that "Daily at the vesper hour, / Mary's name is praised," and she is "Great in her magnificence."[37] The biblical Magnificat is printed in full in the *Newcastle Morning Herald and Miners' Advocate* on Christmas Day 1915 alongside other Christian religious material.[38] In January 1917, *The Register* (Adelaide) published Frederic Warner's poem "Earth's Magnificat" which lists what the speaker cannot know compared with the little he does.[39] Joining the spirit of the divine whirlwind in Job with Luke's Mary, Warner praises "earth's magnificat," with Earth as prompt for and agent of praise. Only at the close does the speaker turn explicitly toward the divine: "And at the feet of God adoring fall."[40] The verse suggests an interesting shift of emphasis, one which has resonance with Lola Gornall's sonnet, "Magnificat," published in *The Australian Worker* (Sydney, 1919), where the speaker's garden is locus of the sacred, and where God looks on the Earth-loving speaker with evident fondness.[41] In 1926, the *Freeman's Journal* (Sydney) presents a more traditional verse narrating Mary's visit to Elizabeth.[42] In this rendition, the writer allows the Earth and its weather, sun and moon, to interact as agents with the travelling woman, leading to the intimacy of the two cousins and the telling lines toward the end: "And then the traveller, full of grace, / Sang, or her heart had died." Amidst the piety and sentimentality of the verse, the song stands on the side of life at a critical point where oppression might occasion despair, and where human

---

34. *The Monitor*, Sydney, Friday 9 March 1827, 8.
35. See, for example, Mr Goodwin, "Church of England Mission," 5.
36. Symons, "Magnificat," *Quiz*, 2.
37. From "Parish Supplement," 4.
38. "Religious Topics," 14.
39. Warner, "Earth's Magnificat."
40. Warner, "Earth's Magnificat."
41. Gornall, "Magnificat," 13.
42. O'Donnell, "Magnificat," 31.

life and action is always more-than-human. In a 1933 verse, the wind seems to sing "Mary's deathless hymn."[43]

These examples suggest that the Magnificat, recited or sung daily, captured the imaginations of settler Australians as an important part of their colonial and religious heritage. It formed a kind of template for exploring experiences of the sacred sometimes in a more-than-human frame. The instances also pick up on the issues of death and life central to the Lukan Magnificat, and the way the song itself, in its performance, can be empowering for life. To what extent did these settler sentiments re-inscribe or resist the colonial mindset of British settler-dom? In this settler tradition, Henrietta Drake-Brockman's short story "Magnificat" poignantly juxtaposes the song with the horror of war.[44] While alert, however, to the grief of a European woman whose child is dying, is she aware of the grief of Indigenous mothers in Western Australia where she resides?

Reading the Magnificat in Relation to Colonial Invasion of Ballardong Country

My mother, descended from English, Irish and possibly Scottish migrants, was born on Ballardong Country in 1925 on a farm in Goomalling, Western Australia. Taking into account the question of relationship between settler women in my own ancestry and the Indigenous women they encountered (Ballardong Noongar and perhaps others from neighboring groups moved off their lands), I offer the following reading and creative response, a kind of setting for the Magnificat in the Wheatbelt around Northam, Toodyay, York, Goomalling, and New Norcia. I focus on three aspects of the text: Mary's journey in Luke 1; her self-description as enslaved woman (*doule*); and the pattern of reversals.

Mary's Journey

A form of colonialism and resilience is evident in the final verse of Luke's annunciation account, when Mary says "Here I am, the enslaved woman (*he doule*) of the Lord/master (*kuriou*). Let it be with me according to your word (*to rhema mou*)" (1:38, my translation). The Lukan Mary employs the language of empire when she refers to herself as enslaved woman and the divine as Lord/master. Her internalized oppression under the imperialism of Rome

---

43. "Wind and Wave."
44. Drake-Brockmann, "Magnificat."

is signalled by this usage. Her agency in addressing the angelic messenger Gabriel, however, points to her resilience and capacity to be collaborator with the materiality of the divine word which is also matter and deed (*rhema*), in effect becoming a material word (*rhema*) which Mary will embody.

Mary's agency spills into the next verse which begins the episode traditionally called the Visitation. Her journey foreshadows the resistances and restorations of the Magnificat and Luke 4:18–19. My somewhat literal translation is: "But rising up in those days Mary went into the hill country, with haste, into a Judean town" (1:39).[45] Like other ancient writers, Luke uses the term for hill country to refer to Judea.[46] The journey from Nazareth, where the annunciation to the Lukan Mary occurs (1:26), to the Judean hill country is about one hundred and twenty-five to one hundred and sixty kilometres and would entail three to four days of travel.[47] Would a woman travel such a journey alone? Would she have brought with her a midwife for Elizabeth?[48] Where would she have stayed on the way? What resources would she have had for the journey? What would she have carried to sustain her? What dangers did the road hold? The parable of the Good Samaritan (10.30–35), suggests that other roads in the region, such as that between Jerusalem and Jericho, carried dangers at that time. For Luke the details of Mary's journey to Elizabeth are incidental and hearers/readers are left with a gap for imagination.

The close of the visitation narrative has Mary returning to *her* house (1:56); in contrast, the house where she visits Elizabeth is denoted "the house of Zechariah" (1:40), Elizabeth's husband.[49] Does this contrast indicate "a theological interest in reference to Mary's virginity" or something else?[50] Mary's agency, signalled not only by *her* house but also *her* yes (1:38), *her* rising up (1:39), and the proclamation of the Magnificat, suggests a kind of freedom which may be understood as "subversive."[51] Mary leaves before the birth of Elizabeth's child, so for Luke she is not there to act as, or assist, the midwife. What is happening is more in the realm of resistance and prophecy; in a country under foreign rule, two women stand in the tradition of their ancestors, especially the women who helped shape their

45. The opening Greek word *anastasa*, rendered in the NRSV as "she set out," has a sense of restoration, resurrection or rising up.

46. Marshall, *Luke*, 80.

47. Marshall, *Luke*, 80.

48. I am grateful to Rosemary Canavan for conversation about the practicalities of the journey Luke has Mary make.

49. Bovon, *Luke*, 64.

50. Bovon, *Luke*, 64.

51. Bovon, *Luke* 64; cf. Trainor, *Earth's Child*, 75.

history (Miriam, Deborah, Jael, Hannah), and they interpret their bodily experience of pregnancy in that context. When she moves from affirming the divine word (*rhema*) in Nazareth to visiting her kinswoman in Judea, Mary brings with her a song which speaks of the material workings of the divine word (*rhema*) in her people's story.

Mary as enslaved woman (*doule*)

It is well-documented that in Western Australia the domestic labour of Indigenous women and girls, who had in many cases been taken from their families and brought up in missions, was unpaid. Wages were kept in trust by governments and never passed on to First Nations workers. Years later, a Western Australian Government recompense offer was woefully inadequate as well as being difficult to access, because the burden of proof of eligibility was demanding for many.[52] It is likely my own maternal grandparents had Ballardong women working for them under this exploitative scheme in the 1920s and early 1930s in the Wheatbelt of Western Australia before the Great Depression. I re-read the Lukan Mary's self-designation as enslaved woman against this context.

Many have noted the problematic nature of Luke's putting the language of slavery in the mouth of Mary, especially from feminist and de-imperialising perspectives. The Lukan narrative presents at least one problem for feminist readings of Mary as liberating for women, namely her self-description as enslaved woman/handmaid (*doule*; 1:38, 48).[53] The songs of Luke's infancy narrative "not only resist, they also imitate and perpetuate the imperial structures that they oppose."[54] A conventional view is that Mary's self-description as enslaved repeats the servant of G-d language used in ancient Israel, and is part of the way the text parallels Mary and Israel.[55] The use of the language of slavery may imply a shift where Mary is characterized as disciple in the Annunciation and as prophet and "interpreter of the gospel" in the Magnificat.[56] Rather than being a figure of a woman who "passively submits," in Luke Mary's "self-designation can function as an ironic indicator of both personal freedom and complete devotion."[57] Moreover, with the designation enslaved person (often translated servant)

---

52. Dingle, "WA's Stolen Wages Shame."
53. Kelso, "Irigaray's Madonna," 177.
54. Reid, "Women Prophets," 42.
55. Gaventa, *Mary*, 57.
56. Gaventa, *Mary*, 58.
57. Levine and Witherington, *Luke*, 37.

of G-d, Mary positions herself in the tradition of "kings, prophets, apostles, and evangelists"[58] But as Amy-Jill Levine and Ben Witherington III write: "While in the biblical tradition only free people identify themselves as slaves of God, the expression today—especially in light of slavery in our own histories and the ongoing devastation of human trafficking—renders the epithet problematic."[59]

It is likely that Mary is not an enslaved person; rather she is using the language of slavery metaphorically, but not from a significant position of power in her world. Did some of those such as David who use this language have enslaved persons themselves? Probably, but not on the Roman model. Did Mary hold enslaved persons? Mary and Elizabeth were perhaps rural peasants, and Zechariah was a "village priest"; their geographic and social situation in rural peasant towns gives them an "unstated identity with Earth" and "this identity . . . emerges in the gestational and birth paradigms that permeate" the opening chapter of Luke's gospel.[60] It is unlikely Mary's household held enslaved persons obtained as the spoils of war or debt. Still, in contemporary terms to use the language of slavery for relationship with the divine is to deflect from its social and political implications. It is as if I were to look at people held in detention for years on end for legally seeking asylum and call myself a refugee, for example from a patriarchal church, though I have a physical home with immediate family and extended family nearby and my direct lived experience is far from that of a refugee who journeys long distances across borders to find a safe place to live, often leaving extended family behind, and sometimes suffering years of indefinite detention. The language of humiliation the Lukan Mary uses in the Magnificat has resonance perhaps with the shame of becoming an enslaved person as a result of war or debt. But does this mitigate the usage—as we would see it now—of a term denoting someone else's experience of oppression? Who benefits from her appropriation of this metaphor? Where is relative privilege situated? What is the force of the reversals/the protest she sings in the light of her self-designation as enslaved?

Reversals

Ironically, while Mary is not likely in actuality an enslaved woman, it is the powerlessness and shame that she takes up in her experience of humiliation—whether through sexual violence, its threat, or through standing in

---

58. Levine and Witherington, *Luke*, 37.
59. Levine and Witherington, *Luke*, 37.
60. Trainor, *Earth's Child*, 77.

for her people under empire or both—that finds resonance in the designation "enslaved person" and gives energy to the protest framed as reversal of oppressor and oppressed:

> G-d has worked power with G-d's arm,
> G-d has scattered and squandered (*dieskorpisen*) the arrogant in the intentions of their hearts and minds
>
> G-d has taken down (*katheilen*) the powerful from (their) thrones
> and lifted up the shamed
>
> Those who are hungry G-d has filled with good things
> and those who are rich G-d has sent forth (*exapesteilen*) empty.
>
> (Luke 1:51–53, my translation)

In the Magnificat three verbs (*diaskorpizo, kathaireo, exapostello*) describe the divine action against the proud, the powerful and the rich. While this action is violent, there are other resonances. In Luke–Acts the verb *diaskorpizo* refers not only to scattering (Luke 1:51; Acts 5:37) but also to squandering property (Luke 15:13; 16:1). Although the divine is the agent of scattering, in the case of Luke 1:51 the echo of squandering allows the reader to hear also the way in which the rich and powerful squander the lives of those on whose subjugated lives and labours they rely. That the divine then squanders the rich in their arrogance, their inability to see beyond their own intentions to the lives of others, is a comment on their dissipation of the people and goods that constitute their own power and wealth.

In Luke–Acts, the verb *kathaireo*, to take down or destroy, refers not only to overthrowing/or taking down a ruler as in Luke 1:52 (see also, Acts 19:27) or nations (Acts 13:19), or destroying a structure (Luke 12:18), but also to taking the body of Jesus down from the cross in preparation for burial (Luke 23:53; Acts 13:29). Echoing, then, beneath the song's imagined divine overthrow of oppressive rulers, is the death of the Lukan Jesus by Roman execution with the collusion of some religious leaders of his own people. A similar echo can be found in Simeon's words to Mary in Luke 2:33–34.

The third verb, *exapostello*, to send away or destroy, also has the meaning of sending (an enslaved person) to achieve a task (Luke 20:10–11) and in a similar manner sending an apostle or missionary (Acts 11:22) or angelic messenger (Acts 12:11); or sending someone somewhere else to preserve their life (Acts 7:12; 9:30), perhaps also because of the trouble that accompanied them (Acts 17:14); *exapostello* is also used for sending salvation

(Acts 13:26). In the context of the Lukan Paul's retelling of his narrative of persecuting the early Jesus followers and his subsequent conversion, *exapostello* is used of Paul's being sent away to the Gentiles, both as a signal of his being sent away from a life in which he stood by approvingly at Stephen's murder, and his being sent forth as an apostle to the Gentiles (Acts 22.21).

While words can be used in multiple ways, the character of the song as poetry (a kind of amplified and complexified talk) allows the reader to hear in the sending away empty of the rich, also their being sent toward another way of living that the Lukan gospel itself will suggest through its emphasis on poverty and riches.[61] I propose that the reversals, especially the halves which use imagery of violence toward the rich and powerful, do not simply reinscribe the oppressions they resist. Rather the reversals, like all binaries, are infused with their own subtle unsettling. The cruciform echoes as a call to oppressors to review their intentions which are evident in their actions, and to live the vision of a world in which oppressive hunger and humiliating poverty, detention, and violence are no more.

Creative Response

The following poem set on Ballardong Country attempts to recognise and attend to the disparity between First Nations and settler longings for an end to oppression. For the oppressor and their inheritors this may be a longing to be free of the shame and inequality in relationship. This experience is rarely life-threatening in the way oppression is to those who are oppressed. The desire for a counter-colonial space is acute in an entirely different way when it is a matter of life and death. I write from the perspective of the inheritor of colonial privilege, recognizing that the colonial longing to be free of the shame of inheritance as perpetrators and ongoing beneficiaries of invasion is also part of the problem.

---

61. Trainor, *Earth's Child*, 79.

"On Visiting Elizabeth in the Western Australian Wheatbelt Mary Sings a Song"

after Luke 1:46–55

1

Tyres hold to gravel. She
takes her   breath

sings   each revolution's puff
of dust. Middle road

a snake suns & wheels' ambit
accommodates her line. Look

back   she chants   see
the reptile still   against

tales she's heard of serpents
clinging to the rim   & found

alive   next stop down
the local access track.

2

All that's left of the school
her nanna ran   & where

married   a lady could
not   hold a teacher's job

is a sign in a paddock. Here
forebears learnt their names.

She reads them now   on
honour boards & on a street

& sings a partway song
of women   white & wanting.

3

This is Ballardong land
where her mother watched

a woman   maybe a girl
work laundry in a copper.

This was a person of Country
in the gaze of a settler child.

She sings recompense
sufficient to the labour

for all unpaid
she lives because.

4

What woman assisted her
nanna   with births at home

on the farm? She sings
their favour   a wisdom

shared on Country   once
more usurped   when a child

is born to inherit. Can
she carol   the

sorry gifts that
made her mother?

5

She psalms a longing
to undo   that cannot

be. She sings to tell
a truth: this colonial

cultivar   this ripped
space   this cleared out

orbit-visible belt whose
indentured labour shames

her family   but does not
threaten their lives. She

takes a breath   sings
out of an old   frontier.

Coda

She stops, she
                listens[62]

In the Magnificat, a young Jewish peasant woman of the Galilee sings a song in the Judean hill country. The political context is Roman empire, and while the song does not directly reference the singer's relation to land, land is there in the reference to the promise or covenant, the ancestors, and in the resistance to the exercises of imperial power that occasion oppression, poverty, hunger, slavery, and debt under Roman occupation. In the context of twenty-first century Australia, reading the Magnificat means seeing it as part of the multiple impacts of invasion, but also as prompting a turn from the hegemony of practices of biblical study that want to "save" the Bible and Christianity. Perhaps indicating its own contingency as a colonial artefact, the Magnificat instead points away from itself, for example, to First Nations women who through their writing, art, and activism tell the truths of invasion and speak the survival, protest, resistance, and resilience of their people. The call to settler readers is to listen carefully and deeply, to hear what responses are appropriate from the perspectives of First Nations.

---

62. Elvey, "On Visiting Elizabeth," 108–11.

Bibliography

Beckett, Jeremy. "Aboriginal Histories, Aboriginal Myths: An Introduction." *Oceania* 65/2 (1994) 97–115.

Briggs, Carolyn. *The Journey Cycles of the Boon Wurrung: Stories with Boon Wurrung Language*. 2nd ed. Melbourne: Victorian Aboriginal Corporation for Languages, 2014.

Burramurra, David, and Ian S. McIntosh. "Motj and the Nature of the Sacred." *Cultural Survival Quarterly* 26/2 (Summer 2002). https://www.culturalsurvival.org/publications/cultural-survival-quarterly/motj-and-nature-sacred.

Boer, Roland. *Last Stop before Antarctica: The Bible and Postcolonialism in Australia*. Sheffield: Sheffield Academic, 2001.

Bovon, Francois. *Luke 1: A Commentary on the Gospel of Luke 1:1—9:50*. Translated by C. M. Thomas. Minneapolis: Fortress, 2002.

Brett, Mark G. *Decolonizing God: The Bible in the Tides of Empire*. Sheffield: Sheffield Phoenix, 2008.

Brewster, Anne. "Oodgeroo: Orator, Poet, Storyteller." *Australian Literary Studies* 16/4 (1994) 92–104.

Cole, Valda. "Settlers, Prayers and Divine Service." *Victorian Historical Journal* 67/2 (1997) 186–95.

Cotter, Richard. *Boon Wurrung: People of the Port Phillip District*. Red Hill South: Lavender Hill Multimedia, 2001.

Dingle, Sarah. "WA's Stolen Wages Shame." *Background Briefing*, ABC Radio National, 6 September 2015. https://www.abc.net.au/radionational/programs/backgroundbriefing/was-stolen-wages-shame/6740068.

Drake-Brockmann, Henrietta. "Magnificat." *The West Australian*, Perth, Saturday 7 January 1939.

Elvey, Anne F. *The Matter of the Text: Material Engagements between Luke and the Five Senses*. Sheffield: Sheffield Phoenix, 2011.

———. *Reading the Magnificat in Australia: Unsettling Engagements*. Sheffield: Sheffield Phoenix, 2020.

———. "On Visiting Elizabeth in the Western Australian Wheatbelt Mary Sings a Song." *Rabbit* 30 (2020) 108–11.

Fitzmyer, Joseph A. *The Gospel According to Luke I–IX: Introduction, Translation, and Notes*. New York: Doubleday, 1981.

Gaventa, Beverley R. *Mary: Glimpses of the Mother of Jesus*. Minneapolis: Fortress, 1999.

Goodwin. "Church of England Mission to the Aborigine." *The Argus*, Melbourne. Monday 23 January 1860.

Gornall, L. "Magnificat." *The Australian Worker*, Sydney, Thursday 20 March 1919.

Jacob, Sharon. *Reading Mary Alongside Indian Surrogate Mothers: Violent Love, Oppressive Liberation, and Infancy Narratives*. New York: Palgrave Macmillan, 2015.

Kelso, Julie. "Irigaray's Madonna." *Feminist Theology* 23/2 (2015) 171–85.

Knopwood, Robert. *The Diary of the Reverend Robert Knopwood 1803–1838*, edited by M Nicholls. Launceston: Tasmanian Historical Research Association, 1977.

Lake, Meredith. *The Bible in Australia: A Cultural History*. Sydney: NewSouth, 2018.

Levine, Amy-Jill and Ben Witherington III. *The Gospel of Luke*. Cambridge: Cambridge University Press, 2018.

Marshall, I. Howard. *The Gospel of Luke*. Grand Rapids: Eerdmanns, 1978.
Monks, Linda. "Knopwood, Robert (Bobby) (1763–1838)." *Australian Dictionary of Biography*. Canberra: National Centre of Biography, Australian National University, 2006 [1967]. http://adb.anu.edu.au/biography/knopwood-robert-bobby-2314/text3003.
Moreton-Robinson, Aileen. *Talkin' Up to the White Woman: Indigenous Women and Feminism*. St Lucia: University of Queensland Press, 2000.
———. *The White Possessive: Property, Power and Indigenous Sovereignty*. Minneapolis: University of Minnesota Press, 2015.
Morgan, Monica. "Colonising Religion." *Chain Reaction* 91 (2005) 36–37.
Nepean Historical Society. "Collins 1803 Settlement." https://nepeanhistoricalsociety.asn.au/history/collins-1803-settlement/.
O'Donnell, C. "Magnificat." *Freeman's Journal*, Sydney, Thursday 4 March 1926.
"The Parish Supplement." Reprinted in *Prahran Chronicle*, Melbourne, Saturday 18 September 1915.
Paulson, Graham and Mark G. Brett. "Five Smooth Stones: Reading the Bible through Aboriginal Eyes." *Colloquium* 45/2 (2010) 199–214.
Presland, Gary. *First People: The Eastern Kulin of Melbourne, Port Phillip & Central Victoria*. Melbourne: Museum Victoria, 2010.
Reid, Barbara E. "Women Prophets of God's Alternative Reign." In *Luke-Acts and Empire: Essays in Honor of Robert L. Brawley*, edited by David Rhoads, David Esterline, and Jae Won Lee, 44–59. Eugene: Pickwick, 2011.
"Religious Topics." *Newcastle Morning Herald and Miners' Advocate*, Saturday 25 December 1915.
Rose, Deborah Bird. *Reports from a Wild Country: Ethics for Decolonisation*. Sydney: University of New South Wales Press, 2004.
Schaberg, Jane. *The Illegitimacy of Jesus: A Feminist Theological Interpretation of the Infancy Narratives*. New York: Crossroad, 1990.
Skye, Lee Miena. *Kerygmatics of the New Millennium: A Study of Australian Aboriginal Women's Christology*. Delhi: ISPCK, 2007.
Symons, A. "Magnificat." *Quiz*, Adelaide, Friday 23 April 1909.
Trainor, Michael. *About Earth's Child: An Ecological Listening to the Gospel of Luke*. Sheffield: Sheffield Phoenix, 2012.
Tuckey, J. H. *An Account of a Voyage to Establish a Colony at Port Philip in Bass's Strait, on the South Coast of New South Wales, in His Majesty's Ship Calcutta, in the Years 1802-3-4*. London: Longman, Hurst, Rees and Orme, 1805.
Warner, F. "Earth's Magnificat." *The Register*, 4–5, Adelaide, Saturday 6 January, 1917.
Wenell, Karen. *Jesus and the Land: Sacred and Social Space in Second Temple Judaism*. London: T&T Clark, 2007.
"Wind and Wave." *Catholic Freeman's Journal*, Sydney, Thursday 5 October 1933, 3.

Part V

Response

Reading the Bible in Australia, Maundy Thursday 2023

Meredith Lake

ON MAUNDY THURSDAY MORNING, on Australian national radio, Indigenous leader Noel Pearson described a political scenario so grievous, he could only compare it to the betrayal of Christ by Judas:

> I couldn't sleep last night. I was troubled by dreams, and the spectre of the Dutton Liberal Party's Judas betrayal of our country.... [It's] kind of symbolic—on the day of the Passover, leading into Easter—that we [First Nations people] should be betrayed like this, and the country should be betrayed like this.[1]

Pearson was responding to the decision by one of Australia's major political parties to oppose the recognition of First Nations people in the Commonwealth Constitution. Pearson and others had championed such recognition for years, in step with the Uluru Statement from the Heart.[2] He had worked and hoped for bipartisanship in favor of recognition and a constitutionally enshrined First Nations Voice to Parliament. But now, in Holy Week, and alert to its resonance, the Cape York leader found that hope had been disappointed.

Distressed as he was, in step with the narrative of Easter, Pearson's deeper hope remained: that attempts to "kill Uluru" would ultimately fail,

1. Pearson, "'A Judas Betrayal.'"
2. First Nations National Constitutional Convention, "Uluru Statement from the Heart." And further, Pearson, "Recognition."

and the Australian people themselves would "rise" to "the historic opportunity that we have." Despite what he saw as a political betrayal, Pearson commended the Uluru Statement directly to the nation. And with an Easter-shaped story of dying and rising, he invited the Australian people to respond in good faith.

By the time this volume finds its readers, the referendum on First Nations recognition will be over. We will have begun the work of responding to the outcome, whatever that outcome may be. Some then may wonder what to make of the way the campaign brought biblical language to the surface. It is certainly striking that numerous Indigenous leaders have invoked the Bible in connection with First Nations recognition. In addition to Pearson, Bidjara Professor Anne Pattel-Gray gave an eschatological view of the significance of the Uluru Statement on the Australian Broadcasting Corporation's *Q&A* program: "We shared with you our pain, but we also shared our hope, and if we don't have that hope recognised, you are then damning us to hell."[3] Wiradjuri journalist and intellectual Stan Grant drew extensively on Scripture to highlight the imperative for justice for the afflicted: "Vindicate me, O God, and plead my case against an ungodly nation" (Ps 43:1).[4] Wiradjuri artist Glenn Loughrey told Radio National that the referendum was analogous to the encounter between Jacob and Esau in Genesis chapters 32 and 33. Would non-Indigenous Australia wrestle with its conscience as Jacob had, and wake up ready to walk differently with the older brother it had defrauded?[5] More locally and within church contexts, too, Indigenous leaders drew on the Bible to explain their view of what was at stake.

What do these examples of biblically-inflected speech suggest about how the Bible is being "read" in contemporary Australia? Most basically, they indicate that the Bible is still being treated as a public text—including in shared spaces that are not ostensibly Christian. Simplistic notions of religion as "private" cannot account for the reality of contemporary political discourse. And to the extent that Australia currently practices a kind of political secularity, it is not hard or absolute, but soft and pluralist. So long as the Bible remains even an occasional reference point in political debate, understanding how it is taken up, by whom, and for what purpose remains worthwhile, even beyond the community of faith. This is arguably an aspect of critical citizenship, which the essays in this book model and cultivate.

3. Johnson, "Leader of Young Liberals will consider supporting Indigenous Voice."

4. Grant, "Listening to Scripture." See further Grant, "Truth that Comes from Love."

5. Loughrey, "Voice to Parliament, a Voice to the Church" and "Jacob & the Statement from the Heart."

These examples also suggest an enduring confidence, at least in some quarters, that biblical references and allusions retain broad communicative potential. Pearson, for instance, assumed his audience would grasp the significance of his allusion to Judas as he mapped political developments onto the narrative of Holy Week. Grant similarly expected that his use of the Psalms to plead for justice in the midst of suffering would resonate beyond any one religious or cultural group. This is notable given that popular levels of biblical literacy in Australia are low by historical standards; patterns of socialization into familiarity with the text have been shifting and shrinking for decades.[6] Yet the possibility remains that the Bible provides a point of meeting between diverse people, a shared reference for at least some Indigenous and non-Indigenous people in this place. Could it be that amidst all the past and present woe, all the divergent interpretations, the Bible affords a bridge to mutual recognition?

The essays in this volume explore diverse possibilities for re-reading the Bible in Australia, in the awareness that "reading," "the Bible," and "Australia" are all fluid and freighted terms. As an historian, it is clear to me that the Bible does not really exist in a static or self-evident way; it changes across time and place, existing in diverse and proliferating forms. With the tools of biblical studies, however, several writers underline the challenge of making meaning from this contingent, composite text. Contributors with expertise in biblical languages and ancient cultures, draw out the possible range of meanings of a single Greek or Hebrew word. Some explore the potential implications of a biblical text's compilation from multiple prior sources, and the multivalence embedded in, say, the opening chapters of Genesis. At the very least, unsettling "the Bible" in this way serves to highlight the specificity (rather than the universality) of any given understanding of the text; it also demonstrates how the Bible can still surprise even the most devoted reader. As a whole, this volume bears out Mark Brett's conviction that biblical studies can contribute distinctive and valuable insights to interdisciplinary efforts to understand the Bible and its reception in Australia.[7]

The focus on "reading" the Bible perhaps affords a clearer subject than the range of encounters and interactions I considered in *The Bible in Australia: A Cultural History*. "Reading" is not treated theoretically, though, nor extensively considered as practice with its own cultural histories—bound up with the material production and form of the text, for instance, which in turn privilege and produce particular literacies. Here, contributors generally approach "reading" as a situated act of interpretation, and sometimes

---

6. Lake, *Bible in Australia*, 405–17.
7. Brett, "Past and Future of Biblical Studies."

also as an exegetical art—involving attention not only to a text, but to the interpretative traditions that have accompanied it in particular contexts, and to the patterns of knowledge and authority that characterize the reading community, including their own.

If reading is a cultural practice inevitably shaped and structured by the contexts in which it happens, the location of reading can be expected to matter to the task of interpretation. To some extent, this volume problematizes "Australia" as a product of a colonizing imagination, keeping in view that the present conversation, too, occurs on stolen land. Contributors also unsettle the hegemony of "Australia" by attending to particular places, to local ecologies, and to human bodies in motion—from pedestrian meditations on Merri Creek to diasporic Pasifika experiences. Attending to these sites and their stories enables several contributors to explore how the Bible might be read differently, and perhaps even to escape historic binaries between black and white, humanity and nature.

※

On Maundy Thursday morning, I listened to Noel Pearson on the radio from my home in the Canterbury district of Sydney on unceded Gadigal Country. In the language of this place, *gadi* means grass tree. The word for bark, *bugi*, is closely related to the word for skin, *bagi*. It is a linguistic clue that the grass tree mob belonged to Country as kin.[8] For Gadigal, Country could not be reduced to mere property, to an object over which to claim possession. And yet, in the late eighteenth century, the English Crown unilaterally took this land as its own—and then granted a tract to the colony's first Christian clergyman, Richard Johnson. Receiving the grant, Johnson renamed this place Canterbury Vale, after the seat of the Church of England—overwriting Gadigal realities, and imaginatively tying the land to his own traditions of sovereignty and spirituality.

Johnson was formally an officer of the Crown, a representative of what Grant calls "white Christendom." As chaplain to the colony, he was the primary advocate of the Bible in early Sydney, a devout and deliberate agent of its transmission among the convicts. An evangelical who desired the spread of the gospel to all nations of the world, he also attempted to evangelize First Nations people, particularly a Burramuttagal survivor of the smallpox epidemic, Booron. By Johnson's own account, he taught Booron to recite the Lord's Prayer, and "endeavor[ed] to instruct her respecting a supreme being"—convinced of her share in the human capacity to respond to God, yet unable to imagine the possibility that in her Country Booron already knew

---

8. Cawthorne, "Learning language in GADI."

a Creator Spirit.[9] In the midst of all this, too, Johnson became entangled in the officers' political efforts to "conciliate the natives" to the reality of invasion.[10] Sovereignty was a spiritual notion to Johnson and the colonists, as well as to First Nations people—though in vastly different senses that have yet to be resolved by Makarrata or by treaty.[11]

Here in the place Johnson called Canterbury Vale, the chaplain oversaw the ecological transformation of Country—clearing the grass trees and the ironbark forest, grazing European animals, and planting European crops. After 1800, when Johnson and his family left the colony, the farm was sold on and expanded by subsequent European owners, before being subdivided again into commercial and residential lots. In the decade after the First World War, a brickworks company dug up and dug over the area just near where I live, to make the materials to construct the houses in which my neighbors and I now reside. The old brick pit has since been filled and levelled out—there is a football ground there now, where local clubs play an annual Indigenous round. On Sundays, depending on the direction of the breeze, you can hear a church bell ringing.

Reading the Bible here, in the wake of these histories, involves grappling with the Bible's place in processes and cultures of colonization. Several contributors to this volume point out that the Bible arrived with colonizing Europeans who read it in ways that cohered with the values of an invading society. And while an argument can be made that attentiveness to the Bible equipped certain colonial Christians to critique the most extreme forms of settler violence,[12] that critique was never thoroughgoing, sufficient, or sustained. In fact, as Anne Pattel-Gray and others attest, colonial understandings of the Bible persist in dynamic ways today. An Aboriginal child attending a white church might still hear the Bible taught in ways that denigrate blackness.[13] On the cusp of National Reconciliation Week, park rangers might still discover "Jesus saves" graffiti scrawled on a sacred site— as they did in Jinibara Country.[14] And settler churches might persist with what Garry Worete Deverell identifies as "an imaginative *terra nullius*" by

---

9. Johnson, "Reverend Richard Johnson to Henry Fricker." See further Deverell, *Contemplating Country*.

10. Lake, "Salvation and Conciliation."

11. First Nations National Constitutional Convention, "Uluru Statement from the Heart."

12. Wolfe acknowledges this in her contribution to this volume. See, also, Lake, *Bible in Australia*, 112–23.

13. On which, see chapters by Naomi Wolfe and Anne Pattel-Gray. See, also Prentis, *Listen, Learn, Love*.

14. Gillespie and Ore, "Sacred Indigenous site on Sunshine Coast defaced."

effectively excluding Indigenous peoples from decision-making, education, and leadership, or by failing to justly resolve the original appropriation of the Aboriginal land they occupy.[15]

It also remains the case that many people in and beyond the churches still encounter the Bible as mediated through English imperial institutions. For instance, the recent death of Queen Elizabeth II, Australia's head of state, catalyzed a series of religious ceremonies that in turn received saturating media coverage. The Queen's funeral and committal service featured the Bible being read, preached, sung, prayed, and recited in the liturgy. Broadcast live by every major Australian television network and watched by at least 3.9 million people in Australia, out of a global television audience estimated at 4 billion, the UK Bible Society described the Queen's funeral as "the largest scriptural event in history."[16] The subsequent coronation of King Charles III likewise asserted—to a mass audience—an enduring, legitimating relationship between crown and Scripture.[17]

Yet the Bible is not and has never been entirely captive to imperial theologies or colonial interests. Anne Pattel-Gray quotes Mennonite scholar Steve Heinrichs with approval: while the Bible has been—and still is—"used as a tool of colonisation, xenophobia, exclusion and cultural genocide . . . this does not have to be." In itself, the Bible has disruptive potential as a composite, multi-voiced text, compiled partly by colonized peoples on the edge of empire. And there are long histories of reading it creatively and critically to "shake the powers from their thrones." Here in this place, for two centuries now, successive First Nations leaders have made their own appeals and allusions to the Christian Scriptures—including to challenge white society, expose its conceits, and call the nation to repentance. Pearson's "Judas betrayal" speech and other biblically-inflected discussions of the constitutional recognition of First Nations people could be seen as part of this potent minority tradition.

The First Nations contributors to this volume see themselves in the biblical text in ways that give rise to a reparative theology for the people of this place. Pastor Raymond Minniecon reads the book of Job as an Aboriginal story, seeing the experiences of suffering endured by his community reflected in the biblical narrative. Like Job, Minniecon rejects the suggestion that their own sin is the root cause of their predicament: "How many times do we have to be saved from our sins . . . when we also need to be saved from

---

15. Deverell, "'For your sakes he became poor . . .'"

16. Bible Society, "Bible, the Funeral—and the Coronation." For an overview of biblical texts referenced in Queen Elizabeth's funeral and committal services, see Woods, "Queen Elizabeth II: The Bible in the Funeral."

17. Woods, "All the Bible verses in the Coronation."

those who have sinned against us?" Taking Creation in Genesis 1, rather than the Fall in Genesis 3, as the biblical foundation for Indigenous theology, he finds that "*Elohim*, to use that old Indigenous name, continues to take us back *inside the beginning* where we find his healing, justice, and consolation."

Centering creation, Minniecon suggests that, just as Job encountered God in the "creation material" of a whirlwind, Aboriginal people encounter God in their ancestral culture and Country. Similarly, trawloolway theologian Naomi Wolfe underlines her grandmother's reading of 1 Kgs 8:57: the Creator was already present with her ancestors, prior to the transmission of colonial Christianity. Anne Pattel-Gray concurs that "the Creator Spirit was with us long before the British invaded . . . our faith has been nurtured over thousands of years." In short, each of these First Nations theologians insist that this was not *terra nullius*, a land belonging to no one, nor was it *terra sine deo*, a land without God.

Given that the Bible was transmitted here by colonial-era Europeans, how do its portraits of God relate to the Creator known by First Nations people? This question has recurred, intermittently, through both missionary and First Nations approaches to reading the Bible in this place. In a remarkable chapter, Mark Brett and Deborah Shuh Yi Tan examine how it exercised William Thomas, the Assistant Protector who attempted to translate passages of King James English into Kulin languages in the 1840s. Learning from Budgery Tom, Old Tottoy, and perhaps other Kulin teachers and informants, Thomas settled on *Pundgyl Marman* (ancestor eagle father) as a translation for God in Genesis chapter 1. Anne Keary has detailed elsewhere that, around the same time, Lancelot Threlkeld and the Awabakal knowledge-holder Eaglehawk Biraban entered into extensive conversations on the subject. That resulted in the missionary's decision to reject the name of the Awabakal creator figure *Koen* for God, as well as the mutual choice to combine Awabakal concepts to translate Holy Spirit as *marai yirriyirri*.[18]

These examples are not exhaustive, but they are rare in the history of Bible reading in colonial Australia in terms of the relationships they reflect, and the conclusions ventured. They point to an exchange of sacred knowledge in the process of translation, which, however uneven, had at least the potential to extend both settler and Indigenous understandings. In these instances, though, Threlkeld despaired of the future of the Awabakal reading community, which suffered a high rate of death following the invasion of Country. In Victoria, even the Kulin survivors who took up Christianity did not embrace the term *Pundgyl Marman*.

---

18. Keary, "Christianity, Colonialism, and Cross-Cultural Translation."

Among colonists and their cultural heirs, the impact of First Nations knowledges on reading the Bible has been limited, uneven, and recent. Perhaps one of many reasons for this is that interactions between settler Christians and Indigenous people on this continent were often mediated through missionary programs or state institutions which, with few exceptions, failed to afford genuinely mutual collaboration in the task of interpreting the Bible.[19] Until the 1980s, the overwhelming majority of formal theological writing and biblical scholarship by non-Indigenous Australians was oriented toward the northern hemisphere.[20] Yet in the wake of Aboriginal movements for civil and political rights, amidst the broader social and cultural shifts that accompanied the end of white, British Australia, there has been growing interest in relating biblical accounts of God to this place and its people.[21]

In 2022, a large glass artwork designed by Wiradjuri man Glenn Loughrey was installed at the entrance to St Paul's Anglican Cathedral in Melbourne. It depicts the Kulin eagle ancestor *Bundjil* (*Pundgyl*) as a permanent acknowledgment that the Cathedral stands on Wurundjeri Country. Is it also an instance of biblical interpretation, perhaps containing an echo of *Pundgyl Marman*? What might it look like, now, to read the Bible in ways responsive to Indigenous knowledge? Beyond the essays in this volume, several recent books of First Nations theology point to the possibilities. Leading voices include Aunty Denise Champion, who has offered an Adnyamathanha reflection on the Bible in *Yarta Wandatha* (2014) and *Anadijt* (2021), and trawloolway scholar Garry Worete Deverell, who reads Country as analogous to Scripture in his multi-volume *Gondwana Theology* (2018, 2023). Crucially, the recent establishment of NAIITS College as a full member institution of the Sydney College of Divinity, and the creation of the University of Divinity's School of Indigenous Studies, provide new institutional homes for ongoing inquiry into First Nations approaches to reading the Bible in Australia.

Reading the Bible in Australia always involves a text in motion across cultures, not only for First Nations people but for everyone, including colonists, missionaries, and more recent immigrants. And, however habituated a reading community may be to any given version of the text, reading always

---

19. For example, Rademaker, *Found in Translation*.

20. As Pattel-Gray notes in this volume. See also, Treloar, "Towards a Master Narrative"; Brett, "The Past and Future of Biblical Studies."

21. This increasing interest is apparent not only in the formal study of theology and biblical studies, but in the formation of the Uniting Church of Australia, and the process of writing and revising the preamble to its constitution. Note Deverell's discussion of this, though, in *Contemplating Country*.

entails the differentiation of concepts in ways shaped by readers' shifting contexts and experiences. In his reflection on the formal work of translation, Sam Freney discusses various positions of authority in ancient Israel as described in 1 Samuel. He notes the likelihood that English readers understand kingly terminology with reference to English monarchical institutions, while Pitjantjara speakers might draw on both their ancestral patterns of authority and recent experiences of more hierarchical forms of power. Freney presents this situation as a challenge for effective translation. In contrast, Brian Kolia, with a different purpose, actively pursues the potential for divergent understandings. His *talanoa* with Exodus 12 brings multiple mobilities to the foreground—mobilities of the divine, the diaspora, and the dispossessed—to question, without resolving, what it might mean to "pass over." Differently again, Megan Turton reads the Bible in conversation with the ecology of her local area. Walking the riverbanks during COVID lockdowns, she develops a more embodied understanding of the Hebrew texts, and of divine immanence in creation.

The mobility of biblical texts in and across different contexts emerges very clearly in Anne Elvey's absorbing interactions with the Magnificat. Elvey attends to Mary's song in its Lukan situation, in its transmission to the colonies, and in its multifaceted cultural "afterlives" here—drawing it into dialogue with contemporary concerns about ecology and how to reckon with the legacies of colonialism. Her own reading practice is marked by contextual self-awareness and a willingness to take up multiple modes of interpretation including translation, exegesis, criticism, and creative response. Elvey also reads to resist what she calls "the hegemony of practices of biblical study that want to 'save' the Bible and Christianity," though she does not elaborate on that here. The result is a vision of the Magnificat as a text that points *away* from itself—not so much towards g-d in worship, as it commonly appears in liturgy, but towards renewed relationships between First Nations people and settler readers, and between human and more than human worlds.

For several authors, reading the Bible in Australia involves getting to grips with what Glen O'Brien calls "biblically inspired social imaginaries." Barbara Deutschmann revisits colonial mythologies about women, as constructed and sustained by post-biblical elaborations on the figure of Eve in Genesis. Michelle Eastwood engages the Australian Christian Lobby's claim to be "a voice for God's truth in the public square" by examining its political theology. Deborah Storie and Jonathan Cornford both consider interpretations of the Bible connected with capitalist cultures of accumulation and consumption. In each case, they indicate why even non-religious people in Australia might have a stake in "reading the Bible": influential patterns of biblical interpretation play out beyond the community of faith, shaping and structuring social relationships in wider Australian life.

In contrast to contemporary culture warriors, who assume easy connections between the Bible and conservative social imaginaries, these contributors are alert to the ways different traditions of biblical interpretation can buttress divergent visions. Attending to the reception of the figure of Eve, Deutschmann finds that European colonists were heir to hierarchical views of gender and a suspicion of female sexuality, which they, in turn, deployed against convict and Indigenous women. Returning to the text of Genesis, Deutschmann highlights how Eve can be and has been read differently—including to subvert misogynistic mythologies and to nourish a more expansive vision of womanhood. Storie takes up the parable of the talents, read in one way by politicians ideologically aligned with neoliberalism, and very differently by the economically marginalized. Storie navigates this contrast by drawing on her own cross-cultural experiences, to locate herself *as if* among Jesus' first disciples. It's a distinctive approach yet similarly concerned to evaluate contemporary readings by returning to the biblical text.

The scholars featured here are interested in gaps between the biblical text and certain culturally dominant interpretations. They are also clearly sympathetic to social justice-oriented understandings of Scripture, and alert to the disruptive potential of multivalence. Yet the diversity of interpretations in itself raises a question that simmers through much of this volume: beyond disruption, beyond making strange, can re-reading the text provide a foundation for liberation? Can we say that a text as complex as this properly bends towards justice?

Several authors are circumspect. Eastwood, for instance, finds the Australian Christian Lobby unappealing, and judges its political theology wanting even in view of its preferred proof texts. But rather than insist on her preferred interpretation of those same passages, or an alternative Christian view of gender and sexuality, she calls for greater biblical and cultural literacy to enable Bible readers to "mind the gap." O'Brien hears echoes of the Hebrew prophetic tradition in bushranger Ned Kelly's self-expression but refrains from elevating Kelly as an icon of folk Christianity. He notes that while the prophetic tradition may inspire advocacy for the poor, it may also provide a "vocabulary . . . of violence, subjugation, and exclusion."

Jonathan Cornford, by contrast, writes in "the unfashionable conviction that the complexity of the Bible does not prevent a coherent moral ethic from being discerned in its pages and across its narrative arc." In his eviscerating essay on settler capitalism and Australia's obsession with material prosperity, he re-reads settler history by the measure of what he calls the "manna economy." He finds that the prevailing forms of Christianity replicated and extended by colonists here were deeply accommodated to European capitalism—readily allied to conquest, the looting of creation as a resource, and a form of enchantment centered on Mammon in an otherwise disenchanted cosmos. In his view, this "hollowed-out" version of Christianity provided moral cover for a national cult of Mammon—but bears no resemblance to "biblical visions of economic commonwealth."

In Cornford's reading, the narrative arc of the Bible bends towards an ethic of universal commonwealth: a "manna economy" marked by shared sufficiency and shared rest, justly enjoyed by all creation. He derives this ethic from diverse Hebrew texts as "radically re-read" by Jesus. In this, Cornford insists that, while the Bible may not "interpret itself," its composite texts stand in relation to each other—with implications for how a contemporary reader might interpret them together. Like Storie and perhaps others, Cornford also seems willing to seriously entertain the possibility that the Bible "reads" Australia—and us. This particular reading practice diverges from that of several other contributors to this book, but I agree it bears a kinship to how many ordinary Christians in this place have approached their sacred texts.

As recently as 2015, Australia's National Church Life Survey found that over 90 percent of church attenders considered the Bible as in some sense "the word of God." While this by no means eclipses or resolves substantial questions of hermeneutics, it is a salient feature of how the Bible has been, and still is, "read" here. Contributors to this volume could hardly have been expected to settle the matter of the text's relationship to any form of divinity, as variously perceived by Christians. Curiously, though, this collection is reticent to engage an idea of the Bible as God's word, despite its relevance to the attempt to describe and explain the Bible's reception here. Whether approaching the Bible as coherent and perhaps authoritative has the potential to "unsettle Australia" remains an open question. At least for Cornford, in reckoning with the consequences of the unbridled pursuit of prosperity—from growing inequality to ecological breakdown to mass extinction—it remains a vital source of hope and wisdom.

On Maundy Thursday evening 2023, many Christians in Australia read the biblical narrative of Judas' betrayal of Jesus. According to John's Gospel, Jesus and his disciples had gathered together on the eve of the Passover festival. And knowing that Judas was about to betray him, Jesus washed the disciples' feet. A short time later, after Judas has gone out, Jesus gave "a new command" to his remaining companions:

> Love one another. As I have loved you, so you must love one another. By this everyone will know that you are my disciples, if you love one another. (John 13:34).

What does it mean to read and respond to this passage of the Bible and pursue the way of love in this place? Naomi Wolfe calls our attention to an earlier occasion, described in the Gospel of Luke (10:25–37), when a lawyer asked Jesus about the boundaries of the obligation to "love your neighbor as yourself." Jesus responded to his interlocutor with the famous parable of the Good Samaritan, linking neighborliness with the practice of mercy. Crucially, the exemplar of righteousness in the parable was not a member of the lawyer's own ethnic or religious community, but a person on the margins nevertheless willing to bind up the wounded. Just as the parable unsettled the lawyer's sense of self-righteousness, Wolfe invites contemporary readers of the Bible in Australia to reconsider the assumptions we bring to this story of neighborly love:

> What might we learn if we see Colonial Christianity as the robber, the violent thief that inflicts harm and disruption? What might we learn if we begin to think about Aboriginal people as the Good Samaritan, the outsider of mainstream society, who stops to assist the broken and beaten victim?

The essays in this book share a longing for healing, for rest and repair, a longing for shalom. There is a widespread willingness, on the part of contributors, to reckon with the legacies of colonial Christianity, and with the particular patterns of biblical interpretation that have shaped and buttressed it. Contributors also find, in reading the Bible, potential resources for renewed relationships—between people, and with Country. Reading here, on Maundy Thursday 2023, the gospel presents to a reader like me an invitation not only to listen, but to love.

Bibliography

The Bible Society. "The Bible, the Funeral—and the Coronation. 24 April 2023. https://www.biblesociety.org.uk/latest/news/the-bible-the-funeral-and-the-coronation/.

Brett, Mark G. "The Past and Future of Biblical Studies in Australia." *Australian Biblical Review* 67 (2019) 84–96.

Cawthorne, Renee. "Learning Language in GADI." Australian Museum, 7 March 2018. https://australian.museum/blog/at-the-museum/learning-language-in-gadi/.

Champion, Denise. *Anaditj*. Self published, Port Augusta, SA: Champion, 2021.

———. *Yarta Wandatha*. Self published, Salisbury, SA: Champion, 2014

Deverell, Garry Worete. *Contemplating Country: More Gondwana Theology*. Eugene, OR: Wipf & Stock, 2023.

———. "'For your sakes he became poor . . .' How the churches can reckon with their colonial legacy." *ABC Religion and Ethics*, 24 October 2022. https://www.abc.net.au/religion/churches-and-their-colonial-legacy-garry-deverell/14091754.

First Nations National Constitutional Convention. "Uluru Statement from the Heart." Alice Springs: Central Land Council Library, 2017. https://ulurustatement.org/.

Gillespie, Eden and Adeshola Ore. "Sacred Indigenous site on Sunshine Coast defaced with religious message." *The Guardian*, 26 May 2023. https://www.theguardian.com/australia-news/2023/may/26/sacred-indigenous-site-on-sunshine-coast-defaced-with-religious-message.

Grant, Stan. "Listening to Scripture.'" Charles Sturt University, 5 April 2023. https://about.csu.edu.au/community/accc/about/latest-news-assets/2023/listening-to-scripture-by-prof-stan-grant.

———. "A Truth that Comes from Love." In *Statements from the Soul: The Moral Case for the Uluru Statement from the Heart*, edited by Shireen Morrison and Damien Freeman, 19–32. Collingwood: La Trobe University Press, 2023.

Johnson, Paul. "Leader of Young Liberals will consider supporting Indigenous Voice to Parliament, despite party stance." *ABC News*, 11 April 2023. https://www.abc.net.au/news/2023-24-11/the-voice-no-vote-young-liberals-leader-considers-yes-vote/102206592.

Johnson, Reverend Richard. "Reverend Richard Johnson to Henry Fricker, 9 April 1790." Library of New South Wales, 11 February 2011. https://www2.sl.nsw.gov.au/archive/discover_collections/history_nation/terra_australis/letters/johnson/index.html.

Keary, Anne. "Christianity, Colonialism, and Cross-Cultural Translation: Lancelot Threlkeld, Biraban, and the Awabakal." *Aboriginal History* 33 (2010) 117–56. https://press-files.anu.edu.au/downloads/press/p74631/pdf/ch0653.pdf.

Lake, Meredith. *The Bible in Australia: A Cultural History*. Sydney: NewSouth, 2020.

———. "Salvation and Conciliation: First Missionary Encounters at Sydney Cove." In *Evangelists of Empire? Missionaries in Colonial History*, edited by Amanda Barry, Joanna Cruickshank, and Andrew Brown-May, 87–102. Melbourne: University of Melbourne, 2008.

Loughrey, Glenn. "Jacob & The Statement from the Heart." 20 April 2023. https://www.redshoeswalking.net/jacob/.

———. "A Voice to Parliament, a Voice to the Church." On *Soul Search* presented by Meredith Lake, Radio National, 4 May 2023. https://www.abc.net.au/

radionational/programs/soul-search/a-voice-to-parliament-a-voice-to-the-church/102232184.

Pearson, Noel. "'A Judas betrayal': Noel Pearson criticises Liberal opposition to Voice." Radio National, 6 April 2023. https://www.abc.net.au/radionational/programs/breakfast/noel-pearson-liberals-no-voice-great-betrayal/102194758.

———. "Recognition: Who we were and who we can be." 2022 Boyer Lecture Series. Sydney: ABC, 2022. https://about.abc.net.au/speeches/noel-pearson-boyer-lecture-series-who-we-were-and-who-we-can-be/.

Prentis, Brooke. *Listen, Learn, Love: Walking with your Aboriginal Neighbour*. Sydney: Bible Society Australia, forthcoming.

Rademaker, Laura. *Found in Translation: Many Meanings on a North Australian Mission*. Honolulu: University of Hawaii Press, 2018.

Treloar, Geoff. "Towards a Master Narrative: Theological Learning and Teaching in Australia since 1901." *St Mark's Review* 210 (2009) 31–53.

Woods, Mark. "All the Bible verses in the Coronation." Bible Society UK, 2 May 2023. https://www.biblesociety.org.uk/latest/news/all-the-bible-verses-in-the-coronation/.

———. "Queen Elizabeth II: The Bible in the Funeral." Bible Society UK, 20 September 2022. https://www.biblesociety.org.uk/latest/news/queen-elizabeth-ii-the-bible-in-the-funeral/.

www.ingramcontent.com/pod-product-compliance
Lightning Source LLC
Chambersburg PA
CBHW070236230426
43664CB00014B/2318